JE '07

FATAL PURITY

FATAL
PURITY

ROBESPIERRE

AND THE

FRENCH REVOLUTION

RUTH SCURR

METROPOLITAN BOOKS

HENRY HOLT AND COMPANY · NEW YORK

Metropolitan Books
Henry Holt and Company, LLC
Publishers since 1866
175 Fifth Avenue
New York, New York 10010
www.henryholt.com

Metropolitan Books® and ® are registered trademarks
of Henry Holt and Company, LLC.

Distributed in Canada by H. B. Fenn and Company Ltd.

Published simultaneously in the United Kingdom by
Chatto & Windus, The Random House Group Limited

Library of Congress Cataloging-in-Publication Data

Scurr, Ruth.
    Fatal purity : Robespierre and the French Revolution / Ruth Scurr.
        p. cm.
    ISBN-13: 978-0-8050-7987-6
    ISBN-10: 0-8050-7987-4
    1. Robespierre, Maximilien, 1758–1794.   2. Revolutionaries—France—
Biography.   3. France—History—Revolution, 1789–1799.   4. France—
History—Reign of Terror, 1793–1794.   I. Title

DC146.R6S38 2006
944.04092—dc22
[B]   2005057694

Henry Holt books are available for special promotions
and premiums. For details contact: Director, Special Markets.

First Edition 2006

Designed by Victoria Hartman

Map of Revolutionary Paris drawn by Edward Weller, 1908

Printed in the United States of America

1   3   5   7   9   10   8   6   4   2

To John

Death is the beginning of immortality

Robespierre's last speech, 26 July 1794

Contents

Chronology   xiii

Map: Revolutionary Paris   xviii

Preface   1

Introduction   5

Part I. *Before the Revolution* (1758–1788)

1   Child of Arras   17
2   The Lawyer-Poet Back Home   36

Part II. *The Revolution Begins* (1788–1789)

3   Standing for Election in Arras   61
4   Representing the Nation at Versailles   78

Part III. *Reconstituting France* (1789–1791)

5   The National Assembly in Paris   111
6   The Constitution   141

Part IV. *The Constitution Fails* (1791–1792)

7   War   177
8   The King's Trial   218

Part V. *The Terror* (1793–1794)

9   The Pact with Violence   257
10   Robespierre's Red Summer   318
     Coda   359

Notes   361
Bibliography   379
Acknowledgments   393
Index   395

Chronology

1758 Maximilien Maric Isidore de Robespierre, born in Arras, May 6

1763 End of the Seven Years War

1764 Death of Robespierre's mother, July 14

1769 Robespierre goes to boarding school in Paris at the Collège Louis-le-Grand

1772 Disappearance of Robespierre's father

1774 Death of Louis XV and accession of his grandson as Louis XVI

1775 Coronation of Louis XVI in the cathedral at Reims, June 11

1778 France supports the American war of independence

1781 Robespierre returns to Arras to practice law

1788 The Lamoignon Edicts fail, May

   Louis XVI agrees to the convocation of the Estates General, August

1789 Robespierre campaigns for election and is chosen as a representative of the third estate, April

The Estates General meet in Versailles, May

The third estate claims the right to represent the nation and renames itself the National Assembly, June 17

Tennis Court Oath, June 20

Storming of the Bastille, July 14

Abolition of feudal rights and privileges, August 4

Louis XVI and the National Assembly move from Versailles to Paris, October

Robespierre rents rooms in the rue Saintonge

The Jacobin Club established in Paris

1790   Proliferation of a network of political clubs throughout France affiliated to the Parisian Jacobin Club

Threat of war over Nootka Sound

Civil Constitution of the Clergy, July

Festival of Federation on the first anniversary of the Bastille's fall, July 14

1791   Death of Mirabeau, April 2

Pope Pius VI condemns the Civil Constitution of the Clergy, April 13

Royal family's flight to Varennes, June 20

Massacre on the Champ de Mars, July 17

Robespierre moves to new lodgings in the rue Saint-Honoré

The Jacobin Club splits and moderate members leave to establish the Feuillants Club

Louis XVI accepts the new constitution, September

National Assembly closes and Robespierre revisits Arras

Pétion becomes mayor of Paris, November 14

Robespierre returns to Paris and opposes war-mongering at the Jacobin Club, November 28

1792   Fall of Louis XVI's Feuillant ministry and appointment of friends and associates of pro-war leader Brissot

Death of Holy Roman Emperor Leopold II, March 1

Festival in honor of the Châteauvieux soldiers, April 15

France declares war on Francis II (Leopold II's son and successor as Holy Roman Emperor), April 20

The guillotine is used for the first time, April 25

Prussia joins Austria in the war against France, June 13

The Duke of Brunswick issues a manifesto threatening Paris if Louis XVI is harmed, July 25

Paris's 48 Sections declared in permanent session, July 27

Fall of the monarchy, August 10

Robespierre elected to municipal Commune governing Paris, August 12

General Lafayette flees France

Longwy falls to Prussia, August 20

Establishment of the first Revolutionary Tribunal

Verdun falls to Prussia, September 2

Prison massacres, September 2–6

Robespierre elected to new National Convention, September 5

French victory over Prussia at Battle of Valmy, September 20

National Convention meets in Paris, September 21

Declaration of the Republic, September 22

French victory at Battle of Jemappes, November 6

Trial of Louis XVI, beginning with his indictment, December 11

Dissolution of the first Revolutionary Tribunal

1793   Execution of Louis XVI, January 21

France declares war on England and the Dutch Republic, February

Enragés food riots

France declares war on Spain, March 7

Revolt in the Vendée

Failed insurrection in Paris, March 9–10

Establishment of the second and infamous Revolutionary Tribunal, March 10

Defection of General Dumouriez after Battle of Neerwinden, March 18

Establishment of the Committee of Public Safety, April 6

Revolt in Lyon, May

Insurrection in Paris, May 31

Expulsion of Girondin deputies from the National Convention, June 2

Jacobin Republican constitution accepted by referendum and adopted, June 24

Danton voted off Committee of Public Safety, July 10

Marat assassinated, July 13

Robespierre voted into the Committee of Public Safety, July 27

Siege of Lyon begins, August 8

Smashing of royal tombs at Saint-Denis, August 10

Toulon surrenders to the English, August 29

Terror becomes the order of the day, September 5

Law of Suspects, September 17

Law of General Maximum, September 29

Adoption of the Republican calendar (backdated to 22 September 1792), October 5

Year I   Fall of Lyon, Vendémiaire 18 (October 9)

Execution of Marie Antoinette, Vendémiaire 25 (October 16)

Execution of the Girondin deputies, Brumaire 10 (October 31)

Festival of Reason in Notre-Dame, Paris, Brumaire 20 (November 10)

Commune decrees closure of Parisian churches, Frimaire 3 (November 23)

Constitution of Revolutionary Government, Frimaire 14 (December 4)

First issue of Desmoulins's *Le vieux Cordelier*, Frimaire 15 (December 5)

French recapture Toulon, Frimaire 29 (December 19)

Rebels in the Vendée crushed, Nivôse 2 (December 22)

Year II   Robespierre ill, Pluviôse 22–Ventôse 22 (February 10–March 12)

Execution of Hébertistes, Germinal 4 (March 24)

Recall of Fouché from Lyon, Germinal 7 (March 27)

Execution of Dantonistes, Germinal 16 (April 5)

Robespierre runs the Police Bureau after Saint-Just leaves on mission to the army, Floréal 9 (April 28)

Cécile Renault attempts to assassinate Robespierre, Prairial 4 (May 27)

Festival of the Supreme Being, Prairial 20 (June 8)

Reorganization of Revolutionary Tribunal, Prairial 22 (June 10)

French victory at Battle of Fleurus, Messidor 8 (June 26)

Fraternal banquets to celebrate the anniversary of the Bastille's fall, Messidor 26 (July 14)

Robespierre's last speech to the National Convention, Thermidor 8 (July 26)

Arrest of Robespierre, Thermidor 9 (July 27)

Execution of Robespierristes, Thermidor 10 (July 28)

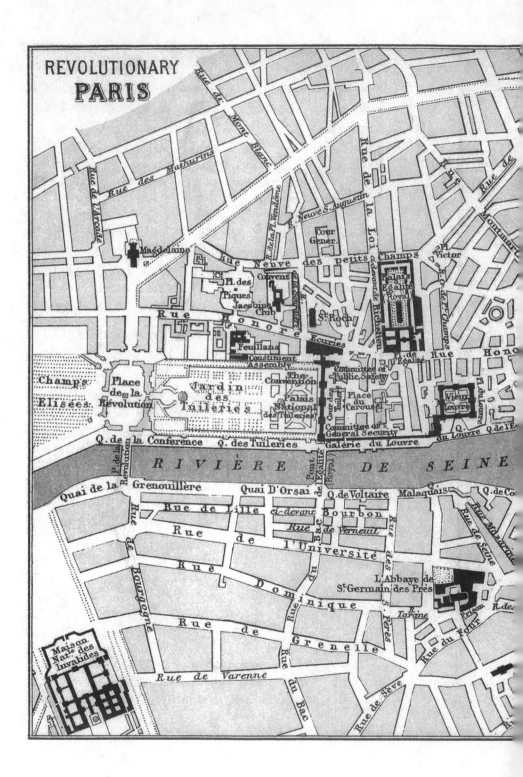

REVOLUTIONARY
PARIS

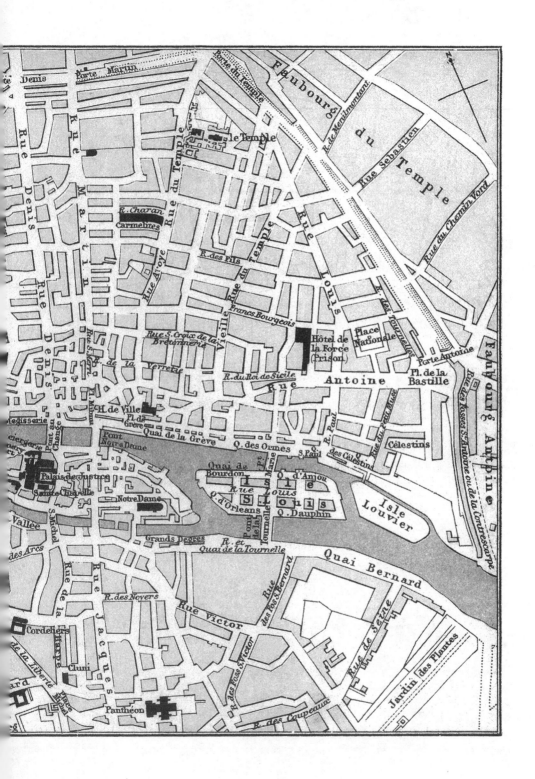

FATAL PURITY

PREFACE

MY DEAR CROKER,

I wish you would think seriously of the History of the Reign of
Terror. I do not mean a pompous, philosophical history, but a
mixture of biography, facts and gossip: a diary of what really took
place with the best authenticated likenesses of the actors.

Ever yours,

ROBERT PEEL[1]

Soon after he received this letter from his friend Sir Robert Peel, the
once and future Tory prime minister, John Wilson Croker packed his
bags for a seaside holiday. Although he was a prominent literary and
political journalist and was hoping to work as he sat on the beach, Croker packed none of his collection of rare and fascinating books about
the French Revolution that are now one of the glories of the British
Library. He took with him only the list of those condemned to death

during the Reign of Terror.[2] He perused it against the rhythmic sound of waves breaking on the shore.

Twenty-two impoverished women, many of them widows, convicted of forwarding "the designs of the fanatics, aristocrats, priests and other agents of England," guillotined.

Nine private soldiers convicted of "pricking their own eyes with pins, and becoming by this cowardly artifice unable to bear arms," guillotined.

Jean Baptiste Henry, aged eighteen, journeyman tailor, convicted of sawing down a tree of liberty, guillotined.

Henrietta Frances de Marbœuf, aged fifty-five, convicted of hoping for the arrival in Paris of the Austrian and Prussian armies and of hoarding provisions for them, guillotined.

James Duchesne, aged sixty, formerly a servant, since a broker; John Sauvage, aged thirty-four, gunsmith; Frances Loizelier, aged forty-seven, milliner; Mélanie Cunosse, aged twenty-one, milliner; Mary Magdalen Virolle, aged twenty-five, hairdresser: all convicted for writing, guillotined.

Geneviève Gouvon, aged seventy-seven, seamstress, convicted of "various conspiracies since the beginning of the Revolution," guillotined.

Francis Bertrand, aged thirty-seven, convicted of producing "sour wine injurious to the health of citizens," guillotined.

Mary Angelica Plaisant, another seamstress, guillotined for exclaiming, "A fig for the nation!"

Relaxing into his holiday, Croker continued reading through the long list of dubious charges against the several thousand victims of the

Revolutionary Tribunal of Paris, from its institution on 10 March 1793 until the fall of Maximilien Robespierre on 27 July 1794. He compiled some grimly fascinating statistics: in the last five months of Robespierre's life, when he supposedly secured tyrannous power over France and the Revolution, 2,217 people were guillotined in Paris; but the total condemned to death in the eleven months preceding Robespierre's Reign of Terror was only 399. On the basis of these statistics, Croker concluded that the executions "grew gradually with the personal influence of Robespierre, and became enormous in proportion as he successively extinguished his rivals."[3] In awed horror he recalled, "These things happened in our time—thousands are still living who saw them, yet it seems almost incredible that *batches* (*fournées*—such was the familiar phrase)—of *sixty* victims should be condemned in one morning by the same tribunal, and executed the same afternoon on the same scaffold."

Although Peel pressed his friend to write a popular and accessible book about the French Revolution, Croker never did so. When he got back from his holiday in 1835 he published his seaside musings in an article for the *Quarterly Review*. Here he acknowledged the enormity of the problem Robespierre still poses biographers: "The blood-red mist by which his last years were enveloped magnified his form, but obscured his features. Like the *Genius* of the Arabian tale, he emerged suddenly from a petty space into enormous power and gigantic size, and as suddenly vanished, leaving behind him no trace but terror."[4]

INTRODUCTION

No backdrop can match the French Revolution. It teems with life and burns with human, historical, intellectual, and literary interest. More than haunting, it obsesses, because it will not lie down and die. When François Furet, its most famous French historian of recent years, proclaimed in 1978, "The French Revolution is over," he provoked great waves of revisionist scholarship across France, beyond the Channel, and on the other side of the Atlantic, proving that it was still alive. With the Revolution's bicentenary in 1989, and the collapse of Communism across Europe the same year, new scholarship brought a young generation face to face with the vivid hopes of 1789—liberty, equality, fraternity, popular sovereignty, representative democracy, rights, and happiness. Hopes that issued, after just four years, in the Terror, the system of emergency government and summary execution with which no one was more closely identified than Maximilien Robespierre.

A pale and fragile man, Robespierre was anxious, hesitant, and principled. Before the Revolution he earned his living as a young lawyer in the northern French city of Arras. He sided consistently with the victimized and fiercely opposed the death penalty. Eloquent in person and on paper, but in a restrained and formal manner, he crossed a great deal out, nervously perfecting his prose, and had difficulty projecting his voice in public. His appearance was meticulously unflamboyant. His eyes were weak, his mind sometimes vague, and his routines colorlessly orderly. He should have drowned in the Revolution's flood of epoch-shattering events and personalities. Instead Robespierre became the living embodiment of the Revolution at its most feral and justified the Terror as an emanation of republican virtue, a necessary step on the path to the ideal society that he was determined to establish in France. However hopelessly utopian, politically misguided, or historically premature Robespierre's vision of this ideal society may have been, he made a unique contribution to events that shaped the future of Europe. To understand him is to begin to understand the French Revolution. It is also to cast light on the uneasy coincidence of democracy and fanaticism present at the birth of modern European politics.

Political turmoil can foster unlikely leaders. The mediocre figure, strutting and fretting on the historical stage in the midst of a revolution, is always more riveting than the one who merely inherits power or gets elected to it in quieter times. But Robespierre's mediocrity is only incidental, a weapon—of sorts—in the hands of his detractors and enemies but never the key to the personal and historical mystery that shrouds him. There were more intellectually gifted revolutionaries. There were better writers and speakers, and more sympathetic characters. Many disagreed politically with Robespierre every step of the way, from his election to the Estates General on the eve of the Revolution in 1789 to his death beneath the guillotine in 1794—often with good reason. But he cannot be explained by what he lacked, or failed to see and do.

Robespierre's private self and his public contribution to the events that inaugurated modern European politics are complex—by all accounts, he was remarkably odd, and the French Revolution was spectacularly complicated. No sooner were his severed remains collected, tossed into an unmarked grave, and covered with quicklime than the struggle began to grasp the connection between Robespierre's personality and his role in the Revolution. While his short career in politics was long enough to win him a lasting place in world history, it was not long enough to show conclusively whether his is rightly a place of honor, one of shame, or something more inscrutable in between.

To his enemies—living and dead—he will always be colored blood red: the first of the modern dictators, the inventor and perpetrator of the Terror who sent thousands to their deaths. One enemy, lucky enough to survive him, predicted, "History will say little about this monster; it will confine itself to these words: 'At this time, the internal debasement of France was such that a bloodthirsty charlatan, without talent and without courage, called Robespierre, made all the citizens tremble under his tyranny. Whilst twelve hundred thousand warriors were shedding their blood on the frontiers for the republic, he brought her to her knees by his proscriptions.' "[1]

Vilification and belittlement were inevitable in the aftermath of the Terror, but "bloodthirsty charlatan" is hardly a satisfactory description of the fastidious lawyer who opposed the death penalty before the Revolution and afterward became France's most articulate pacifist when war loomed with the rest of Europe. On the other hand, the subtler shades with which his friends paint him—reserved, enigmatic, highly principled, the first of the modern democrats—do not suffice either. To them he was an unjustly maligned prophet of the political order of the future. Almost fifty years after his death, one of them wrote: "I would have given my life to save Robespierre, whom I loved like a brother. No one knows better than I do how sincere, disinterested, and absolute his devotion to the Republic was. He has become the scapegoat of the revolutionists; but he was the best man of them all."[2] A sympathetic biographer went so far as to insist: "The more godlike I prove Robespierre's conduct to have been—the greater will be the horror in which his memory will be held by the upper and middle classes."[3]

By the left in France and elsewhere, Robespierre has been cast primarily as the defender of the republic and the ideal of social democracy: a passionate witness to the grievances of the poor and the virtues of the meek or oppressed whom history betrays. He was, after all, the revolutionary who tried to change the Declaration of Rights to limit private property and enshrine the right to life and subsistence for all. It was Robespierre who said, "When will the people be educated? When they have enough bread to eat, when the rich and the government stop bribing treacherous pens and tongues to deceive them. . . . When will this be? Never."[4]

But whatever the view, Robespierre's self and the Revolution cannot be separated. It is not only historians, hostile or sympathetic, who insist on their identity. He claimed himself to represent the pure republic of virtue, and even his adversaries recognized the aptness of the sobriquet "incorruptible." ("He would have paid someone to offer him gold, so as to be able to say that he had refused it," one of them sneered.) His identification with the Revolution grew only closer as the Terror intensified. When Robespierre unveiled a new and perfect religion, the cult of the Supreme Being, at the public festival of the same name, he assumed the central symbolic role of high priest. And when, two days later, he initiated the infamous Law of 22 Prairial, which made summary execution the order of the day, Robespierre and the republic became one and the same tyrant. At what point exactly did the lawyer from Arras begin to believe in the image that the Revolution reflected back to him? Why did that image become so dangerously hypnotic, for him personally, for his contemporaries, and for posterity? And why is it so hard to break the spell, to understand—perhaps imperfectly, but at least clearly—who Robespierre was and what he meant?

Fatal Purity attempts to answer these questions. It expresses neither partisan adulation nor exaggerated animosity; instead it is motivated by the open-minded interest Robespierre deserves. It tries, whenever possible, to give him the benefit of any rational doubt. It differs from what already exists on the subject in three crucial respects. Firstly, it situates Robespierre in the politics of the Revolution, without diminishing, or exaggerating, his personal importance. In this respect, I have heeded François Furet's sagacious warning that: "There are two ways of totally misunderstanding Robespierre as a historical figure: one is to detest the man, the other is to make too much of him."[5] Unlike Furet, however, I have not approached Robespierre as the "mouthpiece" for the Revolution's "purest and most tragic discourse," nor do I share his view that "Robespierre's relation to the Terror is not psychological." Instead I have set out to show that Robespierre's involvement in, and advocacy of, the Terror *was* psychologically motivated in vital respects. The political decisions he made were influenced by the kind of person he was. No matter how complex and terrible the events, individuals—their stories, characters, ambitions, and dreams—are always the most fascinating part of history.

Secondly, I have given equal weight to the successive stages of Robespierre's life. In doing so I have drawn sometimes on detailed scholarship focused on a particular aspect or stage of Robespierre's career (John Hardman's excellent reconstruction of the Incorruptible's daily exercise of power during the Terror, for example). But my own purpose has been to follow the trajectory of Robespierre's story in its entirety and convey this to the general reader.

Thirdly, while I have framed his life, conventionally enough, by the cradle and the grave, I have not followed the cumbersome biographical convention of summarizing all the existing evidence. Instead I have selected carefully the incidents, anecdotes, letters, and speeches that seem to me most revealing of Robespierre's distinctive sensibility. The result is a portrait: my interpretation, based on the evidence, of what he was like. Though Robespierre died over two hundred years ago, he still makes new friends and enemies among the living. I have tried to be his friend and to see things from his point of view. But friends, as he always suspected, can be treacherous; they have opportunities for betrayal that enemies only dream of.

AS FAR AS it goes, the evidence about Robespierre's life is a mass of personal, political, historical, and literary detail, some robust, some not, to be arranged on either side of the argument, for or against: you can tell the story one way, or you can tell it another, as any lawyer knows. The real challenge of explaining him arises not from any paucity of facts but from something deeper—a question of interpretation that reaches down to the roots of modern democratic politics. In 1941 one historian pleaded for a truce: "Robespierrists, anti-Robespierrists, we've had enough. We say, for pity's sake, simply tell us what Robespierre was really like."[6] This is easier said than done.

His astonishing story begins very slowly, deep in the provinces of eighteenth-century France, and only starts to pick up speed with the coming of the Revolution in 1789. Then it accelerates, like the Revolution itself, tearing wildly through ever more frightening personal and political dramas, to end abruptly beneath the guillotine, one warm day in July 1794. The rhythm of his life is a violent crescendo and its shape is extremely lopsided. He was thirty-six when he died. Volume upon volume has been written about his last five years—astounding times by anyone's standard—but little is known about his first thirty-one years, except that they were less than remarkable.

The town of Robespierre's birth and ancestry offers little to balance this deficit. Wandering quiet streets, past buildings dignified by the sense that their time has come and gone, one looks in vain for an image of Arras's most famous citizen, born there on 6 May 1758. There are no pictures of Robespierre in the shops, none in the public library, none even in the Maison Robespierre, identified as the house he lived in as a young lawyer from 1787 to 1789 by a small plaque outside the door. This rather prim stone house in the former rue des Rapporteurs (now the rue Robespierre), with its narrow shuttered windows and tall sloping roof, has been altered over the years but is still typical of those built during Arras's eighteenth-century boom. Robespierre only rented it; he never owned a house of his own. Inside the door, finally, stands a large bust of him, but there are no reproductions of it to take away and it seems inconceivable that anyone might be so indiscreet as to pull out a camera and use it.

The sense that Robespierre is someone to be ashamed of goes back a long way. After his death, one of his contemporaries, Jean Baptiste Dauchez, a fellow lawyer from Arras, suggested an "impenetrable curtain" should be drawn over all that had passed in the local assembly that elected Robespierre as a representative in 1789 and launched him on a career in national politics with such devastating consequences. Dauchez wanted to forget the story, wanted others not to find out. And his suggestion has been taken surprisingly seriously in Arras for over two hundred years.[7] Entry to the Maison Robespierre is free, yet visitors leave feeling shortchanged, hardly any more informed about the young life of the local revolutionary no one is eager to discuss. Inside, in one corner, are three or four photocopied documents (including Robespierre's birth certificate), a brief summary of his short life, and six tiny buttons with embroidered stag heads from an elegant waistcoat he liked to wear. Nothing more.

From Robespierre's later years in Paris, there is of course a wide range of portraits, engravings, and caricatures to give us some notion of what he "was really like." There are also innumerable verbal descriptions of him in the memoirs, diaries, and letters of those who knew him more or less well. One contemporary claimed that he had the head of a cat: "But this face changed its character. At first it had the anxious but rather gentle look of the domestic cat; then the fierce look of the wild cat; and finally the ferocious look of the tiger cat."[8] There is indeed something feline in the surviving images of his face. He had big almond-shaped eyes, high-arching brows, and a long but not peculiarly large or prominent nose that continued the line of his back-sloping forehead, already exaggerated by receding hair and a short and impeccably powdered wig. According to another contemporary, "He had a sinister expression of countenance, never looked you in the face, and had a continual and unpleasant winking of the eyes."[9] He needed glasses but is only pictured wearing them in one unusually disheveled sketch, the last done in his lifetime, on the day he fell from power. At an earlier, quieter time another artist drew him with his glasses carefully balanced halfway up his forehead, far enough below the wig to avoid powder smears, looking every bit as affected as someone in a holiday snapshot with sunglasses on his head. Under the drawing are the words "green eyes, pale complexion, green striped nankeen jacket, blue waistcoat with blue stripes, white cravat striped with red."

Many allude to Robespierre's vanity and fastidiousness about clothes. Before the Revolution he was registered as a customer in a clothing shop in Arras, but he was not rich, and his purchases there were few and modest. Political power did not diminish his preoccupation with appearance. At the height of his career he wore a beautiful sky-blue coat, more suited to the courts of the old kings of France than to a revolutionary assembly negotiating with violent mobs in the streets.[10] But Robespierre would make no sartorial concessions to the times. He was particularly fond of elaborately embroidered waistcoats—an unlikely taste in a political activist who rose to power championing democracy and the rights of the poor in the face of aristocratic privilege.

"He was five feet two or three inches tall"—not especially small by eighteenth-century standards—someone else remembered.

> He held his body stiffly upright; and walked firmly, quickly, and rather jerkily; he often clenched his hands as though by a kind of contraction of the nerves, and the same movement could be traced in his neck and shoulders, which he moved convulsively to right and left. His clothes were neat and fashionable, and his hair always carefully dressed. There was nothing remarkable about his face, which wore a rather discontented expression; his complexion was livid and bilious, his eyes dull and melancholy; whilst a frequent flickering of his eyelids was perhaps a result of the convulsive movements that I have already mentioned. He always wore green-tinted glasses. He had learnt how to give artificial softness to a voice that was naturally sharp and harsh, and to make his Artois accent sound attractive; but he never looked an honest man in the face.[11]

He looked at his audience though. He carried a second pair of large-rimmed eyeglasses to fit on top of the green-tinted ones when he wanted to fix his listeners better with his feeble green eyes. He was both near- and farsighted, so everything he saw was slightly blurred. His glasses helped him focus, they filtered the harsh sunlight, and they were also props used to dramatic effect as he stood at the tribune speaking. As a fellow deputy recalled, "His delivery was slow, and his phrases so long that every time he paused and pushed his glasses up onto his forehead one might have thought that he had no more to say; but, after looking all around the Hall, he would lower his spectacles again, and add a phrase or two to sentences which were already long enough when he broke them off."[12]

For the last years of his life, Robespierre lived in a house in the rue Saint-Honoré with a Parisian furniture maker and his family, the Duplays. They adored him. Here he was surrounded by representations of himself: a little god in a domestic setting. There were many mirrors, his full-length portrait, his bust in metal or terracota, and—rumor has it—print after print of him all over the walls.[13] It was the kind of shrine that Robespierre's remaining friends would still like to have. I hope one day we get it. It would be very interesting to see what it feels like to be in a room dominated by him; to look again at all those images of him; to stand by the window and wonder what it was he saw, gazing at obsessively repeated representations of himself as the French Revolution unfurled outside the door. It is the pictures in Robespierre's mind that are the key to his story. Two of them are more vivid than any of the others: his picture of an ideal society and his picture of himself. The Revolution superimposed the two and he believed, to the point of insanity, that he was the instrument of Providence, charged with delivering France to her exalted future. If the French were not yet worthy of such a future, it was clear to him that they must be regenerated—through virtue or terror—until they became what destiny demanded of them. And yet, even in this extreme and fanatical state of mind, he hesitated, holding something back. He knew that his ideal society was ultimately greater than himself. If his life had coincided with its birth, if he had played his part in realizing it in history, he could go tranquilly to his death, as he did, many times, in his imagination, before his body went under the guillotine.

PART I

BEFORE
THE
REVOLUTION

(1758–1788)

1

CHILD OF ARRAS

Robespierre's story begins in the small city of Arras, in the province of Artois, in northern France. Located on the border between France and the Netherlands, Arras changed hands many times before it was firmly annexed by the French monarchy in 1659. Then the city walls were fortified and Arras settled down to a more peaceful existence as the province's ecclesiastical and judicial center. It was known as "the city of a hundred steeples" because visitors, approaching across the surrounding fields or on the fine gravel road from the nearby town of Béthune, saw from afar the tall spires of Arras's Gothic bell tower, the cathedral, the abbey, eleven parish churches, over twenty monasteries and convents, numerous hospices, chapels, and charitable institutions.[1] Conservative piety pervaded the narrow cobbled streets like the smell of incense, as some twenty thousand men, women, and children went about their daily devotional duties.

Robespierre's birth in 1758 coincided with the beginning of an economic boom in Arras: work had begun to connect the eastern and western sides of the city, which were separated by a branch of the river Crinchon. There were ambitious schemes to clean the river, a seething channel of infection, and to dam or bridge the many places where it seeped insistently into the streets. There were elaborate plans to reconstruct the cathedral, which dated back to AD 687, and to renovate the abbey of Saint-Vaast, which, along with a lavish income and considerable personal power, made the bishopric of Arras an attractive post for the younger sons of France's nobles. Alongside the new public buildings, wealthy investors commissioned new town houses several stories high, to meet growing demands for accommodation. Every Wednesday and Saturday even more people crowded inside the city walls to attend the twice-weekly markets trading in regional produce: hemp, flax, wool, soap, lace, porcelain—and especially grain.

The grain trade was the main cause of this economic vibrancy. In the distant past Arras's wealth had come from the beautiful tapestries that adorned Europe's medieval castles. But while Shakespeare's Hamlet may have immortalized these tapestries by lunging at a rat behind the arras, they were not the source of the city's eighteenth-century wealth. Rather, local landowners, most of them nobles, had grown extremely rich from the rents on their arable land. The facades of their fine new buildings were decorated with stylized sheaves of corn signaling the source of the money that financed them. These well-to-do landowners were responsible, too, for Arras's atmosphere of optimism and urban refinement. Paris was less than twenty-four hours away by courier.

Behind all this prosperity there lay an onerous system of privilege by which the upper classes lived at the expense of the community, a system of taxation that placed the heaviest burden on those least capable of bearing it, outdated restrictions on manufacture and commerce, and the vestiges of feudalism, which weighed heavily on the peasants in the countryside. Along with the economy, crime thrived in Arras. The city's three prisons were crammed full, and processions of beggars, criminals, and prostitutes were often seen leaving the city under armed guard, heading north for the house of correction in Lille.

The de Robespierres, established in the province for over three centuries, were respectable but not noble.[2] They did not own arable land, so did not benefit directly from Arras's economic boom. The family had a coat of arms (which appears on a document of 1462), but the particle "de" included in its name indicated only that they were not manual laborers. One early record mentions Robert de Robespierre, living near Béthune in the mid–fifteenth century and working as *un homme de justice*. In the sixteenth century there was another Robert de Robespierre in Béthune, a grocer. His great-grandson was a notary and attorney, in Carvins, where the main branch of the family lived until the first Maximilien de Robespierre (grandfather of the revolutionary) moved to Arras as a barrister, married an innkeeper's daughter, and through her acquired some property in the city. The first Maximilien proved canny at self-advancement. It happened that in 1745, Charles Edward Stuart, the Young Pretender in exile, spent six months in Arras. On his departure, he bequeathed the city a Masonic lodge, in gratitude for the hospitality he had received, and appointed Robespierre's grandfather an official of the lodge—of all the people in Arras, he had been particularly ingratiating. Everything went well enough—though there were eight children to feed and clothe and never quite enough money for comfort. But gradually it became clear that the eldest son, the second Maximilien (father of the revolutionary), was a bit dissolute and unstable.

Encouraged by his family to begin a novitiate with the Premonstratensians of Dommartin (a religious order founded in northern France by Saint-Norbert in the twelfth century), he gave up when he realized he had no vocation. Sent to Douai to read law, he came home to Arras to work as a barrister but almost immediately got Jacqueline Marguerite Carraut, the daughter of a local brewer in the rue Ronville, pregnant out of wedlock. The shame and scandal associated with illegitimacy in a small conservative city like Arras was considerable. Traditionally it was common for families to ostracize their wayward children or even request their imprisonment. The church was ubiquitous. Public and private libraries were full of religious texts outlining appropriate codes of spiritual and moral conduct, while the homes of nobles, bourgeois lawyers, and artisans were crammed with material objects evoking them: crucifixes, missals, and images of the life of Christ and the saints, before which a pious wife might kneel on an ornate prie-dieu.

Robespierre was rescued just in time from the serious penalties of illegitimacy (which he would help to dismantle in the course of the Revolution) by his parents' hasty marriage on 2 January 1758, when his mother was already five months pregnant. His paternal grandparents refused to attend the wedding. Four months later, they relented and agreed to act as witnesses at the baptism of their grandson, Maximilien Marie Isidore de Robespierre, born on 6 May 1758 to a family whose wealth and status were declining steadily at a time when the city, in general, was flourishing. After her first son, Robespierre's mother gave birth to a baby almost every year: two daughters, Charlotte, then Henriette, another son, Augustin, and a fifth child, who did not survive. She died on 14 July 1764 at the age of twenty-nine, an ordinary eighteenth-century woman defeated by pregnancy and childbirth. Robespierre was six.

In the sentimental memoirs of his sister Charlotte, the death of their mother was the pivotal emotional crisis in Maximilien's life. She remembered that their younger brother, Augustin, not yet two, was still away from home with a wet nurse. So as the older siblings watched the funeral preparations they were at least spared the screams of a hungry infant denied its mother's breast. Robespierre was inconsolable in a more complex and lasting way: he treasured the memory of a gentle woman lost to her young children when they most needed her. Before she died she found time to teach him to make lace skillfully, but little else.[3] Whenever he spoke of her to Charlotte later in life, his eyes always filled with tears.

Soon after their mother's death, their father began abandoning his young and grieving family for long periods of time, sometimes reappearing briefly in Arras to borrow money and on one occasion even renouncing his own and his children's claims on the de Robespierre estate in order to raise some ready cash. Charlotte excuses this behavior by claiming that her father was demented with grief, but it is equally likely that he was still the profligate and unstable character who had caused his own parents so much concern. Deprived of their mother and without any independent means of support, the four siblings whom grief had drawn so close together were soon to be physically separated. The two boys went to live with their maternal grandparents in the brewery, and aunts on their father's side took in Charlotte and Henriette, who went on Sunday visits to their brothers, a few streets away across the smaller of Arras's two market squares. The fact that these children were shared out between their relatives like an unwelcome burden did not escape Robespierre. According to Charlotte, his character underwent a complete transformation: where previously he had been boisterous, careless, lighthearted just like other children, he became serious, poised, responsible, and diligent. From this point on he joined in his siblings' childish games only to explain or enforce the rules. He preferred solitary pursuits like building model chapels and reading. He had a small collection of pictures and engravings that he liked to arrange in exhibitions for his sisters, delighting in their admiration. He was also given some sparrows and pigeons that he raised and cherished as pets. He would place them very gently one after the other into his sisters' cupped hands, during their visits.

Charlotte and Henriette once asked to borrow one of these birds, assuring their brother that they would care for it in their aunts' house and return it safely the following week. Robespierre was hesitant, but they were persistent, begging, promising to look after it, so he agreed. Inevitably, the bird was left in the garden, a storm blew up, and it died. Robespierre was furious. "At the news of this death, Maximilien's tears flowed," Charlotte reported. "He showered us with reproaches, which we more than deserved, and vowed never again to entrust us with one of his precious pigeons." Sixty years later, Charlotte herself recalled this timeless childhood drama, "the tragic end of the poor pigeon," tearfully. How could her brother's detractors imagine that his early years in Arras were spent cutting off the heads of small birds with a toy guillotine? How could they so besmirch the kind and sensitive soul, the character full of *le bon naturel* she had loved all her life?

Besides his bereavement and heightened sense of responsibility, it is reasonable to assume that Robespierre grew up with a vague but persistent sense of familial shame. His father came from a long line of provincial lawyers, but he had wasted his promising start in life, failed to build on the achievements of his own father, and left his sons to build their lives with appreciably fewer advantages than those he had himself enjoyed. In 1772 he disappeared for good and his children never knew where or when exactly he died. On top of the practical difficulties Robespierre faced as an orphan—the uncomfortable dependency and penury—he had three siblings to care for and his father's reputation for irresponsibility to live down. He grew up among relatives who could scarcely utter his father's name without regret and disappointment. Gazing out the window of his grandparents' house in the rue Ronville, down the busy street to the Church Jean-Baptiste, he must sometimes have wished it was his mother's more modest name, Carraut, that he was carrying forward into the unknown future, not that of his disgraced father and disappointed grandfather, Maximilien de Robespierre.

ROBESPIERRE'S FIRST SCHOOL was the local Collège d'Arras, where he went at the age of eight already having learned to read and write. Founded in the sixteenth century and richly endowed, the school had over four hundred pupils, all boys. A small number boarded at the school, but most, like Robespierre, were day pupils, the sons of the province's professional families. One old school fellow later remembered Robespierre as "a conventional good boy," another claimed he had a detestable character and an inordinate love of domination, but these are the trite kinds of characterization anyone might make about a distantly recalled school acquaintance. The Collège d'Arras was governed by a committee that included the bishop of Arras, the teachers were priests, and the pedagogical emphasis was on learning the rudiments of Latin. Robespierre worked hard for three years, then distinguished himself by winning a scholarship to the elite Collège Louis-le-Grand in Paris, whose illustrious alumni included the playwright Molière, the philosophe Voltaire, and the Marquis de Sade. Here he would stay until the age of twenty-three, receiving both the rest of his schooling and vocational training in law.

The scholarship was one of four given by Arras's abbot of Saint-Vaast, who was personally known to Robespierre's pious aunts. Those who doubt Robespierre's natural talents and intellect suspect that it was really these family connections—not merit or achievement—that secured him this first important opportunity. Even his sister Charlotte, whose memoirs are usually so biased in his favor, comments that of her two brothers, the elder was the less academically gifted. He was, however, far more diligent and determined to succeed than the younger Augustin. His siblings saw Robespierre off on the public coach to Paris in October 1769, deeply distraught at the parting. Robespierre cried a great deal, too, but there was already something firm and resolute in his character that helped him focus on the long road stretching out before him. In the emotional last days before he left Arras, he gave his sisters all his toys—the model chapels he had constructed, the pictures and engravings he had collected, everything with which he had amused himself as a child—except his birds, for which he found a more trustworthy home. He loved his sisters, would miss them dearly, but they had already killed one of his pigeons, and there were to be no second chances. He was not the kind of person to forget being let down by anyone.

At the time of Robespierre's schooling, education in France was in an unusually chaotic state. In 1762, only seven years before Robespierre left Arras, the controversial Jesuit order had been expelled from its hundreds of educational establishments. Political and theological opponents of the order—the more puritan and morally severe Jansenists and other detractors who denounced the Jesuits' loyalty to Rome as anti-French—had finally prevailed on a reluctant Louis XV to act against them. Throughout the country Jesuit school buildings, property, and facilities were suddenly deserted, the order accused of teaching dangerous theology, promoting sin, amassing wealth, and perverting young boys. The Jesuits had only a single college in Paris, but it was an important one: the large and prestigious Louis-le-Grand, founded in the mid–sixteenth century in the heart of the Latin Quarter, just across the street from the much older Sorbonne. In the administrative confusion that followed the Jesuits' expulsion, Louis-le-Grand came under the direction of the University of Paris and was reinvented as a college particularly dedicated to the encouragement of scholarship students "whose means do not allow them to enjoy the same advantages as others."[4]

Here, at least, among a throng of other scholarship students from backgrounds as modest as his own, the proud and serious young Robespierre, with his paltry wardrobe and conspicuous lack of familial wealth, would feel not wholly out of place. Twice during his time at Louis-le-Grand he had to apply to his *préfet d'études*, or director of studies, for money to buy decent clothes. Perhaps this meant he was significantly poorer than lots of the other boys, or perhaps he preferred to spend his money on books. As he tried to settle into the new school, with its austere entrance gateway, eight quadrangles, private chapel, and lecture rooms, it might have helped that the Collège d'Arras was one of a number of provincial schools recently affiliated with Louis-le-Grand, making the move to Paris a natural next step for a promising pupil from Arras. From Robespierre's point of view, the expulsion of the Jesuits was a piece of good luck, a benign historical contingency that helped him break free from the restrictive circumstances into which he had been born.[5]

The year of the Jesuits' expulsion, 1762, saw another upheaval in educational thinking with the publication of Jean-Jacques Rousseau's sensational novel *Émile*. Part fiction, part treatise on education, the book was almost immediately condemned by the archbishop of Paris and publicly burnt. Despite this, and perhaps in part because of it, *Émile* became a best seller, plunging the country into debate about the schooling of its young and all that was morally, spiritually, and politically at stake. Rousseau escaped arrest and imprisonment only by fleeing France in the middle of the night. It was the "heretical" discussion of religion in *Émile* that caused so much trouble. The archbishop especially objected to Rousseau's insistence that mankind is naturally good but corrupted by society.

Rousseau was of a particularly sensitive and emotional temperament. Like Robespierre, he lost his mother prematurely, from complications following childbirth, and he spent his early childhood reading her collection of sentimental novels, before moving on to philosophy. In his own words, *Émile* was "merely a treatise on the original goodness of man, intended to show how vice and error, alien to his constitution, are introduced into it from outside and imperceptibly distort it."[6] His aim was to set out the kind of education that might preserve and protect the natural goodness of man from the corrupting influences of society. Thus he emphasized not formal schooling but respect for the child as a being in its own right, and the nurturing of self-worth and self-reliance. This was not a practical program of reform but a bold assertion of the influences that shape a child that remains topical to this day. "We know nothing of childhood," Rousseau insisted.[7] One reason was that people were always "looking for the man in the child, not thinking of what he is before he becomes a man."

Rousseau's discussions cover a wide range of topics. He opens the novel with a controversial argument for maternal breast-feeding. Even comparatively impoverished urban women like Robespierre's mother dispatched their babies to wet nurses, usually in the countryside. Rousseau thought this ill advised and unnatural:

> These gentle mothers, having got rid of their babies, devote themselves gaily to the pleasures of the town. Do they know how their children are being treated in the villages? If the nurse is at all busy, the child is hung up on a nail like a bundle of clothes and is left crucified while the nurse goes leisurely about her business. Children have been found in this position purple in the face.[8]

Any mother would feel panic and guilt reading this. Rousseau wanted to shake a society that seemed to him complacent in its practices, so *Émile* was full of clever, carefully aimed provocation. "I hate books" is an odd statement to find in a treatise on education. And some of Rousseau's advice is so far-fetched it is ridiculous: "The only habit the child should be allowed to contract is that of having no habits." At the center of this important book is the revolutionary idea that mankind is not the being blighted by the original sin that lies at the core of Christianity. "Let us lay it down as an incontrovertible rule," he writes, "that the first impulses of nature are always right; there is no original sin in the human heart, the how and why of the entrance of every vice can be traced."

We do not know when Robespierre first read Rousseau. Very probably it was during his time at Louis-le-Grand. What is indisputable is that when he did he took him into his mind as a companion for life. In the *Mémoires authentiques de Maximilien Robespierre*, a forgery from 1830, there is an account of the young Maximilien's pilgrimage to see the aged, isolated, persecuted author in the final years of his extremely strange life. While the source is discredited, almost no one who writes about Robespierre can simply ignore it: the apocryphal meeting with his lifelong hero, who died in 1778, is too alluring to pass over. Besides, the invented Robespierre sounds remarkably like the real one. He recalls:

> I saw you during your last days, and the memory remains a source of joy and pride. I contemplated your august features and saw on them the marks of the dark disappointments to which you were condemned

by the injustice of mankind. Thus I understood all the pains of a noble life dedicated to the cult of truth. They did not scare me. Awareness of having wanted the good for others is the virtuous man's reward; next comes the recognition of those who surround his memory with the honors that his contemporaries denied him. Like you I want to purchase such goods at the price of an arduous life—even at the price of a premature death.[9]

The meeting might have taken place in the woods near the Parisian suburb of Ermenonville, where Rousseau went to live and think about his final book, *Les rêveries du promeneur solitaire* (*Reveries of the Solitary Walker*). Or indoors in an attic in the rue Plâtrière, the author bedridden, the frail student breathless from climbing the stairs, overwhelmed with emotion when he reached the top. Both scenes are fanciful, but the spell Rousseau cast over Robespierre is not. It can be traced in many different ways throughout his life. In the end its political consequences were devastating, but it began as a personal sentiment, nothing more or less than a temperamental affinity. Rousseau had a profound love of individual liberty and a fear of coercion so intense that he was almost allergic to power. Robespierre identified with the victims of injustice—those misunderstood, isolated, denied, or despised. What the two men shared was compassion for the vulnerable and a fierce censoriousness toward those less principled in their attitudes to power than they were confident of being themselves.

THE REGIME AT Louis-le-Grand gave equal attention to the moral character of the school's charges and their academic attainment. Both objectives were pursued through a rigid daily schedule with strong emphasis on devotional duties.[10] During his school days, Robespierre rose from his dormitory bed, freezing cold in winter, at 5:30 a.m., attended prayers at 6:00 a.m., Scripture study at 6:15 a.m., and Mass at 10:30 a.m. A long day of lessons was followed by more prayers and devotional readings at 8:45 p.m., after which the boys undressed for bed while listening to a reading from the life of the saint whose feast occurred the following day. They were expected to go to confession once a month, and the college brought in clergy from outside for this purpose, hoping perhaps to bolster the boys' trust in the confidential nature of the sacrament. How did Robespierre respond to these devout routines? Some of his enemies have imagined him waging a silent bitter protest: standing with the Book of Hours in his hands, the pages resolutely unturned, refusing to pray or sing, shunning the confessional and Holy Communion. But if his own testimony can be believed, he was a more passive and conventional schoolboy. He later rated himself "a pretty poor Catholic ever since my time at college," which suggests that, whether by force or inclination, he must still have been a practicing Catholic at school.

The pupils were effectively cloistered inside the walls of Louis-le-Grand, their contact with the exciting city of Paris outside the main gate on the rue Saint-Jacques severely limited. Earlier in the century, Rousseau had described Paris as a city of "small, dirty and stinking streets, ugly black houses, an air of filth, poverty, beggars, carters, seamstresses, women hawking tisanes and old hats."[11] But with a population of around 600,000, Paris was the largest city in Europe after London, and it is hard to believe that the students at Louis-le-Grand felt as negatively about it as Rousseau did. The boys went on outings only infrequently and always under the strict supervision of chaperones. Aside from the clergymen brought in to hear confession, the only regular visitors to the school were tailors, shoemakers, launderers, and hairdressers. Some of these could be persuaded to smuggle proscribed books, like Rousseau's *Émile*, into the college, concealed inside washing baskets or under piles of mended clothes. For this reason, pupils were expressly forbidden to commission errands of any kind without official permission. Despite these strictures, soon after he arrived in Paris Robespierre managed somehow to develop a close friendship with a canon of Notre-Dame, M. Delaroche. He was a distant relative, and Robespierre's aunts encouraged Maximilien to get in touch in hope of securing a sympathetic confidant in the big city. According to Charlotte, their relationship got off to an excellent start, with Robespierre finding a mentor in the older man and M. Delaroche discerning rare qualities in the young boy. Within two years, however, the canon was dead, and Robespierre had lost yet another adult protector. Once again, he consoled himself with the solitary pursuit of reading.

The college library where he spent so many hours was beautiful. Light streamed in through its twenty-five large windows and fell across the desks and open books. Looking up from his page, a dreamy or distracted schoolboy might grow fond of the paintings that adorned the library walls. Robespierre already loved paintings, but these were far more intriguing than any he could have owned, or perhaps even seen, in Arras. Also in the library stood two pairs of globes, made by the Italian cartographer Coronelli for Louis XIV in the seventeenth century, reminders of the immensity of the world beyond the college walls. When he wasn't dreaming, Robespierre could choose from an impressive range of approved books. The Jesuits had begun the collection of over thirty-five thousand volumes. When they were expelled from the college, most of their books were repurchased for the library. All of them were confiscated during the Revolution when Louis-le-Grand was renamed Equality College, but the revolutionary librarian in charge of the operation was moved to acknowledge that the books were "an assortment of the best works in all fields. It is evident that the library was brought together by men of learning." The books were later returned to the University of Paris, where they have remained ever since. The report on the confiscation also lists two old microscopes, good quality lenses, a strong magnet, a glass case for natural history specimens, and some animal horns and claws. But, in Robespierre's day the curriculum still centered, as it had done for decades, on the classic literatures of Greece and Rome. These were what really interested him, not the newer, tentatively introduced opportunities to study experimental science.

The most detailed account of Robespierre's school days can be found in an embittered early biography that still turns up in Arras from time to time. It drew on the memories of the abbé Proyart, who taught at Louis-le-Grand during Robespierre's time there and was first published in 1795 by Le Blond de Neuvéglise, then amended and reissued in Arras in 1850 by the abbé Proyart's nephew. According to this source, Robespierre was the kind of boy with whom parents preferred their sons not to associate. He was seething with envy and a subversive egoism that constantly put him at odds with the school rules. When he troubled himself to conform, it was only because his pride made him dread humiliating reprimands. He viewed his school as a prison, its pupils as captives, and the teachers (priests or lay clergy) as despotic oppressors of liberty. But he was far from audacious in the face of this oppression. One day, for example, the biography recounts, a prefect, Yves-Marie Audrein, came upon Robespierre reading a forbidden book in an unfrequented corner of the school—*Émile*, perhaps, or another of Rousseau's works illicitly smuggled in. The frightened boy threw himself at the prefect's feet, begging not to be exposed. Since the prefect was himself interested in new and progressive ideas, he had mercy on the young boy. If this incident, or something even remotely similar, actually occurred, abject panic would almost certainly have been a histrionic response. The proscription of books at Louis-le-Grand was taken seriously and covered by the institutional statutes drawn up after the Jesuits were expelled. Article 10 under title 5 stipulates: "Each assistant master will often examine the books that his pupils are reading; he will take away those that are dangerous to morals or religion and not allow even those that are simply useless or might engender a taste for frivolity. He will prevent his pupils from lending books to each other without his consent." There were many such statutes, excessively detailed, covering everything from religious exercises to personal hygiene and behavior on school outings, where pupils were to "walk neither too fast nor too slowly, nor raise their voices, nor offer provocation to anyone." But those who found themselves in contravention of the statutes (and there must have been many) were unlikely to suffer corporal punishment as drastic as that dealt out in some other Parisian colleges. Article 5 under title 1 directs that masters "will use no severity until they have exhausted all other means of making an impression on an honest and sensitive mind."

The statutes were normative, not descriptive, and Robespierre's school doubtless had its fair share of sadistic masters ready to vent their frustrations on vulnerable children. But at least some of the teachers were open to progressive thinking and keen to encourage it in their pupils. Before the Revolution, the abbé Proyart wrote in defense of this aspect of Louis-le-Grand and the nine other colleges that had come under the direction of the University of Paris:

> I have looked everywhere for the Émile of Jean-Jacques Rousseau, and I find him nowhere but in his book. But the Émiles formed by the University of Paris I can find at the head of church and state; I can show them to you, standing out from the crowd, in every walk and condition of society.[12]

Serenely unaware of the revolution to come, Proyart even praised the sense of equality that prevailed at Louis-le-Grand, which he fondly termed a "little republic." No wonder he became so bitter. Looking back in 1800, Proyart insisted that Louis XVI had been effectively dethroned, before even becoming king, by a godless and subversive generation nurtured in the Parisian colleges. He wrote a retrospective diatribe against the expulsion of the Jesuits in which the revolutionary careers of Robespierre, the prefect Audrein who supposedly surprised him with the forbidden book and turned a blind eye, and other famous ex-pupils are presented in apocalyptic terms. Imagining himself back in 1762, he wrote:

> Remember that it is the educational establishment called Louis-le-Grand, from which you are today expelling the Jesuits, that will send forth twenty-five years from now furies armed with torches to burn their country, firebrands who will sound the tocsin against kings and their ministers. The same establishment will send forth an apostate priest whose sacrilegious hand will violate the secret portfolio of his king to draw from it charges justifying regicide and forge capital crimes: his name will be Audrein. And it is from this establishment that there will come, in human form, a more atrocious being than any known to the barbarism of antiquity, who, after having, more than anyone else, determined the murder of his king, will himself rule over you and yours by daggers and assassinations, and will drink the blood of a million men. . . . His execrable name will be Robespierre.[13]

IN 1793, AS the Revolution slid into the Terror and the republican constitution of France was suspended, Robespierre looked back on his schooling. He claimed that the colleges directed by the University of Paris had been "nurseries of republicanism, which formed the mind of the Nation and made it worthy of liberty." This was overstating the case, as he of all people must have been aware: on the brink of the Terror the mind of France was incoherent with factional strife, far from ready for the particular brand of liberty that Robespierre espoused. But his friend and fellow pupil Camille Desmoulins said similar things about their shared experience at Louis-le-Grand, citing masters who taught them to hate their own government and love republican liberty.

> We were brought up in the schools of Rome and Athens, and in the pride of the Republic, only to live in the abjection of the monarchy. . . . It was foolish to imagine . . . that we could admire the past without condemning the present.[14]

One master in particular may have played such a part—the abbé Hérivaux, nicknamed the Roman, whose subject was rhetoric. Well respected and holding a responsible position at the college, Hérivaux apparently saw no glaring incompatibility between his ardent admiration for the heroes of ancient Rome and the confident teaching or practice of Catholicism. Robespierre spent two years in his class, possibly because his performance in the first year was mediocre and he longed to assuage his injured pride and redeem his reputation. With characteristic determination and application, he did manage to win a prize in the second year. But in the meantime his amour propre had been further inflamed by Hérivaux's repeated and only partly playful assertions that there was something distinctively Roman in Robespierre's character and countenance. Robespierre was clearly flattered by Hérivaux, glad of the attention from an approving teacher, and perhaps further reinforced in his fondness for classical literature.

One day in 1775, Louis-le-Grand all but exploded with excitement: Louis XVI had decided to pay a state visit to the school on the way back from his coronation at Reims. The news quickly spread through the corridors, classrooms, and dormitories—everyone talked of it. Louis XVI was just four years older than Robespierre, twenty-one at the time of his accession. He set out with youthful optimism to win acclaim and affection from his subjects. As he put it, "I wish to be loved." France, unfortunately, was not in a particularly loving condition. Public spending was spiraling out of control. Attempts to reform and liberalize the grain trade during the first year of his reign led to panic buying, rioting, a dramatic rise in the price of bread, and unrest that ended with a spate of public executions. In the circumstances, the new king had been advised to scale down and modernize the traditional coronation ceremony that was planned for June 1775—perhaps even move it to Paris, where it might raise more revenue from public participation.

There were limits, however, to Louis XVI's willingness to please public opinion and the coronation was duly enacted in full accordance with ancient custom in the cathedral at Reims, where French kings had been anointed and crowned for a thousand years. He had, in fact, already ruled for ten months by the time of his coronation, and many of his subjects were already seriously querulous. The ceremony was supposed to disguise such rifts in a show of unity and religious respect for the absolute monarch of France, God's representative on earth, in whom sovereign power resided. Instead it inadvertently highlighted the deepest source of the nation's discontent. French society was divided into three orders: the clergy, the nobility, and the third estate (or commons). Everyone who was not a member of either the clergy or the nobility was a member of the third estate, which included professional families like Robespierre's, as well as artisans, manual laborers, and peasants. There were approximately 130,000 members of the clergy, 110,000 members of the nobility, and 24,750,000 members of the third estate. The clergy and the nobility each owned about a fifth of the nation's land but paid no taxes, while the third estate shared the rest of the land and carried the entire tax burden. This unjust arrangement was deeply resented—it meant privileges for the minority and poverty for the majority of French people. At the king's coronation the third estate was further insulted by being barred entry to the cathedral. Afterward Louis XVI was not even presented to them in his full regalia for fear they might get ideas above their station. Among the disappointed crowd outside the cathedral was the young George Jacques Danton from Arcis-sur-Aube, playing truant from his school in Troyes. He had come all the way to the cathedral on foot, hoping to see for himself "how they made a king." But rather than greet the crowd, the new king chose to participate in a series of smaller, more controlled encounters with his public. He laid a commemorative stone at the University of Reims before leaving the city, and he stopped on his way back to Versailles at Louis-le-Grand.

Out of five hundred pupils in the school, Robespierre was chosen to deliver a ceremonial speech of welcome to Louis XVI and Marie Antoinette. He was the master of rhetoric's favorite prize-winning student, so hardly a contentious or unlikely choice. But the abbé Proyart read more into it, suspecting that in choosing Robespierre for such a prominent encounter with the new king, Hérivaux (the Roman) hoped to inspire the heart and soul of a future assassin like Brutus or a conspirator like Catiline. On the day of the visit, Robespierre, much rehearsed and very nervous, knelt outside Louis-le-Grand at the head of the assembled body of the University of Paris, which was also kneeling and waiting for the royal party to arrive. It was June, but it was raining. Possibly it was for this reason that the royal couple remained inside their coach, acknowledged the speech of welcome with polite smiles, and promptly drove on toward the Church of Sainte-Geneviève. Robespierre, along with everyone else, had probably been waiting in the street for many hours. The new or borrowed clothes he was wearing would have been soaked through. It's plausible to assume he felt a sense of anticlimax mingled with relief that his speech was over, or perhaps a twinge of disappointment that the king had not spoken directly to him.

While he was away at school, Robespierre's younger sister Henriette died. In her memoirs, Charlotte remarks that their childhood was awash with tears, almost every year marred by the death of someone close and dear: "This fatal destiny influenced Maximilien's character more than one would think. It left him sad and melancholy." He threw himself into his work, redoubled his efforts to succeed, and, according to Charlotte, "always carried off first prize," which is certainly not true. She claims that despite his sadness and his devotion to his studies, her brother was affable and popular with both his teachers and peers: "his disposition was so even and sweet that he never had a single fight with his fellow pupils; he appointed himself the protector of small boys against older ones, intervening on their behalf and even fighting in their defense when his eloquence did not prevail." Charlotte was so biased in her brother's favor she did not notice the contradiction here—one minute he never quarreled, the next he was brawling to defend the vulnerable in the courtyards of Louis-le-Grand. He was, however, protective of younger boys: Camille Desmoulins, two years his junior, was one of the students who came under his wing. This clever, attractive boy from Guise in Picardy, whose lieutenant-colonel father saved hard to buy him a superior education, became Robespierre's closest companion. Their friendship deepened dramatically during the Revolution—until it went disastrously wrong.[15]

Another schoolmate with a revolutionary future was Louis Marie Stanislaus Fréron, whose memories of Robespierre were distinctly unfavorable:

> He was the same [at college] as he was in later days—melancholy, bilious, morose, and jealous of his comrades' successes; never taking part in their games but going for solitary walks, striding along in the manner of a dreamer and an invalid. There was nothing young about him. His restless face already showed the convulsive grimaces we came to know so well. Uncommunicative, reserved, unbending, secretive, he was marked by a self-centered amour propre, invincible stubbornness, and fundamental dishonesty. I can't recall seeing him smile, not once. If anyone offended him he never forgot it. Vindictive and treacherous, he had already learned to conceal his resentment.[16]

This retrospective account is hostile and sour, but it echoes many of the characteristics attributed to Robespierre by his friends and sister. He was melancholy, serious, reserved, and stubborn: a loner, a dreamer, someone who never forgot an offense or participated in games. Charlotte insisted that she often saw him laugh until he cried, but the haunting judgment that "there was nothing young about him" could be drawn as easily from her own account of Robespierre's childhood as from Fréron's. Friends and enemies see different things in a person, and when they see the same things they interpret them differently. For Charlotte and Desmoulins there was nothing sinister in Robespierre's reserve. For the abbé Proyart and Fréron there was nothing admirable in his stubbornness.

Whatever the character he exhibited at school, not even Robespierre's worst enemy could doubt his academic success. When he left Louis-le-Grand with his law degree at twenty-three, he was awarded a special prize of six hundred livres (a value in excess of a whole year's scholarship). The college's administrative board gave him this prize in recognition of his outstanding abilities—twelve years of good conduct and sustained academic achievement. Even more flattering was the rare concession allowing Robespierre to transfer his scholarship to his younger brother, Augustin. The abbé Proyart, looking back after the Revolution, insists that those who gave Robespierre such honors did not really know him, had no idea how his misshapen character would one day bring a blood-drenched France to her knees. Yet at the time, the board's decision was unanimous. Everyone believed that the young lawyer going home to Arras, with enough capital to set himself up in practice and to offer his sister a home of her own at last, was a credit to the charitable institution that had formed him.

2

THE LAWYER-POET
BACK HOME

Robespierre moved back to Arras in 1781, the same year his sister Charlotte finished her schooling at a charitable institution for impoverished girls in Tournai, the religious center of medieval Flanders, sixty miles northeast of Arras.[1] Throughout most of their childhood the two had seen each other only in the summer holidays, but even so the bond between them was very strong. It was strengthened further by the changes they found in Arras. Together they grieved for their sister Henriette and missed Augustin, who had taken up his brother's scholarship at Louis-le-Grand. They grieved, too, for their maternal grandparents, who had both died recently, and for the family brewery in the rue Ronville, which had been sold. The sale of the Carraut brewery resulted in a legacy, but before it could be made available to the three surviving orphaned grandchildren—Maximilien, Charlotte, and Augustin—who were greatly in need of it, their aunt and uncle on their father's side, with whom Robespierre had been planning to live, laid claim to a share. The de Robespierres were still trying to recover the debts accrued by the children's father, whose irresponsibility and misfortune had left them so close to destitution.

This painful reminder of his father's shame and his own vulnerability at a point when he was deep in mourning must have stung Robespierre for he refused to support his aunt and uncle in their claim and hurried to rent a house of his own in the rue du Saumon, just around the corner from the old brewery that had been his childhood home. But the rent here proved too high for a newly qualified lawyer, so a year later Robespierre and Charlotte moved into rooms opposite the abbey of Saint-Vaast, in the home of the aunt and uncle whose tactlessness had caused such offense. No one can tell if this was because the quarrel had healed or if Robespierre, unable to make ends meet despite his legacy, handsome school prize, and growing legal practice, moved there with resentment and humiliation in his heart. It was another five years before he settled in the rented house in the rue des Rapporteurs that is known today as the Maison Robespierre.

His daily routine as Charlotte remembered it was rigid and austere. Rising early, he worked at home until one of the town's many hairdressers arrived at eight. He had bread and milk for breakfast and then worked before dressing and leaving for the courts by ten. He dined lightly in the afternoon, watering down his wine, consuming lots of coffee (which he could not do without), and displaying a particular fondness for fruit, especially oranges. Some infer from this that he was dyspeptic or frequently constipated, but his sister, unsurprisingly, offers no comment. He took a walk before resuming his work and ate again late in the evening. He often seemed absentminded or preoccupied. Charlotte recalls his indifference to food: "Many times I asked him what he would like to eat at dinner, and he would reply that he had no idea." Not noticing a missing bowl, he once served himself some soup straight onto the tablecloth. Uninterested in games as he had been in childhood, he often sat in the corner during the after-supper cards or conversation—thinking, planning, or perhaps just dreaming. It has become commonplace to claim that, without the Revolution, Robespierre would have continued on this sensible path, living out his natural life as an increasingly respected provincial lawyer. Eventually he might have developed a stomach ulcer, bowel cancer, a respiratory illness spread by the river Crinchon, or some other contagious disease. After a couple of ineffective trips to local doctors and pharmacists (one of them still, in the mid-eighteenth century, stocked "common dragon blood," oil of scorpion, toad powder, and human brains), he would have disappeared into obscurity forever after receiving the last rites of the Catholic Church.[2] But the rigidity of Robespierre's daily routine, far from restricting his prospects, left him free to take advantage of any opportunity for self-betterment or advancement that came his way, and he stuck to it.

During Robespierre's short life he lived in only two places, Arras and Paris. He was briefly in Versailles at the start of the Revolution, but otherwise there were remarkably few changes of scenery. This partially explains the high-spirited excitement with which he described a short trip to visit friends or relatives in Carvins in a letter of June 1783:

> We started at five in the morning. Our car quitted the gates of the city at precisely the same moment as the chariot of the sun sprang from the bosom of the ocean. It was adorned with a cloth of brilliant white, one portion of which floated on the breath of the zephyrs.[3]

The letter continues in hyperbolic mode. Robespierre leans out to raise his hat and bestow a gracious smile on some watchmen who have been on duty all night or else are still half asleep on the early shift. They respond with surly indifference. He remarks, "I have always had an infinite self-love; that mark of contempt cut me to the quick; and for the rest of the day my temper was unbearable." He can, it seems, laugh at himself. At Sens, while his traveling companions pause for breakfast, he avoids visiting the tourist sites and climbs a hill to survey the plains over which the Prince of Condé, still in his early twenties, led France to victory against the Spaniards in 1643. Then he rouses a porter with keys to the Hôtel de Ville. Of all the things to see in Sens—the famous cathedral where Saint Thomas à Becket spent time in exile, the Palais Synodal, with its rose windows and battlements—the Hôtel de Ville was a curious choice. The building, Robespierre notes, is neither remarkable nor grand, but he is fascinated to see where the great T—— (he does not give the name), who combined the roles of judge and medical doctor, administered justice and afterward prescribed medical treatment for the criminals:

I rush into the hall. Seized with a holy awe, I fall on my knees in this august temple and kiss with transport the seat that was formerly pressed by the rump of the great T——. It was thus that Alexander knelt at the tomb of Achilles and that Caesar paid his homage to the monument that contained the ashes of the conqueror of Asia![4]

The identity of "the great T——" is unclear, but the reason Robespierre was so impressed by him is explicit in the letter: "This great man enjoyed, by virtue of his double office, the most extensive power that a man ever exercised over his compatriots." Achilles, Alexander, Caesar were conquering heros of a kind, but the sort of power Robespierre admired was more sophisticated and philanthropic. He was excited by the idea of intervening in the lives of criminals and sick people—making a difference for the better.

Arriving at last at Carvins, Robespierre is immensely flattered by the interest and enthusiasm with which his party is greeted:

How pleasant it is to travel! I said to myself. It is a great truth that one is never a prophet in one's own land. At the gates of one's own town one is despised; six leagues beyond it one is a personage worthy of public curiosity![5]

Robespierre is certainly sending himself up, but at the same time his florid rhetoric is an evident source of self-regarding delight. The letter also captures his readiness to suspect others of disrespecting him. The surly watchmen are a minor example, and even Robespierre could see the joke. Yet the theme of misunderstood, unrecognized, or slighted greatness haunts his early writings just as it recurs over and over again in later speeches, pamphlets, and letters. As he says in one of his poems:

> The just man's torment, at his final hour,
> The only pang he feels—and I shall feel—
> Is the dark breath of calumny and blame
> Breathed by a grimmer ghost than death himself:
> The hate of those for whom he gives his life.[6]

Law was the traditional profession of the de Robespierre family and in Arras there were still contacts and patrons to help Robespierre at the beginning of his career, despite the disrepute into which his father had fallen. While at school he had written to the head of the Paris bar for advice: "I want to be a lawyer. Of all the qualities needed for distinguishing oneself in that profession, I at least possess keen ambition and an unqualified desire for success."[7] According to Charlotte, though, Robespierre's attraction to the law was motivated by more than familial tradition, pragmatism, or ambition: he had a personal predilection for what he believed to be the most sublime profession in the world, when practiced impartially and humanely. She remembers him saying:

> To defend the oppressed against their oppressors, to plead the cause of the weak against the strong who exploit and crush them, this is the duty of all hearts that have not been spoiled by egoism and corruption. . . . It is so sweet to devote oneself to one's fellows that I do not know how there can be so many unfortunates still without support or defenders. As for me, my life's task will be to help those who suffer and to pursue through my avenging speech those who take pleasure in the pain of others. How happy I will be if my feeble efforts are crowned with success and if, at the price of my devotion and sacrifices, my reputation is not tarnished by the crimes of the oppressors I will fight![8]

Even if it is true that Robespierre made such declarations in the privacy of his home, in front of the mirror, or in the hearing of his sister, her account was composed long after the Revolution. At the time, Robespierre's motives for choosing the law were more likely a mixture of high-minded principle and straightforward personal ambition for ordinary things like status, respect, income, and independence. It is possible, too, that he wanted to prove to his de Robespierre relatives that he could be every bit as impressive as his grandfather had been, and considerably more so than his father ever was.

The judicial system, like so much else in old regime France, was extremely intricate and confusing. Arras had nine separate courts and Robespierre's work generally took him to three of them: the Conseil d'Artois (Council of Artois), the *Echevinage* (Magistrate's Court), and the *Salle Episcopale* (Bishop's Court). The courts met in the morning—

after Mass—in expansive halls connected by dark passages and arcades: here the counts of Flanders had resided before Artois became part of France; now the walls were hung with portraits of distinguished local nobles and public officials. Illicit lovers, duelists, beggars, and criminals took refuge in the shadows, just feet away from the rooms in which justice was done. The arcades were a particularly dangerous place to be at night and the rubbish strewn about festered on hot summer days. Robespierre, adequately patronized and intent on advancement, quickly established himself in his chosen profession, losing relatively few cases. His sister claims people often asked her to explain the secret of his success. He had some natural talents: he was fluent and logical, but according to Charlotte it was his choice of cases that contributed most of all to his growing reputation. "He took on only just cases, never unjust, and he almost always won them." He preferred to represent the poor. When opposing parties approached him, he chose to represent the poorest of them, even if it meant he might never be paid. "The supporter of the oppressed and the avenger of the innocent," Charlotte called him, making a direct connection between the boy who protected the vulnerable at school and the young lawyer.[9]

One of Robespierre's friends in Arras was a lawyer, twenty years older, nicknamed "Barometer" Buissart on account of his keen interest in experimental science. Robespierre corresponded with Antoine Buissart and his wife throughout his political career—a fact overlooked by his detractors, who insist he was incapable of lasting friendship and eager to renounce his provincial provenance. Buissart helped to bring Robespierre his first taste of fame beyond the city walls by involving him in the legal defense of one M. de Vissery de Bois-Valé. M. de Vissery was a lawyer, painter, botanist, amateur scientist, and inventor: among the many forgotten things he invented was a technique for preserving pure water for over a year. In 1780 he designed and positioned a lightning conductor on the roof of his house at Saint-Omer. This consisted of a pointed piece of a gilded sword screwed onto a sixteen-foot iron bar, decorated with a weathercock at the join, and connected to a metal pipe running the length of the neighboring house. The neighbor complained and a rumor spread that the conductor threatened the lives of all in its vicinity. One woman started a petition to have it removed, provoking an early example of Robespierre's sarcasm: "Many refused the glory of associating themselves with this initiative," he commented dryly. There were, in fact, only six or seven signatories. G. H. Lewes, one of Robespierre's English biographers, joined him in sneering at "these obese and stupid citizens of Arras."[10] It is more charitable, though, to assume that the ordinary, provincial neighbors simply failed to understand the purpose of the eye-catching novelty on M. de Vissery's roof. The fact that the decorative weathercock featured figurative bolts of lightning cannot have reassured those of nervous dispositions.[11]

When the Magistrate's Court decreed that the conductor must come down, M. de Vissery appealed to the higher Council of Artois, engaging Robespierre as his advocate on Buissart's advice. Barometer Buissart himself wrote a detailed paper on the subject after seeking guidance from experts in the field, among them the distinguished philosophe the Marquis de Condorcet, then secretary to the Academy of Sciences in Paris, and the future revolutionary journalist Dr. Jean-Paul Marat, a candidate for the directorship of the new Academy of Science in Madrid, known at the time for his experiments with optics and electricity. Robespierre drew heavily on Buissart's carefully researched paper in his pleadings of 1783—science, after all, had not been his subject at school. In court, however, he gave the performance of his early career, evoking the persecution of Galileo, Harvey, and Descartes and calling on the judges to side with the forces of progress and enlightenment. Scathingly he belittled those who thought lightning conductors disturbed the peace and threatened public safety; appealing to national pride, he insisted that such instruments were already commonplace in England, and France must not lag behind. French scientists had contributed to the discovery of electricity—M. Dalibard, for example, had proved Benjamin Franklin's theory that lightning and electricity are one and the same during an experiment at Marly-la-Ville in 1752. Ignorance must not deprive the nation of its right to benefit from scientific advances.

Robespierre won the case and his success was reported in the Parisian newspaper *Mercure de France*. M. de Vissery was pleased, despite renewed threats of prosecution or vandalism by his still disquieted neighbors, and he offered to finance the publication of the pleadings to make them available for wider circulation. Robespierre gratefully accepted the offer and sent a personal copy to Franklin, who was in Paris at the time, addressing him as "one whose least merit is to be the most distinguished scientist in the world." Franklin's reply, if there was one, is lost.

While the lightning conductor case shows Robespierre as an ambitious lawyer, his defense of Marie Sommerville in 1786 shows him championing the poor and oppressed. Marie Sommerville was an Englishwoman, the young widow of Colonel George Mercer, lieutenant governor of South Carolina. She had lived in Saint-Omer as a child, returned many times during her marriage, and moved back permanently after her husband's death. Here she fell into serious debt. Unfortunately for her, the adoptive town, of which she had always been so fond, was one of a small number in the province of Artois where it was legal both to seize a debtor's belongings and imprison him or her without a warrant, even when the debtor in question was a foreigner. Sommerville was duly taken into custody on May 24, 1786. She complained that she had been humiliatingly arrested in her own home, escorted roughly to prison, followed by a crowd of curious onlookers, and refused medication during her few days of incarceration. Robespierre argued her case flamboyantly, claiming that women should be exempt from Saint-Omer's draconian debtors law:

> The gullibility and inexperience of their sex allow women to enter too lightly into contracts detrimental to their liberty; their weakness and sensibility render them more vulnerable to the shame and rigor of imprisonment; there is also the terrible effect imprisonment has on their natural timidity, and the fatal consequences of such treatment, especially during pregnancy—what more can I say? Women's delicate honor is publicly, legally, irreversibly debased in the eyes of men, whose tenderness disappears along with their respect. . . . What compensation could there be for such inconvenience and cruelty, beyond simply expediting the payment of a civil debt?[12]

Robespierre's opponents were skeptical of his gallantry. Truth and justice, they complained, would not have required such decorative rhetoric. Allegedly, Sommerville had been spotted leaving prison happy and well in the company of a doctor, and the only change in her condition was that she had been forced to settle some of her debts. In the event, there was no ruling on the case because the special privilege of arresting debtors in Saint-Omer was revoked in August that year. Perhaps this was one of the many occasions on which Robespierre, according to his sister, received no payment. Instead there was the satisfaction of seeing the law, to which he had so eloquently objected on his client's behalf, abolished. Even before the Revolution there were many such attempts to rationalize the legal system of the old regime, and Robespierre was fast forging a distinguished, if controversial, career through his own efforts in this direction. Already he tended to be long-winded and markedly sentimental. But he also had a ready sneer and could be cuttingly condescending—skills required by his profession. He was an adversarial advocate, so even though he invoked the principles of eternal truth and justice, it was not his job to be impartial.

Very soon after he began practicing law in Arras, Robespierre was chosen as one of five judges in the Bishop's Court. In the course of his routine work for this court, Robespierre was required to sentence a murderer to death. The death was to be a hanging, possibly preceded by a protracted breaking on the wheel, nothing like the comparative speed and merciful efficiency that the guillotine would bring. Before the Revolution, decapitation was considered a privilege, reserved for noble criminals who died as they had lived, carefully segregated from commoners. Robespierre went home that evening to Charlotte in a terrible state with "despair in his heart."[13] He did not eat for two days and paced the house muttering over and over again, "I know he is guilty, that he is a villain, but even so, to cause a man to die!" Intent on proving that Robespierre was anything but the bloodthirsty charlatan vilified by his detractors, Charlotte claims that he was so disturbed by this case that he resigned his post immediately—a claim not borne out by the facts, since he still held the position in 1788.

Charlotte perhaps exaggerates her brother's qualms about capital punishment, yet there is no reason to believe that she invented them. Robespierre prided himself on progressive and enlightened views, he would have been familiar with the strong arguments against the death sentence made by eighteenth-century philosophers such as Cesare Beccaria, and he was squeamish by nature. In an essay published in August 1784, he argued for extending the privilege of decapitation—"a punishment to which we have come to attach a sort of éclat"—to commoners.[14] Here he anticipated the revolutionary demand for the right to efficient, dignified, and equal capital punishment. "Crimes of the same kind will be punished by the same kind of punishment," Dr. Guillotin would assert in 1789, "whatever the rank and status of the guilty man may be."[15] In the meantime a reluctant Robespierre went ahead and condemned the murderer to a hideous end—his signature is on the death warrant.

As much as this incident discloses Robespierre's attitude toward capital punishment, it also reveals his habitual response to nervous strain. Throughout the Revolution he suffered periods of physical and mental collapse, usually precipitated by the need to make an important decision. Sometimes these seem strategic; his enemies were (and remain) convinced that feigning illness was one of the many manipulative techniques he used to get his own way. But even in Arras he suffered at least one episode of psychosomatic illness. In this early example, as in many later ones, Robespierre struggled to reconcile his public actions with his personal principles and convictions. When this proved impossible, he collapsed, stopped eating, and brooded obsessively. The demands of public responsibility and power filled him with anxiety. He was, in important respects, constitutionally and temperamentally ill suited to assume either—but nevertheless intent on pursuing them both.

ANTOINE BUISSART'S PATRONAGE did not stop with bringing Robespierre legal cases; he also helped him win election to the Academy of Arras, a gathering of the city's "best brains," who met regularly to present and discuss academic papers. Established in 1773 on the foundations of a local literary society, the academy thrived for a decade before Robespierre was invited to join. His inaugural speech in 1784 was devoted to attacking the tradition of bad blood whereby a criminal's family was shamed and disgraced by association with his or her crime. He wrote up his speech afterward and entered it in a prize competition organized by the Academy of Metz. Undoubtedly, the subject of bad blood evoked the circumstances of Robespierre's childhood and the injured pride that dogged him throughout his life. Professionally, too, he was drawn to ponder the individuation of guilt and the principles and processes through which people apportion blame. Shame by association, he insisted, was simply an extension of the natural tendency to regard all individuals as intimately connected to their family, friends, and fellow citizens, but its implications varied depending on the form of government. It was characteristic of democratic government to treat people as individuals, to liberate them from shame by association, or at least provide them with opportunities to regain personal dignity through independent acts of merit, heroism, and public service. The key to republican or democratic government was patriotic virtue, Robespierre argued: the triumph of the general good over private interests or personal relationships. "A man of high principle will be ready to sacrifice to the State his wealth, his life, his very nature—everything, indeed, except his honor."[16]

In his essay, Robespierre drew directly on the political theory of the Baron de Montesquieu, who, in his *De l'esprit des loix* (*The Spirit of the Laws*, published in 1748) argued that honor was the mainspring of a well-ordered monarchy, virtue the mainspring of republican government, and fear the mainspring of despotism. Honor and its opposite—shame—made sense under a monarchical form of government where individuals were closely connected to one another through personal and familial loyalties. But what place was there for honor in a democratic republic of patriotic individuals ready to sacrifice their personal relationships to the public good of the state? This question would return to trouble Robespierre during the Revolution as he tried to put theory into practice, but in this early essay he answered it abstractly, introducing a curious distinction between "philosophical honor" and "political honor." Philosophical honor, as he defined it, was none other than a pure soul's exquisite sense of its own dignity—an entirely private sentiment based on reason and duty, existing in isolation, far from the vulgar gaze of mankind—a matter of purely personal conscience. It was, no doubt, Robespierre's own "philosophical honor" that caused him to suffer so much when passing the death sentence on a murderer. In contrast, "political honor," of the kind Montesquieu identified in monarchies, was the desire for social distinction, grandeur, and esteem—more to do with vanity than with virtue at an individual level, even if it was useful in producing unintended social benefits. Here Robespierre showed off his learning, echoing Francis Bacon: "No nobles, no monarchy: no monarchy, no nobles."[17] And he made the link between the temptation to respect someone merely because he came from a grand or noble family and the equally irrational or unjust tendency to despise the children of a condemned man.

As a young lawyer, Robespierre was far from calling for a new social and political system based on philosophical honor. His essay did suggest that there were serious limitations to monarchies founded on political honor, but if he harbored ideas about the kind of system that might one day replace the monarchy in France, he kept them to himself. Like almost everyone else, he argued for incremental reform and insisted that "there is no need for us to change the whole system of our legislation; it is dangerous to look for the remedy for a specific ill in a general revolution."[18] What is more distinctive, however, in this early essay, is the close connection Robespierre envisaged between politics and morality. He regretted politicians' habitual contempt for moral precepts and instead insisted that:

> The laws of God [*l'être suprême*] need no other sanction than the natural consequences he himself has attached to the audacity of those who infringe them and the fidelity of those who respect them. Virtue produces happiness as the sun produces light. Crime results in unhappiness as certainly as filthy insects issue from the heart of corruption.[19]

The Academy of Metz's judges had some reservations about Robespierre's essay, but while they could not bring themselves to award him first prize, they decided to give him a second, equal in monetary value though not in glory. Robespierre spent the prize money (four hundred livres, approximately 230 dollars today) getting his essay printed.[20] In retrospect, it is ironic that it was Pierre-Louis Rœderer, an enterprising member of Metz's supreme court, who donated funds for the prize awarded to Robespierre. Later, looking back on the Revolution, Rœderer would argue that the French, with their love of social distinctions, were "more antipathetic than any other people to democracy."[21] Robespierre, in contrast, would stake his career and his life on the opposite view.

In his essay, Robespierre ranked the personal purity of philosophical honor far above the social benefits of political honor. But was he deceiving himself? From an early age, social distinction meant a great deal to him. Competitive, determined, ambitious as he was, how else could he hope to measure his own success if not in relation to that of his peers? An incident at the Academy of Arras gave a hint of his competitive streak. After the death of the academy's permanent secretary, Alexandre Harduin, in 1785, elections were held to select a replacement. Of the twelve academicians present, ten voted for a distinguished local landowning noble, Dubois de Fosseux, one for Robespierre, and one for another candidate. On the same occasion, three other officials were elected, Barometer Buissart among them, but once more, Robespierre was passed over with only one vote. Perhaps he voted for himself.

Things became tense with the creation of an additional three chairs soon after Dubois de Fosseux assumed his post. Someone proposed Le Gay, a talented young lawyer already winning a reputation as an accomplished poet. At twenty Le Gay had founded his own literary society in Arras, the Rosati; at twenty-four he was a practicing lawyer in the Council of Artois, and it seems that he played some small role on the opposite side from Robespierre in the famous lightning conductor case.[22] When Le Gay's name was put forward, Robespierre and Buissart were strongly opposed. The evening before the vote was to take place Dubois de Fosseux received a visit from Robespierre to discuss the matter in private. The next day, when the vote went ahead, the two friends absented themselves from the proceedings. After Le Gay was elected, Buissart threatened to resign his chair. However, Dubois de Fosseux, proving himself a felicitous choice as permanent secretary, refused to be discouraged by such squabbles and diplomatically restored peace to the academy. Why were Robespierre and Buissart so adamantly against Le Gay? Robespierre's motive may have been simple loyalty to his chief friend and supporter in Arras. Or it might have been more personal rivalry or irritation over Le Gay's part in the lightning conductor case. But whatever it was, he showed no reluctance to engage in factional strife. His visit to Dubois de Fosseux the evening before the academy's vote foreshadows many such personal visits during the Revolution: "If Monsieur Robespierre comes to call, tell him

I'm not at home!" said the great political theorist the abbé Sieyès in his dotage, years after Robespierre was dead, still haunted by the fear of a knock on the door.

ROBESPIERRE'S NEXT ATTEMPT to win a literary prize came in 1784 when, for the fourth year running, the Academy of Amiens announced a competition for the best eulogy of the town's most famous poet, Jean Baptiste Gresset. None of the submissions had been deemed of high enough quality to merit an award, so Robespierre thought it prudent to solicit some strategic advice from Buissart, who had an influential friend in Amiens. This time the prize was worth twelve hundred livres (approximately seven hundred dollars), and Robespierre doubtless needed the cash as much as he yearned for the glory. Gresset was best known for his mock-heroic poem *Ver-Vert*, published in 1734 while he was still a Jesuit priest teaching at Louis-le-Grand. Soon afterward he was expelled from the order and led a successful secular life writing for the stage, before retiring to Amiens, where he lived austerely, atoning for the frivolity of his youth. (Voltaire quipped: *"Gresset se trompe, il n'est pas si coupable"*—Gresset is wrong, he is not as culpable as all that.[23]) *Ver-Vert* is about a parrot, the cloistered pet of one convent that is sent on a visit to another, learns profane expressions on the way, shocks the nuns on arrival, and is sent back in disgrace to repent and die. Aside from money and glory there was much to attract Robespierre to Gresset as a subject: the connection to Louis-le-Grand, literature, the theater, birds, and the poet's celebrated visit to Arras in 1740, when he attended a meeting of the literary society that later became the academy. Robespierre's essay drew a flattering comparison between Gresset and Alexander Pope, pointing out that *The Rape of the Lock* relied on the formulas of epic convention, whereas in *Ver-Vert* Gresset challenged his imagination to slip through the convent grille and animate the sedate life of the cloister. Robespierre also claimed to find Gresset's verse natural, unaffected, and more appealing than Voltaire's. He stopped short of placing him on the same level as Rousseau but insisted that he stood far above the crowd of lyrical poets.

Somewhat wistfully, Robespierre quoted Rousseau's enthusiastic praise of Gresset earlier in the century: "What marvel in a man of twenty-six years! How dismaying for our supposed modern wits!"[24] Such affirmation from his revered hero is what Robespierre would have wanted for himself—in 1784, he, too, was twenty-six years old. He also praised Gresset's respect for religious sentiment. Criticizing poets whose work, by unleashing irreligious passions, jeopardized the peace and tranquillity of their own and future generations, he held Gresset up as the exception, the defender of religion in the face of its detractors. Robespierre sincerely approved—the fact that Gresset was expelled from the Jesuit order only added to his admiration: here was a fellow spiritual loner, unafraid to follow his conscience. Nevertheless, with a backward glance perhaps to the beloved library at Louis-le-Grand, he described the Jesuit order in very fond terms as "this famous society . . . offering such a gentle retreat to men who are devoted to the charms of study and literature," such as "the poet of the Graces [Gresset]."[25]

Despite advice from Amiens via Buissart (overdo the praise since Gresset "is never spoken of here except with veneration, and they think it a crime if one expresses any doubts as to his celebrity"), Robespierre chose to concentrate more on the poet's outstanding character than on his literary achievements:

> I have counted it a merit in Gresset to have drawn upon himself the sarcasm of a number of literary men; for I have been so bold as to insist upon his virtue, upon his respect for morality, and upon his love of religion. This will undoubtedly expose me to the ridicule of the witty majority; but it will win me two votes which are more than a recompense—that of my conscience and that of yours.[26]

Not for the first or last time Robespierre identified with a great man whom he believed to be despised, slighted, and isolated. There was something more than faintly risible in Robespierre's repeated insistence that Gresset should be admired for choosing duty over glory and eschewing worldly trophies that only the vulgar prize, while striving so hard himself to win a literary competition. Besides which, the judges in Amiens could hardly be expected to view their town's literary celebrity as a vulnerable victim of sarcasm in need of a valiant and virtuous advocate. Robespierre's eulogy protested too much and failed to concentrate on the merits of Gresset's verse. He did not win the prize but paid to have his essay published even so—perhaps in the hope of making some money from it, perhaps out of wounded pride or vanity. On receiving a copy, Dubois de Fosseux wrote to thank Robespierre in lighthearted verse, politely expressing astonishment that he had not been awarded the prize, which may or may not have been a comfort to the sensitive and disappointed author.

ROBESPIERRE'S LITERARY INTERESTS also led him to try his hand at poetry. Surviving examples reveal his talent as modest and his sensibility as effete, even silly on occasions. His sister evidently thought so when she advised against publishing a poem about spitting and nose blowing that might undermine his growing reputation as a lawyer.[27] Most of his poems are addressed to women. The only one published in his lifetime was a madrigal to "young and beautiful Ophelia." It exalted innocent modesty and ended with the unworldly, indeed positively misleading, piece of advice: "You will only be better loved / if you fear you are not."[28] Another began, "Do you want to know, O charming Henriette / Why Love is the greatest of gods?"[29] There were melancholy lines concerning the marriage of a girl named Emilie to someone else, and more of the same addressed to the shy beauty Sylvie. Unless Robespierre was using a number of synonyms for the same woman or simply addressing figments of his imagination, the young lawyer was busy composing gallant poetry for any and all— he was either frivolously self-indulgent, narrowly focused on improving his poetic skill, or far cooler at heart than his words imply. An early portrait depicts him with a rose in one hand and the other on his heart, above the motto All for my love. "Which one?" a cynical recipient of his missives might ask.

Beyond the safe allusiveness of verse, Robespierre's interaction with women was markedly stilted and formal. In December 1786, for example, he wrote this letter to accompany a copy of one of his professional speeches—not everyone's idea of a courting gift:

> Madame
>
> I have dared to think that a speech dedicated to the defence of the oppressed would be an homage not unworthy of your acceptance, so I have decided to present this to you. The interest you were kind enough to take in the matter that is the subject will suffice to justify this homage, were justification required. In the midst of the painful labors necessitated by this work, you, Madame, were with me during some moments that I shall never forget, and your presence renewed my courage. Today, when I have finished my work, I seek the reward that is its due, and find it in offering this to you.[30]

There is considerably more in this letter about the sender than about the recipient. His gratitude is well expressed, but the woman concerned is not invoked personally; her contribution is defined solely in relation to Robespierre's own work. And yet, if he was emotionally self-absorbed, his theoretical views were egalitarian and feminist far ahead of the times. A woman's contribution to academic discussion, he argued in one of his papers to the Academy of Arras, was the natural complement to a man's and of equal value. For this reason he thought members of both sexes should be admitted to the academy.[31]

Shy and reserved in character, busy and ambitious at work, socializing primarily with other men, Robespierre must have had limited opportunities to build friendships with women, romantic or otherwise. One friend of Charlotte's bred some canaries for Robespierre and received in return a letter of thanks that was both mildly flirtatious and faintly disturbing:

> What was our surprise when, approaching their cage, we saw them dash themselves against the wires with an impetuosity that made us tremble for their lives! That is what they do whenever they see the hand that feeds them. What plan of education have you adopted with them, and from where have they acquired their wild character? . . . A face like yours, has it not reconciled the canaries to the human countenance? Or is it that they can support the sight of no other, having once seen it?[32]

According to Charlotte, many women were interested in her brother and he could have easily made an advantageous marriage with one of the local heiresses. But at the time there was only one girl he wanted to marry, his sister claims. This was Anaïs Deshorties, the stepdaughter of one of their aunts on the de Robespierre side of the family. Perhaps Robespierre, being sensitive and awkward, found it easier to contemplate intimacy with a member of his extended family. Even so, he courted Anaïs for two or three years without making much progress, in strong contrast to his father's conduct at a similar age. Two letters sent in June 1787 to an unnamed girl, who may have been Anaïs, show Robespierre sad and dejected. The first alludes to a rejection:

> As to the cruelties that your letter contains, I will respond by honestly exposing my feelings. The interest I take in people does not have a fixed term, when they are people like you. That which you inspire in all those who know to appreciate you will not cease in me until I do, because I do not know anyone more deserving of it than you. In addition, the goodness that is always clear in your dealings with me places me under a sort of obligation, and to abjure such a feeling would make me unjust and ungrateful, and I wish to be neither.[33]

This is the letter of someone with rather contorted emotions. The undying fidelity in response to the beloved's perceived cruelty, the peculiar sense of duty, the self-righteous integrity, and, above all, the self-regard, are all highly reminiscent of the love letters in Rousseau's *La Nouvelle Héloïse*.[34] Published in Paris in 1761, this astonishingly popular novel—in France alone there were seventy-two editions before the end of the century—tells the story of Julie, who loves the unsuitable Saint-Preux but in the end renounces passion in favor of a virtuous life of marriage and motherhood. Rousseau described the process of writing it in his *Confessions*:

> Forgetting the entire human race, I invented for myself whole companies of perfect creatures, whose virtue was as celestial as their beauty, and of true, tender, and faithful friends such as I had never known here below.[35]

Rousseau projected his own romantic passions onto Saint-Preux, whose letters could have served as models for Robespierre's:

> An indefinably sweet and consoling idea eases my suffering in being far from you, when I think that you have commanded it. The pain you cause me is less cruel than if fortune had sent it. If it serves to make you happy, I would be sorry not to have felt it. It is the guarantee of its reward, for I know your soul too well to believe you capable of cruelty for its own sake.[36]

Robespierre's second letter to the unnamed woman from June 1787 further suggests the influence of Rousseau:

> The situation in which you are does not matter to me, providing you are happy. But are you? I doubt it a little and this doubt afflicts me, since when one is not personally happy, one consoles oneself with the happiness of others, one wants at least to see those who most deserve it enjoy happiness.[37]

So much earnest renunciation! Yet if these letters were addressed to Anais, as Charlotte's testimony suggests, what were the obstacles to Robespierre's love? Were his feelings not reciprocated? Did he think he had to further establish himself professionally and financially before proposing marriage? Or did he, like Rousseau, project his most intense feelings into a one-sided relationship that was really only part of his fantasy life and elaborate self-image? Charlotte claimed that when he returned to Arras in 1791 for his first visit since the Revolution and found Anais married to another local lawyer, he was heartbroken. In his sister's eyes, Anais, fickle and cruel, was entirely to blame for the failure of the relationship. But it seems possible that Robespierre gave her only scant and confused grounds for hope. He was—as Rousseau had been—exceptionally self-absorbed.

Robespierre's early love poems may have had little or nothing to do with actual romantic entanglements in Arras, but one certain source of his inspiration was his membership in the Rosati, the elite literary society founded by Le Gay, with whom Robespierre had probably patched up his quarrel. The Rosati met every June in a garden at

Blanzy on the banks of the river Scarpe. The meetings were languid and foppish affairs involving the ceremonial smelling of roses, courteous exchanges of lighthearted verse, singing, a bit of dancing perhaps, and elegant al fresco consumption of good food and wine. Dubois de Fosseux said of Robespierre at this time:

> One cannot but acknowledge his fitness for membership in the Rosati when one sees him taking part in the pastoral revels of the village and enlivening the dancers by his presence. See! The god of eloquence himself mixes familiarly with mortals and reveals, beneath the shepherd's smock, the gleam of his divinity.[38]

Queen Marie Antoinette, organizing her courtly attendants into charming pastoral tableaux in the woods around Versailles, was aiming for similar aesthetic effects, though the image of Robespierre prancing on the village green in a shepherd's smock is considerably more incongruous.

Rosati is an anagram for Artois, and with its stylized rituals the society may have been linked to one of the local Freemason lodges—both Robespierre and Le Gay were members of the Hesdin Lodge, and Robespierre's grandfather had been a prominent founder of Freemasonry in Arras.[39] However, the evidence suggests that whatever else might have been going on (and it is notoriously difficult to tell, where Freemasonry is concerned), Robespierre's participation in the Rosati was largely motivated by personal friendship and literary interest. Elaborate initiation rites involved the postulant's waiting in a private bower to be presented with a rose, inhaling the fragrance three times, pinning the flower to his jacket, and downing a glass of wine flavored with rose petals before receiving welcoming embraces and hearing speeches by the other members. The Rosati adopted cross-gendered pseudonyms: one lawyer was known as "Sylvie"—the shy beauty, perhaps, addressed in Robespierre's poem, which also evoked "the noble and brilliant rose," queen of flowers. His long acceptance speech to the society, *Eloge de la Rose*, concludes:

> It is happiness that I wish for you. Such happiness awaits you if, true to the charm of your vocation, you prove zealous in fulfilling the

sacred obligations it imposes on you. In short: love the rose, love your brothers; these two precepts contain the whole law. . . . *In his duobus tota lex est.*[40]

The manuscript of this affected piece of mumbo-jumbo is full of careful crossings-out and rewordings. Robespierre evidently cared about impressing his fellow society members. He was hardly a natural sybarite and the image of him lying on a river bank composing love poems and joining in drinking games is difficult to reconcile with the nervous austerity that characterized him from early youth to the end of his life. But at this stage he was open to every opportunity for bettering himself that came along. If friends he had made through the Academy of Arras invited him to join their Rosati Society, he joined it. If this meant writing silly poems, he wrote them. Maybe he even enjoyed it; Rosati meetings were not the only occasions on which he participated enthusiastically in sentimental rituals—during the Revolution he even invented several of his own.

EARLY IN 1789 Robespierre had another opportunity to align himself with the forces of progress. The soldier M. Dupond was a victim of familial injustice. Having deserted the French army and served in those of Sweden and Denmark for over twenty years, he returned home to Artois to claim his share of a wealthy uncle's legacy. His relatives flatly refused to recognize his claim, and when it became clear that the outraged Dupond could not be silenced, they obtained a lettre de cachet against him. Once issued, this notorious document allowed imprisonment without trial for an indefinite period of anyone deemed a nuisance: insistent creditors, cuckolded husbands, errant children, and so forth. It was a form of privilege very easy for noblemen to obtain and, as such, one of the most hated abuses in old regime France—the means by which so many innocents found themselves locked up in prisons like the Bastille. When Dickens's Dr. Manette is "recalled to life" at the beginning of *A Tale of Two Cities*, he has been buried inside the Bastille for almost eighteen years by a lettre de cachet, "a privilege that . . . the boldest people are afraid to speak of in a whisper."[41]

After Dupond was at last released from prison, he engaged Robespierre to press his original claim on the family money. The ambitious young lawyer seized this opportunity for a broadly focused attack on the lettres de cachet and the corrupt system that issued them. In pleading Dupond's case, Robespierre called upon Louis XVI to complete the work of his illustrious predecessors and move France forward to reasonable, virtuous reform:

> To lead men to happiness through virtue, and to virtue by legislation founded on eternal principles of justice and so framed as to restore human nature to all its rights and all its dignity; to renew the immortal compact that is to bind man to his Creator and to his fellow citizens, by removing all the causes of oppression that now create throughout the world fear, distrust, meanness, selfishness, hatred, and cupidity; behold, Sire, the glorious mission to which you are called.[42]

Robespierre wrote this plea in February, just months before the outbreak of the Revolution. In 1789 he was far from alone in expecting, or at least hoping, that the king would play a major part in bringing about the changes that were so urgently needed in France. What isolated him from his contemporaries was the degree to which, over the following five years—extraordinary years of revolt, turmoil, hunger, war, and execution—he strove to make the project he had outlined for Louis XVI his own.

PART II

THE
REVOLUTION
BEGINS

(1788–1789)

3

STANDING FOR
ELECTION IN ARRAS

Between 8 May and 8 August 1788, France changed forever. A chasm opened at the center of power—a void from which the unimaginable might arise, even a revolution to shake the world. On 8 May the monarchy, in a desperate effort to reaffirm its authority after years of mounting fiscal and administrative disarray, sent the Parlement of Paris a set of edicts outlining comprehensive reforms to the structure of the state. These edicts sought to remodel and diminish the powers of the parlements, the thirteen supreme courts of law spread throughout the kingdom. The Conseil d'Artois in Arras, the grandest of the courts in which Robespierre worked, was a distinguished judicial body, exercising some of the same functions as the parlements, but unlike them it did not have supreme jurisdiction.

Under the old regime, the parlements had legal, policing, and political responsibilities. They were composed mainly, though not exclusively, of nobles, who had often used personal wealth to buy themselves public office. The parlements were highly privileged, conservative in disposition, self-interested, and profligate. To their critics, they seemed to go out of their way to defend brutal and inefficient criminal laws and oppressive feudal rights, while responding with re-actionary suspicion to innovation in the arts and sciences. Notoriously, the Parlement of Paris had banned inoculation against smallpox within its area of jurisdiction—a third of all France. The parlements were also a thorn in the side of the monarchy because they had the power to deflect or impede royal edicts by simply refusing to register them as laws. Often they produced inflammatory *remonstrances*, and over the course of the eighteenth century they became the focal point for opposition to the monarchy. When Louis XVI inherited the crown in 1775, he found that his predecessor had resorted to exiling the trou-blesome parlements. The new king immediately recalled them, declar-ing, "It may be considered politically unwise, but it seems to me that it is the general will."

Louis XVI's words proved prescient, because as the century drew to its close, conflict between his government and the parlements (and the doctrines that lent them legitimacy, the *thèse royale* and *thèse nobiliaire*) reached a dangerous deadlock. Successive royal governments had at-tempted to institute programs of desperately needed fiscal and admin-istrative reform, only to founder, sooner or later, on resistance from the parlements. The Parlement of Bordeaux, for example, refused in May 1788 to register edicts introducing freer trade in grain until they were clarified.[1] But while the parlements could obstruct royal edicts, they had no power to initiate change for the better in France. This was the crux of the problem: even well-intentioned and progressive royal edicts were treated with suspicion by the parlements, determined as they were to retain and exercise their right to oppose the monarch. Since France was an absolute monarchy, rights of opposition were few and far be-tween. The parlements attracted popular interest and support for standing up to Louis XVI's governments, even when the reforms they obstructed were sensible. In the meantime, the country teetered on the brink of bankruptcy, with a public debt of well over four billion livres.[2]

This immense public debt was incurred by a system of taxation that exempted members of the two privileged orders—the clergy and the nobility—and burdened everyone else, the third estate, with taxes that many could not afford to pay. The debt had been aggravated by the ex-pense of the Seven Years War (which ended in 1763) and France's involvement in the American Revolution. Lavish public spending, at the court in Versailles and elsewhere, had further compounded the problem. Taxation was at the center of the protracted and damaging struggles between the monarch and the parlements. After the end of the Seven Years War, for example, the parlements vigorously opposed the continuance of wartime taxes. Later they opposed the extension of stamp duty and the establishment of any new permanent taxes. They did so under the popular mantle of objecting to the monarch's absolute power, but the outcome was the ongoing oppression of the third estate and the frightening prospect of state bankruptcy.

The king's spokesman, Chrétien François de Lamoignon, aimed to break this deadlock once and for all on 8 May 1788. Lamoignon was the keeper of the seals, a prominent and well-connected nobleman, an intellectual who found himself in Louis XVI's ministry at the worst of times. Six months earlier, with the nearly bankrupt royal treasury forced to borrow an additional 420 million *livres* but haughtily unwilling to explain precisely why, Lamoignon had stood before the Parlement of Paris outlining "the principles of the French monarchy":

> These principles, universally acknowledged by the entire kingdom, are that the King alone must possess the sovereign power in his kingdom; that he is answerable only to God in the exercise of his power; that the tie which binds the King to the Nation is by nature indissoluble; that the interests and reciprocal obligations between the King and his subjects serve only to reassure that union; that the Nation's interest is that the powers of its head not be altered; that the King is the chief sovereign of the Nation and everything he does is with her interests in mind; and that finally legislative power resides in the person of the King independent of and unshared with all other powers. These, sirs, are the unchanging powers of the French monarchy.[3]

This was a clear, bold statement of the basis on which Louis XVI held power, or at least thought he did. In retrospect it seems mere wishful thinking. On 8 May Lamoignon set out from his grand house in the Marais Quarter, where literati like Racine and Mme de Sévigné had once come to dine, across an elegant courtyard and through the strong arched gate, to break the power of the institutions that had long formed the bastions of noble privilege in France. He intended to defeat the parlements by introducing an attractive program of reform but simultaneously reasserting the absolute power of the monarchy.

The edicts that Lamoignon presented to the Parlement of Paris on 8 May introduced much-needed reform of the criminal code, substantial restructuring of the judicial system, and an attempt to centralize the legislative process. But they also revived earlier attempts to transfer ultimate judicial authority from the parlements to the royal council, or, as Lamoignon proposed, a new plenary court, and spelled the end of the parlements' involvement in legislation. As a precaution, the Parlement of Paris was dismissed soon after these edicts had been announced and told not to reconvene until further notice. At first, in Paris and the provinces, there was shock, a stunned realization that the long-threatened coup against the parlements had finally occurred. Then there was uproar. Lawyers throughout the country rejected the new judicial arrangements. People took to the streets and some demonstrations turned riotous— mobs controlled parts of Rennes, people were killed in Grenoble, lettres de cachet were flying everywhere, trying in vain to silence the parlements and their supporters. Amidst the chaos, there was mounting clamor for a meeting of the Estates General, the nation's largest representative body, which had not met since 1614. By now, it was widely hoped that the fiscal and administrative crises in the kingdom could be resolved by this extraordinary representative assembly, as had happened, allegedly at least, on several occasions in the very distant past. On 5 July the royal government tried to deflect attention from the contentious Lamoignon Edicts by announcing that the king would welcome his people's views on how the Estates General should be organized when—and if—they finally met.

As a member of the Bishop's Court in Arras, Robespierre joined his local legal colleagues in protesting the Lamoignon Edicts. In recent years, Robespierre had argued passionately for reform of the criminal code and judicial system, yet in siding with the parlements against the government, he was in fact arguing for the perpetuation of privilege— against the erosion of the parlements' established rights and against the government's attempted reforms. This made sense in a situation where the parlements were still the most promising sites of opposition to the absolute monarchy. The full scale of imminent change in

France was still unimaginable, so in May 1788 Robespierre dutifully—perhaps even somewhat cynically—joined the demonstration of support for the parlements, knowing, as everyone knew, that they were highly improbable promoters of a less corrupt regime.

Looking back in 1792, Robespierre presented his behavior in Arras rather differently to his revolutionary colleagues, claiming that even though he was nothing more than a humble official in a provincial court, he had challenged the Lamoignon Edicts on the grounds that they contravened the sacred principle of the sovereignty of the people.[4] He compared himself favorably with members of larger, grander judicial bodies, who had opposed the edicts on more superficial grounds, objecting merely to the form of the administrative changes. In this way, Robespierre backdated his revolutionary career, his unswerving commitment to the people, his incorruptible patriotism, to the spring of 1788, when signs of the gathering political turmoil first reached Arras. Yet the people were far from sovereign in France in 1788. It was the king who possessed the sovereign power, as Lamoignon had recently reminded the Parlement of Paris, and he answered only to God. When Robespierre joined the protest in support of the parlements, he could not have known that the country was months away from a revolution that would alter everything by seizing power from the king and transferring it to the people.

On 13 July bad weather added to the disruption unleashed by the Lamoignon Edicts. A violent summer storm rained enormous hailstones over northern France, killing people and livestock caught in fields without shelter and destroying most of the grain awaiting harvest. The harvest of 1788 was going to be meager even before the disastrous storm, and the previous year's harvest had been poor, too. Now the country was facing its second severe winter in a row; there would be hunger, destitution, and the threat of starvation; peasants would be unable to pay their taxes, and the royal treasury would once again find itself bankrupt. Nevertheless, attention was temporarily distracted from these harsh prospects on 8 August, when Louis XVI agreed to convene the Estates General. The meeting was set for 1 May 1789 at Versailles. The king's announcement was quickly followed by a flood of speculation about how exactly the Estates General should or could be organized. Within weeks, the downfall of the king's ministers, Lamoignon included, and the realm's anticipated plunge into bankruptcy lent still more urgency—and hope—to these popular speculations.

Ever since he had raised the enormous loan of 420 million livres in November 1787, Lamoignon had been able to reassure his colleagues, whenever they nervously asked him, "Do we have the cash?" But by August 1788 the cash was completely gone. The royal treasury had no choice but to suspend payments, government funds plummeted, and the markets panicked. On 24 August, Louis XVI recalled the Swiss banker Jacques Necker from exile, in the hope that he could rescue the regime from its wreckage. Though foreign and a Protestant, Necker had risen to high office as director-general of finances earlier in Louis XVI's reign. His policy of borrowing rather than raising taxes to finance state expenditure had proved successful in the short term but had not solved the country's ongoing financial crisis, and so he was dismissed in 1781. Now Paris was jubilant at his recall after Lamoignon, the scourge of the parlements, fell from power. While Necker's portrait swayed through the unruly streets above a triumphant procession, an effigy of Lamoignon was reviled and burned outside the splendid family residence in the Marais, from which the man himself had fled. The following year Lamoignon shot himself, whether deliberately or by accident has never been determined.

When the Parlement of Paris was recalled in September 1788, after Lamoignon's fall, it discredited itself once and for all as an advocate of progress by calling upon Louis XVI to reconvene the Estates General exactly as it had been composed in 1614. Then the Estates General had met in three almost numerically equal, but separately elected, chambers representing the orders of the clergy, the nobility, and the third estate. They had voted separately by order, and it was easy for the nobility and the clergy to defeat the third estate: two against one. Since 1614 the third estate had grown exponentially in numbers and wealth: it now represented 98 percent of the population, including the rising taxpaying bourgeoisie. So it would be severely underrepresented if the earlier composition of the Estates General were maintained, as the Parlement of Paris demanded. The popular credit the parlements had won through their clashes with the monarch disappeared overnight. Suddenly Robespierre was vitriolic in his denunciations of these old legal institutions. His fury marks the speed with which things were changing, some personal chagrin at the part he had played in shoring up the old order, and a passionate desire to exchange it for something new. Such sudden and violent feelings were far from unique at the time; they were everywhere, and the anger to which Robespierre seemed particularly prone was widespread in the last months of the old regime.

Robespierre was one of thousands to publish a pamphlet with ideas on how the new Estates General should be organized, many of them calling for doubling the number of third estate representatives and for counting the votes by head, not by order. Instead of arguing for the historical, constitutional, or theoretical rights of the third estate nationwide, Robespierre's pamphlet had a specific, local focus. It was preoccupied with the Estates of Artois, the provincial governing body grandly accommodated inside the city walls of Arras, and its standing claim to represent the province of Artois. This claim had to be undermined if the province's deputies to the Estates General were to be newly elected. More precisely, unless the claim of the Estates of Artois to represent the province could be overridden, Robespierre had no hope of going to Versailles as a representative of the third estate the following year. What a difference in just three months! Instead of turning out for a local demonstration under the old regime, where there were such unbreachable limits to his ambitions, Robespierre was now within reach of a role in national politics. His recognition of this opportunity—and the ferocity of his determination to seize it—was amazing. In the past he had commented on politics when it intersected with his legal work or arose in the context of his prize essays, and he was certainly well schooled in the political theory of both Montesquieu and Rousseau, but he had never had any hope of even a minor role in national politics. Contemporaries in Arras noted with surprise (and some distaste) the vigor with which Robespierre started campaigning for election. He had had very limited, and largely dismaying, experience of elections before, in the Academy of Arras and the legal profession. He knew there was only one outcome that counted— winning—and in his circumstances, luck was not going to be enough.

* * *

WHAT WAS ARRAS like on the eve of the Revolution? We can visit it as it was if we travel with Arthur Young, an English gentleman farmer from Norfolk and a pioneer of political science. In 1788 Young bought a mare in Bury Saint Edmunds, confidently assured that she would be fit for at least a year. He had traveled in France before as the guest of a noble family, but this time he went like a farmer, alone, on horseback, without servants. On 30 July he left his estate in Bradfield, crossed the Channel, and arrived in Calais. Then he took the road to Saint-Omer, where he found "little deserving of notice," and from there to "Aire, and Lillers, and Béthune; towns well known in military story."[5]

By 8 August Young was on the "admirable gravel road" between Béthune and Arras. When he reached Arras later that day, it proved another disappointment, and he noted in his journal, "There is nothing but the great and rich Abbey of Var [Saint-Vaast], which they would not show me; it was not the right day, or some frivolous excuse."[6] He went off grumpily through the narrow streets. If he turned left, then left again, he would have walked past Robespierre's front door on the corner of the rue des Rapporteurs and might unknowingly have passed him returning from work. But Young's mood was ruined and he refused to be impressed, even by the town's imposing Gothic cathedral. At the end of his long day, he wrote dismissively in his journal, "The cathedral is nothing," and blew out his candle, tired and disgruntled. The next morning he woke to a city transformed by market day:

> Coming out of the town I met at least an hundred asses, some loaded with a bag, others a sack, but all apparently with a trifling burden, and swarms of men and women. This is called a market, being plentifully supplied; but a great proportion of all the labour of a country is idle in the midst of harvest, to supply a town which in England would be fed by one-fortieth of the people. Whenever this swarm of triflers buzz in a market, I take a minute and vicious division of the soil for granted.[7]

Young was a serious agronomist with strong views on the merits of large-scale farming over small—hence his disapproval of the petty farmers converging on the market with their meager burdens. He also had wider criticisms of the society and politics he found in France. He despised the despotic government that seemed to take no account of public opinion and the oppressive system of privilege by which the first and second estates lived at the expense of the third. On his travels in the south of the country, he noted, "All the country girls and women are without shoes or stockings; and the ploughmen at their work have neither sabots nor stockings to their feet. This is a poverty that strikes at the root of national prosperity. . . . It reminded me of the misery of Ireland."[8] These glaring grievances, so obvious to an attentive English visitor, were prominent causes of the revolution that was just months away as Young prepared to leave Arras. From there, he continued on his way across France—wry, sarcastic, disabused, refusing whenever possible to be remotely impressed. He was still in France when the Revolution came. He welcomed it, suspended his sarcasm, and hoped the problems he had noticed on his travels were about to be resolved.

WHEN THE PROVINCIAL government, the Estates of Artois, met in Arras in December 1788, the price of grain was rising dramatically and a winter of misery was setting in. Poverty was a widespread and complex problem in old regime France—there was an extensive and nuanced vocabulary to refer to different levels of deprivation, but the blanket term was *pauvre*. The poor made up over a third of the total population and were identified as "the family of a working man where such an individual cannot earn enough to support every member and where the individual members cannot support themselves."[9] At best the poor lived at subsistence level. A bad harvest would plunge many into destitution, and without adequate food, clothing, and shelter, they would soon die. These were the circumstances in which Robespierre began his election campaign. His pamphlet, *A la nation artésienne, sur la nécessité de reformer les États d'Artois* (To the Nation of Artois, on the Necessity of Reforming the Estates of Artois), argues that everything wrong in Artois is the fault of the provincial estates and that the only hope of purging corruption from local politics is popular election of

the people's own representatives.[10] The provincial estates had monop-
olized for their own benefit public powers that rightfully belonged to
the people.

In this early pamphlet, Robespierre's two most prominent political
ideas are already present. It is here that he first presents the principle of
election that was to characterize so many of his interventions early in
the Revolution. This principle was based on a simple and consistent understanding of what representation must mean in politics: in order to
represent a person, or a group of people, you must first be chosen by
them. According to him, the bishops in the Estates of Artois represented no one because no one had chosen them for the purpose. The
nobles and members of the third estate, chosen by the elite, represented
only the elite. The poor, meanwhile, were so preoccupied with scraping
together a living that they had no time to reflect on the causes of their
discontent or the natural rights of which they were being cheated by the
unrepresentative Estates of Artois. This sense of the poor as deserving
claimants of justice in a corrupt and unfair world is the second of
Robespierre's prominent political ideas. In Artois, he argued that the
tyranny of wealthy elites excluded the poor from litigation. In recent
years, he had built a certain professional reputation in the courts for
taking on unprofitable cases for impoverished clients, but here already
the poor have become a collective abstraction, enshrined in his rhetoric,
soon to be unleashed in debates that reverberated far beyond Arras.

As this early piece of writing shows, unscrupulous, abusive, and
egotistical "enemies of the people" were vividly present to Robespierre from the start of his political career. He called on justice, reason, and humanity to vindicate the oppressed: the moment had come
at last for vice to tremble and for virtue to put Arras, Artois, France,
perhaps even the world beyond, to rights. In the thick of his election
campaign, he attacked the members of the Estates of Artois for refusing reasonable requests for public expenditure on education or sanitation to alleviate public misery, while approving the refurbishment of
their own offices to the sum of twenty-four hundred livres although
they occupied them for just six weeks a year. He scorned the officials
who refused to allot public funds for repairing important roads, imposed forced labor on peasants to maintain the roads free of charge,

and then provocatively approved the construction of a new trunk road across the province—a completely pointless expenditure, except that the road passed by a château owned by a member of the provincial administration. The corruption was so transparent that once the road had reached the château, work on it stopped. And this was far from an isolated instance of abuse.

In his pamphlet, Robespierre also denounced these enemies of the people for oppressing their victims with lettres de cachet and imprisoning them. He championed the rights of citizens rotting unjustly inside the Bastille of Artois (as he titled the city prison), thanks to the odious caprice of provincial officials who were no better than local despots. He lamented the fate of men, women, and children thrown into prison like animals—even pregnant women, "innocent victims of vile persecution"—and claimed there was not a mother in the province who could not make her son cower merely by mentioning the Estates of Artois. Once having seen the truth about the provincial government, the people of Artois, Robespierre was certain, would elect to change their representatives. The choice facing the people, as he presented it, was between liberty and slavery, happiness and oppression, victory or defeat. But the pamphlet's implicit message was: Vote for Robespierre. Essentially, he conducted his election campaign as if he were already living in a democracy, as if there were popular suffrage, as if politics were open to anyone the people had chosen. None of this was true, but through sheer force of imagination Robespierre managed to suspend his own disbelief. Into his mind there had come the first of many pictures: Robespierre, delegate to the Estates General. He was greatly helped in realizing his ambition by the king's decree on 7 March that Artois was to select its representatives to Versailles by holding new elections, in line with the rest of France; it was not simply to rely on the Estates of Artois to choose them. And so, the Estates of Artois, the long-time emblem of regional privilege and independence, had been superseded; the first great obstacle in Robespierre's path had melted away.

Nevertheless, his chances of election were slight. Because the Estates General had last met in 1614, no one remembered exactly how its delegates had been chosen. Louis XVI told his ministers to consult the archives, but this did not get them far since much had been left to local discretion in 1614: there was no coherent codification of the procedures. So the king's minister Necker had to invent one. The electoral statute that resulted was an uneasy attempt to reconcile "respect for customary practice" with "current circumstances".[11] It decreed that the clergy and nobility would choose their delegates through direct elections. The third estate, however, was to elect deputies indirectly, through a series of preliminary assemblies that would allow rural communities and traditional artisan guilds to participate. The number of deputies for the various regions was to be decided on the principle of proportional representation, "according to their population and resources." Necker made an exception for Paris, designing a special, even more complicated electoral procedure. Those eligible to participate in the third estate's elections included all male commoners, born or naturalized in France, aged over twenty-five, and listed on the tax rolls. Voting was commonly by open ballot, and an absolute majority was required to win.

On Monday, 23 March, Robespierre attended a meeting at his old school, the Collège d'Arras, for all members of the third estate who did not belong to one of the city's thirty-nine trade guilds or corporations (apothecaries, carpenters, tailors, wig makers, and so on). Whereas the corporations met calmly and elected their representatives without any trouble, the meeting in the college chapel was chaotic. It got off to an unpromising start with people slowly filtering in between seven and nine-thirty in the morning. Soon afterward, a bitter fight erupted between the ordinary people who comprised the third estate and the *échevins*, or town councillors—who, in Robespierre's opinion, were at least as suspect as the members of the old Estates of Artois had been.[12] He attacked these councillors for corruption by association with the Estates of Artois, which had allowed them to attend meetings of the third estate. This practice was continuing despite the recent demise of the Estates of Artois. In their defense the councillors argued that they were as entitled as any other members of the third estate to a part in the election of its deputies.

After two long days of deliberation, twelve deputies were chosen to draw up a list of the third estate's grievances (*cahier de doléance*) and go on to the next electoral assembly. Robespierre was one of the twelve and so was his friend Buissart. As Robespierre put it, "People expressed their joy loudly in multiple applause, imposing, no doubt, a great responsibility on those whom they honored with these touching and energetic proofs of their confidence." In this rapturous account, however, Robespierre was getting ahead of himself—this was just the first stage of elections for the third estate and there were still three to go.[13] The next election meeting took place a few days later, again in the college chapel, where the twelve approved candidates were joined by fifty-three deputies from the corporations. At this time, as well as helping to draw up the general grievances of the third estate, Robespierre agreed to draft a list of specific grievances for the corporation of cobblers. Since this was one of the most impoverished and illiterate of the corporations, he may have been motivated by his habitual sympathy with the poor. But he was also eager to broaden the base of his potential supporters. So early in the electoral process, no effort was too speculative, no publicity or source of support too insubstantial.

The fight with the town councillors came to a head in an argument between Robespierre and his old mentor at the academy, Dubois de Fosseux, over a procedural issue. Dubois de Fosseux, himself a councillor, was also a member of the *noblesse non entrante*, a person whose family had attained nobility comparatively recently. He was wealthy and less provincial than Robespierre, having spent six years at court in Versailles and developed a taste for literature and the theater about which he corresponded with Beaumarchais (already famous for his play *Le Mariage de Figaro*, the inspiration for Mozart's opera). As secretary of the academy, Dubois de Fosseux had connections with cultural figures all over France.[14] In Arras, he was highly respected for his public service, his involvement in improving roads and canals, and his attempts to monitor and resolve local economic crises. Since he held municipal office, he attended the assembly of the third estate as well as the assembly of nobles. He disputed the relentlessly pejorative terms in which the councillors were characterized by Robespierre, in particular, and insisted on their right to vote in the third estate. This bitter dispute raged for three days, and on 29 March the third estate of Arras had still not elected its deputies to the key meeting of the third estate of the whole district, or *bailliage*, which was scheduled for the following day. The election was finally held in the middle of the night. Of the twenty-four who were chosen, four were councillors and the majority were lawyers. Robespierre came fourteenth on the list.

The next morning the tired new deputies returned to the college church (if they had left it at all overnight) to welcome representatives of the other 245 constituencies of the *bailliage*, with a view to further amalgamating the province's extensive lists of grievances. The list presented by the twenty-four representatives of the third estate of Arras bore signs of Robespierre's influence, including a complaint against the shaming of the families of criminals by their association with bad blood, the subject of Robespierre's inaugural speech at the Academy of Arras, and several other suggestions for reform of the criminal code. Perhaps it is true, as one hostile biographer claims, that Robespierre had organized his country relatives in Carvins into campaigning on his behalf. Or perhaps the representatives from the countryside, suffering from a stronger sense of oppression than their counterparts in urban Arras, proved more responsive to Robespierre's dramatic rhetoric. Whatever the reason, when the 550 representatives from across the whole province voted, he was one of just forty-nine chosen to draft the final, most comprehensive list of grievances for the third estate. Even Robespierre could not tell whether it was luck, strategy, or a combination of both that had won him this opportunity.

Within the electoral assembly, he continued to align himself with radical democratic proposals, defending, for example, the idea of reimbursing those delegates who usually lived off their earnings for income lost during the elections. Never one to drop a fight, he asked sarcastically: "Do you think the councillors will not find an objection to this demand? They will reply that it appears just but that they oppose it on form." Only a quarter of the 550 delegates could go through to the next stage—the final assembly of the third estate, from which the representatives to Versailles would be chosen. Robespierre's name went forward for the final meeting, and as he waited nervously, to see if he would be chosen for Versailles, he wrote a second political pamphlet. Characteristically entitled *Les ennemis de la patrie démasqués* (The

Enemies of the Country Unmasked), it recounted his experiences of elections in recent months and reviled anyone who had stood in the way of his candidacy. It ended in high style:

> One trembles when one sees the reasons given for the choice of representatives who will decide the destiny of the nation. May God keep us from such hollow reasons, and inspire in all citizens the spirit of righteousness, truth, courage, and disinterestedness, the celestial love of humanity, and that healthy passion for the public good on which depend the happiness of the people and the safety of empires.[15]

Because of the timing of Easter, an important consideration in devout Artois, it was not until 20 April that the third estate met with the nobility and clergy to hear Mass in the abbey of Saint-Vaast, swear a solemn oath before the bishop, and separate again to choose their representatives by ballot.[16] There had been no assembly on this scale at Arras within living memory. Considerable sums of money were spent preparing the cathedral and perfuming the halls in which the estates would meet, surrounded by tapestries. When the chairman of the third estate proposed sending an amiable greeting to the other two orders, Robespierre immediately opposed it: what was there to congratulate them on? In his retrospective account of 1792, he cited this episode as another instance of his having upheld the principle of the sovereignty of the people, just as he had done against the Lamoignon Edicts.

Divisions not merely *between* but also *within* each of the three orders dominated the elections in Artois, as they dominated elections elsewhere in France. Across the country the higher and lower clergy were divided. Differently ranked nobles were divided. And the third estate, as Robespierre had seen, was riven with conflict. In all three estates the deputies elected to the Estates General, Robespierre among them, were chosen primarily because they were known to have opposed government directives in recent years. Dubois de Fosseux attended the meeting of the nobility and helped draft their grievances, but he did not stand as a candidate for election because his mother was gravely ill and he did not want to be separated from her for months to come. He remained behind and resumed the wide network of correspondence he had developed since becoming secretary of the Academy of Arras. In this role he was invaluable as witness and recorder of revolutionary change across France.

By 30 April Robespierre was sure at last that he had been chosen as one of the third estate's eight representatives from Arras. The elected deputies were due in Versailles in a matter of days for the ceremonial opening of the Estates General on 4 May. Robespierre would have been happy to leave even sooner. The maid who helped him pack remembered that he had very few clothes and belongings: a bag of powder and a puff for his meticulously maintained hair; perhaps the shaving bowl that is now in the Musée Carnavalet; some very clean linen (six shirts, six collars, six handkerchiefs); three pairs of stockings (one almost new); one pair of well-worn shoes and a newer pair; a satin waistcoat (probably pink) and a waistcoat of *raz de Saint-Maur* (a very fine shaven cloth) which was threadbare; three pairs of trousers, one black, one green, and one black velvet; a black cloth coat; and his lawyer's gown. There were also clothes brushes, shoe brushes, needles and thread (his mother had taught him to sew and make lace before she died).[17] Everything fitted easily into the trunk he borrowed from one of his sister's friends. He may also have needed to borrow money; the journey cost about thirty-five livres.

Some say that the coach waited for him outside the theater in the place de la Comédie, since it could not enter his narrow street, and that a small crowd of well-wishers gathered to see him leave. But these were hard times in Arras and there was little optimism in the streets, where there had recently been riots over bread shortages. During the past few months, as the electoral assemblies had argued among themselves in their perfumed halls, hungry mobs had marauded outside, with no reason to believe that the changes imminent in France would benefit them personally. It is more likely that Robespierre took his place in the public coach to Paris that changed horses in Arras at the merchant Lefebvre's and that his siblings and a few of his small circle of friends waved him off from there. According to one story, he turned to the servant who carried his bag to the coach and boasted that he would one day make him mayor of Arras. In another version Robespierre threw a celebratory dinner for his friends before leaving and said to a servant nicknamed Lantillette, "Remember, my dear friend, that everything is going to change in France. Yes . . . The Lantillettes of this world will become mayors and the mayors will be Lantillettes."[18] There is more personal spite in this than revolutionary foresight, yet when he left Arras in 1789, Robespierre certainly had reason to expect that he would return to find it dramatically altered.

4

REPRESENTING THE NATION
AT VERSAILLES

With a population of about fifty-five thousand, Versailles was nearly three times the size of Arras and almost one-tenth the size of Paris. By eighteenth-century standards, it was a modern European city, with a carefully planned symmetrical grid of streets, avenues, and monuments (which was later borrowed as a model for Washington, D.C.).[1] When Arthur Young visited Versailles on his travels in 1789, he noted that "this town is absolutely fed by the palace."[2] He had heard stories of the grandeur of what had been France's unofficial capital since the Sun King Louis XIV moved there with his court in 1682. Versailles was only about ten miles southwest of Paris, but it was at a higher altitude and surrounded by attractive wooded hills, very convenient for royal hunting parties. Young, however, was unimpressed:

> The palace of Versailles, one of the objects of which report had given me the greatest expectation, is not in the least striking. I view it without emotion; the impression it makes is nothing. What can compensate the want of unity? From whatever point viewed, it appears an assemblage of buildings; a splendid quarter of a town, but not a fine

edifice. . . . The great gallery is the finest room I have seen; the other apartments are nothing; but the pictures and statues are well known to be a capital collection.[3]

Later Young rambled through the gardens and by the Grand Canal "with absolute astonishment at the exaggerations of writers and travellers"—he found no beauty anywhere. An earlier visitor was even harsher:

> The unpleasant odours in the park, gardens, even the château, make one's gorge rise. The communicating passages, courtyards, buildings in the wings, corridors, are full of urine and faeces; a pork butcher actually sticks and roasts his pigs at the bottom of the ministers' wing every morning; the avenue Saint-Cloud is covered with stagnant water and dead cats.[4]

The stench must have reached the royal apartments where Louis XVI and Marie Antoinette were living with their young family. And it can only have got worse with the arrival of well over a thousand delegates to the Estates General, plus friends and spectators, all swelling the population of Versailles and further straining its sanitation.

LIKE LOUIS XVI'S coronation in 1775, but even more so, the meeting of the Estates General was a spectacular reenactment of the history, tradition, and pageantry of France. On Monday, 4 May 1789, the deputies of all three estates first assembled in Versailles's neoclassical Church of Notre-Dame for the roll call of the *bailliages*. There were 302 clergy, 289 nobles, and 576 third estate: 1,167 deputies in total (this number rose by 35 when the third estate deputies from Paris, delayed by complex elections, arrived a month later).[5] The chancel was covered in ceremonial drapes and there was a throne to the right of the choir screen, awaiting the entrance of the king, who was distracted because his eldest son was ill (and had just weeks to live). Louis XVI finally appeared at ten o'clock, wearing his coronation robes and heralded by trumpets, fifes, and tambours. The third estate was expected to kneel in his presence, as it had in 1614, but it refused to do so. He took his seat and the high-ranking officers of the realm took theirs below him on velvet benches embroidered with fleurs-de-lis. The queen and other ladies of the court sat opposite, to the left of the choir screen, beautifully attired and sparkling with jewels. Two by two, the deputies approached the king, candle in hand, bowing to him and then to his queen. Outside, the king's Swiss Guard lined the short route from Notre-Dame to the Church of Saint-Louis, where the estates would reassemble for Mass. Proceeding with the Eucharist, the deputies moved past buildings hung with tapestries, watched by an adoring crowd, sometimes respectfully silent, sometimes applauding and shouting, "Long live the king!" First came the clergy wearing cassocks and square bonnets, then the nobility in garments of black silk and gold brocade with magnificent hats plumed à la Henri IV, and finally the third estate—far less resplendent—in black coats and batiste cravats. Preparing for the ceremony, one liberal-minded noble from Saumur, the Marquis de Ferrières, wrote to his wife, "My crimson vest will be superb; I still need the trimming for the garment and for the coat. But the hat is expensive. The cheapest one cost 180 livres."[6] On the day, he was surprised to find himself spiritually moved far beyond such mundane concerns:

> Soon I ceased to see the spectacle that I had before my eyes; thoughts that were more intoxicating and yet at the same time melancholy offered themselves to my spirit. France, my fatherland [*patrie*], revealed itself in all its splendor. And I asked myself, what muddled minds, what ambitious, vile men, for their own interests, are trying to break up this whole, so great, so respectable, and dissipate this glory like insubstantial smoke dispersed on the wind? Love for my country has made itself very powerfully felt in my heart. I was not previously aware just how far the mutual ties extend that unite us all to this soil, to the men who are our brothers, but I understood it in that instance.[7]

Somewhere in this procession was Robespierre, walking with the seven other third estate deputies from Arras. They were only just in time, having left Arras late and struggled to find accommodation in crowded Versailles, until they were lucky at The Fox (Hôtellerie du Renard) in the rue Sainte-Elisabeth.

From a window overlooking the main street of Versailles, Necker's grown daughter, Mme de Staël, was watching the procession. She could see her father, the king's chief minister, walking stiffly past. She could see the king and queen gloriously attired. But her attention was caught by one of the deputies of the third estate—the comte de Mirabeau, a nobleman who had been elected to the third estate. Mirabeau was hard to miss. When he arrived in Versailles, aged forty, he was accompanied by a varied and outrageous reputation. He had been many things under the old regime: a man of letters, a journalist, an infamous son of a re-spectable father, a rivetingly ugly seducer of women, a pornographer, a prisoner alongside the Marquis de Sade, and an accomplished orator. Condemning him to death in his absence for seduction and abduction, the Parlement of Besançon had gone so far as to behead a paper effigy of him. Mirabeau had been rejected as a representative of the nobility so had appealed to the third estate, which elected him in both Aix and Marseille. Looking down on him, Mme de Staël reflected:

> You could not but look at this man, when once you had noticed him: his immense black head of hair distinguished him among them all; you would have said his force depended on it, like that of Samson: his face borrowed new expression from its very ugliness; his whole per-son gave you the idea of an irregular power, but a power such as you would figure in a Tribune of the People.[8]

Robespierre—whom next to no one had heard of, and who never stood out in a crowd—went unnoticed.

The following day was the official opening of the Estates General in the Salle des Menus-Plaisirs, a hall specially constructed on the grounds of the Hôtel des Menus-Plaisirs, which housed the adminis-trative office responsible for arranging royal festivities in Versailles. The new hall was spacious and provided abundant spectator seating (three of the four walls supported public galleries). Under the inter-ested gaze of the excited audience, one old man arrived in his farming clothes, ostentatiously rejecting the austere black costume of the third estate. His fellow deputies, already restless amid the noble and clerical pomp and ceremony, applauded loudly. Necker, still the popular idol on whom the hopes of Paris were resting, read his opening address. It was a very disappointing speech, conservative in idiom and content. One contemporary described it as the product of "a mind intoxicated with vanity, displaying an incapacity or unwillingness to explain or illustrate: a composition indecent, unmanly, out of place, betraying a narrow understanding and a timorous heart."[9] At the end of Necker's long disquisition, the king ceremoniously raised and replaced his hat. The nobles did the same. So did some of the third estate, but then, one after another they took their hats off again—an impromptu expression of belligerence. Confused by this unscripted development, the king removed his own hat again. The queen leaned over to ask him what he was doing and there was an unscheduled pause in the proceedings during which the nobles started hesitantly uncovering their heads as well.

Subtle signs of intransigence turned rapidly into open defiance. On 6 May the third estate refused to take a roll call of its deputies or to verify their representative credentials separately from the clergy and nobility. The concern was that separate verification would lead to separate voting by order. Instead, the third estate demanded a joint assembly with the other two estates, where votes would be counted by head and it would stand a chance of outvoting the nobility and clergy. Among the delegates to the third estate were many close students of the recent debate over how the Estates General should be organized, a debate that Louis XVI had publicly welcomed a year ago and was now sorely regretting.

The nobility and clergy went off to their separate assemblies, in nearby halls built for the purpose, but the third estate remained in the Salle des Menus-Plaisirs. All the third estate had to do to maintain the impasse arising from its refusal to verify its representative credentials was nothing, which was just as well considering the chaos in which it found itself. Friends, relations, journalists, and other members of the public spilling over from the spectator galleries filled the seats vacated by nobles and clergymen. From the big central table no one could make a speech without turning his back on half the deputies. Eventually, practical-minded Dr. Joseph-Ignace Guillotin—a Parisian physician and philanthropist—resolved the problem by rearranging the seats in a semicircle. Even so, it was hard to follow the disorderly debates echoing around the high-vaulted hall, competing with chatter from journalists and members of the public mingling with the delegates.

In these unpromising circumstances, Robespierre, Robes-pierre, Robesse-pierre, Robertz-Pierre, Rabesse-Pierre, Robests-piesse, Robespienne—the journalists found it hard to catch his name and even harder to spell it—made his first contribution. To one acquaintance he confided that he was shaking with fear as he approached the table, that the hall went dark before him and he could see or hear nothing as he raised his voice: "He told me that he was prey to the most childish timidity, that he never approached the tribune without trembling, and that when he began to speak, his faculties were entirely overwhelmed by fear."[10] But to Buissart, back in Arras, Robespierre wrote in proud, confident tones, explaining how only bad luck had come between his first intervention and lasting glory. He spoke about the third estate's urgent need to decide how to proceed in its impasse with the other two orders. One possibility was to nominate and dispatch negotiators to the other assemblies; another was to stay put but invite the nobility and clergy to return and reunite with the third estate. Robespierre had a third idea, unoriginal but politically powerful: divide and rule. He suggested inviting only the clergy to return in the first instance. The nobility would be left isolated and under more pressure to join the rest of the nation. Because he outlined this plan at a comparatively late stage in the debate, delayed perhaps by his nerves or merely by the number of other speakers ahead of him, it was not voted on. Afterward, Robespierre criticized the voting procedures but took comfort in the fact that many delegates came up to him to comment favorably on his plan and claim they would have voted for it if only they had been allowed to.

During these early days, as Robespierre developed his fledgling reputation, he was invited to dine with Necker. Allegedly, this was one of the occasions when Robespierre had to borrow smarter clothes than he owned. Necker's wife regularly held supper parties for friends of her husband and admirers of her glamorous daughter, Mme de Staël, and took to inviting along some of the deputies newly arrived in

Versailles. Robespierre admired Necker. A few years earlier he had called him "a great man who seems to have been shown to the people merely for them to glimpse the full extent of the happiness they might enjoy, whose elevation was a triumph for genius, virtue, and the nation."[11] We don't know whether he admired Mme de Staël, an imposing figure for anyone encountering her for the first time; married to the Swedish ambassador, Baron de Staël-Holstein, she was accustomed to being at court, attractive, flirtatious, intellectual, and extremely well connected. What we do know is that Robespierre did not make a favorable impression on her. She later recalled her first meeting with the Incorruptible: "His features were mean, his complexion pale, his veins a greenish hue."[12] She also noted the radicalism of his democratic views. Considering the differences in their circumstances, it would have been peculiar if Robespierre had seemed anything other than common and unappealing to Mme de Staël. Provincial, puritanical, inexperienced, Robespierre was worlds away from her sophisticated way of life, as was immediately obvious when he sat down at her parents' table.

While still a provincial rather than national representative, Robespierre identified strongly with his fellow delegates from Arras, for whom he had become the unofficial spokesman. Boasting to Buissart, he claimed that their group was distinguished for their close rapport with the forty-four deputies from Brittany, with whom they formed a progressive faction, radical and especially patriotic (ready to die for their country, according to Robespierre). The concept of patriotism had a long history in France, appearing in the preambles to royal edicts since the end of the seventeenth century.[13] Involvement in America's struggle for freedom in the 1770s transformed French notions of patriotism into a secular ideology opposed to despotic government, although the crippling cost of these wars somewhat tarnished the glamour of the idea.[14] By 1789 a new version of patriotism was taking root: in the wake of the recent nationwide elections, and fervent public interest in what the Estates General would achieve, the concept increasingly became a label for third estate aspirations.[15] Robespierre's own understanding of patriotism was also influenced by Rousseau's definition: "There can be no patriotism without liberty; no liberty without virtue; no virtue without citizens. Create citizens and you have everything you need; without them you have nothing but debased slaves, from the rulers of the state downwards."[16]

If not all the third estate deputies were as committed to liberty and virtue as Robespierre, he nevertheless deemed most of them enlightened and well intentioned. There were exceptions, of course. In particular, he singled out Pierre-Victor Malouet, a deputy from the *bailliage* of Riom in Auvergne, whom he described to Buissart as "the most suspect, the most odious of all the patriots."[17] Here was a dangerous intriguer, a notorious conservative intent on promoting the aristocratic faction in the midst of the third estate. In his letter to Buissart, Robespierre related an occasion on which Malouet proposed an insidious motion "worthy of his servile soul" and the other deputies from Auvergne disassociated themselves, protesting that he represented only Riom, not their whole province. Interestingly, Robespierre did not say what the motion was, only that it went down very badly.

He went on to summarize for Buissart his observations on the workings of the assembly—how and why speeches succeed or fail, the ways in which reputations can be made or lost. He was particularly interested in Guy-Jean-Baptiste Target, the leading Breton deputy, who arrived in Versailles with an established reputation and was prominent in the assembly from the start. Listening closely to his every word, Robespierre noticed that the points he made were ordinary, nothing but a summary of prevailing opinion delivered with great emphasis and eloquence, yet this was enough to win great applause. With a touch of glee Robespierre described Target as already "hors de combat" despite his promising start. One of Target's motions had been so ridiculous the whole assembly immediately rejected it; Robespierre suspected him of having "versatile principles" and doubted his representative credentials. On the most famous man in the third estate assembly, Robespierre's verdict was startling: "Mirabeau is nothing." He thought Mirabeau's dissolute moral character would make it impossible to trust him—or ought to. These opinions about Target and Mirabeau were eccentric, to say the least. In the short term, Robespierre could not have been more wrong: both men were to play prominent parts in the politics of the third estate over the coming weeks. But in the long term he proved to be right: neither was to put his stamp on the Revolution as he would. Robespierre would certainly have explained this difference in terms of moral character and firmness of principle—the strength of his own and the weakness of theirs—but this, too, would have been somewhat eccentric.

Around the time of Robespierre's election, the local newspaper in Arras had run a satirical article describing the character of each of the city's deputies as though they were horses entered in a race. The entry for the horse Robespierre was longer and more detailed than the others: "impetuous, intolerant of bit and stick, vicious, only dares to bite from behind, fears the whip. Its inclusion was a surprise but it is said to be destined to provide a comic turn after the brilliant performances of Mirabeau, Bergasse, Malouet, etc., whose actions it has been trained to mimic in a ridiculous fashion."[18] The article meant to be cruelly amusing and it certainly underestimated Robespierre's talent for politics, even if the full significance of his election would only become apparent years later. What it very accurately predicted, though, was his determination to transform himself into a successful politician. He knew he had much to learn from the delegates who arrived in Versailles with some political experience, and he set about studying diligently the techniques by which they influenced the assembly.

The radical faction of deputies, to which Robespierre was so proud of belonging, started meeting to agree on objectives and to coordinate strategies. After each meeting of the third estate, this faction, known informally as the Breton Club, would repair to the nearby Café Amaury to discuss the implications of what had happened.[19] Here, over the weeks to come, Robespierre, the deputies from Brittany, and other radicals distanced themselves from the constitutional ideas of the royalists in the third estate, like Malouet and the Grenoble patriot Jean-Joseph Mounier (another of the small number to come to Versailles with an established reputation). The Breton Club's objectives were to obtain voting by head and not by order, the destruction of privileges like the tax exemptions that favored the clergy and nobility and harmed the third estate, and the creation of a nationwide network of patriots. During these early days, there were many future enemies drinking coffee together in the Café Amaury, united in their hopes for the third estate. As well as making contacts and developing a taste for club politics, Robespierre was also mixing with a more diverse set than he had encountered before. His fellow deputies from Arras watched as he grew in confidence and became gradually less withdrawn.

Incipient factionalism, provincialism, chaos, confused ideas, and political uncertainty were escalating in the Salle des Menus-Plaisirs, when the deputies from Paris, who had been delayed by an electoral process even more complicated than the rest of France's, at last reached Versailles on 3 June—a whole month late. Paris was always a case apart. When asked by the King to codify procedures for electing deputies to the Estates General, Necker had produced special guidelines for the capital. However, the sixty Parisian districts disregarded these guidelines and took the radical step of establishing their own electoral college to choose deputies for the third estate. One of the candidates for election, the astronomer Jean Sylvain Bailly, felt revived and exhilarated by the city's new political climate: "I thought I could breathe fresh air," he wrote. "It was truly a phenomenon to be something in the political order and by virtue alone of one's capacity as a citizen."[20] Born in Paris in 1736, Bailly was over fifty when the Revolution began. A member of the French Academy of Sciences, known for his research on the planet Jupiter, he interrupted his studies to preside over the new electoral college and was elected as a deputy to Versailles. No sooner had he arrived than he was chosen as president of the assembly of the third estate. The late-arriving deputies brought with them new vigor, the expectations of all Paris, and the brilliant analytical mind of the abbé Sieyès, who had chosen to stand for election not as a clergyman but as a member of the third estate.

Though he lacked a religious vocation, Sieyès had spent ten years in a seminary, consoling himself with scientific and philosophical study. Finally ordained a priest in 1773, two years before Louis XVI's coronation, he proved to be a genius at the theory of politics: the nature and principles of representative government became his lifelong preoccupation. According to one contemporary, he was far from modest: "Politics is a science that I think I have mastered," Sieyès allegedly confided to a friend.[21] His self-confidence was well-founded. Early in 1789 he published the clearest of all the statements of the third estate's predicament, beginning famously with three questions and answers: What has the third estate been until now? Nothing. What should it be? Everything. What does it aim to become? Something. With devastating rhetoric and lucid reasoning he argued that the third estate simply *was* the nation and, as such, had the inalienable right to provide France with a new system of fundamental rules and principles by which the country would be governed. From this point, the third estate deputies explicitly asserted what many had hoped before arriving in Versailles: that they had been elected to endow France with a written constitution that would transform the old absolute monarchy into a constitutional monarchy. Sieyès insisted that anything or anyone that stood apart from the third estate was parasitical, a canker in the body politic that required excision. In this way he provided the theoretical basis for the third estate to seize the initiative from the clergy and nobility and remake the nation in its own image. Though others shared some of Sieyès's ideas, no one expressed them with such coherent vehemence. His was "the explosion of a talent that, long concealed, at length appears in all its splendor, arrests attention, and extorts applause," as Mirabeau put it.[22] His talent had indeed been long concealed. When Sieyès first arrived in the Salle des Menus-Plaisirs he experienced the problems often characteristic of intellectuals in politics—wry, brusque, conceptually elaborate, infuriatingly inaudible, he had a hard time projecting the distinctive clarity of his vision into the noisy and diffuse debates going on around him. "His voice is thin, his gesture insignificant, his expression slow, his conception difficult, his method unintelligible; he is incapable of ardent and animated language, and he prefers correctness of form to energy of diction," a contemporary remarked.[23] Despite all this, Sieyès had an early, epoch-defining success on 10 June when he persuaded the third estate that the time had come to "cut the cord" and arrogate to itself the power and identity of the nation. Delegates of the nobility and clergy were to have one last chance to join the third estate—and if they refused, the new national assembly he was proposing would simply leave them behind.

Robespierre had played a part in moving the assembly toward Sieyès's position. Three days after the exhilarating arrival of the Paris delegates, Robespierre, no longer feeling like a nervous child, had burst into a passionate denunciation of the clergy. The archbishop of

Nîmes had come to the Salle des Menus-Plaisirs to plead with the third estate to break its deadlock with the other two orders for the sake of the poor and destitute, who were starving while the Estates General remained paralyzed, achieving nothing. Well fed, richly attired, and condescending, the archbishop stood before the third estate hoping to shame them into cooperation. Robespierre lost his temper. He had seen how the wealthy clergy in Arras lived. As a schoolboy he had had to borrow clothes good enough to appear before the archbishop in Arras. Much of his early legal practice had come through the ecclesiastical court. He knew and was indebted to the worldly power of the church in France. "Sell your coaches, give up your horses," he demanded, reminding the assembly of the early church's austerity and the principles of Christian humility:

> Go and tell your colleagues that if they are so impatient to assist the suffering poor, they had better come hither and join the friends of the people. Tell them no longer to embarrass our proceedings with affected delays; tell them no longer to endeavor by unworthy means to make us swerve from the resolutions we have taken. But as ministers of religion, as worthy imitators of their masters, let them forego that luxury which surrounds them and that splendor which makes indigence blush; let them resume the modesty of their origin, discharge the proud lackeys by whom they are attended, sell their superb equipages, and convert all their superfluous wealth into food for the poor.[24]

The assembly was stunned. There was no applause but a confused murmur, which was much more flattering. The question "who is that?" passed along the benches and round the echoing hall. Sitting up and taking notice, some of Robespierre's fellow deputies began to predict a prominent career: "This young man has not yet practiced, he is too wordy and does not know when to stop, but he has a store of eloquence and bitterness that will distinguish him from the crowd."[25]

Following the advice of the abbé Sieyès, the third estate issued its final invitation to the other two orders, received no response, and proceeded to the long-postponed roll call of its deputies, which signaled the formal beginning of its work. There was tremendous excitement on 13 June when three parish priests from Poitou defected from the assembly of clergy and joined the third estate. Sixteen more clergy followed suit over the next few days. On 17 June, after a week of verifying the credentials of its deputies, the third estate changed its name and formally declared itself the National Assembly. There was no turning back now, no more possible negotiation or rapprochement with the other two orders: the Revolution had arrived. Louis XVI was no longer absolute sovereign of France answerable only to God in the exercise of his power. Instead, he confronted a National Assembly asserting the principle of popular sovereignty. More than this, Target (still a leading radical despite Robespierre's low opinion) proposed that existing taxes be declared illegal and only sanctioned provisionally until a completely new system could be instituted. This meant that, if the National Assembly was dissolved prematurely, taxation would come to an end. The Revolution was holding the king to ransom. Louis consulted Necker and Necker advised conciliation, unlike the queen, who thought the time for firmness long overdue and was secretly encouraging the king's army to converge on Paris. Necker suggested a royal session—a public consultation between the king and the deputies of all three orders—at which Louis would reassert his authority, sweetened by lots of concessions to the third estate. Necker drafted some speeches to this effect for the king, but Marie Antoinette modified them behind his back.

Early on Saturday, 20 June, deputies arrived at the Salle des Menus-Plaisirs expecting to welcome the rest of the clergy, who had finally voted as a body to join the third estate. They found themselves locked out. Soldiers guarded the bolted doors and posters everywhere announced a forthcoming royal session of which no one had previously heard. Dr. Guillotin, practical as ever, suggested that the angry crowd of deputies reassemble in a nearby indoor tennis court belonging to a friend of his. They did so, then swore a passionate oath never to disband until "the constitution of the realm and public regeneration are established and assured," however long, however difficult that course might be. The revolutionary painter Jacques-Louis David commemorated the scene on an unfinished canvas in 1789. David had already caused a sensation in the Paris Salon with his depictions of classical republican virtue and patriotism,

The Oath of the Horatii (1785) and *Death of Socrates* (1787). Now he pictured the impassioned deputies on the tennis court, crowding around their president, Jean Sylvain Bailly, raising their right arms, holding their hats high, standing on chairs to swear the revolutionary oath as a welcome summer breeze swept through their impromptu meeting place. Among those prominent in the foreground are an enormous Mirabeau, a refined-looking abbé Sieyès, and Robespierre, clasping both hands to his breast, pledging twice over a heart beating passionately for liberty.

Louis XVI's royal session went ahead on 23 June, a day later than the posters had promised.[26] Necker was absent. Aware of the king's intentions, he had advised strongly against any attempt to dissolve the National Assembly and was, once again, ignored. All the political and fiscal concessions that the court and government could think of were overshadowed by the king's uncompromising declaration that the divisions between his realm's three orders must remain. At the end of his speech, he ordered the deputies to return to their separate assemblies. The clergy and nobles obeyed, some of them smirking with pleasure at what looked like the demise of the National Assembly. But Mirabeau leapt to his feet and declared: "We are here by the power of the people, and we will not leave except by the force of bayonnets."[27] These words signaled a rapturous renewal of the Tennis Court Oath. Meanwhile, the king was informed of Necker's resignation. The third estate's truculence seemed temporarily less important and for the rest of the day Louis XVI's priority was to get Necker to return to his post. He did, but it was too late: Paris had exploded in disgust. Necker, whose portrait had been paraded by a jubilant crowd after the fall of Lamoignon in 1788, once again inspired the people, but this time they wanted and demanded the National Assembly, which he viewed only as an inconvenient compromise in the circumstances. On June 27 a tearful Louis XVI finally gave in and ordered the nobility and clergy to join the third estate. Fireworks lit the sky over Versailles and Paris. Given Mirabeau's prominent role it is not surprising that Robespierre, in his next letter to Buissart (dated 23 July), entirely revised his opinion: he no longer saw Mirabeau as dissolute and negligible but as the charismatic unofficial leader of the National Assembly. "The present Revolution," his letter began, "has produced greater events in a few days than the whole previous history of mankind."[28]

DESPITE THE KING'S climb down, the royal troops now assembling in and around Paris—which included some regiments of foreign soldiers willing to fire on French civilians if necessary—were making the newly triumphant deputies very nervous. By early July there were more than enough soldiers present to quell an uprising in the capital. Mirabeau drew up a petition of protest and Robespierre was one of the deputies who presented it in person to the king. The petition, he assured Buissart, was "sublime, full of majesty, truth, and energy." It had no effect whatever. The ominous military buildup continued, and on 11 July, despite his popularity and public standing, Necker was dismissed and sent into exile, blamed for the Revolution by many in Louis XVI's court. At this Paris, predictably, rioted. Robespierre's close friend from school, Camille Desmoulins—at twenty-six an attractively boyish man always known by his first name—addressed the crowd in the Palais-Royal gardens. Standing on a table in the Café de Foy, which had become a center of political discussion to rival the National Assembly, he cried: "Citizens, you know that the Nation asked for Necker to be retained, and he has been driven out! Could you be more insolently flouted? After such an act they will dare anything." As the crowd cheered and applauded, Camille raged against the monarchy, comparing himself to Othryades, a warrior of the ancient world who wrote "Sparta has triumphed" in his own blood on a captured standard: "I, too, would write in my own blood 'France is free!' "[29]

Later, in his letter to Buissart, Robespierre described the mounting fear in the National Assembly as it went into permanent session for three days and nights, ready to respond immediately to events as they unfolded.[30] He told of a patriotic army of 300,000 rising, as if by magic, from the streets of Paris, including every class of citizen, of French and Swiss Guards and other soldiers going over to the people's side. He marveled at the speed with which, on 14 July, this people's army took the Bastille, the chief fortress in the "tax farmers" customs wall around Paris—a symbol of oppression before the Revolution, an iconoclastic triumph ever since its fall. Under the old regime most of the Bastille's prisoners had been snatched from freedom by lettres de cachet and detained indefinitely inside the imposing fortress with its eight round towers and walls five feet thick. A recent vogue for anti-Bastille literature—lurid accounts of life inside by ex-prisoners—had further secured it as a place of horror in the popular imagination.[31] By 14 July 1789, however, there were only seven prisoners left inside. The most famous of all, the Marquis de Sade, had been transferred elsewhere on 5 July after adapting his slop and urine funnel into a megaphone for haranguing passersby with lurid revolutionary bulletins: massacre was imminent inside the prison; its governor, de Launay, was butchering the inmates; the people must storm the walls before it was too late. Despite such colorful incitements, the infamous fortress had to wait its turn while first the people attacked the tollgates, the city wall that impeded free trade, the abbey of Saint-Lazare, where firearms were stockpiled, and the Invalides for its cannon and other weapons.

The siege of the Bastille did not begin until early in the morning of 14 July and it was all over by early evening. It involved only about nine hundred citizens, many of them tradesmen—joiners, carpenters, cobblers, and so forth—from the Saint-Antoine district of Paris, which lay outside the city wall. Ranged against these patriots were apprehensive prison officers, regular prison guards, and some reinforcements from the Swiss Salis-Samade regiment that had arrived on 7 July. Lieutenant Deflue was in charge of these reinforcements and for a whole week he observed Governor de Launay's preparations for defending the Bastille with surprise and dismay:

> I could see clearly, from his perpetual uneasiness and irresolution, that if we were attacked we should be very badly led. He was so terrified that at night he mistook the shadows of trees and other objects around him for enemies, and on this account we had to be on the alert all night. The staff officers, the lieutenant du roi, the regimental adjutant and I myself often argued with him, on the one hand to reassure him about the weakness of the garrison, of which he complained constantly, and on the other to induce him not to bother about insignificant details while neglecting important matters. He would listen to us, and seem to agree with our advice; then he would

do just the reverse, then a minute later he would change his mind; in a word, his whole behaviour gave proof of the utmost irresolution.[32]

On 14 July the two sides at first negotiated for control of the fortress. Fighting broke out in the afternoon, but the morale of those inside was low. Their leader was hopelessly indecisive, they had neither the food nor the water supply to survive a real siege, the moat between them and their attackers was dry, and anyway many of the guards really sympathized with the assailants. Soon after five o'clock the Bastille fell.

The people promptly punished Governor de Launay for having fired the Bastille cannon "at those deputed by the inhabitants of Paris to seize the firearms and gunpowder that menaced them."[33] They also punished the city's chief magistrate, Jacques de Flesselles, *prévôt des marchands*, who was widely suspected of conspiring with the court against the people and attempting to hide the city's ammunition stores. Governor de Launay died in the street from multiple stab and shot wounds, and de Flesselles was murdered on the steps of the Hôtel de Ville. The "livid and bloody" severed heads of both men were carried through Paris on pikes for twenty-four hours and only thrown into the river Seine on 15 July.[34] In his account to Buissart, Robespierre seems entirely comfortable describing their fate as the people's unmediated justice. He comments enthusiastically that "the terror inspired by this national army, ready to present itself in Versailles, determined the Revolution."[35] In a postscript, he explicitly sanctions mob violence. "M. Foulon was hanged yesterday by the people's decree," he writes, referring to the fate of Joseph François Foulon, one of the ministers chosen by Louis XVI to replace Necker. Allegedly, Foulon had claimed that "the country would be best governed where the common people should be compelled to feed upon grass" and had boasted that when he was minister "he would make the people of France live upon hay."[36] He was lynched by the Parisian mob, then his severed head was paraded through the streets, the mouth stuffed with grass because people blamed him for the famine now sweeping the country, even though it had been predicted long before he came to power. In truth, Robespierre's calm assessment of these deaths at the

hands of the mob was not unusual among the deputies in the National
Assembly, still meeting in Versailles days after the revolutionary initiative had moved to Paris. Antoine Barnave, a deputy from Grenoble
and a future enemy of Robespierre's, quipped: "What, then, is their
blood so pure?"[37] Against this, Robespierre's understanding of revolutionary violence, justice, and terror looks sophisticated. In his account,
Governor de Launay, de Flesselles, Foulon, and others were lynched
by the will of the people; the status of their blood, whatever Barnave
meant by it, was irrelevant. From now on the will of the people was to
be everything.

ON LEARNING OF the day's events, the National Assembly expected
Louis XVI to recall Necker. This he failed to do, despite expressing
regret for the bloodshed in Paris and beginning to withdraw his troops
from the city center. On the following morning, 15 July, Mirabeau had
just finished delivering a brilliant speech on the threat of foreign invasion, when Louis XVI himself arrived at the Salle des Menus-Plaisirs,
unexpectedly on foot, accompanied only by his two brothers, the
Counts of Provence and Artois. There was still no mention of recalling Necker, though the removal of troops from Paris was enough
cause for celebration. Robespierre tells of the king returning to his
palace amid "demonstrations of enthusiasm and intoxication that are
unimaginable."[38] Then on the evening of 16 July the Count of Artois
and other members of the court suddenly fled the country. The following day Louis XVI and his family returned to Paris: the Parisians
wanted him back in their city. The king was not yet a prisoner, but he
was in a plain coach drawn by six black horses, at the mercy of the National Assembly and flanked by a hundred of its delegates, walking
solemnly with a slightly funereal air. One of the hundred was Robespierre, who later evoked this journey to the Hôtel de Ville for Buissart.
"It is," Robespierre wrote, "impossible to imagine a spectacle so august and so profound, and even more impossible to convey the im-
pressions it made on a responsive spirit."[39] "Imagine for yourself," he
continued, "a king whose name only yesterday made the entire capital

and nation tremble, who hears for the first time cries of 'Long live the Nation! Long live Liberty.'" As he processed to Paris, Louis XVI could see his own soldiers amid the newly formed citizen militia lining the route. Just weeks ago the crowd's cry was "Long live the king" as he arrived to open the Estates General. Now the nation with its claim to liberty had displaced him.

Paris was jubilant, with joyous citizens hanging from buildings and trees, women leaning out of high windows, all welcoming, applauding, and delighting in the procession. Robespierre called it a national festival. His responses were deeply emotional, his heart and imagination engaged. He noticed with particular pleasure some monks who had pinned on their cassocks the new patriotic cockade—a rosette of red and blue, the twin colors of Paris. (In the Café du Foy, the incendiary Camille Desmoulins attached a different significance to these colors: red for the blood shed for freedom and blue for the celestial constitution that would enshrine it.) Passing churches on the way, Robespierre saw robed and surpliced clergy competing with the crowd in their displays of patriotic gratitude. There were even cockades attached to stoles and this, he promised Buissart, was fact, not fiction. Why was he so thrilled by these signs that the clergy endorsed the Revolution? Perhaps because he had not expected it and was pleasantly surprised or simply because what the clergy thought or felt still mattered a great deal to him.

Robespierre already knew the astronomer Bailly as the president of the National Assembly, but now he watched him take on a new role as the mayor of revolutionary Paris, welcoming Louis XVI. Bailly had been elected by the capital's electoral college, originally established to choose deputies to the third estate but now the de facto municipal government in permanent session in the Hôtel de Ville. In his memoirs Bailly wrote:

> I rose very early, intending to leave for Paris at seven o'clock, and before that to prepare what I was to say to the King on receiving him at the gates of Paris. I was sorry to leave Versailles; I had been happy there in an Assembly whose temper was excellent, and which was worthy of the great functions that it was called upon to fulfill. I had

seen great things done, and had had some share in them. I was leaving all these memories behind: that day, my happiness was over. I have known splendid days since then and moments of satisfaction, but I have not been happy.

I had sent for a carriage. I was kept waiting to leave; I could not conceive why. When I went out, I was met by all the court coachmen, who offered me a tree loaded with flowers and ribbons. . . . I had to allow them to fasten this tree to the front of my coach; all the coachmen accompanied me, letting off fireworks although it was broad daylight. . . . Finally I left them at the end of the avenue, much touched by their friendly pageantry, and much relieved to be able to go on my way freely after being somewhat delayed. I incurred much praise in the newspapers for the simplicity with which, though chief official of the capital, I arrived in Paris in one of those carriages vulgarly known as "chamber-pots."[40]

Bailly met the king at the city gates and presented him with the historic keys to Paris. Then the procession moved on to the Hôtel de Ville. There, on the steps recently stained with the blood of de Flesselles, Bailly welcomed the king again, together with General Lafayette, veteran of the American Revolutionary War and commander of the newly formed citizen militia, now named the National Guard. Lafayette was tall and thin, with a long nose and reddish hair. His background was aristocratic, but at nineteen he had abandoned his comfortable life in France to fight for freedom in America. Here he impressed George Washington, who remarked, "I do most devoutly wish that we had not a single foreigner among us, except the Marquis de Lafayette."[41] Back in France and a popular hero, Lafayette was poised to apply his experience of revolution on home soil. He adapted the red and blue cockade for the uniforms of his National Guard by adding white, the color of the Bourbon monarchy. Outside the Hôtel de Ville, Bailly presented Louis XVI with one of these cockades: "I did not know quite how the King would take this, and whether there was not something improper about such a suggestion; however, I felt that I was bound to present the cockade, and that the king was bound to accept it."[42] This he did, and gamely pinned it on his hat, despite the arch disapproval of his queen, who said, "I did not think I had married a commoner." Robespierre records scenes of great joy and shouts of "Long live the king and the nation!" but nothing could disguise the fact that the terms on which Louis XVI held power had changed dramatically in a matter of weeks. He returned afterward to his court of Versailles, but his visit to Paris was testament to the capital's ascendancy over the Revolution.

ONE OF THE first things the deputies did after arriving in Paris was to go on a guided tour of the Bastille. Mirabeau led them, mindful of his own days of internment for immorality inside the prison of Vincennes, when "the voice of his despair reverberated from dead stone walls."[43] As the crowd in the rue Saint-Antoine parted before the triumphal procession, people threw flowers and poems in its path. Books and manuscripts found in the Bastille were piled into Mirabeau's carriage. Inside the prison, he asked to see the dungeons. His servant, prevented from accompanying him, sobbed hysterically at the entrance to the dungeon, fearing an attack on the leader of the commons in that dark and somber place.[44] But Mirabeau went on boldly, moving slowly through the underground cells, knocking on the walls to check for secret underground passages from which enemies of the Revolution might suddenly burst forth. Then he came blinking into the light, climbed one of the towers, lifted a pickax, and brought it down on the battlements. Robespierre remarked on how delightful the Bastille seemed now, in the hands of the people and under demolition: "I could not tear myself away from the place; the sight of it produced such feelings of pleasure and ideas of liberty in all good citizens."[45]

As Robespierre stood rooted to the spot, his gaze fixed on abstract ideas, the triumph of liberty and demise of oppression, others around him saw commercial opportunities in the Bastille's rubble. The stonemason Pierre-François Palloy had been among the nine hundred who originally stormed the fortress, fighting alongside carpenters and other tradesmen, many from the faubourg Saint-Antoine, where there had been violent riots over bread earlier in the year. After the fall of the Bastille, Palloy and four other construction specialists were put in charge of demolition. Very soon the ground was strewn with debris that would be recycled as Bastille memorabilia; inkwells, paperweights, commemorative daggers, and decorative models of the prison carved from its own stone were to prove popular and lucrative over the coming years. Spectators came to gawk at chains and manacles, to touch instruments of torture and lock themselves in dank cells where their fellow citizens, plagued by rats, had rotted to death. Robespierre was above all that. He was not much interested in money or, as far as we can tell, in sex. He was not commercially minded, not a connoisseur of thrills. He did not, like Mirabeau, have personal memories of imprisonment to lay to rest or fears about the threat the Bastille might still pose. To him the captured fortress was simply a vast monolith onto which his ideas could be projected. Just as when he first stood up to speak in Versailles the assembly went blank before him, so standing at the Bastille he saw only what was already in his mind. The picks and shovels fell silent as did the workers' banter; the gaping crowd disappeared. The glorious figure of liberty appeared to him on the crumbling ramparts and Robespierre stood there hypnotized.

ALL SPRING AND early summer hope helped fill empty stomachs as people throughout France waited on news from Versailles. But after the Bastille fell there was precious little calm left. Angry mobs marauded through the towns and countryside looking for food or work, barely restrained by detachments of the National Guard.[46] This volunteer force of amateur soldiers that had started in Paris after the fall of the Bastille was now being imitated throughout France. The purpose of the National Guard was to contain spontaneous mob violence of the kind that had killed de Flesselles and de Launay—it was, from the beginning, a prorevolutionary but peacekeeping association of civic-minded people, and for this reason membership was generally restricted to taxpaying citizens who were eligible to vote. Lafayette reduced the number of Parisian National Guardsmen to twenty-four thousand and stipulated that they must buy their own uniforms (which necessarily excluded the poor from joining). He also integrated six thousand professional soldiers into the guard.[47] But outside Paris, Lafayette had less control. Following the Parisian example, the citizens in Versailles and other cities organized their own people's army.

"We hope all France will adopt this essential institution," comments Robespierre in a letter to Buissart, before urging him to promote it in Arras.[48]

Since the new battalions of National Guards, springing up all over France in a piecemeal, spontaneous, and chaotic fashion, had suddenly become the main instrument of law and order in a nation succumbing to revolution, Lally-Tollendal (a conservatively minded member of the National Assembly) suggested excluding anyone likely to be reckless, anyone with nothing to lose, anyone too poor to have an interest in avoiding anarchy. Robespierre at once objected. "It is necessary to love order but not to harm liberty," he began. Insurrection, he argued, had saved Paris and the nation from despotism. To his mind it was wrong—or perhaps just too early—to condemn insurrection or distinguish it sharply from patriotism. There had been deaths, he admitted, a few heads had been lost, but they were guilty heads and no cause for reproaching the insurgent mob. Whatever he had understood liberty to be in the past—an idea, a legal concept, a beleaguered individual right more often breached than observed—it was now linked inextricably with the Revolution. He saw that insurgency was useful to the Revolution, so defended it in the name of liberty.

The right to privacy, on the other hand, was not particularly useful to the Revolution—it might indeed be downright dangerous where its enemies were concerned. And Robespierre had no qualms about overriding the right to privacy when Bailly forwarded from Paris to the National Assembly a packet of sealed letters addressed to the Count of Artois, who had recently fled abroad. These letters had been dramatically snatched from the French ambassador to Geneva in the middle of the night and probably contained details of a counterrevolutionary plot. As the scrupulous deputies stood about discussing whether or not it was permissible to open them, Robespierre was incredulous; to him it was obvious that the Revolution must come first—in circumstances where national liberty was at stake, crime itself could "become an action worthy of praise." Similarly, he agreed with other radicals in the assembly, just days after the crowd murdered Foulon outside the Hôtel de Ville on the place de Grève, that extraordinary courts to try crimes against the state were now needed; what was wrong in a time of peace and stability might be justified during a revolution. The original aim of the Revolution may have been civil liberty, but already in 1789, this was far from being its primary means. Robespierre grasped early, rapidly, intuitively the conflict between ends and means that was destined to blight the Revolution, cause tens of thousands of deaths, and haunt the consciences of the survivors. His response was passionate and political. He was vehemently committed to the Revolution and anything it entailed, passing quickly over moral scruples, intellectual incoherence, and political doubts. In short, he behaved like someone with nothing whatever to lose outside the Revolution itself—the kind of person more conservative members of the Assembly thought unsuited to the citizen militia, let alone positions of power.

As unrest spread through France and pillaging increased in the provinces, the assembly launched into lengthy theoretical discussions about the new constitution that would not have been out of place in the Sorbonne. At the top of the agenda was the Declaration of the Rights of Man and Citizen, which was to head the constitution and serve as both the death certificate of the old regime and the birth certificate of the new. "I well remember the long debate on the subject, which lasted many weeks, as a period of mortal ennui," wrote one witness. "There were silly disputes about words, much metaphysical jumbling, and dreadfully tedious prosing."[49] Even before 1789, many in France had watched the revolution in America with intense interest, and the deputies were well aware of the bills of rights preceding many of the constitutions adopted by the American states between 1776 and 1783, as possible models for the French.[50] Thomas Jefferson was in Paris and a good friend of General Lafayette's; Benjamin Franklin was still alive and corresponding with his many friends in France; opportunities for personal and intellectual exchanges between the two countries were increasing all the time. But when, after long discussion, the National Assembly settled on a draft for the French Declaration of Rights, it differed considerably from the American—it was more condensed, more abstract, and more suited to France's specific circumstances. It morally condemned the old regime and its vestiges of feudalism and laid the ethical foundations for France's new constitution. "Men are born and remain free and equal in rights," it asserted, repudiating legal and hereditary differences of rank or order.[51] In the vision of the future embodied in the declaration, social distinctions could only be justified to the extent that they served the nation: France must become a meritocracy, sovereignty belonged to the nation, and the law would express the general will. There was also a hint of an international crusading mission, since the declaration proclaimed the universal rights of all, not just French men. By the time Mirabeau presented the projected declaration to the assembly, however, he had become skeptical about it: "I can safely predict," he said, "that any Declaration of Rights ahead of the constitution will prove but the almanac of a single year!"[52]

On 4 August, in the absence of both Mirabeau and the abbé Sieyès, the assembly abruptly decided to intervene to halt the widespread discontent that had been growing during the weeks since the fall of the Bastille. Hoping to reassure the people that, contrary to appearances, they were really going to benefit from the Revolution, the delegates decided to abolish formally the remaining traces of feudalism in France. As the assembly went into extraordinary session, a spirit of abandon took over. All day and all night, deputies, weeping tears of joy, renounced the offending features of the old regime, demolishing it piece by piece, like the Bastille. When he heard about their decisions, Mirabeau reflected, "The assembly resembled a dying man who had made his will in a hurry, or, to speak more plainly, each member gave away what did not belong to him and prided himself upon his generosity at the expense of others."[53] The payment of church tithes was stopped; seignorial relations between landlords and tenants ended; manorial forms of income and property were no more; differences in the taxes and legal penalties applied to nobles and commoners disappeared; the special exemptions and liberties of particular provinces were abolished; hunting rights and game laws favorable to landlords were dissolved. There was to be no more confusion between public authority and private position, no more purchasing of public offices; the trade guilds would be radically reformed and the parlements abolished. Rarely has so much legislative work been accomplished in such a short space of time. Yet, in the sober light of morning, Mirabeau and

Sieyès were dismayed. "This is just the character of our Frenchmen, they are three months disputing about syllables, and in a single night they overturn the whole venerable edifice of the monarchy," complained Mirabeau.[54] For his part, Sieyès was most annoyed by the abrupt abolition of church tithes, which, as he saw it, would simply further enrich private landowners at the expense of the church. The two disgruntled men went for a walk together, lamenting that the assembly had failed to act in accordance with their wishes or advice. "My dear Abbé," said Mirabeau to Sieyès, "you have let loose the bull and you now complain that he gores you!"[55]

It took weeks for the assembly to work out the fine details of all its decrees. Robespierre did not play a prominent part in the debates. He intervened to insist that executive officers should be held accountable if they abused the power entrusted to them.[56] He championed freedom of conscience when members of the clergy tried to limit provisions for religious freedom in the new Declaration of Rights.[57] And, inspired by the American example, he argued for unlimited freedom of the press.[58] He envisaged government through legislative and executive powers, carefully separated from one another, both strictly responsible to the sovereign people and financed through equitably distributed taxes. In the moderate newspaper the *Courier français*, he was commended as someone who often made very positive contributions to these discussions without getting worked up or overheated.[59] Clear, precise, and calm as he was, however, there was little to distinguish him from other radicals in the National Assembly, patiently fighting their more conservative colleagues over the new constitution, line by line, article by article, day after day.

ON 4 OCTOBER Paris awoke to find no bread in its bakeries. To add insult to injury, the newspapers were full of inflammatory reports of revelry at Versailles the night before. The papers claimed that there had been a raucous and unpatriotic banquet for the Flanders Regiment, which had recently arrived in Versailles to reinforce the royal bodyguard. Allegedly, the national cockade had been trampled beneath the aristocracy's well-shod and contemptuous feet. One witness, Mme de la Tour du Pin, remembered the event very differently. She noticed Marie Antoinette's nervous anxiety when a Swiss officer asked permission to carry the five-year-old dauphin, like a trophy, around the crowded hall. Understandably fearful in such uncertain times, the ashen-faced queen, who was still mourning the death of the child's elder brother, was visibly relieved when he was returned to her arms.[60] Nevertheless, on the morning of 4 October, hungry and outraged, Paris rioted. A baker was murdered by the mob and General Lafayette and his cockade-wearing National Guard struggled to keep order. The next day a mob of about seven thousand women set off from the Hôtel de Ville for Versailles through driving rain, led by a man named Stanislas Maillard, who bore the unofficial title "Captain of the Bastille Volunteers." They reached their destination in the evening and it was Robespierre who received them: 5 October was crucial to his revolutionary career.

A delegation of twelve of the women plus Maillard, all drenched and mud-splattered from their long walk, entered the National Assembly, demanded food for Paris, and insisted that the king's bodyguard be forced to adopt the patriotic tricolor cockade. The rest of the mob waited, hungry and restless, outside. Robespierre, standing neat and composed at the tribune, answered the delegation by ordering an inquiry into the food shortages that menaced Paris. He supported Maillard's complaint against one particular miller who played the market by refusing for weeks to grind his flour, despite having been paid two hundred livres for it. In this way, he made common cause with the poor, echoing their customary fear that there was a plot against them—that their hunger and suffering were no accident but instead the result of a deliberate and despicable conspiracy.[61] The prospect of an inquiry did nothing to calm the expectant mob, though it did deflect their anger from the National Assembly. The ensuing night was uncomfortable and full of anxiety: Versailles was already crammed with people and there was nowhere for the women to sleep; some bedded down on benches in the Salle des Menus-Plaisirs; pistol shots rang out in the darkness. Inside the palace the court was in panic, barricaded behind doors that there had been no reason to close for decades. Some of the Parisian women found, or were shown, a small door opening onto a secret staircase into the palace, and as they emerged into the royal precincts surprised bodyguards opened fire on them. More enraged and frightened than ever, the destitute women then rampaged through the palace, eating any food they could lay their hands on. Eventually, after midnight, General Lafayette and twenty thousand National Guardsmen arrived in Versailles, soaking wet from the continuing rain.

General Lafayette said to the king, "Sire, I thought it better to come here and die at the feet of Your Majesty than to die uselessly on the place de Grève"—which was histrionic but honorable.[62] Then he explained that the people were rioting for want of bread and urged the king to let the National Guard replace the royal body-guards. The king, who had been hesitating all night over the best course of action, frantically eliciting opinions from everyone he could find to ask, and repeating all the while, "I do not want to com-promise anyone," gave in immediately on the replacement of his bodyguard.[63] The next day, after a mob had nearly broken into the queen's apartments, the royal family agreed to return to Paris for good. They found themselves accompanied by an unruly procession of some sixty thousand people, many chanting triumphantly that they were bringing the baker, the baker's wife, and their boy back to the capital. As a gesture of goodwill, the king had ordered sacks of flour to be transported from Versailles to Paris. Yet on the journey he heard himself derided as a baker and could see, outside the car-riage windows, the severed heads of murdered palace guards ghoul-ishly bobbing alongside on pikes.

"Men had captured the Bastille," wrote the historian Jules Michelet, "but it was women who captured the king."[64] Entering Paris, the royal family were prisoners in all but name. On the morning of 7 October, they tried to settle into their new accommodation—the dusty Tuileries palace on the right bank of the Seine that had been unused since the Sun King, Louis XIV, abandoned Paris for Versailles—while

Jean-Paul Marat's daily paper, *L'ami du peuple* (*The People's Friend*), gleefully celebrated their arrival:

> The king, the queen, the dauphin, etc., arrived in the capital at about seven o'clock last night. It is indeed a festival for the good Parisians to possess their king. His presence will promptly change the face of things: the poor people will no longer die of hunger; but this benefit will soon vanish like a dream if we do not keep the royal family in our midst until the complete consecration of the constitution. The People's Friend shares in the joy of his dear fellow citizens, but he will not give himself over to sleep.[65]

Marat, a physician and scientist admired by Benjamin Franklin, had begun writing revolutionary pamphlets in 1788. His *Offrande à la patrie* (*Offering to the Fatherland*) had some points in common with the abbé Sieyès's more famous *Qu'est-ce que le Tiers Etat?* (*What Is the Third Estate?*), arguing for the identification of the third estate with the nation. Marat, like Sieyès, had a deep knowledge of eighteenth-century political thought, but he soon switched to more direct ways of communicating with the public. He stood on street corners reading aloud from Rousseau's *Social Contract*, and he issued his daily paper under the motto "Truth or death." He preached insurrection to all who listened and helped instigate the women's march to Versailles. Indeed, he went with them on 5 October but had to rush straight back to Paris to keep up his running commentary on revolutionary events. "Marat flies to Versailles and returns like lightning, making as much noise as the four trumpets of the Last Judgment summoning the dead to rise," commented Camille Desmoulins in his own newspaper, *Révolutions de France et de Brabant*.[66] For his pains, Marat was arrested by the Parisian police on 8 October and imprisoned for about a month. Afterward he resumed his provocative journalism, giving voice to "the wrath of the people" and evading arrest by hiding in the cellars and sewers of Paris, where he caught a disfiguring skin disease. The People's Friend, wracked by migraines, his head wrapped in a vinegar-soaked handkerchief, his body covered with open sores, worked relentlessly to ensure that the ordinary people of Paris played their part in the Revolution. If Marat wanted to keep the king in the Tuileries palace until the new constitution came into effect, he seemed to believe he could bring it about by shouting, as loudly as possible, day in day out, into the ears of the Parisian mob.

THE NATIONAL ASSEMBLY did not immediately follow the king to Paris; it stayed behind to debate the new constitution and only closed its sessions at Versailles on 15 October. Buoyant with success, Robespierre was very active in the debates. By now he had made a name for himself—one that most journalists recognized and could even spell. He insisted, against Mirabeau, that the king's list of state-funded employees should be subject to annual approval, not permanently funded by the treasury.[67] He argued vehemently that all those still imprisoned by the old regime's notorious lettres de cachet should be unconditionally released. The case of the ex-soldier Dupond, whom he once defended in Arras, may have been in his mind, but this stance also fitted his growing reputation for radicalism, his passion for the application of clear, uncompromising principles, and the sublime emotions he had felt as he stood amid the rubble of the Bastille. With characteristic seriousness, Robespierre entered into discussions about the form in which the National Assembly's decisions should be published. It was not appropriate for them to read like old-style royal proclamations, he argued, especially since the parlements, once responsible for registering the king's edicts, had now been abolished. He suggested an alternative formulation that was somewhat ponderous and prolix: "Louis, by the Grace of God, and by the Will of the Nation, King of the French: to all citizens of the French Empire: People, here is the law which your representatives have made, and to which I have affixed the royal seal."[68] According to newspaper reports, Robespierre read this out to the boisterous and disorderly assembly in such a pious and earnest tone of voice that someone called out, "Gentlemen, this formula is of no use; we want no psalm singing here!" and he was laughed off the podium. He was sensitive and extremely easy to wound or offend and still rather gauche: a painfully self-conscious provincial with a heavy Artois accent who had thrown himself into the Revolution as he might, in different circumstances, have thrown himself into an important love affair, reckless, unreserved, completely devoid of ironic distance from the events on which he was staking his life. To be laughed at in such circumstances can only have stung him deeply.

After closing its sessions at Versailles, the National Assembly reconvened in the archbishop's palace in Paris on 19 October. Located on the Ile Saint-Louis in the river Seine at the heart of the city, very close to where the old parlement had met, the palace was never a suitable venue, and when a gallery collapsed in midsession, injuring members of the public and a number of deputies, the assembly had to move again. This time it convened in the Manège, a long, narrow building originally designed as Louis XV's riding school, prominently situated on the right bank of the Seine, between the Tuileries garden and the Feuillants monastery. Here, too, there were problems—overcrowding, bad acoustics, and inconveniently small public galleries. At Versailles there had been room for around three thousand spectators, but now there were just two galleries, one at either end of the Manège, with only a hundred seats each. There was a third gallery halfway down the hall, but admission to this was by ticket only. Soon an avid traffic in these tickets developed, along with a new practice of strategically positioning "claques" of people in the gallery to hiss, applaud, or throw missiles at the speakers. It was amid this chaos that Robespierre resumed his struggle to make something of himself and the Revolution—projects that had already converged in his mind. His new lodgings at 30 rue Saintonge, in the Marais Quarter, were comparatively cheap and tranquil. Living some distance from the city center, however, Robespierre had to travel two miles to reach the assembly, by foot or carriage, through congested streets. One acquaintance remembered being stuck in traffic with Robespierre one morning, en route to the Manège: "Our cab stopped at the corner of the rue Gréneta owing to a crowd that was hurrying to the rue Saint-Denis. He was impatient so I got out to see what was stopping us. I came back and told him, 'It is a deputation of the 84th Section that is going to present the assembly with a model of the Bastille made from one of its stones.' 'Pay,' he said, 'and let us get down and go on foot. A Bastille, all the Bastilles in the world, will not hinder me from going to my post.' "[69]

PART III

RECONSTITUTING
FRANCE

(1789–1791)

5

THE NATIONAL
ASSEMBLY IN PARIS

Robespierre's lodgings in the rue Saintonge were on the second floor, a sign of relative impoverishment in status-conscious Paris, where ground or first-floor apartments were highly prized, as they still are today.[1] Since 12 August, he had been paid eighteen livres a day as a deputy to the National Assembly, plus arrears backdated to 27 April, which would have amounted to a lump sum of over twenty-two thousand livres—more money than he had ever had in his life. And yet he still felt himself to be poor and seemed so to others. A penurious journalist and playwright named Pierre Villiers, who claimed to have worked as Robespierre's secretary for seven months in 1790, included some rare domestic details about Robespierre's life in his memoirs.[2] Villiers remembered: "He was very poor and had no proper clothes. When the assembly decreed mourning for Benjamin Franklin I asked a young friend of mine to lend him a black suit, which he wore, though its owner was four inches taller than he was."[3] The secretary's memoirs, like those of Charlotte Robespierre, are unreliable and should be treated cautiously, as suggestive rumors—not robust facts—about Robespierre's home life. "I had some quarrels with him," Villiers recalled, "and later he would have killed me if he had remembered me."[4] As in more ordinary households, some of the bitterest fights were over money. Charlotte had noticed her brother's lack of interest in money when she kept house for him in Arras, and his renowned indifference to bribes was one of the sources of his nickname, the Incorruptible. Villiers, who claimed to have worked for Robespierre free of charge, was irritated by his unworldly attitude to finances: "Several times I have known him to refuse offers of money that required from him no return, not even thanks, and if sometimes I allowed myself to insist on his accepting, he abused me. He was of a fiery temper that he always fought to control, and nearly every night he bathed his pillow in blood."[5] Perhaps Robespierre had nosebleeds (people with high blood pressure and fiery tempers often do). These certainly would have left him anemic and contributed to the unusual pallor of his skin that many contemporaries noticed.

Each morning, Villiers arrived to help him with the volume of correspondence he received as an increasingly prominent member of the National Assembly. Deputies could frank letters or reclaim their expenditure on postage associated with the assembly's business. Robespierre, parsimonious by nature, was fastidious about his record keeping. He always took the assembly's business seriously, which was more than could be said for some of its other members. Villiers remembers one of them, a deputy from the Department of Mont Blanc, franking a parasol for his mother "that traveled in consequence free of cost."[6] It was inconceivable that Robespierre would behave like this—his principles forbade it. And yet admirable as they were, there was already something unnervingly vehement about these principles. "One morning I arrived at his house earlier than usual," Villiers writes. "He was striding about his room. 'Good heavens!' I said. 'Your Assembly held a regular witches' Sabbath last night, a fine piece of work!' 'What is the matter, my fine aristocrat?' he responded. 'Your colleagues,' I said, 'have abolished titles of nobility as well as ribbons and sashes.' 'Ah,' he said, 'you should have been there to shout out *Hang yourself, Robespierre!* Too bad you weren't there to do it.'"[7]

According to Villiers, one of the first things Robespierre did when he got to Paris was to find a mistress, a woman of twenty-six who worshiped him. In the assembly and the public press he was already acquiring the reputation for irreproachable purity (another source of his enduring nickname). Perhaps this was why his relationship with his mistress, whoever she was, came to an abrupt end. As Villiers remembers, the end was ugly. For a time, Robespierre diverted about a quarter of his modest funds toward supporting this woman (which suggests that she was even poorer than he was), then suddenly he cut her off after refusing to admit her into the house.[8] Perhaps he sat at his desk and pretended, as many do in the aftermath of a failed or indiscreet love affair, that nothing had happened. Villiers says he found himself repeatedly in the unenviable position of facing the distraught woman on the doorstep when she came to talk to Robespierre; he concluded that she had been "treated quite badly." No other trace of the affair remains, but someone embarrassed, priggish, callous, or frightened enough to refuse kindness to his former lover would surely have destroyed any material evidence well in advance of posterity.[9] Throughout his short life, Robespierre was loved by women: his combination of strength and vulnerability, ambition and scruples, compassion and refinement attracted women with strong defenses against obviously vulgar men but none against the seemingly sensitive.[10] It is entirely plausible that, after an initial rush of tenderness, Robespierre felt guilty and ashamed of his emotional or sexual liaison, so ended it with brutal efficiency, sparing his own feelings first and reminding himself that he was, after all, a public figure with responsibility toward the future of France. If so, his behavior was not admirable but at least understandable.

About his busyness at this time, however, there can be no question. In November 1789 he wrote again to Buissart after an interval of many months: "My dear friend, I know you are sulking about me; and I cannot blame you. Despite all the good reasons I could give you to justify the long silence there has been between all my friends and me, I am forced to recognize that you deserve to be an exception, and I ought to do the impossible and find the time to write to you. There is nothing more I can do except ask your forgiveness and make good my negligence."[11] Buissart can hardly have been as much in need of a word from Robespierre as the distraught woman outside his door. But this was a far more agreeable letter for him to write, detailing as it did the steady rise in his reputation within the National Assembly and his precious contributions to its debates. The letter reveals someone entirely devoted to current politics, swept up in the assembly's affairs, and completely out of touch with his former life: "What is going on in Artois? What is said? What is thought? . . . Who is in charge? Please inform me on these matters and tell me if the National Assembly's decrees, especially those concerning provisional reforms in the criminal procedures, are registered and observed by the courts." Robespierre wrote as if he had almost forgotten that practicing law in Artois had once been the summit of his professional ambitions. He had moved very far away in the six months since he left, so after apologies for his long silence and perfunctory inquiries about how the Revolution was going in Arras, his letter soon turned to the constitutional debates.

These debates had begun before the assembly departed from Versailles and followed the king to Paris. They were conducted in an inefficient manner; instead of arguing their points against one another and advancing their understanding of the constitutional question under discussion, the deputies spent their time reading out prepared speeches. Repetition, redundancy, refutation of points that no one had yet asserted, and so on abounded. At the heart of these poorly mediated discussions, there was the problem of Louis XVI. How could he be incorporated into the new constitution? Could he be trusted? Would a monarch who was accustomed to absolute sovereignty play the limited role of constitutional monarch in good faith? In his letter to Buissart, Robespierre was moved to raise a deep and politically subversive question that seemed to him no less urgent in the autumn of 1789 than it had ever been: "Are we free?"[12] The new constitution was beginning to take shape. The assembly had already firmly rejected the British constitutional model with its dual legislative chambers, the House of Commons and House of Lords. A separate aristocratic chamber would have been too inflammatory and dangerous in France, where noble privileges had only recently been abolished. So the deputies decided that, under the new constitution, legislative power should be entrusted to a single body of 745 elected representatives. This decision raised the question of an executive veto over legislative decisions. What was the best way to build safeguards into the legislative process? Should the king be given an absolute veto or only a suspensive veto? The latter would allow him to delay new laws for a fixed period of time but not to permanently prohibit any he disagreed with. Would Louis XVI use either kind of veto in the interests of the people?

Mirabeau thought that an absolute executive veto over legislation was essential to the future of the monarchy—he did not see how any kind of constitutional monarchy could be viable otherwise, and he intended to argue the case before the assembly. Mirabeau was a brilliant orator. Unlike Robespierre's weak, wheedling voice, Mirabeau's was "full, manly, and sonorous; it filled and pleased the ear. Always powerful, yet flexible, it could be heard as distinctly when he lowered as when he raised it."[13] His intellect was flexible, too, and he could so easily incorporate penciled notes passed to him from the floor as he spoke that one contemporary compared him to a magician who tears a piece of paper into twenty little bits, swallows each of them separately, then produces the piece whole again. But as he mounted the tribune to deliver a speech on the veto, his gifts failed him. Working and playing harder than ever, despite bad health, Mirabeau had fallen into the habit of relying on other people to write most of his speeches and articles, and was now faced with a text he had not read. Later he confided to a friend that this was the only time in his entire political career that he broke into a cold sweat at the tribune. The speech before him was almost unintelligible, dry, obscure, and completely unsuited to the general mood in Paris, where, urged on by the popular press, people were frenziedly opposing the "monstrous" prospect of an absolute veto. Mirabeau tried to extemporize. He digressed. He inveighed against despotism in general. Then he cut his speech short. The prime opportunity for strengthening Louis XVI's position under the new constitution had just been lost through the inattentive overconfidence of the king's most powerful ally in the assembly.

The abbé Sieyès argued that the king should have the power to sanction the law but that any law he refused to sanction should be subjected to an alternative checking mechanism—it was, after all, the people who were sovereign. Earlier in 1789, Sieyès's lucid intellect had had a dramatic effect on the deputies, altering the terms and course of their debates, by redefining the third estate as the nation. Now he was trying to redirect them again by attacking the widespread assumption that, in the absence of a House of Lords to regulate legislative decisions, the king must be given a veto of some kind. Robespierre was one of the few who immediately recognized the radical potential of Sieyès's argument—not the finer details of his ideas for organizing legislative power but his forthright assertion of the principle of popular sovereignty. This was one of the political principles to which Robespierre was vehemently attached, and he was inspired to compose a passionate and lengthy speech of his own on the veto question.

He began by berating the misguided pragmatism of many of his fellow deputies. Thinking that some kind of executive veto was inevitable in the circumstances, they were prepared to vote for the lesser of two evils: a suspensive rather than absolute veto. Instead, Robespierre recalled his colleagues to fundamental principles: the power of truth, the safety of the people, liberty, equality, justice, and reason. He insisted that the assembly must remain faithful to these principles when making its constitutional decisions—anything else would be a disgraceful abuse of its authority. The all-important power to make the laws belonged to the sovereign people and must be exercised only by their representatives. Of course it was important to make sure that the laws created were good, fair, and useful, but that outcome could not be achieved by executive veto, only by true democracy. To that end, Robespierre outlined some alternative methods: representatives elected to the legislature should serve for only short periods of time, after which they would once again become ordinary citizens and so have an interest in passing only impartial laws; citizens should be elected only on grounds of virtue and merit, with no other distinctions taken into consideration; no representative should continue in the legislature beyond the initial period for which he was elected.

Having worked hard to set out his principles with clarity, Robespierre was frustrated to find himself prevented from delivering his carefully planned speech. Increasingly desperate to do so, he tried convincing the assembly that every deputy should have the opportunity to speak on a matter as important as the veto, before voting could begin. A number of members of the assembly, keen to move on to other constitutional questions, were impatient with his suggestion and so, despite some dissent and disorder, the voting soon went ahead without benefit of Robespierre's speech. The proposal for the king's suspensive veto was passed, 673 votes in favor, 325 against. This meant that when the constitution came into effect, Louis XVI would be able to delay new laws for the duration of two successive legislative sittings (a maximum of three years).[14] Robespierre consoled himself by publishing his speech as a pamphlet at the end of September and applying his political principles rigorously to the remaining constitutional questions facing the assembly.

Some months later, in the rue Saintonge, there was yet another early morning fight. Villiers arrived, keen as always to gossip about the assembly's constitutional debates before settling down to work. "I cannot conceive how any subjects can treat their king so unworthily," he remarked to Robespierre, sure, no doubt, of provoking a testy response. "They will finish by killing him like the English did their unhappy Stuart." "So you see yourself as a subject, do you?" Robespierre asked him. "Yes, I do," replied Villiers, provocatively. "You speak of Charles," came Robespierre's reply. "Well, the English freed by his death should have put an end to his line."[15] It is likely that Villiers embellished this anecdote. Publicly, Robespierre was working hard to establish a constitutional monarchy. Like everyone else, he could see that the presence of Louis XVI made it impossible to draft a constitution with a wholly new executive power, as the Americans had done in their revolution. Instead the assembly had to compromise and design a new role for their existing monarch. The radical deputies did so grudgingly and with a great many suspicions. Even so, there was never any suggestion in the assembly (and almost none outside it either) that the king should simply be deposed, still less executed, and France declared a republic.

IF ROBESPIERRE WAS not overtly republican in 1790, he was nevertheless the assembly's leading advocate of democratic principles. He passionately opposed the plan to divide French citizens into two groups, active and passive (*citoyen actif* and *citoyen passif*), according to whether or not they paid a prescribed amount of direct taxation, equal to the proceeds of two days' labor. Despite Robespierre's protests, the assembly went ahead, limiting the franchise to active citizens. In this way an estimated 39 percent of male citizens were denied the vote, most of them *pauvre*, vulnerable, and disadvantaged—the very people Robespierre was determined to help.[16] He was further appalled by the suggestion that only active citizens should be eligible to join the National Guard. To his mind the distinction between active and passive citizens contravened the Declaration of Rights, and the assembly, in accepting it, had betrayed the fundamental principle of equality to which it had only recently committed itself. Similarly, he objected to the *marc d'argent*, a qualification the assembly thought of imposing on those who wished to stand for election, restricting eligibility to those who paid taxes worth about fifty-three livres, well over ten times the amount of direct taxation necessary to become an active citizen. Thus Robespierre began the long campaign for universal suffrage in France. Using the example of Artois, he showed that the distinction between active and passive citizens would disenfranchise most residents of the region, who were currently paying more indirect than direct taxation. And he pointed out that there were very few in Artois who would be eligible for election if the *marc d'agent* were introduced. His argument was strong enough to win Artois, and other regions similarly affected, exemption from the electoral qualifications until the country's whole system of taxation could be reorganized. But he was not universally applauded. In the assembly he was accused of encouraging his constituents not to pay tax, and in Arras he was accused of slandering the region by claiming it had not paid tax.

Indignant, Robespierre drafted a spirited reply to his detractors and had it countersigned by his fellow delegates from Artois: "Although M. Robespierre needs no other testimony to his patriotism than that of his conduct, and of his public reputation, we have much pleasure in giving him proof of the esteem and affection with which he is regarded by all his colleagues. . . . He has always zealously defended the cause of the people at large, and of public liberty, as well as the special interests of Artois."[17] Be that as it may, it was quite clear that Robespierre's regionally focused arguments and concerns came second to his passion for abstract political principles. Artois provided him with a convenient argument against the assembly's electoral proposals, but the people, public liberty, and the inalienable right of every citizen to vote were closer to his heart. Already isolated for his commitment to universal male suffrage, he went on to argue for the rights of excluded groups like actors, Jews, and West Indians living under French colonial rule.

THE RATIONALIZATION OF French administration that had been so long postponed under the old regime was happening at last. The assembly went from strength to strength, its committees working overtime to come up with suitable proposals for this, that, or the other part of the new constitution, which was slowly but surely coming into being. If the new regime was to be genuinely representative of the people, it would need to be securely founded on a nationwide system of carefully organized elections. In the light of the chaos that had characterized the elections to the Estates General in 1789, most deputies agreed that there was a strong case for reorganizing France into new departments, districts, and cantons. Future elections could then be conducted and local government administered in a clearer, fairer, more convenient fashion. The abbé Sieyès was especially interested in these plans and very influential in shaping them. Unlike most—perhaps even all—of his colleagues in the assembly, he had definite ideas about how to institute representative government. In fact, he had been turning them over in his mind for years. "For a long time I have sensed the need to divide the surface of France afresh. If we let this occasion pass, it will never return, and the provinces will keep their esprit de corps, their privileges, their pretensions, their jealousies forever."[18] After much discussion, the assembly fixed the boundaries of eighty-three new departments and restructured municipal power throughout the country.

Restructuring municipal power in Paris proved more complicated. During the elections to the Estates General in 1789, the city had been divided into sixty electoral districts. After the elections were over, the electoral assemblies in each of these districts ought to have disappeared. In the course of the eventful year that followed, however, many of them transformed themselves into lively debating clubs and even assumed some of the responsibilities of local government. In this

way, the districts became permanent and provided a focus for the political activity of many ordinary Parisians. After the storming of the
Bastille, they converged on the Hôtel de Ville and established a new
municipal committee for governing revolutionary Paris. The driving
force behind this committee (or *Commune de Paris*, as it was known)
came from the vocal crowd of political activists who had brought it
into being. Some of these activists, George Jacques Danton, for example, and others from the Cordeliers district on the left bank of the
river Seine, were far more radical than the moderate majority on the
new committee. As captain of the citizens' militia, or National Guard,
in the Cordeliers district, Danton was fast becoming a rabble-rousing
force to be reckoned with in his own right. A tall, broad, athletic man
with a rugged face and rough, loud voice, he clashed bitterly with
General Lafayette, the commander in chief of the National Guard,
over the organization of Paris. Lafayette wanted to see a strong municipal authority at the city's center, supported by well-disciplined National Guardsmen whereas Danton championed the right of Paris's
sixty districts to a greater amount of representative and administrative
independence. Danton saw no reason to back down.

At first it was unclear whose side the assembly was on. Many of the
deputies were grateful to the radical Paris districts for bringing about
the fall of the Bastille and thus augmenting their own authority over
the king. But when it came to discussing the reconstitution of Paris's
municipal power, the assembly proposed abolishing the sixty districts
and replacing them with forty-eight sections that would elect the municipal authority. This seemed a deliberate attempt to break up groups
of political activists; certainly Danton saw it as a direct attack on his
local power base. Inside the assembly, Robespierre was a staunch defender of the districts. Addressing his colleagues, he argued for retaining the sixty districts, at least until the new constitution had come into
effect, especially for the purpose of surveillance:

> In this city, the home of principles, and opposed factions, it is not
> possible to rely on ordinary resources against those who menace lib-
> erty; it is necessary for the city in general to conserve its achievement
> and yours. Think of where you are: although you have done a great

deal, you have not done everything yet. I dare say that you ought to be more anxious now than if you had not already begun your [revolutionary] work. Who among you can guarantee that without the active surveillance of the districts, those who seek to obstruct your projects won't use more efficacious means? Do not be seduced by a deceptive calm—peace must not be mistaken for the sleep of carelessness.[19]

If he hoped to frighten the assembly or help the Cordeliers with such rhetoric, Robespierre failed. Mirabeau answered him in an ironic, scornful tone: "M. de Robespierre has brought to the tribune a zeal that is more patriotic than reflective. . . . We must not mistake the exaltation of principles for sublime principles." In other words, Mirabeau warned his colleagues to be careful, to identify the actual content of Robespierre's arguments and not merely merely respond to his passionate presentation. Several of the newspapers commented on Robespierre's hysterical and anxious tone. In the assembly, reactionary deputies who usually opposed him applauded loudly on this occasion. Maybe they thought he had discredited himself by intervening so bizarrely or perhaps they believed that retaining the sixty districts would lead to a backlash against radical deputies like him. By the end of the debate, however, the districts were a lost cause. The assembly voted to abolish them, and the Cordeliers were merged into the new section of the Théâtre français before the end of the year. Since the Cordeliers had a policy of deferring to the assembly's decisions, they focused their hatred and resentment elsewhere—on General Lafayette, on Bailly, the mayor of Paris, and on the Commune. Their constructive energy went into forming the Cordeliers Club, to keep alive the district's revolutionary spirit. It met on the left bank of the Seine, in the monastery church of the Cordeliers (or Franciscan Observantists). Danton, who lived nearby, went there every morning at nine, when the tocsin was rung. Already it was his club, a rallying point for workingmen, who paid just a penny a month to belong. Its doors were always open.

THE FUTURE OF the church and its enormous wealth (sixty million livres, according to one mid-eighteenth-century estimate) was the next divisive issue facing the assembly. When the deputies dismantled the remnants of feudalism on the euphoric night of 4 August 1789, they had agreed to redeem church tithes, instead of simply abolishing them without compensation. But since then there had been signs of reneging on this promise. "They wish to be free, but they do not know how to be just," complained the abbé Sieyès about some of his colleagues in the assembly.[20] It was obvious to everyone that the clergy could not continue as a separate privileged order now that the nation had asserted its inviolable right to sovereignty. But, Sieyès insisted, this did not mean that its property could be appropriated illegally— the right to property, after all, was one of those recently enshrined in the Declaration of Rights. Besides which, the clergy (unlike the nobility) was not simply a parasitical elite: it provided crucial services in areas of health and education and cared for the poor, in addition to organizing the religious ceremonies still central to the lives of most French people. From this perspective, the church was a branch of public administration that would need to be incorporated into the new constitution or remodeled under it: the assembly must reconcile the remnants of the old regime's religious institutions with its new revolutionary principles. These arguments drew down torrents of abuse on Sieyès's head. Could the radical theorist of 1789 have turned reactionary overnight? Was the author of the incendiary pamphlet *What Is the Third Estate?* first and foremost a conservative priest after all? "Are you going to abandon the role of legislators to reveal yourselves as— what? Antipriests?" sneered Sieyès in response to his critics.[21] But as so often, his biting cleverness and sharp reasoning were wasted on the unruly assembly, cheered on by anticlerical journalists and spectators in the public gallery.

Robespierre was neither antipriest nor anticlerical. Indeed, it is often hard to tell where he stood on the future of the church. On the motion to confirm Roman Catholicism as the state religion he was silenced: "M. de Robespierre was about to speak, when someone demanded a vote."[22] Tantalizingly, we will never know what he might have said. On other occasions, when he did manage to make himself heard, Robespierre's interventions were idiosyncratic. Sometimes he was as vehemently critical as he had been when he lost his temper with the archbishop of Nîmes back in Versailles, and often he returned to the interpretation of Christian doctrine he had put forward on that occasion. Christianity, in his view, was the religion of the poor and the pure at heart—conspicuous wealth and luxury should have no part in it. Sell everything and give to the destitute—this was the advice Jesus Christ gave his followers, and Robespierre echoed it in the assembly's constitutional debates. When the question of what was to be done with church lands and revenues arose, he urged the nation to appropriate them: "Church property belongs to the people; and to demand that the clergy shall use it to help the people is merely to put it to its original purpose."[23] In itself this line of argument was common enough, but Robespierre added his peculiar stamp to it—according to him, the poor were oppressed not only by their hunger and other neglected needs but also by the spectacle of self-indulgent clerics insensitively squandering what was rightfully theirs. The poor were scandalized and their moral outrage was more than justified.

A few weeks later he made another characteristically odd intervention, arguing that ex-monks were entitled to more generous pensions than they were being offered by recently suppressed religious orders. It was impossible, he said, to estimate the real wealth of these orders. They had been living in fear of the Revolution and had long been preparing for it by carefully concealing their wealth. Here was an early example of Robespierre's growing tendency to suspect hidden conspiracies. Church wealth was indeed difficult to quantify, but more because it took so many different forms and was diffused throughout the whole country than because counterrevolutionary monks and clerics had been scheming to conceal it. Later in 1790, the assembly published a list of the revenues of all the archbishoprics, bishoprics, and abbeys, including the information that the abbey of Saint-Vaast in Arras had an income of 400,000 livres and the bishop of Arras drew a stipend of 92,000 livres. Such figures would have confirmed Robespierre in his perceptions of ecclesiastical decadence.

Robespierre made his longest and most interesting speech on the church in May 1790, when the assembly was embroiled in discussions about the new Civil Constitution of the Clergy. This document had taken a year to draft and would—it was hoped—reconcile what remained of the church with the Revolution. In fact, it plunged France into violent strife and would later be regarded (by the abbé Sieyès, among others) as the assembly's first really serious mistake. In essence, the proposals rejected the pope's authority over the church in France, reduced the number of dioceses from 137 to 83 (thus aligning them with the country's new administrative departments), stipulated that the clergy would now be paid by the state rather than through tithes, and provided for the election of priests and bishops by the people. Robespierre spoke in support of all these changes. As usual, he argued from clear principles to destructive effect. He defined priests as public officials, "simply magistrates whose duty it is to maintain and carry on public worship."[24] Any aspect of the church that was not useful to society must go. Cathedrals, religious colleges, even bishops or priests, if they were not publicly useful, would have to disappear. Robespierre was especially pleased by the prospect of the people electing their own church officials. In accordance with his strict democratic principles, he dismissed the suggestion that the existing clergy might play a prominent role in such elections; instead the clergy should be chosen through the pure, unmediated expression of popular will.

Toward the end of his speech, Robespierre suddenly did something outrageous: he raised the issue of married priests. Many of his colleagues agreed with him that the clergy could not continue as a privileged order, that ministers of the church were not substantially different from any other public officials and should be chosen by the people—but an end to celibacy, and all the trouble it would cause with the pope in Rome, was a step too far for the assembly: a barrage of disapproval cut off Robespierre's speech. It is somewhat puzzling that he took it upon himself to propose something so contentious. One possible explanation is that he was attempting to steal Mirabeau's thunder because he had designs on the radical leader's mantle. The great orator himself had commissioned one of his several ghostwriters (a Swiss man named Reybaz), to prepare a speech on priestly celibacy, and he was furious when Robespierre preempted him by ineffectually raising the matter in the assembly.[25]

Back in Arras, Augustin was particularly unnerved by this development. He wrote warning his brother that "your motion for the marriage of priests has given you the reputation of an unbeliever among all our great philosophers in Artois. . . . You will lose the esteem of the peasantry if you renew this motion. People are using it as a weapon against you and talk of nothing but your irreligion, etc. Perhaps it would be better not to support it anymore. . . . Let me know if you would like me to come to Paris."[26] Though Augustin was highly concerned with protecting Robespierre's local reputation, he was desperate to join his brother in Paris at the center of the Revolution. Meanwhile, at his desk in the Marais, Robespierre was inundated with letters on every side of the issue, sometimes in verse. "Poems in Latin, French, Greek and even Hebrew arrived from the four corners of France, poems of 500, 700, 1,500 couplets rained down upon the rue Saintonge."[27] Wry as ever, he remarked to his secretary across his bursting mailbag, "Do you still believe there is a shortage of poets in France? They are, at any rate, pouring forth from the cloisters and monasteries." According to Villiers, Robespierre dutifully acknowledged all these missives and meticulously reclaimed the postage. Whether or not the correspondents supported his views, the letters were evidence that his reputation outside the assembly was continuing to grow. "I doubt if a single law that he has proposed has ever been carried," said his old school friend Camille, as the constitutional debates drew to a close in 1791.[28] Even so, Robespierre was fast becoming a figure in national politics.

THE JOURNALISTS AND spectators who came to observe the Assembly from the public galleries at the Manège were not the only source of Robespierre's growing reputation. He also owed his fame to the Jacobin Club, an outgrowth of the Breton Club that had met in Versailles at the Café Amaury. After the move to Paris, some of the original members of the Breton Club rented the refectory of a Dominican monastery, conveniently close to the Manège, as their new meeting place.[29] In Paris, the Dominicans were nicknamed the Jacobins because their first religious house in the city was in the rue Saint-Jacques. Over time this nickname was transferred to the political club meeting in the monastery, but initially the remnants of the Breton Club called themselves the Society of the Friends of the Constitution.[30] Whereas the organization of the Breton Club had been obscure, the new club established clear rules and regulations. There was to be a president, four secretaries, and a treasurer, and all these offices were to be rotated. While the club would admit members who were not deputies to the National Assembly, the relatively high membership fees (twelve livres to join and twenty-four livres annual subscription) assured that only educated and serious-minded male supporters of the Revolution would join (women were restricted to spectator seats). Aside from covering the club's running costs, the membership subscriptions were used to finance the publication of important speeches, which broadened the club's influence. The candlelit meetings in the old monastery gradually acquired a central role in revolutionary politics. At the Jacobins, most evenings a week, there was the opportunity to analyze in close detail the progress of the assembly's constitutional debates. It was here that the self-appointed guardians of the Revolution continued to define its objectives. Any member of the club whose revolutionary principles were deemed inadequate could be expelled. From 1790 political clubs all over France began affiliating themselves with the Paris Jacobins, and a nationwide correspondence network came into existence. Robespierre rapidly grasped its political potential. The counterrevolution was gathering momentum throughout the country following the Civil Constitution of the Clergy. He could see that a network of affiliated clubs of active revolutionaries was just what was needed to combat the threat posed by recalcitrant clergy and their supporters.

In Arras, Augustin helped establish a patriotic club and wrote to Robespierre seeking affiliation with the Paris Jacobins. He painted an alarming picture of counterrevolution in Artois, where the patriots were strong but isolated and embattled. Exaggerating wildly, Augustin claimed that they were surrounded by flames after a series of unexplained arson attacks throughout the region. "We are not able to discover the instigators of these fires but are convinced that they are enemies of the public good."[31] He complained of the local government's indifference to libels launched against the National Assembly. In particular he recounted an anecdote about Robespierre's ex-friend Dubois de Fosseux, now mayor of Arras. A road builder in the village of Aire had received a libelous document that he reported at once to the mayor. "You have done well to bring it to me, it is very bad," said Dubois de Fosseux. Upon returning home, however, the road builder found an anonymous letter explaining that the libel against the National Assembly had been sent to him so that he could read it to other peasants in his village, not report it to the mayor. Augustin implied that Dubois de Fosseux himself had sent the letter encouraging libel against the National Assembly. Robespierre was only too willing to think ill of Dubois de Fosseux after their falling out in Arras during the elections to the Estates General in 1789, so Augustin's insinuation would not have been unwelcome. Even more striking, though, was Augustin's hatred of the local clergy. "It is absolutely necessary to ransack our abbeys," he wrote to his brother. "For it is among the monks that one finds monsters wanting to stain France with blood."[32] In another letter, Augustin mentions plans to convert the resources of the abbey of Saint-Vaast into more scholarships for local children, of the kind both he and Robespierre had benefited from, but comments that it would be more fitting to use the money to alleviate the suffering of the indigent over the coming winter. If he echoed his brother's preoccupation with the plight of the poor, Augustin also shared a penchant for dark foreboding: "I cannot hide my fears from you, dear brother. You will seal the cause of the people with your blood."[33]

Even at this comparatively early point in the Revolution, Robespierre was so suspicious of "spies in every quarter of the city, and murderers assigned to assassinate patriots" that he feared the name Robespierre on the outside of an envelope would attract malicious attention. The intoxicating paranoia that would eventually permeate almost all his tactical decisions is already evident. "Reply to me, and put your letter in an envelope marked President of the National Assembly," he tells his friend Buissart in March 1790.[34] In April he writes, "Put your letters in an envelope addressed to the Deputies of Artois to the National Assembly."[35] And in May he tells Buissart, "I am going to send you a letter for my brother. I do not want to address it to him directly from fear that my name will entice aristocratic hands to violate the privacy of the post."[36] Still, it is important to note that Robespierre was not alone in entertaining such concerns. The daily newspaper *Chronique de Paris* carried this advertisement in October 1790:

CODED MESSAGES

> Anyone who wants to procure a method for rendering correspondence impenetrable, contact M. Loppin, rue l'Evêque. . . . By this method you can confidently dictate a letter to your secretary, or any public scribe, without fearing that he will be able to guess your thoughts. Five minutes suffices to put this method into operation.[37]

Given the political climate of the time, it is not surprising that Robespierre grew more suspicious by the day. Like many other patriots, he feared an aristocratic plot. He had made an irreversible personal commitment to the Revolution, so anything that menaced it menaced him too. At the center of his suspicion was the fear that if the Revolution's enemies succeeded in plunging France into a foreign war, all would be lost.

IN THE SPRING of 1790, the threat of war was suddenly real. Back in 1778, toward the end of his last voyage of discovery, Captain Cook had sailed his ship, *Resolution*, into Nootka Sound in the Pacific, to what is now British Columbia. Though the Spaniards had arrived before Cook and taken formal possession of the coastline, English ships followed in his wake and set up a lucrative trade in animal pelts. These English adventurers had the full approval of their government and Prime Minister Pitt. So when Spanish forces arrived to reclaim possession of Nootka Sound, Pitt prepared his fleet for war. Spain demanded French support under the Bourbon alliance that united the two countries. Louis XVI acknowledged his obligation and ordered his foreign minister to ready the French fleet for action. There was only one problem: if Louis XVI was still in charge of foreign policy and could single-handedly commit the country to war, where did that leave the National Assembly? Somewhat surprisingly, from the point of view of his radical colleagues, Mirabeau urged the assembly to accept the king's exclusive right to declare war and make peace. Still hoping to reconcile the king and the assembly, he thought such a move would be a step toward establishing a secure constitutional monarchy. Robespierre, among others, vigorously opposed him.

Robespierre wanted to see the assembly take foreign affairs into its own hands and act in a conciliatory manner that would bring about peace. Beyond this, he disputed the king's right to declare war on behalf of France, referring to him as a delegate of the nation who must do what he was told. As so often, his contentious intervention was greeted by both murmurs and loud applause. Mirabeau, however, rose to the occasion and gave one of the most brilliant oratorical performances of his— by now—distinguished career. He insisted that even if decisions on war and peace were to rest ultimately with the assembly, the right to initiate or propose such decisions must remain with the king. Mirabeau won this point and the assembly went on to decide that "war can be declared only by a decree of the legislature, passed after a formal proposal by the king, and subsequently sanctioned by him."[38] Though this outcome was not as radical as Robespierre would have liked (and, in the event, France did not go to war to help Spain), it was still a blow to the monarchy, and on the evening of 22 May Robespierre, his friend and fellow radical Jérôme Pétion, and other leading Jacobins processed through the Tuileries gardens escorted by a jubilant crowd. Pétion, the son of a lawyer at Chartres, was two years older than Robespierre and, like him, had been a lawyer with literary ambitions before the Revolution. In the assembly the two were increasingly paired as the up and coming leaders in Mirabeau's wake. As the friends walked through the gardens, enjoying the spring blossoms on the cherry trees, the evening light, and the admiration of the crowd, they saw someone watching at one of the tall windows of the Tuileries palace. It was the small figure of the dauphin, waving and clapping his hands.

Louis XVI and his family were already effectively prisoners in the Tuileries, the magnificent palace on the right bank of the Seine. Commissioned in 1564 by Henry II's widow, Catherine de Médicis, and named after the tile kilns or "tuileries" that had previously occupied the site, the Tuileries palace, for all its splendor, was certainly not a desirable abode. It had stood vacant, and been used only as a theater, for a century before the royal family were dragged from Versailles and forcibly installed in it. Connected to the even older Louvre palace by a riverside gallery, the Tuileries was within spitting distance of the Manège where the assembly and its throng of interested onlookers met every day, including Sunday. And there were many service buildings—porters' lodges, barracks, domestic offices, and stables—clustered against the walls of the palace, so that almost all its doors and windows opened onto a public thoroughfare. There was little chance of privacy for the royals. Marie Antoinette complained that even in high summer she "could not open the windows for a little fresh air without being exposed to the grossest invectives and menaces."[39] For the same reason, it was difficult for her family to take any exercise, except on the terrace next to the river, and here the air was soon thick with insults and jeers from the angry Parisian mob. Louis XVI's relations with the assembly were becoming more and more fraught as the weeks went by and rumors of foreign invasion, or "the aristocratic plot," multiplied. Yet, to the noisy crowd accompanying Robespierre and Pétion through the Tuileries gardens that evening in May, the innocent applause of the six-year-old dauphin at the window seemed a good omen: here was the heir to the throne cheering the radical deputies. Here was hope, perhaps, that the constitutional monarchy might be made to work, that king and assembly could agree to a stable form of government for France.

In Camille Desmoulins's report of these events, he has Robespierre sneering at the revelers: "Why, gentlemen! Upon what are you congratulating yourselves? The decree is hateful—as hateful as can be. Let that brat at the window clap his hands if he will: he knows what he is doing better than we do."[40] When he opened the paper and read this version, Robespierre was indignant. He wrote at once to Camille, pointing out that he had spoken his mind in the assembly but had left it at that and would never have been so indiscreet in public. In fact, he had not addressed the crowd in the garden at all. At Robespierre's request, Camille printed his complaint, but he added a long editorial note:

> If I insert these errata, my dear Robespierre, it is solely to display your signature before my fellow journalists and to warn them not to mutilate in future a name rendered famous by the patriotism of its

bearer. There is a righteousness about your letter, and a senatorial weightiness, that hurts me, as an old college friend. You are proud, and you have a right to be, to wear the toga of the National Assembly. I like this noble conceit, and I am only sorry that all the deputies are not as conscious of their dignity as you are. But you might at least have given an old comrade like myself something more than a nod of the head—not that I love you any the less for it, because you *are* faithful to your principles, however it may be with your friends. All the same, why this insistence on my recantation? I may have slightly altered the facts in the story I told; but it was all to your credit, and if you never actually used the words I put in your mouth, still they certainly express your thoughts. . . . Surely you are not one of those wretched creatures described by J. J. Rousseau who hate to have their thoughts revealed, and who only say what they really think in the presence of their butler or their valet but never before the National Assembly or in the Tuileries gardens.[41]

Camille was still Robespierre's closest friend in Paris. At the end of the year, Robespierre acted as a witness at his wedding to Lucile Horace. Their old headmaster, a priest from Louis-le-Grand, officiated. (Civil marriages had not been introduced at this stage in the Revolution, so the ceremony was a traditional Roman Catholic one, even though Camille had recently made some disparaging remarks about Christianity in his newspaper. When questioned about them before the wedding, he cheekily expressed surprise that the clergy read his paper. "Only sometimes," came the priest's wry response.)[42] There was even talk of Robespierre's marrying the bride's sister and making it a double wedding. Yet despite the continuing friendship, Robespierre's newly acquired ponderousness was beginning to irritate Camille. While Camille was a poet and a journalist, Robespierre was a deputy to the National Assembly; if at Louis-le-Grand they had been equals, now Robespierre seemed to think he was more important. In these circumstances, it was clever of Camille to quote Rousseau. He knew how strong an impression Rousseau's books—with their emphasis on equality and integrity—had made on Robespierre. This was also a sly way of warning his friend against the vice of hypocrisy, another of Rousseau's obsessions. But the charge "You are faithful to your principles, however it may be with your friends" is serious. Had Robespierre really been disloyal to his friend? In this instance there is no evidence against him. Camille was hurt and his accusation exaggerated. Robespierre was certainly not the only revolutionary vulnerable to injured pride.

Not long after this public tiff with Camille, a letter arrived on Robespierre's chaotic and heavily laden desk that marked the beginning of another important friendship with a younger man. The letter was from an officer in the National Guard of the Aisne, Louis Antoine Léon de Saint-Just, who was nine years younger than Robespierre and four years younger than Camille. Wild, handsome, transgressive, he was a most unlikely friend for Robespierre. Before the Revolution, Saint-Just had written a long, obscene poem called *Organt* and mischievously dedicated it to the Vatican. He wrote it while languishing in prison for six months, having been convicted for stealing and selling his widowed mother's silver. His completely ludicrous excuse for mistreating his mother was that he needed money to consult a doctor about a disease brought on by overwork. Nevertheless, the preface to his poem was penitent: "I am twenty; I have acted badly; but I shall do better." With the Revolution came Saint-Just's chance at a fresh start. He became involved in local politics, specifically the issue of choosing the new capital of the new Department of the Aisne, as the assembly's plans for reorganizing and redividing France were taking shape. Like many others throughout the country, he swore the new patriotic oath of "Fidelity to the Nation, the Law, and the King." He had already contacted Camille Desmoulins, when he decided to write to Robespierre as well:

> You who uphold our tottering country against the torrent of despotism and intrigue, you whom I know, as I know God, only through his miracles—it is to you, Monsieur, that I address myself, to entreat you to unite with me in saving my poor land. . . . I do not know you, but you are a great man. You are not merely the deputy of a province, you are the deputy of the Republic and of mankind.[43]

All Saint-Just actually wanted Robespierre (whom he had never met) to do was to sign a petition supporting his village in the Aisne,

Blérancourt, in a trade dispute with the neighboring town of Couci—it would have been hard to find a more parochial problem. So why did Robespierre keep this short letter, from someone he did not know, on a topic of little interest to him? It was found among his papers after he died when so many other letters had been lost or disposed of. Perhaps it was true, as Camille claimed, that Robespierre in 1790 was already getting above himself. And Saint-Just had, after all, just compared him to God! Still, the friendship that later developed between these two men centered on their shared ideas and political passions: they had an intellectual affinity aside from any more personal emotional or sentimental attachment. "You are the deputy of the Republic and of mankind," said Saint-Just, and this is exactly how Robespierre saw himself, even if he had not yet put it so clearly. He might simply have been flattered by the letter. Or it could be only an accident that it survived. Or perhaps Robespierre somehow sensed the beginning of a deep and mysterious friendship that would last until the day he died.

THE FIRST ANNIVERSARY of the fall of the Bastille was coming up. How would Paris celebrate? Ever since Louis XVI had agreed to become a constitutional monarch, so-called Festivals of Federation had been in vogue throughout France. They varied greatly in size and grandeur but centered on ordinary citizens and members of the National Guard, who, jubilantly swearing patriotic oaths, were happy for any excuse for a public holiday as revolutionary optimism swept across the country. Why not celebrate the fall of the Bastille with a grand-scale Festival of Federation? Why not turn the Champ de Mars parade ground, a vast open space close to the center of Paris, into an amphitheater with tiered seating for spectators, a triumphal arch at one end, and an "altar of the fatherland" in the middle? The king and National Assembly deputies could sit together in a specially built pavilion and watch the National Guards pass beneath the arch and swear their patriotic oath at the altar. The only difficulty was that things had been left until very late and these plans were approved just three weeks before the anniversary. However, there was public spirit and goodwill in abundance at this point in the Revolution, so volunteers from all walks of life flocked to the Champ de Mars to clear and level the ground. Robespierre would have been pleased to see monks with cockades pinned to their cassocks trampling the earth alongside soldiers, laborers, and well-dressed women. Excitement, cooperation, and holiday spirit accomplished the necessary and by 14 July everything was ready.

In the midst of these last-minute preparations, Augustin wrote to Robespierre hinting, as he had done before, that he would like to come to Paris. He thought he should try to join the local delegation to the national Festival of Federation, since he was sure to be deprived of any patriotic celebrations in conservative Arras. Life there for him and Charlotte was hard, Augustin complained.[44] They had little money and no prospects. There is no record of Robespierre's response, but if Augustin got his way and arrived in Paris for 14 July, he would have been proud to catch sight of his brother at the heart of the celebrations. On the day, it rained, so Louis XVI and the National Assembly deputies were glad of the shelter of the pavilion as they watched mud-splattered battalions of National Guards troop past the Altar of the Fatherland and swear allegiance to "the best of kings." One of the deputies later remembered, "I was standing behind His Majesty's seat and almost cheek by jowl with that famous rascal Robespierre." Had Louis XVI turned to glance over his shoulder, he might have noticed the pallid, feline features of the lawyer from Arras whose reputation was growing steadily, week by week. Probably Louis XVI could not have said when exactly he had started to recognize the name Robespierre and attach importance to it. Certainly he did not recall the very first time he had set eyes on him, fifteen years earlier, when Robespierre was kneeling in the street outside Louis-le-Grand to greet the king on the way back from his coronation. But Robespierre surely remembered. Standing beneath the sodden canvas, so close to the king on this first anniversary of the fall of the Bastille, he could feel confident that he would not have to get down on his knees before anyone ever again. "All mortals are equal; it is not by birth but only virtue that they are distinguished. In every state the Law must be universal and mortals whosoever they be are equal before it."[45] These were the words inscribed on the Altar of the Fatherland. Robespierre was too nearsighted to read them from where he was standing, but the sentiments they expressed were emblazoned on his heart.

Despite the weather, Charles Maurice Talleyrand-Périgord, bishop of Autun, said Mass at the open-air altar and blessed the tricolor banners flapping hard against their poles like great wet towels. Talleyrand was lame, and for this reason had been forced into a clerical career by his family.[46] After the Mass, General Lafayette, emblematic citizen-soldier and head of the National Guard, took over. The sun broke through the clouds and the rain—almost miraculously—stopped. Glamorously mounted on a white charger, Lafayette looked down his long nose and surveyed the assembled ranks below him: forty thousand National Guardsmen, a battalion of children, one of veterans, companies of professional soldiers and sailors, and delegates from France's eighty-three new departments. He turned his horse toward the pavilion, the guards parted to let him through, and there he dismounted to receive the king's permission to administer the patriotic oath. This he did back at the altar. The heady blend of religious sentiment and militarism went down well with the crowd, and in this symbolic way the whole country gave its support to the revolutionary actions of Paris. Afterward, the king, in turn, swore to uphold the decrees of the National Assembly. Lafayette was acting as the intermediary between the people and their king. All eyes were on him. For someone who had volunteered to cross the Atlantic and fight in the American Revolution at the age of twenty-one, he remained remarkably sanguine—his motto was still "Why not?"[47] He wanted harmony between Louis XVI and the Revolution; he believed it possible; he fancied himself the man who could bring it about. "Royalty can only preserve itself by being in unison with the Revolution: otherwise it must be destroyed, and I will be the first to contribute to its destruction. The king is king neither of the aristocrats nor of the factions; he is king of the people and of the Revolution; otherwise he may be dethroned either by the former or by the latter."[48] Robespierre agreed, but he already disliked Lafayette—and within a year he would hate him.

THE FESTIVAL OF Federation did not impress everyone. In his newspaper, *Révolutions de France et de Brabant*, Camille Desmoulins derided it as an opportunity for Lafayette to show off, then mocked the ceremony by depicting a humiliated, supplicating king being dragged through the mud behind the chariot of his conquerors. A leading reactionary deputy, Pierre-Victor Malouet (who had been identified by Robespierre at the very beginning of the Revolution as "the most suspect, the most odious of all the patriots"), decided that radical sectors of the Parisian press had gone too far. In addition to Camille pouring scorn on the Festival of Federation, there was also the poisonous Marat, who day after day vehemently denounced the National Assembly in his paper. IT'S ALL OVER FOR US ("*C'en est fait de nous*"), screamed the *Ami du peuple* on 26 July, when a detachment of Austrian troops asked permission to cross the border into France. This was not yet an invasion but a sharp reminder that the Revolution had foreign enemies. Austria, France's old rival for territory in Europe, was now poised to take advantage of the chaos the Revolution had brought; in addition, Marie Antoinette's brother, the Holy Roman Emperor Leopold II, was anxiously watching events unfold in France, prepared to intervene, if necessary, to save the monarchy. Just in case anyone had missed the paper, Marat posted placards all over Paris with the same message, ending with ominous forebodings of war: "Five or six hundred [aristocratic] heads lopped off would have assured you repose and happiness; a false humanity has restrained your arm and suspended your blows; it will cost the lives of millions of your brothers."[49] Marat claimed that he was only trying to make a strong impression on people and destroy their complacency or "fatal" sense of security in the face of the growing counterrevolution—and was not really calling for bloodshed in the street.[50] However, his tactics appalled most of the deputies in the assembly.

On 31 July Malouet urged his colleagues to censor Marat's paper along with that of Camille Desmoulins. He moved that all authors, printers, and distributors of writings inciting the crowd to revolt against the law or disrupt the drafting of the constitution should be prosecuted for crimes against the nation. Marat responded with vitriolic fury in his paper, but Camille, who was a somewhat milder character, sent an address to the assembly defending himself. After it was read, Malouet thundered, "Is he innocent? Let him prove it. Is he guilty? I will conduct the case against him, and against anyone who takes up his defense. Let him justify his conduct if he dare." From the public gallery, Camille shouted, "Yes, I dare!" This was an unprecedented flouting of the assembly's protocol, and the president (whom the deputies elected from among themselves each month) ordered his immediate arrest. In the ensuing chaos, Robespierre came to his friend's defense. "Do not confuse imprudence and inconsiderateness with crime," he entreated his colleagues.[51] Camille managed to escape and no charges were pressed. Robespierre could sleep soundly that night, knowing that he had proved his loyalty to his friend and that Camille now had reason to be ashamed of having doubted him back in May.

But if Marat was chastised for having spread panic with his apocalyptic posters, the fact remained that Austrian troops were waiting to cross the border into France. Who was to blame? Who was behind this threat to the Revolution? Discussion in the assembly now turned to these questions. Louis XVI's war minister was one possibility; he was suspected of hoping war would help reverse all the changes the Revolution had brought. Another was the leader of the émigrés in exile, the Prince de Condé. Robespierre dismissed both suggestions. He argued that the assembly must not be too hasty in identifying a single individual as respon sible for the plot against the nation. Instead, it should urgently address the problem of how to deal with "all the enemies of the Revolution."[52] The royalist press was delighted that Robespierre, of all people, had deflected blame from Louis XVI's ministry and the Prince de Condé and derisively congratulated him on his new aristocratic credentials. This, no doubt, irritated him; but he was more worried by his suspicion that the most dangerous enemies of the Revolution were not the most obvious ones but rather those with the best disguises. Prominent individuals hostile to the Revolution were less menacing, he insisted, than the hidden enemies who appeared as friends but were in truth the vanguard of counterrevolution. People were beginning to notice and remark on his recurring paranoia: Robespierre "once again enlarged on the plots and conspiracies of which he alone held the secret," reported the *Mercure de France*.[53] "M. de Robespierre, as usual, spoke of plots, conspiracies, etc., etc.," remarked a fellow deputy earlier in 1790, bored but slightly amused.[54] This distrustfulness was not, however, just a passing whim of Robespierre's or further evidence of his peculiar personality; it was a political obsession that would intensify throughout the rest of his career:

> I blame those less who out of romantic enthusiasm justify their at-
> tachment to former principles they cannot abandon [i.e., defenders of
> the old regime] than those who cover their perfidious designs with
> the mask of patriotism and virtue.[55]

Seek first the enemy within, he enjoined his colleagues. Beware of hypocrisy and corruption. He was more prescient than he knew, since, just weeks before the Festival of Federation, Mirabeau (still the most famous deputy in the assembly) had accepted a substantial retainer from the court, plus payment of the overwhelming debts he had ac-crued over a lifetime of drinking and womanizing. In return, Mirabeau agreed to secretly advise the king on how to strengthen his standing with the assembly. The king had promised him a further million francs when the assembly was at last disbanded. The historian J. M. Thompson argues that it is unlikely that any of the deputies would have re-fused such an offer at this point in the Revolution—except, of course, Robespierre. Whether or not that is the case, Robespierre, for all his concerns about corruption and plots, seems not to have suspected Mirabeau. In Versailles he had been wary of Mirabeau's close connec-tions with the court. But over the intervening months his admiration for him had grown, even when they disagreed—as they often did— over a particular decree or detail of the constitution. The royalist press was quick to notice; "Mirabeau's monkey" was one of its many nick-names for Robespierre, and he was even accused of copying the older man's hairstyle and following him about in the street like a puppy. Mirabeau wore an enormous quantity of false black hair, which dra-matically increased the volume of his already enormous head: "When I shake my terrible locks, no one dares interrupt me!" he bragged.[56] It seems highly unlikely that neat, slight, fastidious Robespierre set out to copy him in this way. Really their relationship was more distant and mutually respectful. "He will go far because he believes everything he says," is what Mirabeau said of Robespierre—conscious certainly that the same was not true of himself.[57]

When the royal family was brought to Paris from Versailles back in October 1789, Mirabeau had been quick to note that they were effec-tively prisoners in the Tuileries palace. As winter approached and Paris was in chaos, he wondered what the city would be like in three months' time. And he offered his own grim answer: "A hospital, for sure, perhaps even a theater of horrors."[58] He foresaw strife between radical Paris and the more moderate provinces—he understood the "profound immorality" of Paris, as only someone who had led his kind of dissolute life could; and he concluded that the king would have to leave the capital if there was to be any hope of recovering his power and dignity. Once this proved impossible, Mirabeau tried to reconcile the king to the constitution as it was taking shape in the assembly. But in this he had no more success than General Lafayette and was soon wringing his hands, exasperated by the incessant intrigue at court: "What woolgatherers they are! What bunglers! How cowardly! How reckless! What a grotesque mixture of old ideas and new projects, of petty scruples and childish whims, of willing this and not willing that, of abortive loves and hates!"[59] Now, almost a year had passed and conditions were little better. There was a serious threat of war: civil war, war with a foreign power, or both. Discontent was mounting in the provinces. There was terrible trouble brewing over the Civil Constitution of the Clergy and the oath to uphold it imposed on the recalcitrant priests. The assembly was increasingly fragmented and frustrated. The country was even more bankrupt than it had been before the Revolution. And Mirabeau was seriously ill, his personal degeneration a match for the general disintegration of France.

At the beginning of the Revolution, Mirabeau suffered from jaundice, hereditary nephritis, intestinal troubles, rheumatism, swollen legs, and a recurrent infection in his left eye. His friend Dr. Cabanis remembers his drinking vast quantities of lemonade, the only treatment he had time for. The assembly's long daily meetings were extremely insalubrious. At the best of times, the Manège was very poorly ventilated, but the quality of the air deteriorated still further in winter, when the doors and windows were kept closed and heating stoves belched smoke into the atmosphere. Eye and stomach infections were epidemic, affecting everyone from the most robust deputies to the frailest members of the public crowded into the spectator galleries. At one point, Mirabeau's infected eyes were so sore that he covered them with bandages when he addressed the assembly. The soiled bandages came off for his secret audience with the queen on 3 July, when he kissed her hand and declared, in the face of all evidence to the contrary, "Madame, the monarchy is saved!" But even so, Marie Antoinette shivered in horror at the sight of the huge, vulgar sick man on whom her family's future had come to depend. "You know not all the power of my ugliness!" Mirabeau liked to boast to his friends. Yet for all his bravado, he was desperate by the end of 1790, and his advice to Louis XVI became increasingly harebrained, unpatriotic, even treasonous. Stir up trouble between the National Guard and the Paris mob, he suggested; embarrass the assembly so as to suborn it; undermine General Lafayette; tamper with the press; and revive the royal army, starting with the Swiss and German regiments. Exacerbate, in other words, the extent to which France was already ungovernable, so that power might, by default, be returned to the throne. Robespierre, in his darkest nightmares, scarcely imagined such treachery.

6

THE CONSTITUTION

At the beginning of 1791, Mirabeau was elected president of the assembly, despite his deteriorating health. His friend the Swiss jurist and political writer Etienne Dumont remembered:

> The irritation of his system produced violent attacks of ophthalmia, and I have seen him, while he was president, sometimes apply leeches to his eyes during the adjournment between the morning and evening sessions and attend the assembly with his neck covered with linen to stanch the blood.[1]

Mirabeau was suddenly—very suspiciously—flush with money, and far from discreet with it. Marat, vigilant as ever, kept drawing attention to this new wealth: "Two years ago, Riquetti [Mirabeau] was obliged to send his breeches to the pawnshop to get six francs; today he swims in opulence . . . and has three mistresses whom he showers with gifts."[2] Among other flamboyant extravagances, Mirabeau bought a large property in the Marais (quite close to the building in which Robespierre rented his humble second-floor flat). Here he retired on weekends, enjoyed overseeing the restoration and refurbishment of his grand new home, and looked forward to the coming of spring with the special delight of an ex-prisoner whose life has come right again. It was at his Marais retreat, on the night of Sunday, 27 March, that he was taken seriously ill. Nevertheless, he insisted on getting up and going to the assembly the next morning to defend the property rights of mine owners. He had a friend who owned a mine, to whom he remarked afterward, "Your case is won, but I am lost." The next day, the news that he was dying spread through Paris.

It is often said that Mirabeau had syphilis, which was known in eighteenth-century Britain and Italy as "the French disease" and in France as "the Italian disease" but also as "the great imitator" because its symptoms were so difficult to distinguish from those of other illnesses. With typical candor, he often bragged about his venereal disease. Dumont reported Mirabeau's boasting "that a statue ought to be raised to him by the physicians because he had discovered in the stews of the Palais-Royal the germ of a disease thought to be extinct—a kind of leprosy or elephantiasis."[3] His friends were not so frank or unabashed. Dumont thought Mirabeau had acute enteritis, whereas Dr. Cabanis, who treated his last illness, wanted to believe that Mirabeau died of systemic complications arising from ophthalmia. But between the two of them they recorded many of the symptoms of syphilis in its later stages. Ever since the assembly had moved to Paris, Mirabeau had taken to traveling the short distance between his lodgings and the Manège by cab because he found it increasingly difficult to walk. His joints and his sense of balance were affected. In the autumn of 1790 a large swollen gland developed in his neck, just below his right ear. Dr. Cabanis noted that when the gland softened and shrank, Mirabeau's left eye deteriorated, and vice versa. From this he concluded that there must be a connection between the two sites of infection and prescribed mercury, the conventional treatment for syphilis since the sixteenth century. The infection spread across Mirabeau's face and neck. His energy declined rapidly, his color was bad and his body lethargic, and his thoughts were increasingly morbid. His liver weakened. His breathing was often labored, a sign of heart disease, very typical of advanced syphilis. In the early months of 1791 Mirabeau started showing evidence of mental confusion and memory loss: "He was slow finding ideas or expressions and sometimes could not find them at all."[4] His sufferings, in the final days of his life, were hideous.

All Paris was interested in Mirabeau's decline. Crowds of people gathered beneath his windows, grabbing and frantically reading the regular health bulletins that were printed on demand. At the Tuileries, Louis XVI asked for news of the dying man to be brought to him twice a day. Marie Antoinette had tears in her eyes. Complete strangers offered Mirabeau their blood. Out of premature grief, Mirabeau's secretary stabbed himself several times—not fatally—with a penknife. Deputations from the Jacobin Club and the assembly arrived, Robespierre very likely among them. Talleyrand, the bishop of Autun (last seen saying Mass at the Festival of Federation but excommunicated by the pope since then on account of his support for the Civil Constitution of the Clergy), came to visit, and Mirabeau entrusted him with his final speech to the assembly. This turned out to be an offering on testamentary law, written by someone else, which proposed significant changes to the inheritance laws. "It is a very remarkable fact that, on his very deathbed, Mirabeau preserved his thirst for false fame, when he had so much personal glory," reflected his friend Dumont.[5] Talleyrand came away observing that Mirabeau was intent on dramatizing his death, which was certainly true but hardly reprehensible in the circumstances. "No weakness unworthy of you and of me," he said stiffly to Dr. Cabanis, who could not stop sobbing. On the morning of 2 April, Mirabeau got out of bed, opened the window, and said, "My good friend, in a few hours I shall die. Give me your word that you won't leave me. . . . Give me your word that you won't let me suffer pointless pain. I want to enjoy, without interference, the presence of those I love."[6] By nightfall, he was dead and Paris was rioting. The crowd suspected that the leader of the third estate, the most famous deputy in the assembly, had been poisoned, and they wanted vengeance. "I go wearing mourning for the monarchy," quipped Mirabeau on his deathbed: witty, politically astute, and, in his own rough way, an admirable human being to the last.

The next day, grief-stricken and painfully conscious of Mirabeau's empty chair, the assembly received a delegation from the Department of Paris asking that the ashes of the nation's greatest men be housed beneath the dome of the recently completed neoclassical Church of

Sainte-Geneviève in the Latin Quarter and that Mirabeau be the first revolutionary honored in this way. One deputy suggested referring the proposal to the committee appointed to draft the constitution, but Robespierre demanded an immediate vote on whether or not Mirabeau was a great man. Who could doubt it the day after his death? In recent months, Robespierre had had his disagreements with Mirabeau, but now he urged the assembly to recognize the claim of one "who opposed despotism with all his might at the most critical moments."[7] Plans for turning the Church of Sainte-Geneviève into a national mausoleum dated back well before the Revolution, but now the assembly's subcommittee approved them. And so the church became the Pantheon, Mirabeau's final destination after a sumptuous funeral that brought the city to a standstill on the evening of 4 April. An estimated hundred thousand mourners took part in the league-long procession. Battalions of National Guardsmen, all twelve hundred or so of the National Assembly deputies, the Jacobins, the king's ministers, journalists, and saddened members of the public all accompanied the great orator's remains—his heart inside a leaden urn—to his resting place on the left bank of the Seine. There were many orations in his honor, including one by Robespierre. There was music by Gossec, with haunting mournful notes for the wind instruments. The ceremonies lasted well into the night and were somber and grand enough to satisfy the most overblown aspirations for funereal fame, even Mirabeau's: "torchlight, wail of trombones and music, and the tears of men; mourning of a whole people—such mourning as no modern people ever saw for one man."[8]

It is hard to overstate the impact of Mirabeau's death on Robespierre's future. A wide political vista opened out behind that black-draped hearse. Into the large vacant space stepped the slim figure of Robespierre—much too small for Mirabeau's clothes; like Macbeth, he would have felt them "Hang loose about him, like a giant's robe / Upon a dwarfish thief." He had coveted Mirabeau's ascendancy over the assembly. He had envied his stentorian voice, confidence, agile intellect. He might even have envied his easy candor, because, for all the progress he had made since 1789, the lawyer from Arras remained awkward and painfully shy. But as it turned out, Robespierre was spared the effort of working to usurp Mirabeau's position. It was enough to wait patiently in the shadows, hone his own talents, and let the diseases that racked the unrepentant old roué do their worst. Now that Mirabeau's tormented body was ashes in the Pantheon, Robespierre was eager to get back to the business of the Revolution. On 13 April, when one of the Jacobins proposed that the club's plaster bust of Mirabeau should be cast in bronze, he interjected brusquely, "A bust, a mausoleum, a civic crown, an oak leaf, all are equal [honors], but may I remind you that your real work relates to the public good."[9] He was notably less impatient when Mme Labille-Guyard, an artist preparing an exhibition of portraits of public men for the Salon later that year, wrote asking if Robespierre would sit for her. "They tell me that the Graces wish to paint a likeness of me," he replied. "I should be quite unworthy of such kindness if I did not keenly appreciate its value."[10] So there was certainly a touch of jealous pique in his insistence that the time had come to move on from honoring Mirabeau. "Mirabeau's death gave courage to all the factions. Robespierre, Pétion, and others who dwindled into insignificance before him immediately became great men," remembered Dumont.[11] "Immediately" is too strong. There were still some months to go before Robespierre would be considered a great man. But what is true is that Mirabeau's death was an enormous opportunity for Robespierre, just as consequential to his career as his election to the Estates General. He did not let it pass unnoticed.

ROYALISTS WERE INCREASINGLY annoyed by the Arras lawyer. Who was he? Why was he so radical, so vexatious for them in the assembly? Rumors began to circulate. The most outlandish claimed he was the nephew of Robert-François Damiens, the most infamous person to have emerged from Arras before him. Damiens had been an unemployed domestic who tried to assassinate the previous king of France on 5 January 1757 (the year before Robespierre was born). He chose the eve of the Epiphany for his attempt. Swathed in a cloak, he sauntered past the Swiss Guard on the palace steps at Versailles and stabbed Louis XV in the side as he was climbing into his coach. It was an improbably naïve and simpleminded plan, and it very nearly worked. The king clutched his ribs, saw blood on his hands, announced, "Someone has touched me!" and was carried back up the palace steps to die.[12] He had already called for a Jesuit priest and hastily confessed his last sins, when it became clear that the wound was superficial and not at all life-threatening thanks to the shortness of Damiens's blade and the number of clothes the king was wearing to protect himself against the cold air. Damiens was arrested, interrogated, tortured, and condemned to a gruesome death on the place de Grève in Paris. As one eyewitness recalled:

> After the tearings with the pincers, Damiens, who cried out profusely, though without swearing, raised his head and looked at himself; the same executioner dipped an iron spoon in the pot containing the boiling potion, which he poured liberally over each wound. Then the ropes to be harnessed to the horses were attached with cords to the patient's body; the horses were then harnessed and placed alongside the arms and legs, one at each limb. . . . The horses tugged hard, each pulling straight on a limb, each horse held by an executioner. After a quarter of an hour, the same ceremony was repeated and finally, after several attempts, the direction of the horses had to be changed. . . . This was repeated several times without success.[13]

Damiens's horrific suffering became an iconic representation of the arcane and ritualized cruelty of old regime France. There was no truth to the rumor that Damiens, the would-be regicide, and Robespierre were blood relations, but it gathered a flimsy credibility nevertheless. The royalist press was so keen to defame the Incorruptible that it seized on any opportunity. Yet there was a self-defeating irony in attempting to blacken Robespierre's name and provenance by linking him with Damiens. Why should a radical revolutionary shun identification with the emblematic victim of old regime cruelty? No matter what the crime, had the accused been punished thirty-five years later, after the Revolution, there would have been no flesh ripped from his breast, arms, thighs, and calves with enormous custom-made pincers, no molten lead, boiling oil, burning pitch, wax, and sulphur poured on his wounds, no horses, four and then six, straining for interminable hours to pull his bleeding limbs apart. Instead Damiens would have suffered a cleaner, more humane end, in keeping with the Revolution's penal code: "Every man condemned to death will have his head cut off."

The assembly finally got around to discussing a new penal code in May 1791. The issue had first arisen in Versailles just before the assembly's move to Paris, in a series of proposals put forward by Dr. Guillotin:

I. Crimes of the same kind shall be punished by the same kind of punishment, whatever the rank of the criminal.
II. In all cases of capital punishment (whatever the crime), it shall be of the same kind—i.e., beheading—and it shall be executed by means of a machine.
III. Crime being personal, the punishment of a criminal (whatever it may be) shall inflict no disgrace on his family.
IV. No one shall be allowed to reproach any citizen with the punishment of one of his relations. The judge shall reprimand anyone who dares to do so, and this reprimand shall be posted on the door of the delinquent and moreover shall be posted on the pillory for three months.
V. The property of a convict shall never be confiscated.
VI. The bodies of executed criminals shall be delivered to their families if they demand it. In all cases the body shall be buried in the usual manner, and the registry shall contain no mention of the nature of the death.[14]

Because of the imminent move and other pressing business, the assembly postponed discussion of Dr. Guillotin's principles and only took them up again several months later. The first proposal was approved without any problems, following as it did from the abolition of old regime privileges—there was no question of reserving decapitation for nobles under the new constitution. The second article, however, provoked more discussion. Was it or was it not desirable to extend the practice of decapitation to all cases of capital punishment?

One of the assembly's leading royalists, the abbé Maury, thought not. A brilliant preacher, a stalwart match for the stentorian Mirabeau, and the great hope of those who opposed the Assembly's more radical initiatives, Maury argued against routine decapitation "because it might deprave the people by familiarizing them with the sight of blood."[15] Maury's very interesting point was brushed aside by Dr. Guillotin, who insisted that hanging was a far worse public spectacle and confidently reassured the Assembly that decapitation had never been simpler or more humane: "Now, with my machine, I'll knock your head off [*je vous fais sauter la tête*] in the twinkling of an eye, and you'll never feel it."[16] At this the deputies collapsed in helpless laughter. As the acerbic historian John Wilson Croker pointed out, "amongst the laughers there were scores who were destined to be early victims of the yet unborn cause of their merriment."[17] Despite his crude boasting, Dr. Guillotin's machine was not ready for use, nor, strictly speaking, was it his own invention. His name became associated with the new machine because he avidly promoted it, but around the corner from the assembly, at the College of Surgeons, it was a M. Louis who was busy reinventing the Halifax gibbet, which had cut off heads in seventeenth-century England.[18]

In the light of his earlier writings, we might expect to find Robespierre supporting Dr. Guillotin's proposals. Before the Revolution he had himself argued for extending the privilege of decapitation—"a punishment with a certain éclat"—and putting an end to the tradition of bad blood that tainted a criminal's whole family with his or her shame. In 1791, however, he distinguished himself by insisting that the time had come to abolish the death penalty altogether. He began his speech with a classical reference: on learning that the death penalty had been introduced in either Athens or Argos (the newspaper reports of his speech differ over which), the citizens ran to the temple to ask the gods to intervene and save man from such cruelty to man. For rhetorical flourish, Robespierre pointed out that his prayers had the same content but were addressed not to gods but to his fellow legislators in the assembly. He was against the death penalty for two reasons: first its injustice; second its ineffectiveness as a deterrent. He thought it unjust because society could not have rights that individuals lacked, and individuals had the right to kill only in self-defense. This, of course, left open the questions as to when a society had the right to kill in order to defend itself and how its enemies, internal or external, could be defined. Such questions had long preoccupied Robespierre, and would soon come to obsess him, fearful as he was about the threat of counterrevolution, but on this particular occasion he set them aside to present a clear argument against the death penalty:

> Note well one circumstance that decides the matter: when society punishes a culprit, harming him is out of the question; instead it holds him in chains, it judges him peaceably, it may use its limitless authority to chastise him and make it impossible for him to make himself feared in the future. A conqueror who butchers his captives is called barbaric. [Murmurs from the floor.] Someone who butchers a perverse child whom he could disarm and punish seems monstrous. [More murmurs from the floor.][19]

At this point the abbé Maury interrupted, sarcastic as ever: "Tell M. Robespierre to go and deliver his opinion in the forest of Bondy." This was slang for the badlands, haunts of bandits or outlaws, and a real forest too, just outside Versailles, where an Austrian king had once been assassinated. Ignoring Maury, Robespierre went on to consider the death penalty as a deterrent and here his argument became more idiosyncratic. No one, he insisted, was as afraid of dying as they were of calumny—in fact, good citizens would prefer to die rather than merit the scorn of their fellows. According to him, integrity was the most dominant of human passions, stronger even than the desire to live. The death penalty confused severity of punishment with efficiency, when what was really needed was a system of punishment finely attuned to the passions that drive human nature. Robespierre was further concerned that the death penalty might discourage the innocent from denouncing the guilty, for fear of depriving them of life. He did not elaborate on the kinds of punishments he thought suitable for those denounced by their fellow citizens. Instead, he cautioned the Assembly against allowing the sword of the law to run with innocent blood. One royalist newspaper, the *Journal de Louis XVI et de son peuple*, referred to him as "the democrat Robespierre," but no one seems to have noticed that his arguments against the death penalty were all compatible with the most stringent social repression, should this be required to safeguard the interests of good and innocent citizens; everything he said was compatible with the famous maxim *Salus populi suprema lex* (the safety of the people is the supreme law).

Despite Robespierre's intervention and the applause it won him, the assembly voted on 3 June 1791 to retain the death penalty: "Every criminal condemned to death will have his head cut off." At this point in the Revolution, hanging had also been discredited by mob violence, lynching, and brutal murders *à la lanterne*, in which aristocratic or counterrevolutionary suspects were set upon and strung up from lampposts. Camille Desmoulins, tastelessly, had gone so far as to style himself *procureur de la lanterne*.

ON 7 APRIL, less than a week after Mirabeau's death, Robespierre proposed and carried a decree prohibiting any member of the assembly from becoming a minister of the king for four years after the new constitution became law. He was inspired by the earlier decree in November 1789—aimed against Mirabeau—that had prevented assembly deputies from simultaneously accepting posts as ministers of the crown. Now that Mirabeau was dead, why was Robespierre bothering to extend the prohibition for another four years? As so often, it was a point of principle for him. He had studied the writings of Montesquieu and Rousseau; both had insisted on the political importance of separating legislative and executive power. The assembly was a legislative body, so its members could not be ministers of the executive without confusing the two kinds of power. Not content with this step, Robespierre went one further and proposed that members of the existing assembly should also be ineligible to stand for election to the new legislature under the new constitution. In an astonishing act of political self-denial, he effectively ensured that he and all his colleagues in the assembly would be thrown out of power when the new constitution was enacted.

Even at the time, it was unclear what exactly Robespierre hoped to achieve by this move: further proof of his incorruptibility; protection against the possibility that his reactionary colleagues might be re-elected and he might not; some other inscrutable scheme; or simply the relentless application of one of his political principles for its own sake. Some historians have argued that, irrespective of what he thought he was doing, the result of Robespierre's decree was the disastrous exclusion from political life at a crucial juncture in the Revolution of the only people who had any relevant experience: those deputies who had been there from the beginning. Others disagree and think that amid the tumult spreading through Paris and all France, any elections would have returned only the most extreme candidates: "factious lawyers—infidel sophists—club orators—newspaper writers—and unprincipled adventurers of all disreputable classes and characters."[20] Robespierre could not have been aiming for either of these outcomes. He was, more likely, remaining rigorously true to his ideals—whatever the consequences.

A few weeks later he addressed the Jacobin Club on the freedom of the press. Drawing inspiration from the American example, he argued for complete absence of censorship in both public and private life; perfect liberty, he insisted, was the best, indeed the only, way to ensure that what got published was "as pure, serious, and healthy as your morals."[21] In an age as prone to pornography and libel as any other, there was something unworldly about Robespierre's expectation. Yet he was nothing if not consistent. Amusingly, he thought there was no future for pornography in France, but he nevertheless opposed restrictions on the exhibition or sale of obscene images: "The Law must be founded on principle," he argued, and there must be absolutely no limits on liberty. He had already intervened in the assembly in defense of the incendiary journalism of Marat and Camille Desmoulins, but now he set out a theoretical case for freedom of the press. In a free state, he explained, each and every citizen acts as a guardian of liberty. Everyone must be completely free to protest, in person or in print, anything endangering liberty. If, as a consequence, public officials find themselves exposed to calumny, so be it:

Incorruptible men, who have no other passion besides the well-being and glory of their country, do not dread the public expression of the sentiments of their fellow citizens. They know only too well that it is not easy to lose their esteem, when one can counter calumny with an irreproachable life and proof of disinterested zeal; if they are sometimes victims of a passing persecution, this is, for them, the badge of their glory, the brilliant testimony of their virtue; they rest assured with gentle confidence in the suffering of a pure conscience and the force of truth, which will soon reconcile them with their fellow citizens.[22]

The influence of Rousseau, that "eloquent and virtuous citizen of Geneva"—his emphasis on integrity, individual conscience, natural goodness, and dignified independence from a gross and uncomprehending world—is stronger than ever in this passage. At this point, Robespierre was still acting on principle and according to ideals, adopting the kind of uncompromising stance on freedom of speech and freedom of the press that might have won him an essay prize before 1789. This stance was to prove much harder to sustain in practical politics than on the printed page: within two years he was to change his mind dramatically.

In the same speech, Robespierre also made the remarkable suggestion that libel suits arising from unrestricted liberty of the press should be adjudicated not on the legal merits of each case but on the general character of the litigants concerned. In revolutionary circumstances, what could be more dangerously appropriate? The possibility of denouncing public officials not on account of some precise transgression of the law but on grounds of their general attitudes or reputation would soon become an indispensable—and merciless—way of dealing with the real and imaginary forces of counterrevolution. Without this opening to trial by character, it would not have eventually become possible to convict citizens "of hoping for the arrival in Paris of the Austrian and Prussian armies and of hoarding provisions for them" or to execute them for exclaiming "A fig for the nation!"—two examples of the "crimes" later brought before the revolutionary tribunals and punished with the guillotine. While, by contemporary standards, Robespierre's advocacy of complete freedom of speech was unusually liberal, his suggestion that litigants should be judged according to their characters was the exact opposite. After all, who, beside himself, could lay claim to an irreproachable character? Who, except Robespierre, was beyond suspicion? This more ominous nuance of his argument was probably lost on the Jacobins that night in 1791, and for the time being he remained their champion of untrammeled liberty.

It is testimony to how hard Robespierre was now working that he attended other political discussion groups on the few nights a week that the Jacobins did not meet. At one of these, the Cercle Social, he heard another discourse on the freedom of the press, two days after he had delivered his own to the Jacobins. He borrowed the text—which had been composed by one François-Xavier Lanthenas from Lyon and read to the assembled company by the radical bishop Claude Fauchet—so he could study it more closely at home. At about nine-thirty that evening, he caught a cab on the quai des Augustins and headed back to the rue Saintonge. Robespierre, as his sister remembered, had always been absentminded. This time he left Lanthenas's manuscript behind in the cab. Fauchet had read only part of it aloud to the Cercle Social, so there was a real danger that much of it would be lost forever as a result of Robespierre's inattentiveness. Mortified, Robespierre offered a reward in *L'orateur du peuple* for anyone who helped trace the speech, hoping that "patriots will do their best" to recover it.[23] Paris, for him—unworldly as always—was full of vigilant patriots, hanging on the words of revolutionary orators, committing them lovingly to memory, and tracking down precious manuscripts gone astray in the city's filthy streets.

CONTRARY TO ROBESPIERRE'S vision, many in Paris in 1791 were going about their everyday lives with little regard to the Revolution. The number of marriages and baptisms had risen significantly since the previous year and the mortality rate was falling. Judging by the small ads posted in the daily *Chronique de Paris*, the people still had plenty of mundane concerns. One Mme Gentil of the rue de Richelieu offered a handsome reward for her lost greyhound. There were elegant apartments to rent with facilities for stabling horses or parking carriages, as well as plenty of more modest accommodations. Opticians, hairdressers, pharmacists, dentists specializing in teeth whitening, and chiropodists all promoted their skills. An Italian singer just arrived in the city offered home tuition. Exchange visits between French and English children were still being advertised. Oysters, oranges, and other luxury comestibles continued to be imported. In the theaters and opera houses, the Revolution was being culturally assimilated. Jean-Baptiste Pujoulx wrote a play about the death of Mirabeau (*La mort de Mirabeau*) and Luigi Cherubini's instrumental music for it was performed in the Théâtre Feydeau for the first time in May.

There were, however, ways in which Paris had not recovered from 1789. The rearrangement of the city's sixty districts into forty-eight new sections had not destroyed local loyalties, and in poorer sections like Saint-Antoine and Saint-Marcel popular militancy did not disappear with the fall of the Bastille. Even though day-to-day policing was probably as effective in 1791 as it had been before the Revolution, tension between patriots and aristocrats, together with anticlerical feelings exacerbated by the disputes over the Civil Constitution of the Clergy, led to many incidents of violence.[24] In April, for example, rampaging patriotic women in the rue Saint-Antoine broke into local convents and dragged the nuns into the street for public whippings. Of course, the scurrilous press was delighted by this, exaggerated what had happened, and inspired repetitions of the incident in other parts of the city. There was also widespread fear of brigands, or troublemakers, recently arrived in the capital. Such "enemies of the people" could easily conceal themselves among Paris's transient population: six out of ten people in the city at the time had been born elsewhere. The growing fear of malicious outsiders led to demands for a new census, and the municipal police department ordered a survey of the city's *logeurs*, or people letting furnished rooms, who might be harboring suspicious newcomers.[25]

In this context, the National Guard became all the more important. People throughout France had imitated the Parisians and formed local battalions of national guards, but the relationship of these citizen militias to the Revolution was increasingly vexed. In theory, the National Guard was designed both to protect the Revolution and to maintain public order. In practice these two objectives sometimes conflicted. Soon after the fall of the Bastille in 1789, Robespierre had been horrified by the move to exclude nontaxpaying citizens (*citoyens passifs*) from the National Guard, and he never ceased to oppose it. In his newspaper, on 5 December 1790, Marat—who had heard but still could not spell Robespierre's name—had written, "Robertspiere, Robertspierre alone in vain raised his voice against the perfidious decree regarding superior conscripts, but his voice was muffled."[26] Afterward, Robespierre composed a speech on the topic, read it to the Jacobins at Versailles, then published and circulated it through the network of affiliated clubs across France. In February of the following year, he wrote sarcastically to the newly wed Camille Desmoulins, reminding him to advertise the published speech in his newspaper:

> May I remind Monsieur Camille Desmoulins that neither the beautiful eyes nor the beautiful attributes of charming Lucile [Camille's wife] are reasons for not announcing my work on the National Guard. . . . There is not at this time anything more urgent or important than the organization of the National Guard.[27]

Camille did as he was told and a notice about Robespierre's recent work appeared in *Révolutions de France et de Brabant* a week later, on 21 February. Even so, it was not until the end of April that the assembly got around to discussing the subject again.

Robespierre argued that the institution of the National Guard was an unprecedented revolutionary act, resulting from a kind of patriotism previously unknown among free peoples. The assembly was busy formulating constitutional laws intended to protect the people's liberty, but only force—force deployed in the name of the people—could ultimately guarantee that liberty:

> The National Guard cannot be other than the whole nation armed to defend, when necessary, its rights; all citizens of an age to bear arms must be admitted without distinction.[28]

This idea was straight out of Rousseau, and when he spoke in the assembly, Robespierre mentioned the philosopher by name:

The free cantons of Switzerland offer us examples in this area, even though their militias have a more extensive purpose than our National Guard, since they [the Swiss] do not have any other troops to direct against external enemies. All the inhabitants are soldiers, but only when it is necessary for them to be, if I may paraphrase J. J. Rousseau.[29]

The French still had a professional army and Robespierre was particularly insistent that it must be kept separate from the National Guard. He argued that the king, as nominal head of the professional army, must not be allowed to nominate the heads or officers of the National Guard, that officers in the professional army must not hold posts in the National Guard, and that the king and his ministers must not be allowed to deploy or discipline the National Guard either. Robespierre was mindful of recent problems inside the army. During the summer of 1790, at Béthune (near Arras) and Metz, there had been a series of conflicts between rank-and-file soldiers sympathetic to the Revolution and aristocratic officers intent on maintaining old-style discipline. In Nancy things had gone completely out of control when a cousin of General Lafayette's, the Marquis de Bouillé, used severe military discipline to suppress a rebellion in the Châteauvieux regiment.

The rebellious soldiers had the support and encouragement of their local Jacobin Club. But this did not save them from the draconian measures of General Bouillé's military tribunal: one soldier was broken on the wheel, twenty were hanged, and forty-one were sentenced to the galleys for life—all of which astonished enlightened citizens, who thought such barbarism had been banished from France along with the old regime. Even more astonishing, though, was the assembly's decision to praise Bouillé for this pitiless repression. At first, only Robespierre, Pétion, and a handful of other radical deputies protested. Robespierre was shouted down at the tribune. Outside the assembly, however, he had the support of the Jacobins, and soon there were public demonstrations of solidarity with the heroes of the Châteauvieux regiment. To show their sympathy with those forty-one soldiers now toiling their lives away in the galleys, some patriots took to wearing the *bonnet rouge*, the cap of the galley slaves.[30] Robespierre himself disdained this fashion and was extremely irritated when, at the Jacobins one evening, someone leaned over and dumped a bonnet on top of his meticulously maintained wig.[31] Nevertheless, events in Nancy had made an impression on him, and he was adamant that there must be no confusion in the future between the National Guard and what remained of the old regime army. He wanted to see the former organized along rigorously democratic lines, free of the authoritarian hierarchy that had caused such suffering at Nancy. Throughout his speech in April, he kept referring to "the people" until someone interrupted, demanding to know what he meant exactly. "I myself protest against all manner of speaking that uses the word *people* in a limited sense," he said:

> It is the people that are good, patient, and generous. The people ask for nothing but peace, justice, and the right to live. The interest, the will of the people, is that of humanity: it is the general interest. The interest of that which is not the people, of that which separates itself from the people, is mere ambition and pride.[32]

This was all very well in theory, but in practice the National Guard's dual responsibilities—to protect the Revolution, and to maintain public order—were bound to come into conflict, sooner or later, with particular sectors of this much-invoked people. Robespierre, following Rousseau, could define the people and their National Guard as one and indivisible, but theirs was not a definition that would hold up in a public brawl, still less a Revolution.

AS EASTER 1791 approached, the king and queen, eager for a rest and change of atmosphere, hoped to be permitted to leave Paris for Saint-Cloud. In this suburb west of Paris, Marie Antoinette owned a splendid château, surrounded by twelve hectares of gardens and terraces overlooking the Seine. It was here that she had held her secret audience with Mirabeau, the occasion on which his ugliness overwhelmed her. Now Mirabeau was dead, the king was wracked by terrible headaches, and Marie Antoinette longed more than ever to escape the confines of the Tuileries palace, where privacy was impossible and she scarcely dared open a window for fear of the abuse that would greet her. Back in December 1790, the king had finally given in and signed the proposed Civil Constitution of the Clergy despite the pope's disapproval, but now his conscience was troubling him. At Saint-Cloud it might be possible to celebrate Easter in the old way, without political interference. However, for the last few weeks Marat had again been spreading panic, this time telling his readers that a hostile foreign army was massing at the Austrian border. "It is all up with liberty, it is all up with the country," he warned, "if we suffer the royal family to quit the Tuileries."[33] It was true that during the nine months that had passed since a battalion of Austrian troops asked permission to cross into France, foreign troops had been gathering at the border.[34] It was also true that it would be much more difficult for the Parisians to influence the course of the Revolution if the king abandoned the capital. So when the royal party tried to set off on 18 April, it was stopped by the mob. The next day, Louis XVI strode purposefully across the Tuileries gardens to the Manège and addressed the Assembly:

> Gentlemen, you are informed of the opposition expressed yesterday to my departure for Saint-Cloud. I was unwilling to overcome it by force, because I feared to occasion acts of severity against a misguided multitude, but it is of importance to the nation to prove that I am free. Nothing is so essential to the authority of the sanction I have given to your decrees. Governed by this powerful motive, I persist in my plan of going to Saint-Cloud, and the National Assembly must perceive the necessity of it.[35]

This was a strong and dignified speech, but to no avail. Over at the Hôtel de Ville, the municipality of Paris, urged on by Danton with the Cordelier Club behind him, decreed that the king was not to go to Saint-Cloud. The assembly decided not to interfere, there was nothing General Lafayette could do to help, so the king, who had behaved well and wisely, had no choice but to walk back despondently across the garden and break the news to his disappointed wife.

Marie Antoinette had been planning an escape for many months.

Mirabeau had fully shared her belief that removing the king from Paris was the only way to restore royal authority over the Revolution. All sorts of schemes had been auditioned—getting him out was, obviously, a difficult project—but now even the famously indecisive king was determined to try. He was equally determined, however, not to leave France, not to flee as so many nobles had done and abandon what he still thought of as a kingdom entrusted to him by God. This narrowed his list of possible destinations down to one: he must try to reach the loyal troops under the command of General Bouillé, who were encamped at Montmédy, near the Austrian border, about 170 miles away. Bouillé was highly regarded by Louis for his successful 1778 campaign against the English in the West Indies during the American Revolutionary War, and, much more recently, for suppressing the controversial rebellion in Nancy, with cavalry that remained under his control even as insubordination spread through the rank and file. Bouillé could not reach the king in Paris, but if the king could get to Bouillé, they could together start to assemble forces for reasserting royal authority, with or without reinforcements from abroad.

The most direct route from Paris to Montmédy ran through Reims. For this reason, the king rejected it, convinced he would still be widely recognized in the place of his coronation fifteen years ago. Unfortunately, the alternative road was not only longer but also less remote, passing through many small towns, where the royal fugitives might easily arouse suspicion. Nevertheless, that was the road chosen, and the departure date was set for 20 June. The decision to travel in an unusually shaped, extra-large custom-made coach capacious enough for at least eight people did nothing to lower the risk of attracting attention. Since this striking vehicle could hardly pull up outside the Tuileries, on the night of 20 June it was parked discreetly near the city wall, while a more ordinary coach waited close to the palace on the corner of the rue de l'Echelle, the royal party's first point of assembly. Shortly after ten, the king's two children, heavy with sleep and dressed in disguises, were carried out and left in the coach with their governess. The princess asked her young brother what he thought they were going to do that evening. "Act in a play, I suppose," he replied, "since we have all got these odd dresses."[36] An hour later, their aunt,

Mme Elisabeth, joined them, stepping on the dauphin, who had fallen asleep on the floor as she entered the carriage: "He had the courage not to cry out," his sister loyally recalled. Then the king and queen arrived, separately, Marie Antoinette shaken because her face had been caught for a few fleeting seconds in the lights of General Lafayette's carriage, sweeping past unexpectedly at that late hour.

The royal family were conveyed successfully to their special traveling coach and set off for the border accompanied by three guards in flamboyant yellow livery. If they were stopped and questioned, the plan was to pass themselves off as the family and traveling companions of a Russian woman, the Baroness de Korff, played by the governess. Marie Antoinette would assume the now-vacant role of governess, the king's sister would pose as a friend named Rosalie, and Louis XVI—most improbably of all—would take the part of a valet. The dauphin had been quite right to guess that amateur dramatics were in store. As the sun rose behind the carriage window blinds, the occupants settled into their journey, practiced their parts, and began on a picnic breakfast that lifted their spirits. It was pretty funny to think of the shock on Lafayette's long face when he learned of the empty beds in the Tuileries that morning. The king, always keen on lists and maps, was suddenly in his element, providing a running commentary on the group's progress for the benefit of his children. By the afternoon he was relaxed enough to get out and engage people in pleasant conversation about the weather and crops as the horses were changed at relay stops. As far as the town of Varennes, fresh horses were ordered in the ordinary way by sending a courier ahead. But at Varennes arrangements had been made for a special relay of horses to be protected by a small detachment of Bouillé's troops. These troops drew suspicious comment from nervous locals—many of them newly signed-up members of the National Guard—even before the peculiarly shaped coach arrived in the middle of the night and squeezed through the narrow arch in the town wall. In the twenty-four hours since the escape from the Tuileries had commenced, the royal family had got to within twenty miles of their final destination.

At Varennes everything went wrong. The special relay of fresh horses was nowhere to be seen. As the coach drove into the town, the travelers peeped through the blinds and saw groups of National Guardsmen milling around, some carrying muskets. The yellow livery worn by the three guards accompanying the suspicious coach shone beneath the lamps and moonlight; to make matters worse, the livery resembled that of the Prince de Condé, leader of the émigré nobles in exile, and people stopped to stare. It was exactly like the beginning of a play. None of the party could sustain their assumed identity for long—the king's papers were made out for Frankfort, but Varennes was not on the road to Frankfort—and besides he had been recognized at one of the post houses earlier in the day. At first, there was general excitement—it was quite something to have Louis XVI paying the town an unexpected nocturnal visit—and there was even talk among the townspeople of escorting the coach to Bouillé at Montmédy in the morning. However, Lafayette's orders from Paris arrived by 5:00 a.m. on 22 June, along with a decree from the assembly that the royals must return. And so they set out again, slowly retracing their path, accompanied by the National Guard and an angry, jeering crowd throwing dung at the liveried guards, who were prominently seated on top of the carriage like three bright badges of shame.

Robespierre was not in Paris on 20 June. He was in Versailles for the day, visiting his friends in the local Jacobin Club, tactfully explaining his decision to give up the post of judge on the Versailles tribunal, a position he had held since 1790 but never devoted any time to. Tact was required because Robespierre had recently been appointed public prosecutor in Paris and so had a good job to look forward to once the assembly's business was finished and the new constitution went into effect. However, he remained anxious not to alienate his friends in Versailles. Just as he had cultivated every available source of support when standing for election in Arras, so Robespierre continued in 1791 to value each and every expression of interest in himself and his career, no matter how lowly or improbable. He definitely did not want the Jacobins at Versailles to think badly of him, especially when he was doing so well among the Paris Jacobins, so he went in person to apologize and explain. By happy coincidence, his visit fell on the day of the second anniversary of the Tennis Court Oath, and he joined the local Jacobin Club in its celebrations, amid cries of "Vive Robespierre! Vive the nation! Vive the Friends of the Constitution [Jacobins]!" "No one ever deserved flattery as much as Robespierre," commented a Versailles newspaper approvingly.[37]

The next morning he woke to a city in tumult. Rumors of the royal flight filled the air and Robespierre had to fight his way to work through crowds of people all heading toward the Manège to find out what had happened in the Tuileries. He pushed his way through and was in his seat by nine. There was stunned silence in the assembly. Hoping to save the constitutional monarchy, Bailly, mayor of Paris, was maintaining that Louis XVI had been kidnapped against his will and that there was no reason for the assembly to distrust the king or his ministers. On his desk in the Tuileries, however, the king had left behind—in his own handwriting—a list of his complaints against the assembly and the constitution it was drafting. These ranged from regrets over the formal powers (such as direct control of the army) that he had been forced to relinquish, to more personal slights (especially the Assembly's reduction of his personal revenues). This detailed account of his reasons for fleeing Paris was tantamount to a confession of guilt. There was uproar in the assembly, and Robespierre, urging his fellow deputies to "tell all good citizens to be vigilant for traitors," could not make himself heard at greater length in the chaos. At lunchtime he went home with Pétion, his fellow radical deputy, to discuss the response these unforeseen developments required. The journalist Jacques Brissot was there at lunch, too, along with a newcomer, Manon Roland, both destined for political eminence over the coming year.

Brissot, whose father was an innkeeper in Chartres, was thirty-five when the Revolution began, just four years older than Robespierre. Thirteenth in a family of seventeen children, he had used his outstanding memory to educate himself and escape from his lowly background into the worlds of law and journalism. Rather pretentiously, he had adopted the name of a neighboring village, calling himself "Brissot de Warville" under the old regime. He was not elected to Versailles in 1789 but nevertheless somehow managed to inveigle his way onto the assembly's Constitutional Committee and into Paris's Municipal Assembly. Before 1789 he had founded a society to campaign for the abolition of slavery (*Ami des noirs*) and a newspaper called the *Patriote français*. Now that he was a revolutionary, Brissot dropped the aristocratic sounding "de Warville." However, when he came to write his self-portrait—a popular genre at the time—he followed the fashion for doing so under an assumed name and called himself Phédor:

> Phédor is not very tall: at first glance there is nothing uncommon about him; but one can see in his eyes and face, particularly when he speaks, the active temper of his soul. . . . He sacrifices his family to the cause of humanity. He is too credulous, too confiding. He is a stranger to revenge, as he is to self-interest. To judge from some of his writings, he might be compounded of bile and vengeance, whilst, in fact, he is too weak to hate anyone. He has friends, but not always of the heart-to-heart kind. He is as pleasant and easy-going in society and verbal argument as he is difficult and cantankerous in controversy. Phédor is one of those men who are at their best alone, and who are less useful to the world when they live in it than when they dwell in solitude.[38]

Brissot thought of himself as unworldly, but he kept up with fashion. He attached great importance to dressing the part of a revolutionary. He was a prominent member of the Jacobin Club and one of the first to stop powdering his hair and start wearing the *bonnet rouge*. Active as he was in radical circles, Brissot had recently met and introduced to Pétion the fascinating Mme Roland, a staunch patriot who would soon preside over her own salon. Mme Roland had arrived in Paris early in 1791 on a business trip with her husband, an inspector of manufactures in Lyon. The business completed, he was ready to leave, but she insisted on staying and attending the Jacobin Club, where she could meet and socialize with radical revolutionaries. Manon Phlipon was the daughter of a Parisian artisan, a master engraver who had his workshop on the quai de l'Horloge, very close to Pont-Neuf. Her six siblings had all died at birth or in infancy. Precociously intellectual— she claimed Plutarch had been a major influence before she was nine years old—Manon grew up devouring books, teaching herself foreign languages, memorizing the Bible, and impressing the local parish priest with her knowledge of theology. Whomever would her parents find to marry her? In the end it was Jean Marie Roland, twenty years her senior, who asked for her hand when she was twenty-five. Like Brissot, she composed a self-portrait:

At fourteen, as today, I was about five feet tall, fully developed, with a good leg, very prominent hips, broad-chested and with a full bust, small shoulders, an erect and graceful posture and quick, light step. . . . There was nothing special about my face apart from its fresh softness and lively expression. If one simply added together the individual features one might wonder whether there was any beauty there. . . . The mouth is rather large; one may see hundreds prettier but none with a sweeter or more winning smile. The eyes, on the other hand, are smallish and prominent. The irises are tinged with chestnut and grey. The impression they convey is of openness, vivacity and sympathy, reflecting the various changes of mood of an affectionate nature. Well-moulded eyebrows of auburn, the same colour as the hair, complete the picture. It is on the whole a proud and serious face that sometimes causes surprise but more often inspires confidence and interest. I was always a bit worried about my nose; it seemed to me too big at the tip.[39]

By the summer of 1791, the Rolands, Brissot, and Pétion had become firm friends, so when the king's flight to Varennes was discovered, it was natural for them to meet to discuss the implications for the Revolution. Yet for all the fervent ideas that flew around in their circle, Brissot and his friends were not at all sure how to react to the king's flight. Over lunch chez Pétion on 21 June there was much agonizing. Was this the end of the monarchy? And what about a republic—was it necessary, or even possible, to have one in France? According to Mme Roland, "Robespierre, with his habitual grimace, and biting his nails, asked: 'What is a Republic?'"[40] He suspected a plot to assassinate the patriots and did not expect to survive another twenty-four hours. Nothing was clear. While Pétion later volunteered to go and fetch the king back from Varennes, Robespierre was more preoccupied with what was going on in the Jacobin Club in Paris. It was here, the same evening, that he made the most flamboyant speech of his career so far.

"For me, the flight of the first public functionary ought not to appear a disastrous event. This could have been the best day of the Revolution, and it might still be," Robespierre began. He told the Jacobins, calmly, directly, right at the beginning of his speech, that the assembly had been wrong to present the king's flight as a kidnapping and to reaffirm its faith in his ministers. The assembly had not listened to him and had disregarded his cautionary words. It was obvious, Robespierre continued, that the king had chosen to desert his post at a crucial juncture in the Revolution. The constitution was nearly finished and there was lots wrong with it, not least the ridiculous divisions between citizens who could vote or stand for election and those who could not. Throughout France's eighty-three new departments, treacherous priests were rejecting the Civil Constitution of the Clergy. Foreign powers (Prussia and Austria) were preparing an invasion to end the Revolution, and on top of everything else, the harvest, though ready, was still in the fields: it would take only a small band of brigands to set it alight and starve the whole country. There could be no mistake: Louis XVI—or the prime public functionary, to give him the less glamorous title Robespierre preferred—had chosen to abandon revolutionary France at its most vulnerable. But that was not the worst of it:

> What scares me, gentlemen, is precisely that which seems to reassure everyone else. Here I need you to hear me out. I say once again, what scares me is what reassures all the others: it is that since this morning all our enemies speak the same language as us. . . . Look about you, share my fear, and consider how all now wear the same mask of patriotism.[41]

The real enemy, as he saw it, was right there, in Paris, mingling with the true patriots. "Share my fear" was his invitation to the Jacobins to join him in the next stage of the Revolution. Here he took the dramatic step of turning not only against the king and his ministers but also against the assembly that had affirmed its faith in them earlier in the day. The assembly was wrong—Robespierre dared say it. For the public good, he would take the dangerous step of accusing almost all his colleagues in the assembly of being counterrevolutionary out of ignorance, terror, resentment, pride, or corruption. Let the press term him the new Nostradamus, prophesying the future in apocalyptic mode: he was, he assured the Jacobins, ready to sacrifice his life to truth, liberty, and the fatherland (*la patrie*). At this (according to his own newspaper), Camille Desmoulins leapt to his feet and cried, "We would all give our lives to save yours!" and the audience of eight hundred Jacobins, crammed inside the old monastery, joined in an impromptu oath to defend Robespierre's life. It seems unlikely that Robespierre was genuinely in more danger than any of the other radical revolutionaries, who feared that the forces of counterrevolution might be galvanized into action by the king's flight. Even so, the Jacobins in Marseille wrote to say they would come to Paris and defend him if the need arose. And the Cordeliers Club sent an armed guard to protect him in the rue Saintonge.

Later that night, before going to bed, Robespierre made his will. The assembly and General Lafayette had issued orders for the royal family to return to Paris. But though they could still issue orders and be obeyed, as far as Robespierre was concerned, the assembly and General Lafayette were mutually discredited by the king's flight: neither could be relied upon in the continuing struggle to provide France with a legitimate constitution. In his attempt to persuade the Jacobins of this, Robespierre succeeded in creating a schism at the club: 264 of the members who were also deputies in the assembly left to form the Feuillants, in a disused monastery of that name across the street from the Jacobins. The Feuillants Club, led by Antoine Barnave (a Protestant advocate from Grenoble), was committed to defending the king's role in the forthcoming constitution, despite the discredit brought upon him by the flight to Varennes. Robespierre remained behind in the Jacobins with a handful of radical deputies, dedicated to curtailing the king's powers under the new constitution. Robespierre's break with his more moderate colleagues was decisive; from this point on his political future rested on his influence over what remained of the Jacobin Club and its network of affiliates throughout France. If the king had not fled, Robespierre would probably have settled down to his job as public prosecutor under the proposed constitutional monarchy. It would have been a more glamorous life than he ever hoped for in Arras, but not so very different in kind. However, the king had fled, and Mirabeau, who might have turned the situation around and rescued the monarchy despite everything, was dead. The configuration of power in Paris was changing very fast.

The flight to Varennes had taken one day, yet the return of the royal family to Paris took four; during this time, Marie Antoinette's hair turned gray.[42] They were halfway back by the time deputies from the assembly (Pétion and Barnave) arrived to take charge of the dismal procession and protect it from the mob. Pétion and Barnave climbed into the carriage and the royal children sat on the other adults' laps for the rest of the journey. Despite the presence of the deputies, violent incidents continued to plague the exhausted travelers, including a near miss with brigands in the notorious forest of Bondy. Inside the coach, Barnave did his best to befriend the king, assuring him that it would still be possible to save the constitutional monarchy. Robespierre's friend Pétion was much less ingratiating, but it is hard to tell if his rudeness was deliberate or inadvertent. Afterward he claimed that Louis XVI's sister had fallen in love with him by the time they reached the Tuileries, which seems unlikely, to say the least.

THE SECOND ANNIVERSARY of the fall of the Bastille was nothing like the first. Thursday, 14 July 1791, was a beautiful summer's day without a spot of rain, but the spirit of festive unity that had characterized the celebrations on the Champ de Mars a year earlier was nowhere in evidence. The king and queen did not attend. And the assembly, instead of turning out en masse as it had before, sent a delegation of just twenty-four deputies—one of them Robespierre. General Lafayette remained prominent on his white charger, but even he could scarcely ignore the suspicion and open hostility with which many in Paris now regarded him because of his continued support for the king. On the Champ de Mars the stadium had been expanded to hold more spectators than the year before, and the Altar of the Fatherland had been remodeled. In 1790 its dedication read, "the Nation, the Law, the King"; in 1791 it read, "the Nation, the Law, the——": the last word was effaced.

Gossec composed some music for the occasion: something less mournful than for Mirabeau's funeral and aptly entitled *La prise de la Bastille* (*The Fall of the Bastille*).[43] During the ceremony there were occasional cries of "No more king!" And back in the Manège the Assembly, meeting for business as usual despite the celebrations, heard a petition—one of many—from Danton's Cordeliers Club, demanding a national referendum on the fate of the king who had tried to abandon the Revolution. In his newspaper, Marat wrote that he suspected the assembly had included Robespierre in the delegation to the Champ de Mars to keep him away from the tribune. While his back was turned it might try to exonerate the king, that "crowned brigand, perjurer, traitor, and conspirator, without honor and without soul." Vigilance, vigilance, screamed the *Ami du peuple*.[44]

Robespierre wanted to put Louis XVI on trial. Submitting to the rule of law could degrade no one, he insisted, not even the king. But more moderate deputies were concerned about the impact such a trial would have on the constitutional monarchy, which, after two long years of discussion and disagreement, was at last ready to come into effect. The moderates were helped by the unexpected arrival of a letter from General Bouillé taking the blame for the flight to Varennes on his own shoulders, from the safe distance of Luxembourg. "I arranged everything, decided everything, ordered everything. I alone gave the orders, not the king. It is against me alone that you should direct your bloody fury."[45] This was the excuse the assembly deputies who advocated exonerating the king needed. The day after the Festival of Federation, inside the Manège, they made a case for leniency, for putting the past behind and allowing Louis XVI to assume the role allotted him under the forthcoming constitution. But the Cordeliers Club was outside, banging on the door, again demanding a referendum. Robespierre and Pétion went out to negotiate. They told the petitioners it was too late. They gave them a discouraging letter to take back to their club: petitions like this were not a helpful contribution; please could they stop.[46] This letter—signed by both Robespierre and Pétion—did not have its intended effect. Instead, it inspired the Cordelier and Jacobin Clubs to unite behind a new petition calling for the deposition of the king. This was drafted by Brissot in terms that cleverly avoided calling for a republic by demanding the "replacement of Louis XVI by constitutional means."

Standing at the Altar of the Fatherland, where General Lafayette had stood two days before to celebrate the fall of the Bastille, Danton read the text aloud to crowds assembled on the Champ de Mars on 16 July. The same day, the deputies in the Manège voted to suspend the king, but only until he had approved the new constitution. The petition for his dethronement was therefore now illegal, since it contravened the assembly's decree. Realizing this, the Jacobins rapidly withdrew their support and canceled the printing of the petition before it left the printer's shop. The Cordeliers were less cautious. Reassembling the following day at the Altar of the Fatherland, they drew up yet another petition, demanding the trial of the king. There was a disturbing incident early in the morning, before the crowds arrived: two men were found hiding under the altar, assumed to be spies, and summarily hanged *à la lanterne*. However, since it was Sunday, many of the petitioners arrived later in the day with their wives and children, and the prevailing atmosphere that afternoon was peaceful and festive. By early evening over six thousand people had signed the petition and the crowds showed no sign of dispersing. At around seven, General Lafayette and Mayor Bailly arrived at the Champ de Mars. Authorized by the assembly, they came accompanied by armed National Guardsmen, ready to suppress the demonstration. About fifty of the signatories were shot on the steps of the altar; their blood splattered across what was left of its dedication: "the Nation, the Law, the——" was illegible now. A matching red mark of terror and repression appeared simultaneously above the Hôtel de Ville—the red flag of martial law was flying and the prominent revolutionaries ran for their lives.

Eighty years later, in the middle of another revolution in 1871, a fire in the Hôtel de Ville destroyed the soiled petition of 17 July 1791. Reputedly, Danton's name was not on it, nor was Robespierre's. After the petition on dethronement was outlawed, Danton had had nothing to do with organizing the next one. He may not even have been on the Champ de Mars that Sunday. Nonetheless, on learning that his enemy, General Lafayette, had taken charge of Paris, he fled to Arcis-sur-Aube (where he had been born), then to London, where he lived in Soho on Greek Street for a month, until it was safe to return. Robespierre spent the evening of 17 July in the Jacobin Club. Hearing the news of bloodshed on the Champ de Mars, he wept unapologetically:

Let us weep for those citizens who have perished: let us weep even
for those citizens who, in good faith, were the instruments of
their death. Let us in any case try to find one ground of consolation in this great disaster: let us hope that all our citizens, armed
as well as unarmed, will take warning from this dire example, and
hasten to swear peace and concord by the side of these newly dug
graves.[47]

Was this perhaps ignoble? Given that he had supported—if not actually initiated—the idea of putting the king on trial for his flight to
Varennes, why wasn't Robespierre there among the men, women, and
children on whom the National Guard opened fire? Why was he
weeping at the Jacobins, instead of with the wounded at the Altar of
the Fatherland? Like Danton, Robespierre had had nothing to do with
the petition that had caused the bloodshed. Critical of the Assembly as
he was, he recognized the legal force of its decision on the king and
the forthcoming constitution. In his speech to the Jacobins it was right
and responsible to point out that the National Guardsmen were citizens too—volunteer soldiers following orders. Those who gave the
orders, not those who carried them out, were the proper objects of the
people's anger.

Robespierre was speaking, as darkness fell on the Champ de Mars,
to only a handful of Jacobins. Pétion was still there and so was Pierre-
Louis Rœderer (a lawyer in the Parlement of Metz before the Revolution and afterward a supporter of progressive reform in the National
Assembly). But most of the other liberal deputies—the abbé Sieyès
among them—were in the Feuillants Club, across the street, where
they professed themselves more moderate than the Jacobins and more
unequivocally committed to upholding the proposed constitutional
monarchy. Suddenly there was a disturbance outside—shouting and
the clash of arms in the rue Saint-Honoré. It was the National Guard
returning to the city center in shock and disarray. Some of the citizen
soldiers made their way into the Jacobins' courtyard and shouted abuse
at the radicals within—the radicals whom they blamed for inviting
civil unrest and bringing Paris to the brink of civil war. For the first
but by no means the last time, there was complete panic inside the

Louis XVI in coronation robes *(Musée Bargoin, Clermont-Ferrand: Bridgeman)*

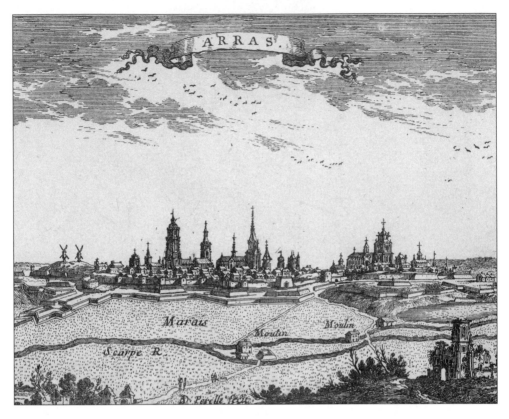

Arras, "city of a hundred steeples," in the mid-eighteenth century *(University of Cambridge Library)*

Robespierre's house in Arras, where he lived as a young lawyer *(from Hippolyte Buffenoir, Les Portraits de Robespierre, 1910)*

Robespierre as a
young man in the
costume of a delegate
to the third estate
(*Château de Versailles:*
Bridgeman)

Robespierre's sister Charlotte,
who kept house for him before
he left Arras (*Buffenoir*, Portraits)

The procession of the opening of the Estates General at Versailles *(Bibliothèque Nationale, Paris: Bridgeman)*

The Tennis Court Oath *(Private Collection: Bridgeman)*

The siege of the Bastille *(Musée du Louvre, Paris: Bridgeman)*

Inside the Jacobin Club *(Bibliothèque Nationale, Paris: Bridgeman)*

Robespierre in his room at Duplays *(Buffenoir,* Portraits*)*

Robespierre: incorruptible legislator *(Buffenoir,* Portraits*)*

The Triumvirs: Rœderer-Pétion-Robespierre, who remained in the Jacobin
Club after it split in 1791 *(Bibliothèque Nationale: Cabinet des Estampes)*

Eléonore Duplay: a self-portrait *(Buffenoir, Portraits)*

The execution of Louis XVI *(Musée de la Révolution Française, Vizelle: Bridgeman)*

club. Robespierre managed, somehow, to talk it down, and Mme Roland was present to hear him do it. Later that evening she sat at home thinking about him, how terrified he had been, but also how brave, and wondered if he had managed to get safely home to the rue Saintonge, "in the depths of the Marais." On a daring but foolhardy whim, she decided to go check. She persuaded Roland to go with her, and they reached Robespierre's lodgings just before midnight, to find him still out. How surprised he would have been to find Mme Roland on his doorstep at that hour! Robespierre, as we have seen, did not do well with women on the doorstep, and it had been an un-usually long and terrible day. Since he was not there, however, there was nothing Mme Roland could do except go home again with her husband and resume worrying that the leader of the Jacobins—on whom she was developing one of her many crushes—had been ar-rested or worse.

In fact, he was fine. Another member of the Jacobin audience that night was a master joiner and cabinetmaker named Maurice Duplay, originally from Auvergne but now living just doors from the Jacobins in the rue Saint-Honoré. As Robespierre was about to leave the club that night and step out into the unruly streets, Duplay intercepted him and offered sanctuary in his home close by. Robespierre, certainly ex-hausted and possibly frightened too, accepted the kind offer. Duplay lived modestly in a two-story house centered on a small courtyard in which he kept the tools and materials of his trade. Stepping over planks of wood and a saw pit on his way in, Robespierre was greeted by Duplay's wife and family, a son and three daughters. In this simple household he felt instantly at home. As his sister Charlotte pointed out, he had been accustomed to her own domestic ministrations in Ar-ras. Since moving away he had lived as a bachelor, but that life did not suit him. "Mme Duplay and her daughters expressed toward him the most vivid interest and surrounded him with their thousand delicate concerns. He was extremely susceptible to all those sorts of things. My aunts and I had spoiled him with an abundance of the little atten-tions that women alone are capable of."[48] Charlotte was jealous at the very thought of the Duplay women looking after her brother. He, however, was very comfortable—close to the Jacobins, close to the

Manège, and living with the kind of skilled artisan whose straightforward work and home life seemed to embody the very essence of the political principles he believed in. After the massacre on the Champ de Mars, Robespierre lodged with the Duplays until he died. He had found his last home.[49]

THE ROYAL FLIGHT to Varennes was tactfully forgotten and the constitution, so long in the making, was finally finished and formally accepted by Louis XVI in September 1791.[50] A hot-air balloon trailing tricolor ribbons floated over the Champ de Mars announcing the fact. The gesture was suitably ephemeral, since the constitutional monarchy relied on a tenuous partnership between the king and the people's new representatives, tied together but no better coordinated than the ribbons flapping in the sky. Because of the self-denying edict put forth by Robespierre, he and his fellow assembly deputies were not eligible to stand for election to the new legislature. On the last day of the assembly, in the atmosphere of relief and celebration overtaking Paris, Robespierre and his friend Pétion, the acknowledged leaders of the radical faction, were crowned with wreaths of laurel and led through the city streets by a jubilant crowd. People who had yet to set eyes on Robespierre went to look at the portrait by Mme Labille-Guyard hanging in the Paris Salon. He had entered the assembly an unknown in 1789 but now left it a popular hero—a bold spokesman for liberty and equality, the defender of the poor, an advocate of democracy, that rare and admirable thing in politics: an incorruptible man. For the time being, however, he was not needed and could take his first holiday in over two years. Robespierre, unlike Danton, Pétion, Brissot, and others whom he knew in Paris, had never been abroad. He could have gone at this point. He had enough money at last and his health, strained by the daily grind in the Manège and the late nights at the Jacobins, might have benefited. Instead, he answered the call of family duty and went home to Arras.

Robespierre wrote to tell his sister that he was coming and that he wanted, if at all possible, to avoid a public welcome. She treated his request with characteristic seriousness but could do nothing to prevent

Augustin's announcing their brother's imminent return from the tribune at the local Jacobin Club. On the designated day, Charlotte and
Augustin set out early in the morning to meet Maximilien, accompanied by Mme Buissart, the wife of his closest friend in Arras.[51] They
hired a coach and took the road to Paris as far as the small town of Bapaume. But though they waited all day, their brother did not arrive.
They went back to Arras that evening, very disappointed. At the city
gates a crowd had assembled, having heard a rumor that the famous
deputy had finally returned. As the coach pulled up, the people began
detaching the horses so as to pull it inside the city walls themselves as
a mark of respect and gratitude. Everyone was quite embarrassed
when they discovered that it was only Charlotte, Augustin, and
Madame Buissart inside. On 14 October, the small welcome party set
off again, even earlier this time, hoping to avoid attracting further attention. Camped at an inn at Bapaume, keeping out of sight, they
waited for Robespierre. Although the inn was on the road from Paris,
they were afraid of missing him so posted a lookout in the street.

Bapaume was already in a turbulent state because a battalion of
National Guardsmen from Paris, among them some of the original
heroes from the fall of the Bastille, were currently garrisoned in the
town. Over the past week, there had been bitter conflicts between
these soldiers, full of revolutionary enthusiasm, and the locals—many
of whom, as Robespierre was soon to discover, were considerably less
enthusiastic. Suddenly the Incorruptible—away for over two long,
eventful years—was in the arms of his nearest and dearest. Outside
the inn the lookout had spread the word. The National Guardsmen
were delighted and gathered to congratulate Robespierre on his
democratic principles, his tireless fight against the enemies of the people, his outstanding political courage. They set about organizing an
impromptu banquet, which detained Robespierre in Bapaume for several hours, so that it was dark before he set off again with his proud
siblings beside him.

At Arras there was an even bigger crowd. The people were in high
spirits; they had waited excitedly all day; and some of them were probably rather inebriated by the time the coach—with Robespierre in it
this time—rolled into view. Once again there was an attempt to detach

the horses at the city gate so the appreciative crowd could pull their returning hero across the city threshold. Seeing this commotion
through the window, Robespierre had one of his attacks of irritation
and got out immediately. He proclaimed priggishly to his brother and
sister that he did not approve of free citizens taking on the role of animals and debasing themselves in this manner—all his hard work in
the assembly had been for nothing if the people of his own hometown
were still so unenlightened. Undeterred by his disapproval, the crowd
at Arras, now joined by the crowd that had followed the coach from
Bapaume, surged through the streets toward his old home in the rue
des Rapporteurs shouting, "Vive Robespierre! Long live the defender
of the people!" This was exactly what he had not wanted. He had
hoped for a discreet private homecoming, fearing that any public fet-
ing would be reported in the Parisian press and turned against him by
his growing number of political enemies. With immense relief he finally closed the front door behind him and was alone again with his
strange small family.

PART IV

———

THE CONSTITUTION FAILS

(1791–1792)

7

WAR

Robespierre got home on a Friday evening. By the end of the weekend, when he wrote to the Duplays, all his irritation had been forgotten and he described his homecoming in glowing terms. "I was enchanted by the patriotism of the National Guard," he wrote. The people of Arras had received him "with demonstrations of such affection as I cannot express and cannot recall without emotion." Even his enemies, the aristocrats, had illuminated their houses in his honor, "which I can only attribute to their respect for the will of the people." (A local newspaper, however, attributed it to the aristocrats' fear of having their windows smashed.) The following day an unarmed battalion of National Guardsmen had danced and sung patriotic songs outside his house. All of this, he gleefully remarked, must have been very disagreeable for Feuillant ears. The split at the Paris Jacobin Club earlier in 1791 had reached Arras. Here as in many other places throughout the country, former members of the local Jacobin Club had followed the Feuillant example and formed new, more moderate clubs on hearing the news of the massacre on the Champ de Mars. According to Robespierre, the Feuillants now dominated the local government, which was increasingly hostile to the people, the patriots, and their Jacobin champions, including the most famous—himself. In fact, once the initial excitement of his homecoming had died down, many in Arras gave him the cold shoulder. He went to visit one old friend, only to find him distant and completely changed. Robespierre was upset to see that the Revolution had destroyed some of his connections from his days as a member of the Academy of Arras and the Rosati literary society.

According to Charlotte, he was also upset to discover that, in his long absence, Anais Deshorties (the stepdaughter of one of their aunts, whom he had courted before the Revolution) had married another local lawyer—but if the news broke his heart, there is no evidence in his surviving correspondence. Instead his mind was full of two political subjects: the National Guard and the church. It was all very well to have battalions of National Guardsmen trooping about, singing and dancing and dressing up in their new uniforms, but were they really ready to defend the country? Some of them were not even armed, let alone trained—how could they repel an invading army? Arras was close to the frontier and Robespierre's sense that revolutionary France was dangerously unready for war grew stronger as he traveled around during his six-week holiday, visiting Lille, Béthune, and environs. He also noticed, on these short trips, that the roadside inns were full of émigrés. Dropping in for refreshment on his travels, he was horrified to overhear wellbred voices at the surrounding tables discussing their discontent with the Revolution and their plans for abandoning the country. As the uncompromising defender of liberty in the assembly, he had argued for freedom of movement—if anyone (except the king) wanted to leave the country, they must be free to do so.[1] When he saw the émigrés for himself, however, he was disconcerted. He interrogated the innkeepers. Was this typical? Yes, they told him, for quite some time people had been leaving in droves. His uncomfortable suspicion that the country's borders were vulnerable and insecure became more intense. The counterrevolution was growing in strength and at Coblenz, just across the German border, the Prince de Condé was continuing to amass troops.

Equally disturbing to Robespierre was the religious resistance to the Revolution gathering strength across provincial France. In Arras he had grown up in an atmosphere pervaded by Catholicism. He owed his education to the church, his intervention in the National Assembly in the interest of the lower clergy might have been an expression of gratitude, and he still sometimes spoke as though residual religious belief were the bedrock of his political convictions. When he returned home to the ecclesiastical center of Artois, he cannot have expected to find it transformed beyond recognition. What he did find, however, shocked him deeply. Months ago, his brother had written to him about the provincial clergy's opposition to the Revolution. But in Paris, where the majority of priests had sworn to uphold the controversial Civil Constitution of the Clergy, Robespierre and his fellow radicals had little direct experience of that opposition. Not so in Arras, where there had recently been a reenactment of the Crucifixion with revolutionaries cast as Roman soldiers offering vinegar to the lips of the dying Christ. Refractory priests (priests who had followed the pope in rejecting the Civil Constitution of the Clergy) were flagrantly turning their congregations against the Revolution. Confronted now with the force of religion, Robespierre wrote to an unidentified friend in Paris:

> Nearly all the orators in the National Assembly were on the left over the question of priests; they spoke rhetorically about tolerance and the liberty of sects; they saw nothing but a question of *philosophy* and *religion* in what is really a question of *revolution* and *politics*; they did not see that every time an aristocratic priest makes a convert he makes a new enemy of the Revolution; since those ignorant people he leads astray are incapable of distinguishing religious from national interest, and, in appearing to defend religious opinions, [the priests] actually preach despotism and counterrevolution. . . . I realize now that in Paris we very poorly understand the public spirit and the power of the priests. I am convinced that they alone would be enough to bring back despotism and that the court need do no more than leave it to them, confident of soon reaping the benefit of their schemes.[2]

Robespierre's view was not so different from that of the Revolution's most articulate foreign critic, the conservative philosopher and politician Edmund Burke, who thought that the counterrevolution could rely on the priests to establish "peace and order in every parish."[3]

Burke's great hope was Robespierre's worst nightmare. To Robespierre's surprise and irritation, this opinion, expressed in a private letter, was published the following week in not one but two Parisian newspapers—whoever Robespierre's friend was, he or she had betrayed him. From Arras he wrote at once to the editors to complain at the infringement of his privacy, but he made no attempt whatsoever to disown the opinion itself.[4]

In a letter to Maurice Duplay—a more reliable friend—Robespierre described another recent religious sensation in Arras. A refractory priest was celebrating Mass in the Chapel of Calvary when a crippled man in the congregation suddenly threw down his crutches and walked freely. The man's wife fainted when she heard the astonishing news and, after she had recovered consciousness, gave thanks to heaven for the miracle. Interestingly, Robespierre does not flatly reject the concept of a miracle, as Mirabeau and other determinedly secular revolutionaries certainly would have done, often with ribaldry. Instead, he comments that it is not so surprising that a miracle should have occurred in that particular chapel, since others had occurred there in the past. There is perhaps a note of sarcasm in his next remark. "I do not propose to stay long in this holy land," he tells his carpenter friend. "I am not worthy of it."[5] But this is not the letter of someone who simply sneers at religion. His provincial holiday had served to remind Robespierre of religion's immense social power. Before the holiday was over, he concluded that the Revolution must harness the church for its own purposes or risk destruction. At the very end of his letter, he sends his greetings to Georges Couthon, another of Duplay's Jacobin lodgers, himself a cripple as well as a prominent member of the circle of friends who now surrounded Robespierre in Paris. In Arras, he was homesick for that circle.

ROBESPIERRE RETURNED TO Paris on 28 November. He went first to the Duplays, deposited his modest luggage, and refreshed himself in his low-ceilinged timber-framed bedroom, which looked out over the carpenter's yard. Later that evening, he went to dine with Pétion. There had been some big changes in Pétion's life since Robespierre last saw him. He had been elected mayor of Paris in the recent municipal elections, receiving 6,728 votes to General Lafayette's 3,126. Perhaps it was general disaffection, perhaps confusion about voting eligibility, but whatever the case about 70,000 people who were eligible to vote abstained and 100 voted for Robespierre even though he wasn't a candidate: flattering or frustrating, depending on how he looked at it. Dinner chez Pétion was a much grander affair than it had been on the day after the king's flight to Varennes. As mayor, Pétion was now living in a magnificent Parisian house, "but his spirit is as simple and pure as ever," Robespierre reassured himself, nervously.[6] He spoke freely in a letter to Buissart of the new configuration of power in Paris: Pétion had taken on an exacting role, but his personal virtue and love of the people equipped him well for it; the recently elected Legislative Assembly, according to Robespierre, was full of promise and a real improvement on its predecessor in the Manège; public opinion was turning against the Feuillants, among them Barnave, who had befriended the king on the difficult journey back from Varennes, and people were rightly suspicious of the king's new Feuillant ministers. Chosen by the king, these ministers were men Louis XVI thought he could trust to bolster his own precarious constitutional role, including the Comte de Montmorin (the foreign affairs minister, who soon resigned) and the Comte de Narbonne (war minister). Popular opinion was increasingly hostile toward the monarch and concerned that he might try to reassert his power and strengthen his position under the new constitution. All in all, Robespierre's first impression on arriving back in the capital was that things looked good for the patriotic party.

Despite his long day traveling, Robespierre visited the Jacobin Club before dining with Pétion. Here he was greeted with rapturous applause. No sooner had he entered the old convent than the Jacobins made him their president: he had truly come home. The following evening one of the club members raised the matter of confession—surely this Catholic sacrament was dangerous and should be discouraged. Robespierre, fresh from Arras, disagreed—it was pointless attacking religious customs beloved by the people, he warned his fellow Jacobins.[7] Better to hope that over time the people would mature and abandon such prejudices. In the meantime, the club should stick to discussing issues raised by the Legislative Assembly, just as it had followed the National Assembly in the past; in this way it was sure to focus on urgently relevant business. And nothing, Robespierre insisted, was more relevant than the threat of war. He was far from alone in worrying about the émigrés at the frontier. Rumors of war, of a royal plot to restore despotism, were circulating wildly. Louis XVI appeared before the assembly on 14 December and promised to send 150,000 French troops to protect the frontier within a month. In fact, he had already written to the major European powers requesting their armed intervention to save his throne. Robespierre did not know this for certain, but he suspected as much and ended the year 1791 as the de facto leader of an antiwar campaign.

Brissot, who, unlike Robespierre and Pétion, had been eligible for election to the new legislative body (never having been an official member of its predecessor), was the leader of the pro-war party. He had not attended a Jacobin meeting for several months when he suddenly decided to confront Robespierre on his own territory. On the night of 16 December, having set the case for war before the assembly earlier in the day, Brissot told the Jacobins that only war could save the Revolution and stop France from becoming a plaything for Europe's tyrants. War, as he saw it, would consolidate the Revolution in France by carrying it into foreign countries in the wake of an invading army. Robespierre intervened to prevent Brissot's speech being printed and circulated to the affiliated clubs until he had had a chance to reply.[8] Two days later he harangued the Jacobins with his twenty-page response:

> Is this the war of a nation against other nations or a king against other kings? No. It is a war of the enemies of the French Revolution against the French Revolution. Are the most numerous and dangerous of these enemies at Coblentz [the headquarters of émigré forces]? No, they are among us. . . . War is always the first desire of a powerful government that wants to become more powerful. . . . Let us calmly assess our situation: the nation is divided into three parts; aristocrats, patriots, and the hypocritical in-between party known as ministers.[9]

On and on he went, insisting that France was teetering on the brink of a foreign, civil, and religious war, all equally menacing to the Revolution. The king and his ministers must not be trusted. But always it was the hidden enemy—the enemy within—that preoccupied Robespierre. Turning on Brissot, he asked what security the journalist could offer against such alarming dangers. None. "Mistrust is a shameful state," Brissot had argued. Now Robespierre riposted that mistrust was a good deal less shameful than "the stupid confidence" (a phrase borrowed from Danton) that might lead the nation over the edge of a precipice. "Patriot legislators, do not slander mistrust," he warned Brissot and the rest of the assembly. Finally, mindful of what he had seen in and around Arras, he pointed out that in any event France could not go to war until it was ready: weapons would need to be manufactured, the National Guard would have to be properly armed, the people themselves would need to be armed too, albeit only with pikes. All of this was a direct development of Robespierre's earlier speech on the National Guard. Now as then, he drew on the idea of a democratic war, waged exclusively in the general interest by the whole people in arms. The war that, for different reasons, Brissot, the king, and his ministers were all proposing could not have been more different.

Mutual friends at the Jacobin Club effected a personal reconciliation between Robespierre and Brissot early in the New Year, but no one could reconcile their positions on war. "I shall continue to oppose Brissot's views whenever they seem contrary to my principles," Robespierre announced. "Let our union rest upon the holy basis of patriotism and virtue; and let us fight as free men, with frankness and, if necessary, determination, but also with respect for friendship and each other."[10] And this is exactly what he did when, against all his warnings, the assembly approved the first ultimatum to Marie Antoinette's brother, the Holy Roman Emperor Leopold II. The ultimatum demanded that Leopold II disassociate himself from the counterrevolutionary émigrés and all European powers hostile to the Revolution. If, by 1 March, he had still not publicly declared his support for France, war would ensue.[11] Snapping straight into his Nostradamus mode, Robespierre prophesied to the Jacobins:

Ah! I can see a great crowd of people dancing in an open plain covered with grass and flowers, making play with their weapons, and filling the air with shouts of joy and songs of war. Suddenly the ground
sinks beneath their feet, the flowers, the men, the weapons disappear;
and I can see nothing but a gaping chasm filled with victims. Ah! Fly!
Fly, while there is still time, before the ground on which you stand
opens beneath its covering of flowers.[12]

Marat himself could have no found more powerful images for an audience still reeling from the shock of the massacre on the Champ de Mars.

THE BUILDUP TO war accentuated the division at the Jacobin Club
between Robespierre and Brissot, and Robespierre had to struggle
hard to secure his ascendancy over what was now his only power
base.[13] He tried to close the club's doors, arguing against the admission
of new members or even the readmission of old members who had left
but wanted to come back. He proposed posting a list of members up
on the club wall, along with their addresses, current occupations, and
status prior to the Revolution, both to discourage people from claiming to be Jacobins when they were not (or were no longer) and to help
keep track of the membership.[14] But he failed to gain control of the
club's Correspondence Committee, which, as he astutely recognized,
was the link between the Parisian Jacobins and their thousands of associated clubs throughout the country.[15] In February it came to light
that the Correspondence Committee, dominated by Brissot's faction,
was on the point of sending a pro-war circular to affiliated clubs without consulting the Parisian club in its entirety. Then, on 10 February,
Robespierre set out before the club his own vision of a war of defense,
still hoping to sway the Parisian Jacobins against the war of conquest
advocated by Brissot. Robespierre began characteristically. "I am going to propose a means of saving the fatherland, that is to say, stifling
the civil war and the foreign war by confounding the schemes of our
internal enemies."[16]

What followed was an outpouring of his obsessions at this crucial
juncture in the Revolution—many of which he would return to, with

far more power at his disposal, two years later. They fell into two categories: internal treason and obstacles to the free expression of public spirit. Again he raised the question of arming the National Guard and the people themselves. The king's war minister had suggested recruiting men from the ranks of the National Guard into the professional army. Treason, warned Robespierre, nothing less than a proposal to annihilate the National Guard, the very opposite of arming it properly in the defense of the people. He reminded the Jacobins of how, over a year ago, he had cautioned the National Assembly against letting the king retain the right to declare war. The deputies had only half listened to him, and now the new Legislative Assembly was paying the price of not being free to make decisions independently of the king and his untrustworthy ministry. To remedy the situation, he called for weapons inspections in all the municipalities, in the presence of the people, so everyone would know exactly what there was to defend the nation with. These weapons should then be distributed to National Guards throughout France, beginning with the battalions at the frontier with the Austrian Netherlands, some of which, as he had seen for himself in Arras, were still unarmed.

The next step, as he saw it, was to arm the people:

> I demand the manufacture of pikes, and that the [Legislative] Assembly commend this almost sacred weapon to the people and exhort them to never forget the important role it has played in our revolution; and I propose that it [the assembly] summon all citizens to the defense of the state and liberty and efface all the injurious and impolitic distinctions that divide them.[17]

Beyond this, he called for the electoral colleges of the forty-eight Paris sections to go into permanent, that is, daily, session. Perpetual vigilance was required to save the state, he insisted, and only the sections could provide it. Here again, Robespierre echoed a speech he had given in 1790 in support of Danton; now as then he wanted to see "a tight and holy" alliance between the people and their representatives. But more was needed. "Do you want to invigorate and regenerate the whole state in an instant?" he asked his amazed audience. This, he thought, could be achieved by organizing a new Festival of Federation, on the model of the original festival, which had commemorated the first anniversary of the fall of the Bastille. Let National Guards all over France freely elect delegations and send them to Paris for the first of March. There, in a patriotic and fraternal festival, they could renew their commitment to the admirable principle "Liberty or death!" They could offer a symbolic sacrifice on the altar of liberty and appease the spirits of the virtuous citizens.

In the middle of this speech—playing dangerously on religious imagery and the memory of earlier revolutionary scenes on the Champ de Mars—Robespierre called upon his friend Pétion to officiate at this new festival:

> O Pétion! You are worthy of this honor, worthy of deploying as much energy as wisdom in the dangers that menace the fatherland that we have defended together. Come, on the tombs of our brothers let us mingle our tears and weapons, remind ourselves of the pleasures of celestial virtue, and die tomorrow, if need be, from the blows of our common enemies.[18]

He called, too, on the members of the Legislative Assembly to join in this festival that he imagined so vividly. Let them come to the Champ de Mars, not as their predecessors had done, overshadowed by the corrupt pomp of an arrogant court (Robespierre remembered how he had sat in the pavilion behind the king on 14 July 1790), but proudly inspired by "all the majesty of the people and the simplicity of civic virtue."[19] This indeed would be proof that the France of 14 July still lived.

After this rhetorical climax, Robespierre returned to the causes of the current crisis in foreign policy. He pointed out that the National Assembly (against his advice) had misjudged the political situation and given too much credence to the king and his ministers. It had, for example, approved of General Bouillé's brutal repression of the rebellious soldiers in Nancy. On this, as on so many other occasions, it had been led disastrously astray. The new Legislative Assembly must do better, must remember that it was in the middle of a revolution, surrounded by traitors wearing masks of patriotism, and must remain ever vigilant and critical of the advice it received. To this end, he proposed that a new hall to house the assembly be built on the site of the razed Bastille. Things would never have gone so catastrophically wrong if in Paris, as in Versailles, the assembly had met in a hall big enough to admit large numbers of the general public. The meager spectator space at the Manège had led to treasonous decisions—like the declaration of martial law that led to the massacre on the Champ de Mars—that would never have been made in the presence of the people. The hall Robespierre envisaged would hold at least ten thousand spectators, and he thought it could be built quickly if as much energy and determination went into the project as had gone into the building of opera houses under the old regime. (In this way, he anticipated by two hundred years the televising of parliaments in the democratic world.)

Finally, he came to the subject of education, obviously extremely important, given the prominent role he envisaged for the people. He favored a centralized national system of pedagogy, which a number of other revolutionaries had already advocated. But for his purposes in this speech he outlined only a handful of simple ideas for rapidly propagating the principles of the revolution. Unsurprisingly, after what he had already said, national festivals topped his list of suggestions. He also wanted to see the theaters used in the service of the Revolution: plays like *Brutus*, *William Tell*, and *Gracchus*, which depicted the charms of virtue and wonders of liberty, would be edifying entertainments for the people.[20] Nurtured in this way, Robespierre was convinced—or said he was convinced—that public spirit would soon converge with the true principles of the Revolution and resolve the problems menacing France. When it came to patriotism, the Paris sections made better judges than the academics in the Académie française, better judges, too, than the administrators in the Department of Paris. In making this unabashed populist argument, Robespierre, as so often, was following Rousseau, who had claimed in the *Social Contract* that all men and groups in positions of power had an interest apart from that of the people. With Rousseau in mind, he argued that the people alone are good: "the spirit of the people is good, and it alone renders justice to its friends and its enemies."[21]

As Robespierre stepped down from the tribune after this remarkable speech, he was applauded as rapturously as on his return from Arras. He had found his public persona and hit his political stride. This was obvious even to a foreign visitor in Paris. The political writer and composer of comic operas William Augustus Miles wrote to the British poet laureate, Henry James Pye, of Robespierre:

> He is a stern man, rigid in his principles, plain, unaffected in his manners, no foppery in his dress, certainly above corruption, despising wealth, and with nothing of the volatility of a Frenchman in his character. . . . I watch him very closely [at the Jacobins] every night. I read his countenance with eyes steadily fixed on him. He is really a character to be contemplated; he is growing every hour into consequence.[22]

The Jacobins acclaimed Robespierre the hero of the Revolution, and, as was now customary in their club, they proposed printing and circulating his speech to their affiliated clubs and to the Paris sections (which would, obviously, be very gratified by it). As so often before, however, this seminal speech that contained in embryo Robespierre's core themes—his suspicion of internal enemies, his trust in the people—had little impact at the time. In January the Jacobin Club had sent a circular to all its affiliates claiming that war was inevitable. Even Danton, who like Robespierre was opposed, said, "If anyone were to ask me, 'Are we to have war?' I would reply (not in argument but as a matter of fact), 'We shall hear the bugles.' "[23] After Robespierre's speech in February there was another club circular announcing that the majority of the Parisian Jacobins strongly favored war. And in March the king gave in to the attacks on his ministers (who were suspected of trying to turn the imminent war to the advantage of the counterrevolution), dismissed them, and appointed instead friends and associates of Brissot's, among them Mme Roland's husband, who became minister of the interior, Etienne Clavière, a Genevan financier and journalist, now minister of finance, and Joseph Servan, minister of war. Brissot was suddenly at the center of a sphere of political influence undreamed of by anyone since Mirabeau, ranging across the Jacobins, the Legislative Assembly, and the executive power. His war-mongering had proved popular with those who resented the émigrés, feared foreign invasion, and suspected the king's commitment to the Revolution. Brissot was emerging the leading advocate of a republic in France. All eyes were upon him—none more warily than Robespierre's.

EVER SINCE THE Revolution began, Robespierre had been suspicious of the king's ministers, whoever they happened to be, because they were entrusted with executive power and thus vulnerable to corruption. Even Necker, whom Robespierre eulogized before 1789, became a target for his attacks afterward. Now that Brissot's friends—Roland, Clavière, Servan—were ministers, executive power was, for the first time, in the hands of people Robespierre knew personally. This only aggravated his hostility. Sneeringly, he criticized Brissot, who had used his influence in the assembly to help his friends to power:

> You have got rid of certain old ministers, but you have filled their places with your own friends. It must be confessed that your patriotism is not without its little consolations. All the world sees the publicity—the ridiculous ostentation—with which you dispose of all the office and employments in the country among your own creatures.[24]

The Incorruptible could not tolerate nepotism. Now, on top of his ideological differences with Brissot over the putative war, there was open personal contempt. In the circumstances, his relationship with Mme Roland also deteriorated sharply. After he returned from Arras she was as effusive and solicitous toward him as ever, but very soon even she could not ignore the distance that had developed between Robespierre and the circle of radicals she presided over so proudly. As the wife of the minister of the interior, she was prouder still: "When my husband was at the ministry I made it a rule not to make or to receive social calls and not to invite any women to meals. . . . Twice a week I invited to dinner ministers, deputies, and others with whom my husband needed to be on good terms. They always talked business in front of me because I did not interrupt and was not surrounded by indiscreet friends. . . . Thus, without any need for intrigue or unseemly curiosity, I found myself at the center of affairs."[25] Mme Roland wrote to Robespierre almost ordering him to come see her so she could pick his brains and decide how to use her supposedly discreet influence, "You are at the head of my list. So please come at once. I am eager to see you and to tell you again of my regard for you—a regard that nothing can alter."[26] If he went, he went only warily, and the decline in their friendship continued. Pétion tried to act as a peacemaker. But it would not be long before Robespierre, who had only recently imagined standing by Pétion's side, pledging liberty or death on the Champ de Mars, fell out with him too. Here began a period of political isolation that Robespierre, determined as always never to compromise his principles, relished. He had no formal power of any kind, except his legal office as public prosecutor, which he resigned on 10 April, giving up its steady income of eight thousand livres a year, to leave himself more time for politics.

All his energy now went into the Jacobin Club, whose support he needed more than ever. In his isolation he identified yet more closely with Rousseau. When Brissot returned to the club to try once again to defeat Robespierre on the question of war, Robespierre retorted that the only legitimate charge ever levied against him was that he had championed the cause of the people by opposing a war that he thought would lead to the defeat of the Revolution at home and abroad. He was proud to admit this charge. From his experience of public life so far he had learned for himself "the great moral and political truth announced by Jean-Jacques [Rousseau], that men are sincerely fond only of those who show them affection; that only the people are good, just and generous; and that corruption and tyranny are the monopoly of those who hold them in disdain."[27] Robespierre claimed to be happy in his isolation, happy even to retire from politics (at this some of the women in his audience gasped), so long as he could remain true to his principles and free to worship the "sacred image of Jean-Jacques." "But where would you have me retire?" he asked his fellow Jacobins. What despotic regime would offer him asylum, and how could he leave France with liberty under attack?

No! One might abandon one's country in the hour of happiness and triumph; but when it is threatened, when it is torn asunder, when it is oppressed, one cannot do so; one must either save it or die for it. Heaven, which gave me a soul passionately fond of liberty and yet ordained that I should be born under the domination of tyrants, Heaven, which prolonged my existence up to the reign of faction and of crime, is perhaps calling me to mark with my blood the road that leads my native land to happiness and freedom. I accept with enthusiasm this sweet and glorious destiny.[28]

It was this peculiar combination of acute political suspicion and personal animosity toward anyone who disagreed with him that carried Robespierre to his lonely and eccentric destination in the Revolution. Tellingly, he quoted a politically pregnant phrase of Rousseau's: *"Le peuple veut le bien, mais il ne le voit pas toujours"* (The people want what is good, but they do not always see it).[29] Robespierre was very sure of himself as an astute interpreter of what was or was not in the interests of the people. And so those whose opinions differed from his were instantly suspect.

On 11 April a member of the Jacobins described a recent invention, a new kind of rifle that could fire twenty-five rounds a minute. Should the club help fund experiments to perfect it? Absolutely not, said Robespierre, such an invention was contrary to humanitarian principles. He said that sometime toward the end of the National Assembly, he had seen this rifle demonstrated in the garden of the house he was then living in. It could shoot nine rounds without needing to be recharged. The inventor asked his opinion, and Robespierre told him to keep silent about it—such a discovery in the hands of a free people might give them a momentary advantage over despots, but the weapon would soon pass into the hands of the despots and become just one more instrument for oppressing the people (a very pertinent and prescient point for all revolutionaries). The majority of the Jacobins, however, were not convinced. The atmosphere in Paris grew more bellicose by the day.

The tide of public opinion ran against him, the Jacobins could not be swayed against the war, but Robespierre refused to back down. He feared that war could only damage the Revolution. If France lost, foreign enemies would crush the Revolution and reestablish a despotic government to suit their own interests. But if France won, Robespierre thought internal enemies, in league with the king and the victorious army generals, were just as likely to destroy the Revolution. General Lafayette was particularly untrustworthy, in Robespierre's view. Lafayette had retired from public life after the king accepted the constitution in 1791. However, with war imminent, he had been recalled to command one of the three armies the French had now positioned on the frontier to attack the émigré forces and Austria, if necessary. Robespierre thought the ambitious veteran of the American Revolution was secretly hoping to lead France to victory, only to perpetrate a military coup and seize power afterward. There was no similarity, Robespierre insisted, between the American War of Independence and the war France was about to become embroiled in. When the Americans fought against foreign despotism, they did not have internal enemies to fight simultaneously. Arguing that the Americans had triumphed (not without cost) over a despot who made open war on them, Robespierre asked, would they still have triumphed if generals loyal to their enemy, George III, had been leading them?[30]

On 1 March, the very day named in the French ultimatum he had received, the queen's brother, the Holy Roman Emperor Leopold II, suddenly died. Robespierre publicly thanked Providence for averting the war in this unexpected way. The Jacobins were astonished. As one of them blurted out, how could someone who had worked for three years to liberate the people subscribe to such superstitious nonsense as a belief in Providence? Instead of letting this rejoinder pass and confining himself to the debate about the international crisis, Robespierre veered off into a vehement profession of religious faith. Perhaps he could not stop himself or perhaps he saw no reason to:

> There is nothing superstitious in using the name of the Deity. I believe, myself, in those eternal principles on which human weakness reposes, before it starts on the path of virtue. These are not idle words in my mouth, any more than they have been idle words in the mouths of many great men, nonetheless moral for their belief in the existence of God.[31]

There was an uproar in the old convent chapel. Robespierre shouted over it:

No, gentlemen! You cannot stifle my voice. There is no call to order that can stifle this truth. . . . Yes, it is hazardous to invoke the name of Providence and express the idea of the Eternal Being who intimately affects the destinies of nations and who seems to me personally to watch over the French Revolution in a very special way. But my belief is heartfelt; it is a feeling I cannot dispense with. I needed it to sustain me in the National Assembly, surrounded by all those passions, vile intrigues, and so many enemies. How could I have carried out tasks that required superhuman strength, if I had not nurtured my isolated soul? . . . This divine sentiment has more than compensated me for the advantages that are gained by those who are prepared to betray the people.[32]

With that the meeting ended. Four days later, Robespierre withdrew his proposal to circulate to the affiliated clubs another controversial address on regenerating the public spirit. For the moment nothing was more important than harmony among the Jacobins, he claimed—in bad faith, since he had purposefully exacerbated division in the club with his antiwar efforts. But he knew his latest speech had gone too far. "M. Robespierrot [*sic*] is completely out of favor, *dépopularisé*. He had the audacity to say in the middle of the Jacobins that he believes in the existence of God," one newspaper reported.[33]

ANOTHER CAUSE OF Robespierre's political isolation, according to Fréron, his former schoolmate, was the Duplay household:

Whilst he lived [in the rue Saintonge] . . . he was accessible to his friends and to any patriot. Once installed at the Duplays', little by little he became invisible. They sequestered him from society, adored, intoxicated, ruined him by exalting his pride.[34]

The family at 366 rue Saint-Honoré consisted of Duplay, his wife, three of their four daughters, a son, and a nephew. Although he was a joiner and cabinetmaker by trade, Duplay's real income came from renting the houses he had bought after moving to the capital from Vézelay. Since the Revolution, his preferred tenants had been Jacobins.

By the time they came to know Robespierre, Duplay and his wife were middle-aged, settled, hospitable people with strong political views and a wide circle of acquaintances that included the artists François Gérard and Pierre Paul Prudhon, the sculptor Pierre Cietty, and the musician Philippe Buonarotti. It is not credible that Robespierre was less accessible living at the heart of the Duplay household, just doors away from the Jacobins and around the corner from the Manège and the Tuileries palace, than he had been when he lived all the way out in the Marais. However, it must have been more difficult for anyone to see him alone. His visitors could reach his rooms by narrow ladderlike stairs from the family dining room or by an external staircase in the yard—something like a modern fire escape. Those who chose the latter could avoid the scrutiny of the assembled company—Buonarotti on the piano if there was one, the Duplay daughters playing with Robespierre's dog, Brount, Duplay himself holding forth on the day's political developments. But footsteps and raised voices would be overheard downstairs through the timber floor. Real privacy was impossible at No. 366, where even the blue-and-white damask curtains around Robespierre's bed had been made from one of Mme Duplay's old dresses.

Since Robespierre often took the Duplay daughters' side when their mother was cross with them (an extension, perhaps, of his political insistence on championing the weak and vulnerable), they were soon extremely fond of Robespierre. The youngest, Elisabeth, recalled:

> I was very young, and rather silly; but he gave me such good advice that, young as I was, I enjoyed listening to him. If I was upset about anything, I used to tell him all about it. He was never censorious, but a friend, the best brother a girl could have, a model of virtue. He had a great regard for my father and mother, and we all loved him dearly.[35]

Her older sister, Eléonore—plain, dark-haired, and serious—had more romantic feelings for the famous lodger. According to the family doctor, Souberbielle—who was in a better position than most to know the household's private business—her feelings were reciprocated. Eléonore and Robespierre were, he remembers, "very fond of each other and they were engaged to be married, but nothing immodest passed between them. Without affectation or prudery, Robespierre kept out of, and even put a stop to, any kind of improper talk, and his morals were pure."[36] Doctors, for all their privileged access to information, are often far from reliable. Souberbielle's testimony, however, seems credible because even if Robespierre was the kind of man to get himself into trouble with a mistress in the Marais, he was hardly the kind to carry on an indiscreet affair with a young girl under her father's own roof. He was neither deeply jaded nor helplessly promiscuous—if anything he was rather romantic—and the idea that he and Eléonore should wait until his public commitments were less exacting would have held a deep appeal. "She had the soul of a man and would have known how to die as well as she knew how to love," he boasted of his intended.[37]

DESPITE THE DIVISION over the war in the spring of 1792, the Jacobins united to celebrate the return of the freed Châteauvieux soldiers, so controversially condemned to the galleys for their mutiny in Nancy. After serving less than two years of their life sentences of hard labor, these mutineers were now officially pardoned and received in Paris as heroes, their broken shackles badges of honor. At first, the assembly hesitated to receive the returning mutineers. The constitution, very reasonably, banned armed men from entering the legislative chamber. But on this occasion the assembly broke the rule and the ex-convicts marched through the Manège, accompanied by a detachment of National Guardsmen with drums, flags, banners, and weapons, to the resounding applause of the Jacobin deputies, in agreement for the first time in months. After the soldiers came a mob of men and women brandishing pikes—some of the thousands that had recently been manufactured in accordance with Robespierre's demands. Over in the Hôtel de Ville, the municipal government decreed a national festival in honor of the Châteauvieux soldiers—exactly the sort of occasion that Robespierre hoped would regenerate the public spirit and propagate revolutionary principles.

On Sunday, 15 April, an excited crowd paraded through Paris pulling a galley wreathed with flowers. With it came women carrying the broken shackles high for everyone to see; then forty placards, bearing the names of the ex-convicts, each adorned with a civic crown of oak leaves (a symbol of patriotism inspired by ancient Rome), and busts of Voltaire, Rousseau, Benjamin Franklin, and the seventeenth-century English republican Algernon Sidney—all prophets of freedom in the eyes of the patriots. Finally there came a float carrying a statue of liberty brandishing, somewhat incongruously, an enormous club. Surrounded by a moving forest of pikes, the parade made ceremonial stops at the site of the demolished Bastille, the Hôtel de Ville, the Champ de Mars, and so on: the ceremony was strangely similar to the Stations of the Cross that had been performed the previous week in Easter Masses throughout France. The crowd sang revolutionary hymns. Some proudly identified themselves as "sans-culottes": ordinary working people, patriots without fine clothes (literally, without the *culottes*, or knee breeches, of the wealthier classes). Pétion officiated in his capacity as mayor of Paris. He did not, however, wield the kind of control General Lafayette on his white charger had commanded at festivals commemorating the fall of the Bastille. This was a popular demonstration, not a disciplined military parade from which the people were carefully excluded. According to some hostile reports, it was a rather debauched affair. The girls carrying broken shackles had been recruited from among the prostitutes in the Palais-Royal gardens, not all the songs were pious revolutionary hymns, and there was apparently some louche dancing as well. But if there was, the Incorruptible did not notice, or turned a blind eye. The press described the event as "Robespierre's Festival," but it is hard to know whether he was really pleased with it. Afterward he proposed a monument commemorating "the triumph of poverty and the people, the National Guard, the soldiers of Châteauvieux, and all good citizens persecuted on account of the Revolution."

Three days later, the king's sister wrote from the Tuileries palace to her friend the Marquise de Raigecourt:

You think perhaps we are still in the agitation of the festival of Châteauvieux; not at all; everything is very tranquil. The people flocked to see Dame Liberty tottering on her triumphal car, but they shrugged their shoulders. Three or four hundred sans-culottes followed her shouting: "The Nation! Liberty! The Sans-Culottes!" It was all very noisy, but flat. The National Guards would not mingle; on the contrary, they were angry, and Pétion, they say, is ashamed of his conduct. The next day a pike with a *bonnet rouge* walked about the [Tuileries] garden, without shouting, and did not stay long.[38]

Mme Élisabeth was not alone in finding the festival absurd, and there was some truth to the rumors she had heard about the ambivalence with which the National Guard and Pétion participated. On 20 April, France finally declared war on Leopold II's son and successor as Holy Roman Emperor, Francis II (Prussia joined in on Austria's side in June). Pétion immediately wrote to Robespierre imploring him to repair the divisions among the Jacobins that had been caused—Pétion dared suggest it—by his friend's frustrated ambition and petty jealousy of those in power:

We have lost the quiet energy of free men. We no longer judge things coolly. We shout like children or lunatics. I simply tremble when I consider how we are behaving, and I ask myself every moment whether we can continue to be free. I cannot sleep at night, for my usual peaceful slumbers are disturbed by dreams of disaster.[39]

Robespierre did not reply.

Nature gave me a strong frame, and she put into my face the violence of liberty. I have not sprung from a family that was weakened by the protection of the old privileges; my existence has been all my own; I know that I have kept and shown my vigor, but in my profession and in my private life I have controlled it. . . . I consecrated my whole life to the people, and now that they are beyond attack, now that they are in arms and ready to break the league [of foreign powers] unless it consents to dissolve, I will die in their cause if I must . . . for I love them only, and they deserve it. Their courage will make them eternal.[40]

This was not Robespierre speaking but Danton, who had returned from London as soon as it seemed safe after the Champ de Mars massacre. Their physiques aside—Robespierre's slight frame, Danton's burly one—the two men had a great deal in common. Both were dedicated to the people, above all. Both were operating outside the Legislative Assembly and extremely active in the Jacobins (Danton was also still prominent at the Cordeliers and had an administrative post in Paris's municipal government). Both were against the war, convinced the country was unprepared, suspicious of the king, and afraid the forces of counterrevolution would triumph with a foreign invasion. Their suspicions were soon justified: after the fighting began at the border, the distressing dispatches that reached Paris, each more alarming than the last, made it clear that the war was not going well and the Revolution was hanging in the balance. Within two weeks the French generals had lost control—French soldiers actually murdered one of them—officers absconded, and the enemy captured entire regiments.

The Jacobins—frightened, angry, hysterical—laid into one another. Their internecine fighting figured so prominently in the press that a letter arrived from the front deploring these distracting divisions at a time of national crisis. It was duly met with hisses in the club. The personal attacks continued. One newspaper held Robespierre singlehandedly responsible for the private vendettas and endless denunciations: "M. Robertspierre [sic] resigned his position as public prosecutor to prove, as he himself said, that he is not ambitious. Does this not prove, on the contrary, that he is devoured by an immeasurable ambition?"[41] On 10 May another letter from the front arrived, accusing Robespierre of sullying the tribune at the Jacobins by attacking General Lafayette. Despite fierce dispute and many disruptions, the letter was read aloud. Afterward, Robespierre went up to the tribune and snatched it from the hands of the reader. Chaos broke out again. On another occasion a Jacobin named Jean Baptiste Louvet, the licentious novelist and poetically gifted son of a Parisian stationery shop owner, accused Robespierre of tyrannizing over the club. Danton stepped forward to defend him: "M. Robespierre has never used any tyranny in this house, unless it is the tyranny of reason. It is not patriotism but base jealousy and all the most harmful passions that inspire the attacks against him."[42] But not even Danton could deny that his friend was always ready with a vicious counterattack.

In the midst of this rancorous strife Robespierre decided to start his own journal. Despite being passionate and opinionated, he was not a natural journalist. Even more long-winded on the page, his speeches also seemed far flatter—almost pedantic—in print. But it was relatively easy to venture into journalism at this time, even with little natural talent; all you needed was a bit of funding and enough stamina to write a couple of thousand words a week. From the middle of May, *Le défenseur de la constitution* (*The Defender of the Constitution*) appeared every Tuesday in an eye-catching red paper cover. As was common practice, the issues were undated. Despite its conservative-sounding name (since when had Robespierre been the defender of a constitution he never ceased to criticize during its drafting in the National Assembly?), what he really wanted was another platform from which to attack Brissot and anyone else who disagreed with him over the course of the Revolution. Readers could subscribe for thirty-six livres a year and were welcome to send in comments or books for review. Initially, the printer was to be another of Duplay's lodgers, an artisan from that close circle devoted to the Incorruptible. But then Robespierre came to an arrangement with a printer and bookseller in the rue de l'Ancienne Comédie Française, who promised to get the paper into every post office in France and all the major bookshops of Europe.

There was something implausible about Robespierre's prospectus for the paper. His pen, he professed, would be directed only by his love of justice and truth. He would descend from the tribune and "mount the platform of the universe to speak not only to an assembly, which might be agitated by the clash of different interests, but to the whole human race, whose interest is that of reason and general happiness." He would be like an actor who, leaving the stage and positioning himself in the audience, is better able to judge the play. He would be like a traveler who flees the tumultuous metropolis—or, in his case, revolutionary politics—and climbs to the summit of a mountain so as to feel "the calm of nature sink into his soul and his thoughts broaden out with the horizon." So *Le défenseur de la constitution* would be nothing like Marat's or Desmoulins's or Brissot's or Louvet's publications: no, Robespierre's was to be modeled on the Sermon on the Mount with romantic overtones. Predictably enough, he promised to use it to unmask the enemies of the people: "Placed since the beginning of the Revolution at the center of political happenings, I have had a close view of the tortuous advance of tyranny, I have discovered that our most dangerous enemies are not those who have openly declared themselves, and I shall try to render my knowledge of value for the safety of my country."[43] For all the declared purity of its manifesto, the journal was really a weapon in a factional fight that Robespierre had no intention of relinquishing.

Brissot and his friends were now openly calling for a republic. In his fight against them, Robespierre went so far as to turn himself into the last defender of the constitutional monarchy. Now that Brissot had made the campaign for a republic in France his own, Robespierre dared to criticize republicanism itself: "I care no more for Cromwell than for Charles I," he announced flamboyantly. "Surely it is not in the words *monarchy* or *republic* that we shall find the solution to the great problems of society."[44] Brissot had recently started a journal entitled *Le républicain*. There was nothing, Robespierre insisted in the first issue of his own journal, truly populist about Brissot's new venture except its title. Furthermore, he argued, the very word *republic* had recently caused division among the patriots and given the enemies of liberty an excuse for claiming that there was a conspiracy afoot against the monarchy and the constitution. Indeed, in Brissot's hands, the word *republic* had led directly to the massacre of innocent citizens, for it was Brissot who had been behind the petition that caused the debacle on the Champ de Mars on 17 July, almost a year earlier. It was Brissot who had insisted on calling for the abolition of the monarchy, when all the Jacobins had wanted was a referendum on the role of the king after his flight to Varennes. This—obviously—was splitting hairs. Robespierre had wanted to put the king on trial in 1791 and the call for a referendum was itself a challenge to the future of the monarchy. Moreover, the Jacobins had joined the call for deposition, however briefly. Here, however, it suited him to implicate Brissot in the bloodshed on the Champ de

Mars—of all the crimes in the Revolution so far, the one that would never be forgotten or forgiven. Not even his worst enemy could claim that Brissot had intended the massacre, but he was nonetheless culpable, in Robespierre's eyes, of inept and impolitic behavior. More recently, Robespierre argued, Brissot was guilty of collaborating with General Lafayette over the disastrous war. According to Robespierre, Brissot's mask of patriotism had slipped and he now ripped it off. So much for rising above the factional strife and publishing a journal with Olympian impartiality!

Also in the first issue of *Le défenseur de la constitution* was Robespierre's recent retort to Brissot in the Jacobin Club, delivered just after the declaration of war. Brissot had come again to the Jacobins to put an end to Robespierre's vituperations. "What have you done," he asked dramatically, "to give you the right to criticize me and my friends?" Robespierre seized the opportunity to summarize his own contributions to the Revolution so far. Now the readers of his journal throughout France (and beyond, if the bookseller kept his promise) would learn the story of his early revolutionary career:

> When I was only a member of a very small tribunal [in Arras], I opposed the Lamoignon Edicts on grounds of the principle of popular sovereignty, when superior tribunals only opposed them on form. . . . In the epoch of primary assemblies [in Arras], I alone insisted that we not merely reclaim but also exercise the rights of sovereignty. . . . When the Third Estate [in Arras] wanted humbly to thank the nobles for their false renunciation of financial privileges, I persuaded them to declare only that they did not have the right to give to the people that which already belonged to them.[45]

In Robespierre's eyes, one overwhelming conclusion followed from these flawless revolutionary credentials: those attacking him three years later, in political circumstances changed beyond all recognition, could only be enemies of the people. By now, Robespierre was personally invested in the public image of himself as incorruptible: he was not and had never been in the wrong. In this context, further comparison with Danton is illuminating. On one of the rare occasions that Danton spoke about himself in public, he was able to say: "If I was carried away by enthusiasm in the first days of our regeneration, have I

not atoned for it? Have I not been ostracized?"[46] Robespierre could
not have spoken these words. Atonement—for all his religious
sensibility—was outside his repertoire; martyrdom made more sense
to him. Like Danton, he had given himself to the people and could en-
visage dying for them; but unlike Danton, he could never admit that
he might have been wrong. Why? Because he was a self-righteous and
hypocritical prig? In some respects, he certainly was. Yet it is the political implications of the differences between the two men that really
matter in the history of the Revolution. Both aspired to be popular
leaders. Danton's identification with the people was objective—when
he could, he left his flawed, colorful, life-loving self out of politics.
For him, the distinction between private and public life was rarely
confused. In contrast, Robespierre's identification with the people was
subjective. If he was wrong the people were wrong, and that, as
Rousseau had assured him, simply could not be the case. Later in the
Revolution, when his wife suddenly died, Danton was plunged into
deep personal grief; despite his many alleged infidelities, he had loved
her passionately. Robespierre wrote to him, "I love you more than
ever, I love you until death. At this moment, I am you. Do not harden
your heart to the voice of friendship."[47] To anyone who did not know
Robespierre, such a letter at such a time might have seemed a bit
gauche and offensively self-centered. Danton, however, did know
Robespierre and recognized that that capacity to channel himself into
someone or something else—to seamlessly identify with something
beyond himself and make it his own—was the very center of his
friend's extraordinary self.

FOR SOMEONE STAKING both his personal and political credibility
on never being wrong, Robespierre's defense of the ailing constitutional monarchy was extremely risky. In 1789 he had argued vehemently but unsuccessfully against giving the king a legislative veto.
Now, over matters of religion and the army, the king was on the brink
of using his veto against the Legislative Assembly. After their appointment in March 1792, Brissot's friends had pursued a policy on religion
guaranteed to antagonize the king. On 24 April, four days into the for-

eign war, Jean Marie Roland (supported or perhaps even inspired by his avidly political wife) called for repressive measures against the refractory priests whom Robespierre himself had already identified as a major counterrevolutionary threat. A month later, on 24 May, the assembly approved a decree to banish and deport all members of the clergy who still refused to swear the oath to the Civil Constitution. Effectively, this action sanctioned a nationwide priest hunt, and it was obvious that Louis XVI, already in trouble with his conscience, would balk at approving the persecution of Catholic priests. A showdown between the king and the assembly, at a time when the ministers it had imposed on him were calling for a republic, would certainly have resulted in the collapse of the constitution. Given his recent defense of it, Robespierre would have been left looking foolish, the hapless defender of a hopeless cause. The fact that he was prepared to risk this is testimony to two things, his confidence in himself as a revolutionary leader and his irreconcilable differences with Brissot's faction, from which he wanted to distinguish himself at any cost.

The view that the refractory priests were a threat to the Revolution was far from eccentric, and it would be unreasonable to blame Brissot's faction for the trouble it caused the king in this respect. But the faction went a step beyond troubling Louis's conscience to menacing his person, when it persuaded the assembly to abolish his personal bodyguard. Holed up inside the Tuileries, pinning their hopes on a foreign invasion, and maintaining a stalwart sense of humor as the tide of hostility flowed round them ("a pike with a *bonnet rouge* walked about the garden . . . and did not stay long") was all very well, but none of the royals could ignore the implications of the removal of their guards. They were even more alarmed to hear that the bodyguards were to be replaced not by ordinary Parisian National Guardsmen (most of whom were headed for the front line) but by members of a new federalist army, called to Paris from the provinces and selected by local Jacobin Clubs. This new institution was as offensive to the National Guard as it was threatening to the king and his family. Many people—thousands of National Guards among them—thus urged him to use his veto and put a stop both to the new army and to the persecution of the priests. On holiday in Arras in the autumn of 1791, Robespierre had fixed on two main sources of revolutionary anxiety: France's armed forces and its refractory priests. Six months later, his twin anxieties were proving prophetic.

The idea of a new patriot army, summoned to Paris to supplement if not actually replace the National Guard, was originally Robespierre's. He had first suggested something of the kind in one of his antiwar speeches to the Jacobins, when he imagined a new federation of civilian soldiers from all over France regenerating public spirit on the Champ de Mars.[48] Since then, in the very first issue of his newspaper, he had called for an army of sixty thousand veteran soldiers to be assembled and garrisoned close to Paris. To his dismay, Brissot's friend in the ministry (Joseph Servan, the new minister for war) was calling for something disconcertingly similar: a new national army of twenty thousand men chosen and sent to Paris by local Jacobin Clubs throughout France. The problem, from Robespierre's point of view, was to determine which of the Jacobin factions would do the choosing—his own or Brissot's? Where would the loyalties of the new troops really lie? For all his exertions on the Jacobin Correspondence Committee, there was next to nothing he could do to ensure the outcome he desired. Instead, he channeled his energy into an elaborate theoretical discussion of military discipline that filled twenty pages of the next issue of his journal. From this it emerged that he was as intent on applying democratic principles to the armed forces as to any other sector of society.

Every soldier was also a citizen and every citizen a member of the human race, Robespierre insisted. He envisaged duties attached to each of these three spheres in ascending order: the professional duties of a soldier were narrower than his duties as a citizen, which in turn were narrower still than his duties as a human being. Yet Robespierre completely evaded the real issue in this area: what would happen if, or when, the spheres of duty collided? The one example of such a collision that he mentioned was ludicrous. He imagined an off-duty soldier chatting up a woman at a party and being ordered by his superior officer to stop: "Your presence here displeases me. I order you to return to barracks and forbid you to talk to this woman. I reserve for myself alone the pleasure of conversing with her."[49] Irritating as such a scenario would no doubt be for the frustrated soldier, it hardly got to the heart of the problem of military discipline in a country slipping into civil war. The first anniversary of the Champ de Mars massacre was just weeks away. In the immediate aftermath of that massacre, Robespierre had done well to remind the Jacobins that the National Guardsmen who obeyed General Lafayette and fired on unarmed civilians were not to blame for their orders, were themselves still citizens and patriots too. But there was a huge difference between struggling to limit the bloodshed in a political crisis and delineating a coherent theory of how soldiers could be held to their duties. Unexpectedly, fragile, bookish Robespierre turned out far more talented at the practice than at the theory of politics. Before the Revolution he had been a competent lawyer and a second-rate essayist; in its maelstrom he was emerging as a quirkily brilliant politician. As the spring of 1792 ripened into summer, he was still overshadowed by Brissot's faction.

The inner circle around Brissot was presided over by Mme Roland, who was growing ever more imperious in her modest parlor. They now planned a republic for part, if not all, of France. "We spoke often," Mme Roland reported,

> about the excellent spirit in the Midi, the energy of the departments there and the facilities which that part of France might provide for the foundation of a Republic should the Court succeed in subjugating the north of France and Paris. We got out the maps; we drew the line of demarcation. Servan studied the military positions; we calculated the forces available and examined the means of reorganizing supply. Each of us contributed ideas as to where and from whom we might expect support.[50]

Roland's wife had come a long way since she married an obscure bureaucrat twenty years her senior out of intellectual respect. Now she was poring over maps of France and helping the ministry to divide it into putative republican and monarchical segments. On 10 June she prompted Roland to write an open letter to the king denouncing his threat to use his veto to delay the assembly's decrees on the refractory priests and the new federal army (due to arrive in Paris in time for the third anniversary of the fall of the Bastille on 14 July). She may even have drafted the words in which Roland effectively accused the king of treason: "Much more delay and a grieving people will see in its king the friend and accomplice of conspirators."[51] Unsurprisingly, the king responded, two days later, by dismissing Roland and his friends from the ministry. They had lasted just three months in office.

General Lafayette heard the news on the front line. The war continued to go badly. Lafayette struggled more than ever to integrate new rank-and-file soldiers recruited from the National Guard with remnants of the old regime army. There were not enough funds or weapons; the frontier moved closer to Paris every day. In an open letter to the capital, he welcomed the fall of Brissot's friends and blamed all France's recent troubles, including the grim news from the front, on the Jacobin Club: "This sect, organized like a district empire, in its metropolitan and affiliated societies, blindly guided by ambitious chiefs, forms a separate corporation in the midst of the French people, whose power it usurps by governing its representatives and proxies."[52] What did Lafayette have in mind—a military coup to coincide with the 14 July observation, as Robespierre feared? Might he sweep down from the north on his white charger and put a stop once and for all to the relentless bickering in the capital when the nation already had its work cut out fighting a foreign war? If so, there would be bloodshed again on the Champ de Mars, for Paris meanwhile was planning a popular protest in support of the dismissed ministers. Robespierre disapproved. He hated and feared Lafayette. "Strike at Lafayette and the nation will be saved," was his improbable advice to the Jacobins.[53] But he hated Brissot's faction just as bitterly, so he stood at the tribune and denounced the forthcoming protest:

> You [friends of Brissot] that are sounding so loud an alarm and giving such an impulse to the public mind on the subject of a change of ministry, why do you not employ your power for a more national object—some object worthy of the French people? If you have grievances lay them before the assembly. No doubt a great country is justified in rising in its own defence, but only a degraded people can allow itself to be thrown into such agitation for the interests of individuals and the intrigues of a party.[54]

He might as well have said that Brissot was not worth a drop of patriotic blood. But no one was listening to him. The demonstration in favor of the dismissed ministers and against the king's veto—widely vilified ever since it was first discussed in 1789—was planned for 20 June, the third anniversary of the Tennis Court Oath. The Jacobin and Cordelier Clubs, the municipal government of Paris, the electoral assemblies of the city's forty-eight sections were all involved. The plan was to present a petition to the assembly asking for the reinstatement of the ministers and plant a tree of liberty in the Tuileries. But the petitioners also wanted permission to bring their weapons, a request refused by the municipal government. As mayor of Paris, Pétion found himself in a very difficult position. He did not want to be blamed for suppressing the protest, but nor did he want responsibility for the bloodshed that might result if the crowd was armed. He referred the problem on to Pierre-Louis Rœderer, now the chief legal adviser of the Department of Paris, which had wider responsibilities than the municipality. Rœderer had the courage to ban the proposed demonstration, calling on the National Guard to stop the protestors from going ahead illegally: another massacre loomed on the Champ de Mars. Pétion, having passed the problem to Rœderer, now disputed his solution, said no power on earth should be allowed to prevent the demonstration, and suggested that the National Guard march alongside the petitioners, rather than against them. The National Guardsmen themselves were divided: some were delighted to join the petitioners, others refused.

At five on the morning of 20 June a mob began to assemble at the site of the fallen Bastille. Later in the day it set off with a tree of liberty in the direction of the Tuileries. Rœderer, furious at the flouting of his advice, got there first, entered the Manège, and told the assembly that had it not recently broken a constitutional rule to admit armed men into one of its own sessions, the impending crisis would never have loomed.[55] One of Brissot's friends stood up and retorted that since the assembly had indeed recently received armed men, when the Châteauvieux soldiers marched through the Manège, it would be a gross insult to the people of Paris if their petition was rejected merely because it came accompanied by arms. Before the deputies could decide how to settle the argument, the mob arrived and forced its way into the hall. The demonstrators were persuaded to leave peacefully, but only on the condition that they would be allowed to march back in later. And so they did, drums, weapons, pikes, banners, and all, and for the second time in three months the assembly applauded the rabble-rousing music of the people in arms. It drew the line only at a bloody bullock's heart skewered on a pike and inscribed, THE HEART OF AN ARISTOCRAT. This was one popular emblem too many for the deputies and they sent it straight outside, where it was paraded instead at the gates of the Tuileries. The single pike, which the king's sister had laughed at in April, was back in the garden in June, covered in blood: DEATH TO VETO AND HIS WIFE, the crowd menaced from below. When it came to the planting of the tree of liberty—which, after the presentation of the petition to the assembly and the king, was the ostensible point of the demonstration—a new problem arose. There were twenty-four battalions of National Guardsmen strategically positioned in and around the Tuileries, and the palace gates were closed.[56] The petitioners had no hope of forcing their way into the gardens, and anyway it would have been absurd to risk a bloody confrontation over planting a tree, even if it was a tree of liberty. They compromised and planted it instead behind the assembly in the courtyard of the Capuchin convent on the south side of the rue Saint-Honoré, almost directly opposite the Duplays' house. If Robespierre was at home in his room that day—and very likely he was—he could have watched the planting from his first-floor window. Otherwise he played no part.

Given the number of National Guardsmen defending the Tuileries—ten battalions on the western terrace of the palace alone—it was, and remains, something of a mystery how the demonstrating mob managed to get inside. One explanation is that a delegation of municipal officers went to the king and complained that the locked gates were offensive to the people, who were merely holding a peaceful demonstration on the anniversary of the Tennis Court Oath. They may, or may not, have pointed out that back in 1789 it was the king's attempt to lock the third estate out of its own meeting hall in Versailles that led to its reassembling on a tennis court and swearing never to be disbanded until the nation had received a new constitution. Three years

later, to the very day, it was locked out again and definitely no less offended. In another letter to her friend the Marquise de Raigecourt,
the king's sister wrote her account of that frightening day, from the
perspective of those trapped inside the Tuileries:

> For three days [before 20 June] we expected a great upheaval in
> Paris, but thought we had taken all necessary precautions to ward off
> every danger. On Wednesday morning the courtyard and garden
> were full of troops. At midday we learnt that the faubourg Saint-
> Antoine was on the march; it brought a petition to the Assembly, and
> did not declare its plan to cross the Tuileries [garden]. Fifteen hun-
> dred people filed into the Assembly; a few National Guards and
> some Invalids, the rest were sans-culottes and women. Three munic-
> ipal officers came to ask the King to allow the demonstrators to en-
> ter the garden, saying that the Assembly was troubled by the crowd,
> and the passageways so crammed that the gates might be forced. The
> King told them to arrange with the commandant to let them defile
> along the terrace of the Feuillants and go out by the gate of the
> riding-school [Manège].
>   Despite these orders, shortly afterwards the other gates of the garden
> were opened. Soon the garden was full [of demonstrators]. The pikes be-
> gan to defile in order under the terrace in front of the Palace, where
> there were three lines of National Guards. . . . The National Guard,
> which had not been able to obtain any orders since the morning, had the
> grief of watching them cross the courtyard without being able to bar the
> way. . . . At this point, we were at the King's window. . . . The doors were
> closed. . . . The pikes entered the chamber like a thunderbolt; they
> looked for the King, especially one of them, who said the most dreadful
> things. . . . At last Pétion and members of the municipality arrived. They
> first harangued the people, and after praising the "dignity" and "order"
> with which they had marched, he enjoined them to retire with "the same
> calmness" so that no one could reproach them for abandoning them-
> selves to excess during a "civic festival." At last the populace began to de-
> part. . . . The King returned to his room, and nothing could be more
> touching than the moment when the queen and his children threw them-
> selves around his neck. The deputies who were there burst into tears. . . .
> At ten o'clock the Palace was empty again, and everyone went to bed. . . .
> The Jacobins are sleeping. These are the details of the 20 June. Adieu; I
> am well; I kiss you, and am thankful you are not here in the fray.[57]

* * *

HEARING OF THE mob's invasion of the Tuileries, Lafayette decided to wait no longer, abandoned his embattled troops on the front
line, and returned to Paris, calling on the assembly to punish the perpetrators of 20 June, destroy the Jacobin Club, and force a return to
law and order. He went to see the king—for the last time, as it turned
out. "The King told me in the presence of the Queen and his family,"
Lafayette reported, "that the Constitution was his safety, and that he
was the only person who observed it."[58] By now this was true. Robespierre was still publishing his journal, *Le défenseur de la constitution*, but
the presence of Lafayette in Paris—the general's open hostility to the
Jacobins and the imminent threat of a military coup—reunited him
temporarily with Brissot's faction. For the time being, the enemies of
Robespierre's enemy Lafayette were his friends. He began to work
with them for "the constitutional rising against the constitution,"
maintaining through this contorted paradoxical phrase the impression
that he had not been wrong to defend the constitution in recent
months and was not wrong now in seeking to overthrow it. By his own
standards, he came dangerously close to admitting he had been wrong
on the war. In the eighth issue of his journal he reflected on it at
length, introducing a strained distinction between a war of liberty and
a war of intrigue or ambition:

> When a powerful nation conducts a war of liberty it arises in its en-
> tirety, it marches under leaders that it has chosen from the most zealous
> defenders of equality and the general interest. At the time it declares [a
> war of liberty] formidable preparations are in place to assure the suc-
> cess of its enterprise. Its object is sublime, its force invincible, its mea-
> sures wise and grand, its attacks prompt and irresistible. . . . It does not
> purchase a painful victory through torrents of blood.[59]

A war of intrigue, conducted by one tyrannous power against another,
was altogether different. It led to oppression and crimes against liberty
on the home front as well as on the battlefield—there could be no
hope of unity between opposed nations if their only point of contact

was clashing armies sacrificing themselves for the despots, the enemies of liberty, who ruled them. For the last three months, according to Robespierre, France had been involved in the second of these two kinds of war, a disgraceful war of intrigue. But the time had come to convert it into an admirable war of liberty. True patriots must replace treacherous generals like Lafayette. Liberty must first be secured at home and then carried triumphantly, effortlessly abroad. Citing famous examples of bloodshed, he promised:

> Unhappy French, Belgian, German slaves of the tyrants who divide the human race like base herds, you will be free, doubt it not. I swear it by the burning of Courtrai, by the children of Brabançons, murdered in their mother's wombs and carried blood-soaked on the points of Austrian bayonets; I swear it by the shades of Avignon who perished at the hands of our common enemies; I swear it by our wives and children slaughtered by cowards on the Champ de Mars, by the defenders of the fatherland, . . . by the patriots; I swear it by the foreign armies . . . and by the traitors who summoned them, . . . I swear it by the Declaration of the Rights of Man, so solemnly promulgated and insolently violated, by the disasters of twenty centuries, by our ancestors, whom we must avenge, by our descendants, whom we must liberate, and by ourselves, whom we must save.[60]

This outburst was characteristically personal, populist, and hysterical. But was Robespierre really now endorsing the war he had so adamantly opposed? Yes and no. He endorsed it but only insofar as it conformed to his vision of a democratic war—the war of a free people against the despots of an oppressed people, in the interests of those oppressed people, who would welcome their invading army with open arms. Robespierre had never been to war. The closest he came to it was brawling in the playground at Louis-le-Grand, where he had a reputation for defending the smaller boys against bullies. His distinction between a war of liberty and a war of intrigue made sense in theory, but how would it look on the battlefield? Is a democratic war—or a war waged in the name of democracy—so very different from any other when it comes to the fighting? Those easy, bloodless, swift, efficient, popular victories Robespierre envisaged are extremely scarce.

When Brissot's party had proposed calling a new federal army of twenty thousand men to Paris, Robespierre had been critical. Despite the king's threatened veto, the new army was now assembling in Paris, ready for the annual celebration of the fall of the Bastille. In the next issue of his paper, Robespierre addressed these federal forces directly. Their mission, he told them, was to save the constitution—not the constitution as drafted in 1791 but the timeless constitution that guaranteed sovereignty and natural rights. "The fatal hour strikes. . . . Let us march to the field of Federation. There is the Altar of the Fatherland! There the place where the French once strengthened the bonds of their political association!"[61] Let them do so again, he entreated, but this time not in the presence of false idols like Louis XVI and General Lafayette: "Let us take no oath but to the country and to ourselves; and let us take it at the hands not of the King of France but of the immortal King of Nature, who made us for liberty and punishes our oppressors." Robespierre had never missed the 14 July festival. He was there in 1790, standing behind the king in the pavilion. He was there again in 1791, when the king was absent, in disgrace, and the assembly was wavering over its response to his flight to Varennes. Now he was there for the third time, mindful of the blood that had been spilled on the Altar of the Fatherland during the Champ de Mars massacre, mindful of the blood that was still being spilled at the front line, and wondering how long it would be before another Parisian insurrection brought the monarchy to an end. From the crowd he heard cries of "Vive Pétion!" But if he was jealous of his friend he did not show it. Pétion was prominent in people's minds because he had been briefly arrested after the invasion of the Tuileries, then quickly reinstated as mayor. At the close of the National Assembly in 1791, and afterward in Bapaume and Arras, the crowd had shouted, "Vive Pétion! Vive Robespierre!" Now it was only "Vive Pétion!"—but not for much longer.

Robespierre hoped that when it came the insurrection would sweep all before it: the king, his ministry, the Legislative Assembly, the army generals, the departmental administrators, the municipal government. In preparation for all the changes to come, the electoral assemblies of Paris's forty-eight sections once again went into permanent session.

Robespierre wrote approvingly to his friend Couthon, who was taking a mud cure at Saint-Amand: "The Revolution is about to take a more rapid course, unless it buries itself in military despotism and dictatorship. . . . The Paris sections are manifesting an energy and prudence worthy to serve as a model for the rest of the state. We miss you."[62] On 30 July armed men from Marseille arrived in Paris, as part of the new federal army. They had threatened to come once before, to save Robespierre after the Champ de Mars massacre. Now they came dragging cannons: a black cloud on the horizon advancing rapidly toward the capital and singing a new song, the "Marseillaise." "If they leave Paris without saving the country, all is lost," Robespierre wrote to his friend in Arras. "We all intend to lay down our lives in the capital rather than shrink from risking everything in a final attempt."[63] Later that evening he was in the chair at the Jacobins as a recent manifesto from the Duke of Brunswick, the commander of the enemy forces, was read out. Brunswick threatened to hold all Paris answerable for the safety of the king: "If the palace of the Tuileries be insulted or forced, . . . if the least violence, the least assault, be perpetrated against Their Majesties the King, the Queen, and the Royal Family," Paris would suffer "an exemplary and never-to-be-forgotten vengeance, . . . martial law and complete destruction."[64] At this grandiose threat, the Jacobins burst out laughing. But Robespierre refused to participate in their frivolity. He suspended the meeting early, appealing for calm. Again and again he cautioned against a premature insurrection that would only play into the hands of the people's enemies and turn public opinion against the true friends of liberty. If it had been up to him to give the signal, to decide that the time had definitely come for the people to rise up and revolt, he might never have done so. He wanted his "constitutional rising against the constitution," but he both feared it and was afraid for it. His fears, in the circumstances, were wholly reasonable.

IN THE EVENT, it was Danton who gave the signal. First he went home to Arcis and settled money on his seventy-year-old mother in case he was killed. Then he came back and called together representatives of the city's forty-eight sections. On the night of 9 August they formed the Insurrectionary Commune and proceeded to take over the municipal government (which Danton himself had belonged to in recent months). Danton briefly lay down to rest as his colleagues rang the tocsin in the tower of the Cordelier church nearby. The tocsin echoed across the city, a call to arms resounding from the churches of central and eastern Paris. Robespierre heard it in the Section of the place Vendôme, where the lights in the houses had been lit again. He sat in the Duplays' cellar, running up the narrow stairs to his bedroom from time to time if his curiosity got the better of him and he wanted to look out a first-floor window. According to Lucile Desmoulins, there had been a recent attempt to assassinate him, so he was even more nervous and suspicious than usual.[65] The bell rang all night, like a troubled infant that cannot sleep—rhythmic, relentless, inconsolable—but it did not, at first, bring the people out into the streets.[66] Perhaps it woke the Desmoulins's baby, now nearly a year old but too young still to know his godfather, Robespierre. Camille had gone out with a gun and Lucile remembered how "the tocsin of the Cordeliers rang, it rang for a long time. Bathed in tears, kneeling at the window, my face hidden in a handkerchief, I listened to the sound of that fatal bell. People came to comfort me in vain. It seemed to me that the day that preceded this deadly one had been our last."[67] From 2:00 a.m. on, Danton was giving orders to the insurrectionists from the Hôtel de Ville. Eventually a crowd for the storming of the Tuileries assembled. Unlike the Bastille, the palace was properly defended, and there was likely to be considerable loss of life. Since 20 June the king had recalled his loyal Swiss Guard and his constitutionally mandated bodyguards. Several battalions of National Guardsmen were on his side, too, and Pierre-Louis Rœderer was there again, giving advice on behalf of the Department of Paris, while pacing nervously around the Tuileries gardens. Louis XVI thought that Paris could be subdued; he regretted not having done so in 1789. He would do it now with belated help from Europe's invading army, whose arrival in the capital was, surely, only weeks away.

At dawn, the king's sister called the queen to the window to see the summer sun rise; allegedly, it was very red that day. The king, like Danton, had not slept, only lain down for a little in his violet breeches, flat-

tening the curls and rubbing the powder from one side of his head. Still
disheveled, he heard of the arrival of an early morning message from
the Insurrectionary Commune demanding that the current head of the
National Guard, a man named Mandat, leave the palace and present
himself at the Hôtel de Ville immediately. He did so and was murdered
on the steps outside (where de Flesselles and Governor de Launay had
been butchered by the crowd after the fall of the Bastille). By 6:00 a.m.,
Rœderer had persuaded the king to seek sanctuary in the Manège—just
a short walk across the garden—where the Legislative Assembly had
been burning candles through the night. The queen was opposed. She
thought they should fight on with their "considerable forces," but
Rœderer dissuaded her with "Madame, all Paris is against you."[68] It was
only 10 August, but the leaves in the garden had started to fall. As they
walked through them the dauphin kicked them playfully into the air and
the king remarked, "What a quantity of leaves! They fall early this year,"
knowing as he did that the popular press had been claiming for months
that the monarchy would not last beyond autumn. In the assembly he
said, "I am come hither to prevent a great crime; and I think I can be
nowhere more secure, gentlemen, than in your midst." The president
assured him he was right, but then one of the deputies drew attention to
the constitutional rule against the Legislative Assembly's deliberating in
the presence of the king. So the royal family was quickly ushered into a
side room, where they could watch the assembly's proceedings through a
grate. For all the president's and Rœderer's reassurances, that room was
the first of their real prisons. Outside, the fighting began. Led by the
contingent from Marseille, on whom Robespierre pinned such high
hopes, the armed mob—estimated at twenty thousand—succeeded in
entering the palace at around nine that morning. But they were driven
out again when the Swiss Guard—a force of nine hundred professional
soldiers—opened fire.[69] The battalions of National Guardsmen that had
remained loyal to Louis XVI now joined forces with the mob, and an
hour later the Swiss Guardsmen were in retreat. Around six hundred of
them were hacked to pieces. Several hundred of the mob—National
Guardsmen, shopkeepers, tradesmen, and artisans among them—were
also killed in the siege. By midday well over a thousand lay wounded or
dead among the fallen leaves. The queen had been right and the defense

of the Tuileries was formidable. Contrary to appearances, however, to the stretchers and screams, the loss of blood and life, this was a victory for the people. Afterward they lit celebratory bonfires to burn not early autumn debris but the naked bodies of the slain Swiss Guardsmen.

That evening Robespierre was at the Jacobins as usual. Here he offered his views on the events of the last twenty-four hours, afterward publishing them in his paper for wider circulation. For him it was a new beginning, like the fall of the Bastille, but better, wiser, purer:

> In 1789 the people of Paris raised themselves tumultuously to repel the attacks of the court, to free themselves of the old despotism, more than to conquer liberty, the idea of which was still confused, its principles unknown. All passions concurred in the insurrection and the signal it gave to the whole of France.
>
> In 1792 they have raised themselves with imposing courage to avenge the fundamental laws of their violated liberty, the infidel mandatories who sought to enslave once again the imprescriptible rights of humanity. They have put into action the principles proclaimed three years ago by their first representatives; they have exercised their recognized sovereignty and deployed its power and its justice to assure their safety and happiness.
>
> In 1789 they were helped by a great number of those who were called great, by a party of men who took back the power of government.
>
> In 1792 they have found their own resources, both their direction and their force; alone, they have protected justice, equality, and reason against their enemies. Not only did the people of Paris give a great example to France, the French people rose up at the same time.
>
> The solemnity with which they proceeded in this great act was as sublime as their motives and object.[70]

Robespierre urged his audience to believe that the promise of 1789 had been redeemed with the fall of the Tuileries. Everything that had gone wrong in the Revolution since the Bastille fell, all those departures from true principles that he had disputed so fervently in Versailles and afterward in Paris, all the compromises of the new constitution and its flawed enactment after 1791, all the disruption, misdirection, and confusion caused by factional fighting at the Jacobins, all the life already squandered in an incipient civil war, all the life wasted on the front line in a foreign war that was going badly wrong— it would all be canceled and redeemed now that the Revolution had recovered its true course. There is no reason whatsoever to suspect Robespierre's revolutionary optimism. He was speaking and writing from his heart, and those who dispute his interpretation of events cannot deny his sincerity. Mirabeau had said of him in 1789, "That man will go far, he believes everything he says." Quite how far, now that the monarchy had finally fallen, not even Mirabeau could have guessed.

8

THE KING'S TRIAL

Several weeks after the storming of the Tuileries, Paris was still in turmoil. Pétion remained mayor. Lafayette had fled the country. The Legislative Assembly continued to meet in the Manège. France was again without a constitution or government. To acquire these a new nationally representative body would need to be elected and invested with constituting power. In the interim, the assembly recalled Brissot's friends Roland, Servan, and Clavière to ministerial office and formed a provisional government. Danton was made minister of justice, in recognition of the part he had played in ending the monarchy. It was possible for Danton to serve alongside Brissot's friends because there was no personal animosity between him and them, but Robespierre could never have done so.[1] Instead, he threw himself into the politics of his section, the place Vendôme, soon renamed Section des Piques (pikes). Meetings were daily and increasingly dominated by sans-culottes determined to further the revolutionary demands of the poor and disadvantaged. From here Robespierre was elected to the Insurrectionary Commune, a body of 288 members formed by the election of six representatives from each of the forty-eight sections of Paris. Like Robespierre's, many of these sections were radical and so sent to the Commune representatives likely to push for radical measures, such as economic redistribution and price controls on essential commodities. But neither the sections nor the Commune, the mayor, the Legislative Assembly, or the provisional government could reliably control the streets, filled with panic after the Duke of Brunswick kept his promise and marched into France on 19 August.

By the beginning of September the invading army was at Verdun (only fifteen miles from Varennes), where the last fortress on the road to Paris surrendered. Less than a month before, the Jacobins had laughed at the duke's manifesto and its threat to raze Paris. But no one was laughing now. Black flags flew from the towers of Notre-Dame and above the Hôtel de Ville, with the word *Danger* (the same in French and English) emblazoned in white letters. The city gates were closed. The prisons were crammed with royalists, refractory priests, and other suspects summarily arrested since the fall of the monarchy. The patriots were afraid to leave the city to fight Brunswick's forces in case the counterrevolution took hold in their absence. Nor could they sit and wait calmly for the destruction of Paris. Toward the end of another restless weekend, there was a sudden crescendo of violence:

- Twenty-four priests, conveyed in four carriages to the prison of the abbey of Saint-Germain-des-Près, on Sunday afternoon, 2 September 1792, were set upon by a mob and murdered.
- One hundred and twenty-two other prisoners inside the abbey were condemned to death later that evening by an informal tribunal. They were taken outside and killed with pikes.
- About a hundred and fifty priests held at the convent of the Carmelites, including the archbishop of Arles and the bishops of Saintes and Beauvais, were murdered.
- Two hundred thieves and debtors held at the Châtelet prison were slaughtered.
- On Monday, 3 September, the queen's friend the Princesse de Lamballe and others held at La Force prison were butchered. The princess's severed head was then paraded on a pike outside the

windows of the Temple, the medieval fortress in the Marais
where the royal family were now incarcerated.

- An unknown number of convicts awaiting deportation were
  murdered.
- So, too, were an unknown number of priests held at the
  monastery of Saint-Firmin.
- One hundred and sixty inmates at the Bicêtre reformatory, forty-
  three of them between the ages of twelve and eighteen, were
  murdered.
- On Tuesday, 4 September, thirty-five women incarcerated at La
  Salpêtrière on charges of prostitution were sexually assaulted
  and killed.

So much then for the people's justice: well over a thousand victims,
some from the weakest and most vulnerable sectors of society, were put
to death in the first weeks of the new republic to satisfy the blood lust of
the mob that brought down the monarchy. Men, women, and children
who did not matter to the Revolution, whose names have been forgotten by history, were sacrificed to the braying crowd. Danton claimed he
saw them afterward in his dreams, shaking their gory locks at him.

How much did Robespierre know about the September Massacres?
Did he, during those horrific three days, do anything to try to stop the
slaughter? He was definitely present at the meeting of the Insurrectionary Commune on 2 September when reports came in about what
was happening at the abbey of Saint-Germain-des-Près. That day, the
Commune did nothing. On 3 September, in response to news of the
killings at La Force, the Commune sent someone to investigate "the
excitement."[2] As the week wore on, the Commune made no attempt to
restrain the violence: it left the most radical of Paris's forty-eight sections to do as they liked, perhaps because restraint was impossible or
perhaps because members of the Commune genuinely thought the
people had earned their right to bloody vengeance. It did, however,
send Robespierre across to the Temple, close to his former residence
in the rue Saintonge, to make sure that "everything was quiet there."
The royal family were potentially valuable hostages if the advance of
Brunswick's invading army could not be stopped; they must not be

perfunctorily cut down in the general bloodletting. When he got to the Temple, Robespierre found everything in order, if not exactly quiet. There was no reason for him to ascend the narrow winding stair of the tower in which the deposed King and his family were imprisoned and guarded by sans-culottes. Outside, the patriot Palloy, who had turned the demolition of the Bastille into such a profitable business, was contemplating demolishing the buildings surrounding the tower and erecting a new perimeter wall for extra security, in case the royal family tried to escape. In 1789 Palloy had destroyed a prison; three years later he was building one.³ Robespierre, who had seen liberty appear like a vision on the crumbling battlements of the Bastille, probably did not linger looking up at the Temple tower.

Aside from checking that no unauthorized acts were being committed at the Temple, Robespierre intervened in the Commune's deliberations for only one purpose: to try and get his opponents—Brissot and Roland—arrested and taken off to prison. There, as he well knew, they would very likely be killed immediately, along with the other prisoners condemned by the improvised tribunals set up by the sans-culottes. These makeshift tribunals inside the prisons acquitted a few fortunate victims, but the rest were hacked to death as they left the temporary courtrooms. Danton saw to it that the arrest warrants for Robespierre's personal enemies were withdrawn. To sanction, or even encourage, the alarming spectacle of the people's vengeance was one thing; to use it to settle personal scores was quite another. As Danton already knew, however, this was a difference lost on Robespierre. Yet the Duplay family doctor, years later, said Robespierre could never speak of the September Massacres without horror. "Blood again! Nothing but blood," he remembered him saying, in the privacy of the Duplay household.⁴

Perhaps Robespierre, like Danton, also had nightmares. After all, he was still the same squeamish man who collapsed in Arras when his legal duties there required him to condemn a man to death. But now he was also a committed revolutionary leader who knew that he owed his power to the people's propensity for violence. Without it, the monarchy would not have fallen on 10 August. Robespierre, for all his refined sensibility, was too astute a politician either to deny this fact or to ignore it: mob violence was there to be compromised with, not censured by the revolutionaries whose careers it had done so much to promote. His solution was to demand the establishment of an official revolutionary tribunal, which, he insisted, would maintain the peace, satisfy the people's impatience for justice, and investigate promptly all counterrevolutionary activities. He got his way, and in the short period between the collapse of the monarchy on 10 August and the end of 1792, this tribunal sentenced a total of twenty-eight people to the guillotine.

The guillotine had first been used publicly in Paris on 25 April 1792, to execute a criminal named Nicolas Jacques Pelletier. Erected on scaffolding, it was positioned outside the Hôtel de Ville on the place de Grève, where Damiens and others had been gruesomely dispatched under the old regime. On that day, anticipating a large crowd at this new public spectacle and worried about maintaining order, Rœderer had written to General Lafayette asking him to ensure that National Guardsmen would remain in place until the execution was over and the scaffolding had been dismantled (when it was first introduced the guillotine was kept in storage and out of sight when not in use). The day had been long in coming. Pelletier had been condemned for robbery and murder soon after the National Assembly made decapitation the only legal capital punishment. He had had to wait in jail for over three months while the guillotine was built in Strasbourg according to the design of the surgeon Antoine Louison, at a cost of thirty-eight livres. Some more weeks passed while the public executioner, Charles Henri Sanson, tested the machine on corpses in the Bicêtre hospital. Sanson favored the guillotine because he knew the practical problems of decapitation by sword—the nobility's old regime privilege:

> How can the executioner have the necessary power over a man who will not or cannot keep himself in a convenient posture? It seems, however, that the National Assembly only devised this species of execution [decapitation] for the purpose of avoiding the protracted executions of the old way [hanging]. It is in furtherance of these humane views that I have the honor of giving this forewarning of the many accidents that executions may produce if attempted by the sword. It is therefore indispensable that, in order to fulfill the humane intentions of the National Assembly, some means should be found both to avoid

delays and ensure certainty, by fixing the patient so that the success of the operation shall not be doubtful.[5]

After 10 August and the establishment of the Revolutionary Tribunal that Robespierre demanded, the guillotine was set up closer to the Tuileries palace, on either the place du Carrousel or the place de la Révolution. As it turned out, very few of the twenty-eight condemned by the new tribunal were executed for political crimes: like the murderer Pelletier, most were just ordinary criminals.

WHEN HE FIRST outlined his idea of a democratic war—a war of defense, not conquest, conducted by the whole people, armed with pikes, if nothing more—Robespierre's was an isolated eccentric voice at the Jacobins. One year on, the people rose up as he had said they would, to grab whatever weapons they could and meet the invading army on the road from Valmy. During those early days of September, as bodies were piled up in the prisons, thousands of patriot volunteers collected on the Champ de Mars, ready to die for the fatherland. Danton urged them on with the most famous speech he ever made, this man with stentorian lungs to equal Mirabeau's who spoke five languages but none so fluently as the language of the crowd. His speech ended: "Audacity! Yet more audacity! Always audacity—and France will be saved."[6] (Danton's heavy engagement in trying to save revolutionary France might account for his reported callousness with regard to the prison victims. When asked what to do about them, he replied, according to Mme Roland, "Let them save themselves.")[7] The tocsin rang out as it had before. The royal family listened to it in their beds in the Temple. They heard it accompanied by Marie Antoinette's anguished cries for her murdered friend, whose beautiful blond head had been paraded on a pike at the window. Fortunately for the Revolution, unfortunately for the royal family, the fighting at Valmy went well— the French forces, an amalgam of old army professional soldiers, National Guardsmen and new volunteers, repelled the Duke of Brunswick's troops, charging into battle and shouting above the cannon fire, "Vive la nation!" The poet Goethe was with the invading army. On the night of 20 September, as the autumn chill was drawing in, he sat with other downcast Prussian soldiers, huddled around a campfire. They asked him what he made of the day's events and he pronounced: "Here and today a new epoch in the history of the world has begun, and you can boast you were present at its birth." Europe's first concerted attempt to end the Revolution had failed.[8]

Robespierre, of course, was far from the battlefield. It is doubtful whether he even knew how to fire a musket or would have lasted an hour in the mud at Valmy. Instead, he was doing something at which he had, over the last three years, become extremely skilled: electioneering. He was in the vanguard of those demanding a new representative assembly to draft France's first republican constitution. Soon after 10 August he had published his own call to arms in his journal:

> You must prepare the success of this convention by the regeneration of the spirit of the people. Let all awake—all, all arise—all arm, and the enemies of liberty will hide themselves in darkness. Let the tocsin of Paris reverberate in all the departments. Let the people learn to reason as well as to fight.[9]

Robespierre now devoted himself to getting elected. The existing Legislative Assembly, diminished in power since 10 August, had nevertheless managed to decree that the new elections must be indirect, like the elections of 1789 and 1791. Primary assemblies would elect members of an electoral body to choose their delegates for them. However, the distinction between active and passive citizens—ones with the vote and ones without—to which Robespierre had always strongly objected, was abolished. Instead there was universal male suffrage: the electoral assemblies were to be chosen by primary assemblies composed of all independent male citizens over the age of twenty-one, and they were to deliberate in public. In the primary assembly for his Section des Piques (which had already elected him to the Commune), Robespierre was chosen first of the sixteen electors. His landlord and friend Duplay was another of the sixteen. Rabble-rousing Marat, who had openly approved of the prison massacres, was chosen in another section. When the whole body of 990 electors for all the sections and suburbs of Paris met, radical patriotic candidates dominated. The electors first assembled on 2 September—the day the massacres began—in the archbishop's palace, where the National Assembly had originally convened for a brief period after moving to Paris from Versailles. Robespierre remembered that this hall had proved very unsuitable and that the National Assembly had soon had to abandon it for the Manège. Indeed, he had been working since the end of August to persuade the electors to ask permission of the Jacobin Club to meet in its more publicly accessible hall, where it would be much easier for the people—and of course the Jacobins—to oversee the proceedings. He succeeded. Not yet content, he also proposed, in the name of the primary assemblies, that any of their chosen electors who had previously displayed monarchist sympathies—who had joined the Feuillants, for example, after the Champ de Mars massacre—should be excluded immediately. The majority of radical patriots hastened to agree and expelled the dubious minority whom the primary assemblies had only just elected. This time, evidently, the Jacobins would take no chances.

At that first meeting of the electors, Robespierre, comfortably out of range of the front line, declared from the tribune that he would "face with perfect calmness the swords of the enemies."[10] In doing so he would take with him to the grave "the certainty that France would remain free and the satisfaction of having served the fatherland." Since he was now accompanied everywhere by a bodyguard, to discourage any repetitions of the alleged assassination attempt earlier in the year, he could not have been as sanguine about going to his grave as he claimed. Two days later he was at the top of the list of deputies elected to the new National Convention. The person standing against him was Pétion. Their friendship had been strained for months, but after 10 August it deteriorated dramatically. Just days after the storming of the Tuileries, Pétion, as mayor of Paris, wanted to disband the Insurrectionary Commune and reinstate the municipal government that it had displaced. The Commune commissioned Robespierre to get Pétion to back down. Their meeting did not go well, Pétion did not back down, and soon afterward Robespierre received yet another disconcerting letter from the man who, only a year ago, had been his closest revolutionary colleague:

You know, my friend, what my feelings are toward you: you know that I am no rival of yours and that I have always given you proof of my devoted friendship. It would be idle to attempt to divide us. I could not cease to love you unless you ceased to love liberty. I have always found more fault with you to your face than behind your back. When I think you too ready to take offense or when I believe, rightly or wrongly, that you are mistaken about a line of action, I tell you so. You reproach me with being too trustful. You may be right, but you must not assume too readily that many of my acquaintances are your enemies. People can disagree on a number of unessential points, without becoming enemies, and your heart is said to be just. Besides, it is childish to take offense at the things people say against one. Imagine, my friend, the number of people who utter libels against the mayor of Paris! . . . Yet it does not worry me, I can assure you. If I am not totally indifferent to what other people think about me, at least I value my own opinion more highly. . . . You and I are never likely to take opposite sides. We shall always be of the same political faith. I need not assure you that it is impossible for me to join any movement against you: my tastes, my character, my principles all forbid it. I don't believe you covet my position any more than I covet the king's. But if, when my term of office comes to an end, the people were to offer you the mayoralty, I suppose that you would accept it; whereas, in all good conscience I could never accept the crown. Keep well. March ahead! The times are too serious to think of anything but the public interest.[11]

When Robespierre on his return from Arras had first visited Pétion in his grand new residence, he had reassured himself nervously that the job would not go to his friend's head, that his spirit would remain "simple and pure as ever." This pompous letter proved otherwise. For almost a year, Pétion had sat on the fence between the rival factions at the Jacobins, believing, perhaps, that his official position enabled him to rise above the hatred between Robespierre and Brissot, who were both his friends. He had played the part of peacemaker to no avail. Who, in the circumstances, did he think might offer him a crown? What reason did he have to believe that Robespierre coveted the role of mayor of Paris? Despite his delusions of grandeur, Pétion's letter captures two of the most prominent features of Robespierre's personality: his perennial distrust—"Share my fear," he had urged the Jacobins in 1791—and his propensity to take personal offense of the most lasting and rancorous kind. Robespierre himself testified to the deep spiteful gratification he experienced in the electoral assembly when he, not Pétion, was chosen as the first of Paris's deputies to the Convention. As he wrote to the self-important mayor:

> Everyone saw the change in your countenance when, in the progress of the ballot, another name [Robespierre's own] seemed to have the advantage of yours. You were aware that it was the Assembly's intention to have you named the next day, but you left the hall abruptly and never reappeared. You would not even keep your dinner engagements, and you have at last confessed the true motive of your vexation by saying, "Well then, to be candid with you, I did think that if I was named at all, I was entitled to be first."[12]

So who was jealous and who was gloating now? Once, Pétion had been all but indistinguishable from Robespierre; his name had been honored alongside Robespierre's after the end of the first National Assembly, and since then his career had gone from strength to strength. But the toast of the crowd at the 14 July celebrations of 1792 was no longer the most popular man in Paris two months later. Pétion's confident belief that nothing could ever come between himself and Robespierre was not unwarranted—just, as it turned out, completely mistaken.

AFTER BEING PASSED over in the capital, Pétion was elected a representative to the forthcoming convention from the Department of Eure-et-Loir (which included his hometown, Chartres). Brissot was also chosen a deputy for Eure-et-Loir. Even before the convention of 749 deputies met, many of those elected from the provinces, especially those from the Gironde department in western France, were concerned that the Paris delegates, backed by the Commune and the city's radical sections, would try to dominate proceedings. On the list of Paris's twenty-four delegates, Robespierre was first. Danton was second, Camille Desmoulins sixth, Marat seventh, the revolutionary artist Jacques-Louis David twentieth, and—rather more surprisingly—

Robespierre's brother from Arras nineteenth. At last, Augustin had a real reason to be in Paris. Let people say what they liked about corruption, Robespierre was convinced that his brother had stood independently and been elected on merit, yet only his own influence could have secured such an unlikely outcome. Augustin had distinguished himself as president of the Arras Jacobins and, since 10 August, been active in the Arras Commune (one of the many provincial imitations of Paris's Insurrectionary Commune), but he scarcely knew anyone in the capital. He wasted no time in packing his bags. It soon became clear, however, that Charlotte was not going to be left behind in an empty house in the rue des Rapporteurs while both her brothers pursued exciting revolutionary careers in the capital. Robespierre's siblings arrived on his doorstep and proceeded to move into the Duplay house, renting from 1 October for a thousand livres a year one furnished and one unfurnished room. Inevitably, their arrival disrupted Robespierre's comfortable Parisian home life. His own rooms at the Duplays' had started filling up with congratulatory letters, statuettes, medals, and prints of himself. For example, there was a medal to commemorate the events of 10 August on which he was represented cupping milk flowing from the breasts of liberty and offering it to a patriot to drink. It would have been ungracious to dispose of these tributes—even if he had wanted to—so instead Robespierre carefully arranged them around his two small rooms, which soon resembled a shrine.

The Duplays were so proud of their famous patriotic Jacobin lodger, so devoted to him both personally and politically, that Robespierre's rooms never struck them as peculiar. But Charlotte was uncomfortable. It was not the emergence of a personality cult focused on her older brother that disturbed her. Nor was it all the pictures of him—he had always been fond of collecting prints, fond, too, of sketching, and he used to organize small exhibitions when Charlotte and Henriette visited him on those long Sunday afternoons of their childhood in Arras. Admittedly, the subject of the pictures had altered dramatically since those far-off days, but Charlotte was at least as fixated on Robespierre as the Duplays were and said nothing about finding his rooms odd. It was the private attentions lavished on him by the smotheringly maternal Mme Duplay that irritated her. Even at an epistolary distance, she had been jealous at the idea of Robespierre cosseted in the home of another woman; she could imagine only too well how responsive he would be to this kind of fussing. She knew his domestic character to be *"débonnaire"* (meek or accommodating), so even before setting foot in 366 rue Saint-Honoré, she feared finding him passively relaxed in a home she could not control. The reality was intolerable. Almost as soon as her clothes were unpacked, Charlotte began lobbying Robespierre to rent a house of his own. Now that he was an important public figure, she said, he ought to have an independent establishment. And who better than his sister to preside over it, unimpeded by the likes of Mme Duplay and her bothersome daughters?

Robespierre, of course, had more important things on his mind than the fight brewing between his sister and his landlady. On 20 September, as Goethe and the rest of the Prussian army retreated before the full force of the French nation, the National Convention gathered to meet in Paris. It had two purposes: to win the war and to draft a republican constitution. The Convention officially opened the following morning, with the newly elected deputies from all over France assembling at the ransacked Tuileries and processing to the Manège, where they filled the vacant seats. It was only a short walk across the garden from the Tuileries to the Manège—there was no celebratory Mass, no ceremonial robes, none of the symbolism that had moved the Marquis de Ferrières to write to his wife in 1789: "Love for my country has made itself very powerfully felt in my heart. I was not aware just how far the mutual ties extend that unite us all to this soil, to the men who are our brothers, but I understood it in that instance."[13] Ferrières had been a noble in the procession at Versailles. Now he was in danger of losing his life, one of the despised enemies of liberty from whom the new National Convention must protect the nascent French Republic.

Danton, Camille Desmoulins, Marat, David, and Augustin were all there in the procession with Robespierre, but none of them had been with him in 1789. Robespierre was one of a minority who could compare the two occasions; Pétion was another, but these days the two men were staying far apart, not walking together reminiscing about the past.[14] They entered the Manège at different ends of the procession and, once inside, Robespierre and his friends made a point of occupying the high seats at the far end of the hall to the left of the president's chair; Pétion had already been chosen as the Convention's first president, which cannot have pleased them. They sat there looking down and soon afterward the group around Robespierre became known as the Mountain; Pétion, Brissot, and his friends became the Girondins (so called because some of them came from the Department of the Gironde). And between these two rival factions—bemused or irritated by their crossfire but inextricably caught up in it—there was the Plain—all those new deputies who had only just arrived in Paris to draft a republican constitution. At four o'clock that afternoon, trumpets sounded outside the Temple and a voice pronouncing the formal abolition of the monarchy boomed through the thick walls and windows of the royal family's rooms. Louis XVI was reading. Between 10 August 1792 and the start of the New Year he read 250 volumes in several different languages and translated Horace Walpole's *Historic Doubts on the Life and Reign of King Richard III*. At the announcement of the republic, he did not even look up from his book.[15]

SINCE 10 AUGUST, Robespierre had been too busy to issue his journal. But once the preoccupying business of electioneering was over, he relaunched it under the new title *Lettres à ses commettans* (Letters of Maximilien Robespierre, member of the National Convention of France, to his constituents). It was, as ever, a platform for both his theoretical and his practical political concerns. In the first article of the first new issue he argued:

> It is not enough to have overturned the throne: our concern is to erect upon its remains holy equality and the imprescriptible Rights of Man. It is not in the empty word itself that a republic consists but in the character of the citizens. The soul of a republic is *vertu*—that is, the love of the fatherland and the high-minded devotion that resolves all private interests into the general interest. The enemies of the republic are those dastardly egoists, those ambitious and corrupt men. You have hunted down kings, but have you hunted out the vices that their deadly domination has engendered among you? Taken together

you are the most generous, the most moral of all peoples . . . but a people that nurtures within itself a multitude of adroit rogues and political charlatans, skilled at usurpation and the betrayal of trust.[16]

Like an austere godfather at the birth of France's republic, Robespierre advised the nation to seek first the enemy within. These were not new sentiments. Before he left Arras for Versailles in 1789 he had written a pamphlet entitled *The Enemies of the Fatherland Unmasked*. Absolutely nothing had happened since then to reduce his fear of surreptitious political foes. Now that everyone claimed to want a republic, he thought the really important distinction was between those who wanted it for their own selfish purposes and those—himself, for example—who genuinely wanted to found it on the principle of equality and in the general interest. Next he revisited another long-standing concern: fear of executive power. As he understood it, overly strong governments had caused most of the misery of human society—he was more frightened of despotism than of anarchy. In this, as in his conception of the general interest into which all private interests could, and should, be dissolved, Robespierre was again following Rousseau. Around this time there was a rumor that he slept with a copy of the *Social Contract* under his pillow. It does not appear in the inventory of his books taken after his death, but his speeches refer to it so often that there can be no doubt about how much it meant to him. Perhaps one of the Duplays took his personal copy as a keepsake before the inventory was compiled.

At one point in the *Social Contract*, Rousseau describes his ideal lawgiver. The qualities required in someone truly worthy of formulating the laws are extraordinary:

> You would need a superior intelligence that sees all the human passions without experiencing them, . . . that earns a distant glory, perhaps even working in one century for the benefit of another; it would take gods to give laws to men.[17]

Robespierre quoted this passage in full in his article. But then he proceeded to gloss it, significantly altering the meaning so that an unusually admirable human being—Robespierre himself, for example—might enact the role of lawgiver that Rousseau had reserved for the gods:

> You would need philosophers as enlightened as they were intrepid, who experienced the passions of man but whose first passion would be the horror of tyranny and the love of humanity, treading underfoot vanity, envy, ambition, and all the weaknesses of petty souls, inexorable toward crime, armed with power, indulgent toward error, sympathetic toward misery, and tender and respectful toward the people.[18]

This was a self-portrait—an extremely flattering one. Despite his shrine of sorts in the Duplay house, Robespierre probably did not think he was above human passions, but he did consider himself more self-controlled than most, more resistant to political temptation, more unambivalently for the people, less selfish, less corruptible, perhaps even incorruptible. Robespierre seemed to share Rousseau's belief in the need for an almost superhuman lawgiver, omniscient, disinterested, and capable of directing the people for their own good. And he may well have been privately preparing himself to assume just that role. In this context, Robespierre's vision of democracy was very different from anything we would recognize today. The rule of the people, as he understood it, was not simply derived from the will of the majority. The point was to ensure the triumph of the good, pure general will of the people—what the people would want in ideal circumstances—and this needed to be intuited on their behalf until they had received sufficient education to understand it for themselves. When it came to drafting the laws, to giving France its new republican constitution, Robespierre believed that he was far closer to Rousseau's conception of the ideal lawgiver than Brissot and his friends could ever be.

ROBESPIERRE'S ENEMIES IN the Convention wasted no time. On 25 September, just four days after the official opening, they accused him of aspiring to be a tyrant. His enemies—many of them friends of Brissot's—were dismayed at his influence and popularity in the capital. They insisted that since Paris was only one of eighty-three departments in France, its representatives' votes should count as only an 83rd of the total within the National Convention. Robespierre, denounced as leader of the Paris deputies in their illegitimate quest for power, hesitated. But Danton leapt to the tribune to defend him as he had done before at the Jacobin Club. He demanded the death penalty for anyone scheming to destroy the unity of France. By this he meant death to anyone scheming to turn France into a federation of independent departments or small republics in order to diminish the power of Paris. This was one of the accusations the Mountain leveled against the Girondins. When Robespierre finally stood up to defend himself, he struck a characteristic note: "I begin by thanking my accusers. Calumny serves the public good when it clumsily unmasks itself." First he appealed, as usual, to his personal patriotic credentials: "I did this . . . I did that . . . ," he reminded the Convention, summarizing his achievements since 1789 until the audience got restless and someone shouted, "Enough!" Then he said he had long suspected that Brissot's faction wanted to divide France into a federation of small republics, leaving it even more vulnerable to internal and external enemies than it already was.[19] He had not been in the room when Mme Roland and her friends bent over the map and discussed the division of the country into monarchical and republican parts. But now that the monarchy had fallen, he was convinced they wanted another kind of division, one that would curtail the influence of Paris, so essential to sustaining revolutionary ideals, and diminish his power base.

Robespierre's intervention was subtle and sardonic but completely overshadowed by the next speaker. Blistering with skin disease and reeking of vinegar, this was the infamous Marat, the so-called *ami du peuple* (people's friend), the indefatigable pamphleteer who, since 1789, had consistently called for blood and anarchy. "I believe in the cutting off of heads," he had declared in his newspaper.[20] Of course, he did not always mean what he said. "My hand would wither rather than write another word if I really thought the people were going to do what I tell them to," he confided to a friend.[21] Even so, he had openly approved of the September Massacres and may have had more to do with arranging them than Robespierre cared to hear about. The two were not close friends. Marat claimed that the only time they had ever met privately, Robespierre was horrified by his sanguinary attitudes:

> Robespierre listened to me with terror. He grew pale and silent for some time. This interview confirmed me in the opinion that I always had of him, that he unites the knowledge of a wise senator with the integrity of a thoroughly good man and the zeal of a true patriot but that he is lacking as a statesman in clearness of vision and determination.[22]

This was high praise indeed from Marat, who so delighted in defamation. The admiration may not have been mutual, but it was nevertheless hard to imagine that Marat, this flagrant travesty of Rousseau's ideal lawgiver, could have been elected to the Convention as a representative for Paris without the Incorruptible's consent. As Marat stood up to speak the hall erupted in hoots of disapproval. When the booing relented he said in his hollow, croaking pantomime villain's voice: "I perceive that I have enemies here." "All, all, all are your enemies," cried his fellow deputies.[23] Undeterred, he addressed the charge of tyranny that had been leveled at Robespierre and the other representatives of Paris, whose election the Jacobins had so vigilantly monitored:

> I owe it to justice to declare that my colleagues, and especially Danton and Robespierre, have always opposed the opinions that I avow on this point; I, first and alone of all public writers in France, have thought of a dictatorship as the only means to crush the counterrevolutionary traitors.[24]

The same day Marat despaired of the Convention in his *L'ami du peuple* and prophesized to the French:

> Fifty years of anarchy await you, and you will emerge from it only by the power of some dictator who will arise—a true statesman and patriot. O prating people, if you did but know how to act![25]

Among the crowd at the Tuileries on 10 August was an unemployed army captain who watched with horror as the Swiss Guards were murdered and burned. "If he had mounted his horse," the young Napoleon Bonaparte wrote of Louis XVI, "victory would have remained with him."[26] Here was the future statesman and patriot whose dictatorship Marat foretold but did not live to see.

THE GIRONDINS' ATTACKS on Robespierre redoubled. The old divide at the Jacobins between Brissot and Robespierre was carried over into the Convention, where it mutated into the hostility between the Girondins and the Mountain. But whereas the previous year Robespierre had struggled to win ascendancy over the Paris Jacobins, now he succeeded in having Brissot and his friends formally expelled from the club. On 29 October, in the Convention, Mme Roland's husband denounced in general terms the proponents of violence and blamed the Insurrectionary Commune for the September Massacres. Robespierre responded with general refutations but also asked rhetorically, "Who dares accuse me?"[27] From the seats at the other end of the hall where the Girondins were sitting came a voice. "I do," called Jean Baptiste Louvet, the licentious novelist married to one of Mme Roland's close friends. Silence fell among the assembled deputies. According to a Dr. Moore (a distinguished medical doctor studying in Paris who had heard a rumor that something exciting was going to happen that day), Louvet, thin, lank, and pale-faced, "stalked along the hall like a specter, and being come directly opposite to the tribune, he fixed Robespierre, and said, 'Oui, Robespierre, c'est moi qui t'accuse!'" (Yes, Robespierre, it is I who accuse you). Robespierre froze. "He could not have seemed more alarmed had a bleeding head spoken to him from a charger." Danton tried to help by causing a distraction—he knew his friend was a skilled yet nervous speaker and could see he was deeply flustered. But Louvet had captured the deputies' attention and they wanted to hear what he had to say. Realizing this, Danton, always so adept, so agile as a public speaker, began to threaten Louvet before he could even begin. "I want the accuser to put his finger into the wound," he said, challenging Louvet to back up his allegations.[28] "I intend it," Louvet replied, "but why does Danton scream beforehand?"

In fact, Louvet had nothing new to say. He accused Robespierre of conspiring to control the Insurrectionary Commune, of complicity in the September Massacres, of trying to include Roland and Brissot among the victims, of associating with Marat, and of dominating the Jacobin Club:

> I accuse you of having produced yourself as an object of popular idol-
> atry, and of having caused it to be rumoured that you are the only man
> capable of saving the country. I accuse you . . . of having tyrannised
> by intrigue and fear over the Electoral Assembly of Paris, and of hav-
> ing aimed at supreme power by calumny, violence, and terror; and I
> demand that a Committee be appointed to examine your conduct.[29]

It had all been said before, and yet, Dr. Moore observed, this speech stirred up so much hostility against Robespierre that he was in danger of being lynched on the spot. Answer, Danton urged him, answer immedi-ately. But either he could not or he would not. Once again, Danton spoke on his behalf, rejecting the charges of tyranny. Finally Robespierre was given a week to prepare his own response. There was cunning behind his reluctance to speak. He knew that he lacked Danton's fluency and that if the Convention turned against him his career was finished. He knew he could use the coming week to write and rewrite in his small, neat hand-writing another finely honed account of his exemplary revolutionary cre-dentials. But there must have been fear as well. Standing there facing Louvet, resolute as Banquo's ghost, he completely lost his nerve. He needed the week to recover, to write his defense, and, above all, to assem-ble the facts of his revolutionary contribution and square them with his conscience. He was not, he never had been, wrong. Much as he needed others to believe this, what he needed still more was to believe it himself.

Robespierre defended himself before the Convention on 5 No-vember. On that day Dr. Moore was at the Manège again, in the crowd of people who went early to secure a place in the public galleries. Looking around, he noticed suddenly that the galleries were "almost entirely filled with women." They applauded Robespierre loudly. Dr. Moore was not the only person to notice Robespierre's female fan club. Later that week the Marquis de Condorcet, secretary of the

Academy of Sciences under the old regime, now a Girondin deputy in the Convention, raised the subject in the newspaper *Chronique de Paris*:

> There are some who ask why there are always so many women around Robespierre: at his house, in the galleries of the Jacobins and of the Convention. It is because this revolution of ours is a religion, and Robespierre is leading a sect therein. He is a priest at the head of his worshipers. . . . Robespierre preaches; Robespierre censures; he is furious, grave, melancholy, exalted—all coldly; his thoughts flow regularly, his habits are regular; he thunders against the rich and the great; he lives on next to nothing; he has no necessities. He has but one mission—to speak—and he speaks unceasingly; he creates disciples, . . . he talks of God and of Providence; he calls himself the friend of the humble and the weak; he gets himself followed by women and by the poor in spirit; he gravely receives their adoration. . . . He is a priest and will never be other than a priest.[30]

Condorcet's characterization was ill intentioned, but there is plenty of other evidence that Robespierre had a peculiar appeal for women. Olympe de Gouges, a butcher's daughter and pioneering feminist, wrote to him at this time, suggesting they drown themselves together in the Seine as an act of extreme patriotism: in this way, she suggested, he could cleanse himself of the stains that had sullied his reputation since 10 August.[31] Robespierre, understandably, preferred to redeem his reputation by more conventional methods.

Before the Convention, he denied outright having played any part in the election of Marat. He confirmed that he had met him privately in January 1792. At that meeting they had spoken of public affairs and Marat had been despondent. "I told him myself what all patriots, even the most ardent, thought of him."[32] Robespierre described to the Convention how he had reproached Marat for inciting extreme violence in his editorials; calling for five or six hundred guilty heads to be lopped off was, he insisted, as repugnant to the friends of liberty as to the aristocracy. After "that first and unique visit" he had encountered Marat next in the Convention itself, where he was amazed to find himself accused of having schemed to get him elected. There were elements of truth in this retrospective account. Strictly speaking, it was

Danton and the Cordeliers, not Robespierre, who had proposed Marat. But certainly Robespierre had not opposed Marat's candidacy; in fact, he had favored it. For the benefit of the deputies, and cheered on by all those admiring women in the galleries, he was expertly managing the truth, staying as close to it as possible while massaging it to produce a particular impression, as all skilled politicians do.

It was when he came to the subject of the September Massacres that Robespierre made a truly staggering announcement:

> It is certain that one innocent person perished [an alleged victim of mistaken identity]; the numbers have been exaggerated, but one [innocent] without doubt [perished]. We should weep, citizens, at this cruel mistake, and we have wept over it for a long time. He was said to be a good citizen and was therefore one of our friends. We should weep also for the guilty victims, reserved for the vengeance of the laws, who fell beneath the blade of popular justice; but let this grief have an end, like all mortal things. Keep back some tears for more touching calamities; weep instead for the hundred thousand victims of tyranny.[33]

The kinds of comparison Robespierre calls for in this speech are morally disturbing. Were the deaths of forty-three frightened children at the Bicêtre reformatory really less moving than the deaths of the many more who never had enough to eat, never had a real hope or start in life under the old regime? Were the deaths of those cornered, defenseless priests any less disturbing than the persecutions inflicted on nonbelievers in the past? Robespierre was defending the Revolution and himself; the two were scarcely distinct in his mind anymore. He argued that the end of the Revolution—liberty—justified its means—bloodshed—and asked a chilling political question, destined to reverberate down the centuries: "Citizens, do you want a revolution without a revolution?"[34] To people who complained that the Insurrectionary Commune of 10 August had done illegal things, he replied, "The Revolution is illegal: the fall of the Bastille and of the monarchy were illegal—as illegal as liberty itself!"[35]

There can be little doubt that however much he preferred to distinguish himself publicly from Marat's tasteless and flamboyant calls for violence, Robespierre was quite prepared to sanction it in practice. He believed violence indispensable for advancing the political experiment on which he had staked his life. The Girondins were no different. Their fight with Robespierre, Danton, and Marat was about who would control the new republic, not whether or not it was legitimate to use violence in bringing it into existence. Louvet tried to reply to Robespierre's speech, but this time he was howled down. Dr. Moore recorded that another of the deputies, Bertrand Barère, a suave lawyer from the Midi soon to be known as "the Anacreon of the Guillotine," brought the venomous debate to a close with incomparable condescension:

> It is time to estimate those little undertakers of revolutions at their just value; it is time to give over thinking of them and their manoeuvres: for my part, I can see neither Sullas nor Cromwells in men of such moderate capacities; and instead of bestowing any more time on them and their intrigues, we ought to turn our attention to the great questions which interest the republic.[36]

That night Robespierre's speech was celebrated in the Jacobin Club as a resounding success. Louvet, unsurprisingly, had been expelled, just like Brissot. The club was now, more than ever, the Incorruptible's domain. But he could not savor his triumph. He went home, collapsed, and did not speak in the Convention again until 30 November. He was ill for nearly a month, not in the Duplay household but in rooms around the corner in the rue Saint-Florentin, to which Charlotte had at last managed to make him move. Why was he ill? His immune system seems to have been weak at the best of times, and this was far from the best of times. The nervous strain of defending himself in the Convention had clearly taken its toll. Overwork, the approach of winter, the rivalry between his sister and his landlady all weighed on him. To make matters worse, Charlotte attempted to conceal Robespierre's illness from Mme Duplay, judging that "his indisposition was nothing serious. He needed a lot of care and I certainly made sure that he got it."[37] When Mme Duplay eventually found out, she was furious and demanded Robespierre's immediate return to the rue Saint-Honoré. According to Charlotte, he resisted at first but soon gave in because he did not want to hurt the Duplays' feelings: "They love me so, they have such consideration, such kindness for me, that it could only be ingratitude on my part to reject them."[38] Years later, Charlotte was still complaining that he had sacrificed her feelings to those of Mme Duplay. Evidently she shared his propensity for lasting personal offense, even when none had been intended. For her, as for him, it was the principle that mattered. "He ought not" to have done it, she says over and over again. While Robespierre's principles were broader and grander than his sister's domestic codes of conduct, the tenacity with which each held fast was remarkably similar.

Throughout this period, Robespierre was absent from the Jacobins. By the time he returned to the club, Mirabeau's posthumous reputation had been ruined by the dramatic discovery of his secret letters of advice to Louis XVI. The ransacked Tuileries were being renovated as the new home for the Convention, and the letters had been discovered in a locked chest on 20 November. It was 5 December before Robespierre addressed the club on the subject of its disgraced ex-leader, whose bust still presided over its meetings and whose remains had been laid to rest with such pomp and ceremony in the Pantheon. At the time of his death popular sentiment had called for Mirabeau to be eulogized and Robespierre, "the organ of the people," had gone along with it. Now he spoke in support of Duplay's suggestion that the bust of Mirabeau should be removed from the Jacobin hall. His bust in the Manège had already been covered with a black veil, pending the report of a committee investigating the discovery at the Tuileries. The Jacobins were less restrained. They fetched ladders and pulled down the busts of both Mirabeau and the philosopher Helvétius, who, Robespierre reminded them, had persecuted Rousseau and shown counterrevolutionary tendencies before his time. The busts were smashed and the Jacobins made a show of trampling the pieces into the floor—a parody of the civic spirit that had prevailed when they trampled the Champ de Mars to prepare it for the first anniversary of the fall of the Bastille. The hostile *Patriote français* reported the incident with some glee:

> This evening the Jacobins broke the bust of Mirabeau in their hall. It was on Robespierre's motion that this execution was carried out, just as it was on Robespierre's motion that Mirabeau was accorded the honors

of the Pantheon. This is how demagogues sanctify popular idols to please worshipers, then break the idols in order to succeed them.[39]

In response, Robespierre composed a letter to the paper that stands out from the rest of his writings and speeches in being an apology, not a personal defense: "I feel remorse today for the first time in my life; for I may have let it be believed that I shared the good opinion of Mirabeau held by the [National] Assembly and by the general public."[40] As apologies go, Robespierre's was hardly abject. But by his own standards—he was not and never had been wrong—it was remarkable. The fact was that not even he could deny that at the time of Mirabeau's death only Marat had dared criticize Mirabeau in public. On 4 April 1791, *L'ami du peuple* had declared:

> People, give thanks to the gods! Your most redoubtable enemy has fallen beneath the scythe of Fate. Riquetti [Mirabeau] is no more; he dies victim of his numerous treasons, victim of his too tardy scruples, victim of the barbarous foresight of his atrocious accomplices. Adroit rogues who are to be found in all circles have sought to play upon your pity, and already duped by their false discourse, you mourn this traitor as the most zealous of your defenders; they have represented his death as a public calamity, and you bewail him as a hero, as the savior of your country, who has sacrificed himself for you. Will you always be deaf to the voice of prudence; will you always sacrifice public affairs to your blindness? . . . Beware of prostituting your incense.[41]

Irresponsible, crazy, disconcerting as ever—still Marat definitely had a gift for prophecy. Robespierre never had his clinical capacity to fearlessly diagnose the pathology of politics. But even now that Marat had been proved so devastatingly right—Mirabeau had been a double-crossing traitor and there were documents to prove it—Robespierre resisted identifying with him. On 23 December the Jacobins circulated a memorandum to their affiliated societies warning true patriots not to confound Robespierre and Marat. The prudent patriotism, statesman-like views, and superior abilities of the former were on no account to be confused with the sanguinary gutter journalism of the latter.

* * *

THE QUESTION OF putting Louis XVI on trial was first discussed in the Convention on 13 November. Ill though he was, Robespierre made a point of attending. The Convention, determined not to get sidetracked by another protracted fight between the Mountain and the Girondins, focused the debate on three questions: Can the king be judged? By whom ought he to be judged? And in what respect may he be judged? Charles Morisson, deputy for the Vendée, was the first to speak in defense of the king. He reminded the Convention that the constitution of 1791 had declared that "the person of the king is inviolable and sacred." For this reason, he could not be brought to trial:

> Citizens, like you I am overcome with the greatest indignation when I consider the many crimes, the atrocities, with which Louis XVI is stained. My first and doubtless most natural impulse is to see this bloody monster expiate his crimes by the cruellest torments that can be devised. I know that he has earned them all. Yet I must deny my impulse: before this tribunal, representing a free people who seek happiness and prosperity in acts that are just, in acts that are humane, generous, and kind, because only through such acts can happiness be found, I must deny my impulse, and heed instead the voice of Reason, consult the spirit and the disposition of our law, seek only the interest of my fellow citizens, for that alone must be the single goal of all our deliberations.[42]

Already in his fifties, Morisson, unlike most of his younger colleagues in the Convention, had adult memories of the reigns of two French kings. He had not been a mere schoolboy, like Robespierre and Danton, when Louis XV died and his grandson was crowned Louis XVI in 1775. It was rumored that, in his heart, Morisson still believed in the sanctity of kingship. But his argument turned on law, not religion. He could see that, in the circumstances, an appeal to the failed constitution of 1791 was Louis XVI's best hope.

Immediately after Morisson, Saint-Just, deputy for Picardy, stepped up to the podium. Twenty-five, handsome, well-dressed, and self-confident, Saint-Just had long coveted a more prominent role in the Revolution—and a closer relationship to Robespierre. "You whom I know, as I know God, only through his miracles," he wrote to him back in 1790.[43] He had tried to stand for election to the Legislative Assembly in 1791 but was disqualified when the irate father of his young mistress pointed out that at twenty-four he had not yet reached the minimum age to stand as a deputy. A year later, a year older, he had at last been elected to the Convention. Now he settled himself, took a breath, and began his maiden speech. It brought him everlasting fame:

> I say that the King should be judged as an enemy; that we must not so much judge him as combat him; that as he had no part in the contract which united the French people, the forms of judicial procedure here are not to be sought in positive law, but in the law of nations. . . . Some day men will be astonished that in the eighteenth century humanity was less advanced than in the time of Caesar. Then, a tyrant was slain in the midst of the Senate, with no formality but thirty dagger blows, with no law but the liberty of Rome. And today, respectfully, we conduct a trial for a man who was the assassin of a people, taken *in flagrante*, his hand soaked with blood, his hand plunged in crime. . . . Citizens, if the people of Rome, after six hundred years of virtue and hatred for kings, if Great Britain, after the death of Cromwell, saw kings reborn despite their energy, what must these good citizens among us fear, those who are friends of liberty, seeing the axe tremble in our hands, seeing a people, from the first day of its liberty, respect the memory of its chains! . . . For myself, I can see no mean: this man must reign or die.[44]

Reign or die—one or the other, Saint-Just insisted, his political logic slicing through Morisson's legal argument like a freshly sharpened blade. Then, as if he had not done enough to dazzle posterity and make the Convention swoon, he pronounced the sentence that would never be forgotten: *On ne peut point régner innocemment*—no one can reign innocently. The king, he repeated at the end of his speech, must be judged as an enemy. He was the murderer of the Bastille, of Nancy, of the Champ de Mars, of the Tuileries. What enemy had ever done more harm? When he had finished, Saint-Just proudly stepped down from the tribune. He walked back to his seat, carrying his head, as Camille Desmoulins scathingly remarked, like a sacred host. Robespierre was electrified. He demanded to be heard at once, even though it was not his turn and he was not next on the list of speakers. He would not take no for an answer and caused an unseemly commotion at the tribune. He was asked if it was for or against the king's inviolability that he wanted so urgently to speak. But he would not give a straight answer, saying only that he proposed to speak "on the king's inviolability," that he must address the Convention in the wake of Saint-Just. He did not get his way and the meeting soon adjourned.

By the time the Convention resumed its discussion, the King's reputation had been even further blackened by the discovery of Mirabeau's incriminating correspondence. Meanwhile, Robespierre, reensconced at the Duplays, was feeling much better. On 3 December a brilliantly incisive speech signaled his complete return to form:

> Louis was king, and the republic is founded. The great question with which you are occupied is settled by this argument: Louis has been deposed by his crimes. Louis denounced the French people as rebels; to punish them he called upon the arms of his fellow tyrants. Victory and the people have decided that he alone was a rebel. Therefore, Louis cannot be judged; he has already been condemned, else the republic is not cleared of guilt. To propose a trial for Louis XVI of any sort is to step backward toward royal and constitutional despotism. Such a proposal is counterrevolutionary since it would bring the Revolution itself before the court. In fact, if Louis could yet be tried, he might be found innocent. . . . If Louis is acquitted, where then is the Revolution?[45]

This was Saint Just's argument, recast in Robespierre's words. Characteristically, Robespierre personified the Revolution. Whereas Saint-Just invoked the law of nations with devastating clarity, Robespierre brought it to bear on a fight to the death between the king and the Revolution. On the subject of the death penalty itself, he did not hesitate to remind the Convention that he had spoken against it at length in May 1791. Lest anyone now accuse him of inconsistency, he explained why the king's case was different:

> Public safety never calls for the death penalty against ordinary citizens because society can always prevent them by other means and render the guilty man incapable of doing further harm. But a deposed king in the midst of a revolution as yet unsupported by just laws, a

king whose very name draws the scourge of war on the restless nation: neither prison nor exile can render his existence indifferent to the public welfare. . . . Regretfully I speak this fatal truth—Louis must die because the nation must live.[46]

As Robespierre presented it, the execution of the king was to be another manifestation of the people's revolutionary justice, very different in kind from ordinary legal justice:

A people does not judge as does a court of law. It does not hand down sentences, it hurls down thunderbolts; it does not condemn kings, it plunges them into the abyss; such justice is as compelling as the justice of the courts.[47]

The justice of the courts had been Robespierre's whole life before 1789, when he exchanged it for the justice of the people: swift, inexorable, revolutionary. He found both compelling, but he knew too, from personal experience, that they were incompatible. There could not be a legal revolution or a revolution without the people's justice. When he began his new career in Versailles, Robespierre had had plenty of revolutionary instincts but no theory of revolution to guide them. After three years' hard learning he was beginning to develop such a theory. "Citizens, do you want a revolution without a revolution?" he had asked after the September Massacres.[48] Now, at the very end of 1792, he was even clearer and more explicit: any revolution must be a transitional period of struggle on the part of an entire people desiring liberty but "as yet unsupported by just laws."[49] To him this was unmistakably what the French Revolution was. He urged the Convention to execute Louis XVI without further delay, "to nourish in the spirit of tyrants a salutary terror of the justice of the people."[50]

THE FRIENDSHIP BETWEEN Saint-Just and Robespierre was spontaneous, profound, and hugely consequential for the Revolution. Beyond the powerful coincidence of their views on the king's trial, they shared an obsession with *vertu*, which can only loosely be translated into English as virtue. *Vertu* in French has the wider meaning of righteousness and is a public as well as a private good. Robespierre had read a great deal about *vertu* and its pivotal role in republican governments in the books of both Montesquieu and his beloved Rousseau. He had mentioned it already in some of his speeches, but the arrival of Saint-Just in Paris brought it to the forefront of his concerns. The two men talked often and at length. Saint-Just was the only person who dared run straight up the outside staircase into Robespierre's rooms at the Duplays'—everyone else tended to approach his quarters more tentatively, through the house. Saint-Just had about him the allure of a reformed sinner—"I have ached badly, but I shall do better," he said, aged twenty—five years later, bursting with political talent, ambition, and ideals, he renounced his mistress.[51] She followed him to Paris, but he would not open the door to her. Robespierre must have approved. The two men agreed about Christianity, too: the early Christians were austere and full of *vertu*, but things had gone badly wrong ever since. As Saint-Just wrote the year before he was elected to the Convention:

> The early Romans, Greeks, and Egyptians were Christians because they were good and kind, and that is Christianity. Most of those called Christians since the time of Constantine have been nothing but savages and madmen. Fanaticism is the work of European priest craft. A people that has suppressed superstition has made a great step toward liberty. But it must take great care not to alter its moral principles, for they are the basic law of *vertu*.[52]

Robespierre's fascination with Saint-Just was inevitable. Their unsuccessful joint attempt to stop the king's trial and have him immediately executed was just the beginning of an intense revolutionary alliance.

LOUIS XVI WAS brought to the Convention for questioning for the first time on 11 December. Inside the tower of the Temple he and the young dauphin had been kept on a different floor from the rest of their family since October. He had been teaching his young son geography and Latin, his own favorite subjects, and had devised a game with maps, an elaborate jigsaw puzzle that required the dauphin to fit countries back in their right place. When guards came to escort him to the Convention that morning, the king was separated from the boy, and he only saw his family again to say good-bye on the eve of his death. At the Convention he was interrogated by the suave deputy Bertrand Barère. Accused, among other things, of deploying troops against the citizens of Paris, he replied: "I was the master then and I sought to do what was right."[53] Afterward, in the carriage back to the Temple, he made polite small talk about the history of the streets through which he passed with the new secretary of the Paris Commune sitting beside him. He had shown similar politeness in the carriage on the way back from Varennes in April 1791, but now as then it did him little good.

The questioning continued for several days, after which the Convention postponed further discussion of the king's fate for ten days to give his lawyers a chance to prepare his case. They presented it on 26 December. Louis XVI was portrayed as a victim of circumstance, not a resolute tyrant, a monarch who had tried to do his best for the people, who had never intended bloodshed. Saint-Just was the first to respond the following day:

> Louis tainted *vertu*; to whom henceforth will it appear innocent? . . .
> Some will say that the Revolution is over, that we have nothing more
> to fear from the tyrant . . . but citizens, tyranny is like a reed that
> bends with the wind and which rises again. What do you call a Revo-
> lution? The fall of a throne, a few blows leveled at a few abuses? The
> moral order is like the physical; abuses disappear for an instant, as the
> dew dries in the morning, and as it falls again with the night, so the
> abuses will reappear. The Revolution begins when the tyrant ends.[54]

Saint-Just was already looking to the future. He wanted the king executed so the Revolution, as he understood it, could truly begin. Ultimately, Robespierre was extremely sympathetic to the thorough regeneration of the moral order that Saint-Just envisaged. But for the time being his own attention was more closely focused on defeating the Girondin deputies, who were demanding a national referendum on the king's fate. In this way, some of the Girondin deputies hoped to save the king's life, others to diminish the influence of Paris by appeal to the rest of France, all to defeat the Jacobin policy that Robespierre and Saint-Just had defined. In a long speech on 28 December, Robespierre reminded the Convention of the mistakes the National Assembly had made following the flight to Varennes, when he alone dared argue for the king to be put on trial. He characterized the demand for a referendum as yet another Girondin plot "to destroy the work of the people and to rally the enemies that they vanquished" on 10 August:

> Yes, doubtless there is a plot to degrade the Convention and perhaps to cause its dissolution as a result of this interminable question [of referendum]. . . . This plot thrives among a score of rascals who abstain above all from announcing an opinion on the question of the last king but whose silent and pernicious activity causes all the ills that trouble us and prepares all those that await us.[55]

To defeat the threatened referendum, Robespierre drew on a principle of representation that had dominated the Revolution since 1789: there could be no appeal against a body that represented the sovereign will of the people. The National Assembly in 1789 was such a body, as was the Convention in 1792. The principle was clear enough, but in his fevered exposition of it, Robespierre's speech became obscure, his logic hard to follow:

> The general will is not formed in secret conventicles or around the tables of ministers. The minority retains an inalienable right to make heard the voice of truth, or what it regards as such. *Vertu* is always in the minority on this earth.[56]

At this, Marat, who was on the same side but as independent and outspoken as usual, shouted: "All this is nothing but charlatanism!"[57] Most of the Jacobins were more appreciative of Robespierre's speech, and two days later the club suspended all other business so he could solemnly read it aloud again. Afterward he published it in his journal, along with criticisms of his old enemy Brissot. But Brissot had certainly not given up the fight against the Mountain. As the unofficial leader of the Girondins (who were sometimes even referred to as the Brissotins), he continued proposing measures to diminish the influence of Paris and its delegates over the Convention. He proposed abolishing the permanence of the Paris sections, which, together with the Jacobins, were the chief support of the Mountain. Robespierre took the tribune in opposition but could not be heard above shouts of "Censure him! Lynch him!" from the other end of the hall. Once again, the Manège resounded with violent remarks, personal abuse flying back and forth between the factions, and in the middle of it all Marat outdoing himself with contributions euphemistically described in the official minutes as "unacademic phrases."[58] The president rang his bell for order until it broke in his hands. When at last he could make himself heard, he censured everyone: Robespierre, Brissot, Marat, the rest of the assembly, and the public in the galleries, too. One observer said the scene far surpassed a cockfight.[59]

On 14 January the Convention unanimously voted the king guilty. On 15 January the call for a referendum on his fate was defeated by 424 votes to 287; led by Robespierre, all twelve deputies from the Department of Paris opposed it. On 16 January voting began on the king's sentence, with each deputy giving his opinion and explaining his reasons. The session continued all day, all night, all the following day and night, and on into the 18 January. An eyewitness said, "It is impossible to describe the agitation, even to madness, of that long and convulsive sitting":

> One would naturally suppose that the Convention was a scene of meditation, silence and a sort of religious terror. Not at all: the end of the hall was transformed into a kind of opera-box, where ladies in charming negligés were eating ices and oranges, drinking liqueurs, and receiving the compliments and salutations of those coming and going. . . . On the side of the Mountain, the Duchess Dowager [a relation by marriage of the king's], the Amazon of the Jacobin bands, made long "Haha's!" when she heard the word "death" strongly twang in her ears.
>
> The lofty galleries, assigned to the people during the days that preceded this famous trial, were never empty of strangers and people of every class, who drank wine and brandy as if it had been a tavern. Bets were open at all the neighbouring coffeehouses.[60]

There was such confusion, such variety of opinion as to what the King's punishment should be, that it was very difficult to collate the results. Of the 721 deputies who voted, at least 361 had to have voted for death for this to be the majority outcome. On the night of 17 January, the president announced that 365 had indeed done so. The next morning Barrère took over as president (the role was routinely rotated) and revised the figure to only 361—the barest majority. To this day there is disagreement about the actual figures but no disagreement at all about the narrowness of the margin that decided the king's fate. When someone questioned whether a mere majority was really enough to condemn him, Danton retorted:

> You decided the Republic by a mere majority, you changed the whole history of the nation by a mere majority, and now you think the life of one man too great for a mere majority; you say such a vote could not be decisive enough to make blood flow. When I was on the frontier the blood flowed decisively enough.[61]

Throughout the whole protracted process, Robespierre worked zealously to ensure the king's execution. On 16 January, as he was polled for his opinion, he gave what was, by his standards, a short speech, advocating death:

> I am inflexible in relation to oppressors because I am compassionate toward the oppressed; I do not recognize the humanity that butchers the people and pardons despots. The sentiment that led me to demand, in vain, in the National Assembly the abolition of the death penalty is the same as that forcing me today to demand that it is applied to the tyrant of my fatherland, and the king in person.[62]

It was not enough for him to argue that Louis XVI was an exception to the general case he had made against capital punishment; for the sake of his own sense of perfect consistency, Robespierre had to go a step further and argue that the same principle underpinned his two conflicting opinions. The following morning, before the first count of the votes, the Convention received a letter from the king's lawyers asking to be heard again. Danton said yes, after the result was known. Robespierre said no, the Convention should proceed straight to other business: "Never when an accused person is definitively condemned do his defenders have the right to an extension; I demand the order of the day." When the result was known later that day, he spoke again, insisting there must be no further appeal beyond the Convention:

> The nation has condemned the king who oppressed it, not simply to execute a great act of vengeance; it has condemned him to give a great example to the world, to affirm French liberty, to evoke liberty in Europe, and, above all, to affirm among you public tranquillity.[63]

After this, the only hope for the king was a reprieve, or postponement of his sentence. For twenty-four hours the Girondin leaders tried to save him this way—tried also to secure their own victory over the Jacobin faction. Robespierre intervened three times to make sure they did not succeed. Most notably, on the night of 19 January, he led the Paris deputies in voting against the reprieve, and it was defeated 380 votes to 310. In the circumstances, 70 votes was a narrow enough margin to mean that, without Robespierre's special exertions, Louis XVI might have lived. Robespierre fought for the king's death with a religious solemnity that had nothing in common with the ribald vulgarity of the brandy-swilling public in the galleries. It is true that he was backed all the way by the radical Paris sections, backed in their turn by revolutionaries throughout France. But his sensibility was all his own. The evening before the execution, scheduled to occur as soon as possible on 21 January, Robespierre told the Jacobins to present in the morning "a calm demeanor, so dignified and formidable that it will freeze with fear the enemies of freedom." The Girondin Condorcet had been absolutely right to identify Robespierre as the high priest of Revolution.

Louis XVI's chief lawyer was Chrétien Guillaume de Lamoignon de Malesherbes, the great-grandfather of Alexis de Tocqueville, who would write one day of the inevitable progress of equality and democracy in France (and America) that Robespierre, in advance of his time, fought for with such passion. After the Convention had counted and recounted its votes, Malesherbes ascended the narrow winding stairs of the Temple tower to tell the king he must die. Halfway through their interview, he broke down and fell weeping to the floor. Recovering himself, he said, "But, Sire, these wretches are not yet our masters, and every honest man will endeavor to save Your Majesty or to die at your feet."[64] The king replied:

> M. de Malesherbes, such proceedings would involve a great many persons and would incite a civil war in Paris. I had rather die. You will therefore, I entreat of you, command them from me to make no effort to save me—the King of France never dies![65]

"The king is dead! Long live the king!" This famous cry had echoed through the centuries down the long line of French monarchs, marking the times when they passed the crown uninterruptedly one to another: to Louis XVI from his grandfather Louis XV, to him from the Sun King Louis XIV, to him from Louis XIII, the successor of Henry IV, the first of the Bourbon branch of the Capetian dynasty founded by Hugues Capet in 987 after the demise of Frankish power.[66] It was this cry that sustained the last of their line when he learned that, like none of his predecessors, he was to die on the scaffold. He saw his family for the final time on the evening of Sunday, 20 January, told his son never to think of avenging his death, and gave both his children his blessing. Marie Antoinette wanted the family to stay together all night, but the king needed to be alone with his priest. He told his wife he would see her again in the morning—the tenderest of marital white lies, for he knew he could not stand to confront her grief on his way to execution. After they left, he asked the guards not to permit his family to return. He spent until midnight with the abbé Henry Essex Edgeworth de Firmont, a Roman Catholic priest of Irish birth whom he had specially requested.

He was awoken by drums outside at 5:00 a.m. The priest said Mass and administered Holy Communion. On his way to execution, Louis XVI read more prayers, the special ones for those at the point of death. He wanted to address the people from the scaffold, but the drums beat loud to prevent him. He was asked to remove his coat and resisted at first—surely they could execute him as he was? When it was explained that the collar of his coat might obstruct the blade of the guillotine, he consented and removed it himself. Then they wanted to tie his hands. Again, he resisted—surely that gratuitous humiliation was unnecessary? The abbé Edgeworth helped him by reminding him that Christ's hands had been tied at the Crucifixion. He helped him again by proclaiming as the blade fell: "Son of Saint Louis, ascend to heaven!" The executioner showed the king's head to the people. Some of them surged forward to dip handkerchiefs or pieces of paper in his blood. One was inspired to mimic a priest blessing the congregation with holy oil:

> One citizen got up to the guillotine itself, and, plunging his whole arm into the blood of Capet, of which a great quantity remained, he took up handfuls of the clotted gore, and sprinkled it over the crowd below, which pressed round the scaffold, each anxious to receive a drop on his forehead. "Friends," said this citizen, in sprinkling them, "we were threatened that the blood of Louis should be on our heads; and so you see it is!"[67]

Alone in her room, Marie Antoinette had not slept, had not even undressed for bed. At 6:15 a.m. guards had come, to take her to the king, she thought, but they were only looking for a prayer book for the King's last Mass. She had waited all morning, still thinking she would see him again, until shouts of joy from the crowd below told her he was dead. Hearing the jubilant cries, Marie Antoinette stood like a statue in a state of silent, choking agony. When at last she roused herself, she asked to see one of the men who had been in the king's rooms until he was taken away. This man gave her back her wedding ring with a message from the king—he would never have parted with it but with his life. She turned it over in her hand. Inside it was engraved: M.A.A.A. 19 Aprille, 1770.[68] Marie Antoinette, archduchess of Austria, had married the heir to the French throne twenty-three years earlier. Now she had to ask his executioners' permission to wear mourning.

Robespierre had breakfast as usual that day with the Duplays. Elisabeth, the younger of the daughters, to whom he was always so kind, asked him why there were so many people out in the street at that early hour. He told her something was happening that she should not see and asked one of the household servants to shut the great outer door that opened from the carpenter's courtyard onto the rue Saint-Honoré. Later in the morning, Louis XVI passed that closed door with his priest, guards, and a vast, silent crowd of the French people. It was in the name of those people that the king was guillotined, just around the corner from the Duplays, on what had once been the place Louis XV and was now the place de la Révolution. Robespierre had counseled solemnity to the Jacobins. He was solemn himself that morning: he turned his back on the public spectacle that he had persuaded the Convention was indispensable for the future of the republic but that he did not himself care to witness.

PART V

THE TERROR

(1793–1794)

9

THE PACT WITH VIOLENCE

News of Louis XVI's execution spread like a stain across Europe. In England Prime Minister Pitt pronounced it "the foulest and most atrocious deed which the history of the world has yet had occasion to attest."[1] In Russia Catherine the Great, shocked and grieving, took to her bed and decreed six weeks' mourning for her whole court. Spain immediately recalled its ambassador. Public opinion in all these countries turned unremittingly against the Revolution. The reaction in America was more ambivalent—distant support for the embattled new republic, mingled with sorrow for its regal victim, who, in his time, had supported the colonists in their struggle to found their own modern republican government on the other side of the Atlantic. "As Americans we regret the loss of the life of the King," wrote the religious minister and diarist William Bentley, "but we remember the liberties of mankind are dearer than any life whatever."[2]

The regicide transformed the war. By November 1792, after the battle of Valmy and one subsequent victory at Jemappes, French forces had overrun the entire Austrian Netherlands. French armies in the south and on the Rhine were also advancing the new republic's borders. Brissot's vision of a proselytizing war to consolidate the Revolution by carrying it abroad seemed realized, and the Convention promised to "accord fraternity and help to all peoples who wish to recover their liberty."[3] It also demanded that the territories it "liberated" contribute to the cost of France's conquests. Danton went on mission to the armies in the Austrian Netherlands in December 1792 and saw blood flowing freely at the front line. He declared that "the limits of France are marked out by nature. We shall reach them at their four points: at the ocean, at the Rhine, at the Alps, at the Pyrenees." Belgium would have to be incorporated into France.

Ten days after Louis XVI's execution, the Convention declared war on England and the Dutch Republic. This was a preemptive strike, since Prime Minister Pitt had already cleared funds with Parliament for war against a country prepared to murder its king, and the Dutch Republic, situated between France and the Rhine, was also preparing for war. In March war was declared on Spain also. Danton—who had rung the tocsin and roused the people to fight before Valmy—left again on a mission to the army in the north, this time burdened by concern for his gravely ill wife, Gabrielle, whom he had once wooed romantically in Italian and still deeply loved. He arrived in Belgium, demanding its annexation to France, on 3 February and began the journey back to Paris on 15 February. He returned to a cold, empty house: no fire, no children, and no wife. In his absence, Gabrielle had died and the children had been taken to their grandmother. Danton went straight to the graveyard and dug Gabrielle's coffin out of the dank earth in which she had been lying for four days. He prized off the lid to hold her and see her face one last time. He summoned a sculptor to the grisly scene and commissioned not a death mask but a bust of the lifeless woman. Then he went home to the letter from Robespierre that said, "I love you more than ever, I love you until death. At this moment, I am you."[4]

His mind macabre and full of battlefields, his heart ravaged by grief, his eyes distracted by hungry, rioting, destitute Parisians, and his ears ringing with reports of the Royalist and Catholic discontent in the Vendée (an especially religious region south of Brittany), Danton now did something that a year later he would beg forgiveness for at the foot of the guillotine. He persuaded the Convention to revive

the Revolutionary Tribunal, with its extraordinary powers to condemn people to death (the Convention had disbanded the Revolution's first extraordinary tribunal at the start of the king's trial). Now
Robespierre fully supported Danton's call for its reestablishment and
further proposed that capital punishment be meted out for counterrevolutionary acts of any kind directed "against the security of the
state, or the liberty, equality, unity and indivisibility of the Republic."[5] A majority of the Convention deputies opposed the reconstitution of the tribunal. After long debate, the project was nearly
abandoned when, toward midnight, Danton hastened to the Manège.
Speaking ominously in the candlelight he warned his exhausted colleagues that there was no longer any alternative to the tribunal, except a bloodbath in the streets. This was not a strong but a desperate
argument. During its first incarnation, at Robespierre's instigation after 10 August 1792, the tribunal had done nothing to prevent the
September Massacres; what reason was there to believe it could—or
would—prevent further bloodshed by resuming its summary powers
over life and death? Danton saw the tribunal as an overwhelmingly
powerful weapon in the hands of the government, the last hope for
restoring order in a starving, anarchic country rent by civil strife and
foreign war. He never expected it would be used against himself, but
on the scaffold before his execution he said: "This time twelve
months ago I proposed that infamous tribunal by which we die and
for which I beg pardon of God and man."[6] The Convention agreed to
the Revolutionary Tribunal on 10 March. It consisted of twelve jurors, a public prosecutor (Antoine Fouquier-Tinville), and two substi-
tutes; there could be no appeal against its judgments. By law the Paris
sections were supposed to elect the members of the tribunal, who officiated wearing dark clothes and black plumes in their hats, but this
never happened. Instead, the Commune chose them.[7] At Fouquier-
Tinville's own trial (in 1795, after the fall of Robespierre) it emerged
that many of the jurors on the tribunal had been unable to read or
write and were often drunk.

Conditions in Paris were indeed deteriorating rapidly. On the evening of 9 March, armed bands had marauded through the city, smashing the print shops that produced Girondin journals.[8] The Girondins

were hated in Paris for trying to diminish the city's role in the Revolution. The next day, the mob attempted another insurrection. The city gates were closed. The tocsin was rung. Disaffected Parisians demanded the arrest of all suspect army generals, ministers, and all the leading Girondin deputies. Even more radical than the sans-culottes, these petitioners wanted a "maximum" price imposed on basic commodities that were increasingly difficult to obtain due to the economic strains of war and rapid inflation; recently there had been a wave of attacks on grocery shops and warehouses. They demanded an end to private property, radical social leveling through price controls and redistribution of wealth. The Girondins blamed Marat for inciting such violence, but the Jacobins and the Mountain deputies distanced themselves from it, referring to the radical petitioners as rabid *enragés*. There is no evidence that Robespierre wanted or approved of the new insurrection, and the Commune decided not to support it. The National Guard was instructed to maintain order, and the insurgent *enragés* failed in their objectives on 10 March.

Meanwhile, the news from the front line was not encouraging. The French were struggling. The invasion of Holland began in February. At first all went according to plan, but then at the battle of Neerwinden on 18 March, French troops under the command of General Charles Dumouriez, the hero of the battle of Valmy, were routed by the enemy and fled headlong from the field. Holland had not been conquered and now Belgium was almost lost. By this point, Dumouriez felt little more sympathy with the Girondin or Jacobin factions than General Lafayette had before him. Unlike Lafayette, Dumouriez had had allegiances with both factions in the past and had accepted the destruction of the monarchy on 10 August. But he remained a royalist at heart and threatened now to march back to the capital and preside over a regency for young Louis XVII, who was currently ailing in the Tower. Amid the panic in Paris the Convention decided to set up surveillance committees (*comités de surveillance*) in every municipality throughout the country to scrutinize the activities of foreigners and suspects.[9]

Soon after the fiasco of Neerwinden, Danton set off to the army for a third time, to meet with Dumouriez and attempt to reconcile him to the republican government. His mission was not successful and he was back in Paris when Dumouriez finally deserted to the Austrians at the beginning of April. The time had come to put the new weapon of the Revolutionary Tribunal into hands capable of wielding it, and to this end Danton, again speaking dramatically by candlelight at midnight, urged the Convention to create the Committee of Public Safety, a provisional revolutionary government briefed to supervise and accelerate the exercise of ministerial power. When the Convention had first met in September 1792 it had established a Committee of General Security with extensive policing responsibilities. But now a smaller, more dynamic executive committee was called for, not to replace the Committee of General Security but to work alongside it.[10] Over time the relationship between the two committees, both of them formally responsible to the Convention, became extremely fraught. Nine deputies were chosen for the new Committee of Public Safety, whose members had to be reelected every month. Danton was one of them. The others were Bertrand Barère, Jean Delmas, Jean Bréard, Pierre Joseph Cambon, Louis Guyton, Jean-Baptiste Treilhad, Jean Delacroix, and Jean Lindet. Significantly, none were Girondins, who opposed the creation of such a committee, fearing in advance that they would be excluded from it. And so the factional fight that had begun when Robespierre first opposed Brissot's war policy at the end of 1791 entered its last phase with the Girondins at a serious disadvantage. They had failed to save the king, failed to prevent the resurrection of the Revolutionary Tribunal, and failed to avert the Committee of Public Safety. These three failures together were soon to lead to the death of Brissot, of twenty of his colleagues in the Convention, and of Mme Roland, who once pored over a map of France imagining how it might be divided.

The new republic urgently needed a bigger army if it was going to recover from recent defeats and win the foreign war. To provide recruits the Convention resorted to conscription—a levy of three hundred thousand—and decreed a quota for each of the eighty-three departments: if there were not enough volunteers, unwilling men were to be drafted by drawing lots. At this, the discontent in the Vendée escalated into horrifying civil war. Earlier in the year the Convention had begun dispatching some of its members to visit and report on the provinces, but now, in the hands of the new Committee of

Public Safety and with the outbreak of civil war, these "representatives on mission" were invested with new repressive powers. Personally entrusted with the exercise of sovereign authority, they were sent out in pairs to designated departments to oversee the levy, mandated to do whatever was necessary to ensure its success. In theory their purpose was to strengthen the republic's centralized government, but in practice the Committee of Public Safety found it hard to control its own representatives on mission, who, in some cases, deviated sharply from official policies, imposing extraordinary taxes, raising private armies, and committing shameful acts of spoliation, violation, and murder.[11] Another emergency measure that would prove hard to control over time was Danton's suggestion for a Revolutionary Army of sansculottes to go out into the countryside and requisition grain and other food supplies.

Robespierre was now more publicly hysterical than ever, obsessed with death, convinced he was about to be assassinated, and constantly offering himself for martyrdom, as though that would resolve any of the Revolution's problems. Fear most the enemy within, he warned the Jacobins again; the most dangerous traitors were not on the front line but mingling in disguise among the patriots in Paris. The time had come to choose between slavery and death: "We know how to die, and we will all die," he announced triumphantly at the end of a speech on 13 March.[12] "All! All!" echoed voices around the hall. Then Marat stood up and said, "No! We are not going to die; we will give death to our enemies, we will erase them!"[13] Two weeks later, Robespierre had imbibed some of Marat's fighting spirit. Speaking again at the Jacobins on the dangers menacing France, and the vigorous measures required to combat them, he asked, "Must we despair of the safety of the republic? No! Tyrants unmasked are nothing. The French people are only betrayed because they want to be; the French people are stronger than all their enemies. One republican who knows how to die can exterminate all the despots."[14] Such flamboyance went down well with his audience, who applauded vigorously, but in itself it hardly amounted to a strategy for saving the Revolution. Yet Robespierre had such a strategy, one that converged with Danton's. He, too, wanted a strong government, an end to the separation of power between the legislature and the executive, in this time of crisis. But here even the Jacobins thought Robespierre had gone too far, while the Girondins accused him of aspiring to dictatorship. He retorted by denying even that he wanted to become a minister. At this someone in the Convention laughed openly.[15]

When news of Dumouriez's treachery reached Paris, Robespierre seized on yet another weapon in the fight with the Girondins, striving to implicate Brissot, Pétion, and their associates in the general's spectacular betrayal of France. His move was both aggressive and self-defensive. The Girondins would happily have held Dumouriez against Robespierre, Danton, and the rest of the Jacobins if they could, and questions were already being asked as to why, when Danton went to the army a third time and met with Dumouriez, he had failed to denounce him as a traitor. Robespierre was exposed, too, for just weeks earlier he had publicly expressed full confidence in Dumouriez and his command of the foreign war. Characteristically, he did not say he had been wrong. Instead he deftly reworked the reasons he had given for trusting Dumouriez so that, in retrospect, they sounded far more conditional and skeptical than they had at the time. Simultaneously he insisted, over and over again, that Dumouriez had been collaborating with Brissot—surely the time had come at last to take action against the man responsible for plunging the country into a disastrous war well over a year ago. "Dumouriez and Brissot were the first apostles of the war," he told the Convention, bending the facts to his advantage.[16] As ever he spoke of plots and hidden enemies. "If you wish, I will raise a corner of the veil," he tantalized his colleagues. "Raise it all!" they pleaded.

This time the conspiracy Robespierre outlined had international components: it connected Prime Minister Pitt with General Dumouriez, the Girondin faction, property owners in France fearful for their assets, and the nobility hoping to recover their old regime privileges. Conspiracy on this scale was a figment of Robespierre's fevered imagination. Yet he was absolutely correct to identify private property as the new focus of contention in the Revolution. The Girondins envisaged a republic with strong protection for private property and differences in the personal wealth of individual citizens. The Jacobins, led by Robespierre, distanced themselves from the radical demands of the *enragés*, but nevertheless proposed limits to private property in the interests of the people, the majority of whom were poor. Robespierre declared:

> All the ambitious persons who have appeared until now in the theater of the Revolution have had this in common: they defend the rights of the people for only as long as seems necessary. All have regarded them [the people] as a stupid flock, destined to be led by the most able or the strongest. All have regarded representative assemblies as bodies composed of men either greedy or credulous, who can be corrupted or tricked into serving their criminal projects.[17]

His fight against the Girondins here emerges as more than personal enmity toward Brissot, who had successfully defeated his passionate crusade against the war. More, too, than hatred for Pétion, formerly his closest radical colleague, who had been—as Robespierre saw it— corrupted by power and public office. Beyond all such considerations lay Robespierre's perception that the Girondins were not as sincerely, thoroughly, uncompromisingly for the people as he was himself. If he was deceived in this—and there is plenty of evidence to suggest that he was not—the very least that can be said in his defense is that he genuinely believed he had committed himself to the people, the poor especially, and was acting accordingly to save their Revolution for them.

Disadvantaged as they now were, the Girondins nonetheless fought on. They turned on Marat, the most outspoken and provocative of all the Jacobins, whose newspaper was now emblazoned with the motto "Let us tax the rich to subsidize the poor."[18] In early April, the Girondin Marguerite-Elie Guadet denounced Marat to his fellow deputies for having plotted against the convention. He was arrested, pending an investigation into the charges against him. Robespierre, reporting these events to the Jacobins, claimed that the move against Marat was a further development in the insidious counterrevolutionary plot he had just unveiled. Guadet had "exhaled the poison of an impure soul"; he had called for the seizure of Jacobin and Cordelier newspapers and an end to the permanence of the Paris sections.[19]

Despite these attacks, Robespierre appealed for calm and cautioned the Jacobins against any actions that would only play into their enemies' hands and be held against them in the provinces where the Girondins had formidable influence. He was far from calm himself, though. On 12 April he thundered from the tribune, "I demand censure of those who protect traitors."[20] "Bravo, bravo," shouted Marat. At this Pétion rose to speak, but before he could do so Robespierre added, "And their accomplices." Pétion retorted, "Yes, their accomplices, and you yourself. It is time at last to end all this infamy; it is time that traitors and perpetrators of calumny carried their heads to the scaffold; and here I take it upon myself to pursue them to death." "Stick to the facts," said Robespierre. "It is you whom I will pursue," returned Pétion (as though anyone were in doubt). At these open menaces there was uproar. Then the painter David ran into the middle of the hall, ripped opened his shirt, and, pointing to his bare breast, cried, "Strike here! I propose my own assassination! I, too, am a man of virtue! Liberty will win in the end!"[21] Madness reigned in the Manège.

The next day, the deputies heard the report against Marat. It proposed his indictment for "pillage, murder, and attempting to dissolve the Convention."[22] They voted 226 in favor of indictment and 93 against (48 deputies were absent, 3 refused to vote, and 7 asked for an adjournment). The new Revolutionary Tribunal awaited Marat. It met inside the Palais de Justice above the Conciergerie dungeon on the small island in the Seine at the center of Paris. It used the same great room that the parlement had used before 1789, but the tapestries had been stripped from the walls, the royal fleurs-de-lys carpet rolled up, and the king's throne and Dürer's painting of Christ removed. Instead there were wooden tables, chairs, and platforms for the judges, jury, prisoners, and members of the public. Prisoners were interrogated and allowed to prepare their defense. In Marat's case this was hardly necessary. His Jacobin colleagues on the tribunal not only acquitted him but also crowned him with civic garlands. Marat was carried into the street on the shoulders of a jubilant crowd who took him straight back to the Convention, where he mounted the tribune again. He was determined on revenge against the Girondins. "I propose that the Convention shall decree complete freedom in the expression of opinion, so that I may send to the scaffold the faction that voted for my impeachment," he said soon afterward.[23]

The Paris sections, for their part, sought to avenge Marat by demanding that the Convention expel twenty-two of its leading Girondin deputies. When they presented their petition on 15 April, a Girondin named Boyer-Fonfrède, who had not been included among the twenty-two, rushed to the tribune asking to be added to the list. Cries of "Include us all! All! All!" echoed through the volatile debating chamber, and a crowd of deputies grouped themselves around the twenty-two, bodily pledging solidarity with the Girondins.[24] Two weeks later supporters of the Girondins took to the streets, marching and shouting, "Long live the law! Down with the Mountain!" In the Convention the Girondins now attacked the Commune, hoping in this way to undermine the support it had provided for the Jacobins since the insurrection that brought down the monarchy. Robespierre retaliated by claiming that the Girondin supporters had actually cried, "Long live the king! Down with the republic!" The Girondin Maximin Isnard was moved to point out that the French words for law and king (*loi* and *roi*) could easily be mistaken for each other. Robespierre ignored this smart remark and went on to defend Paris against its critics in the Convention and the provinces. Reporting his own speech afterward to the Jacobins, he said:

> I demanded that the factions in the Convention cease to slander the people of Paris and that the journalists who pervert public opinion be reduced to silence. . . . I demanded that the people make an effort to exterminate the aristocrats who are everywhere. [Loud applause.] . . . I demanded the existence in the heart of Paris of an army, not that of Dumouriez but a popular army composed of sans-culottes perpetually armed against Feuillants and moderates. I demanded the allocation of sufficient funds to arm the artisans, all the good patriots. . . . I demanded that tomorrow forges be erected in all public squares to make weapons for arming the people. . . . I demanded that the constituted authorities oversee the execution of these measures and not forget that they are the delegates of a city that is the boulevard of liberty, whose existence renders the counter-revolution impossible.[25]

The Departments of France created during the Revolution (*Musée de la Révolution Française, Vizelle: Bridgeman*)

Louis Lafitte: the twelve revolutionary months: Vendémiaire, Brumaire, Frimaire, Nivôse, Pluviôse, Ventôse, Germinal, Floréal, Prairial, Messidor, Thermidor, Fructidor (*Musée de la Ville de Paris, Musée Carnavalet, Paris: Bridgeman*)

ABOVE LEFT: Robespierre at the Tribune *(Bibliothèque Nationale, Paris)*

ABOVE RIGHT: Jean-Jacques Rousseau on a playing card of 1793 *(Musée de la Révolution Française, Vizelle: Bridgeman)*

"All mortals are born equal, it is virtue that makes the difference," 1793 *(Bibliothèque Nationale, Paris: Bridgeman)*

ABOVE: The Desmoulins family: Robespierre's godson, Horace, at center (*Château de Versailles: Bridgeman*)

LEFT: Marat—L'Ami du Peuple (*Musée Lambinet, Versailles: Bridgeman*)

Saint Just: "The words we have spoken will never be forgotten." *(Musée de la Ville de Paris, Musée Carnavalet, Paris: Bridgeman)*

Danton with his hands tied on his way to execution *(Musée de la Ville de Paris, Musée Carnavalet, Paris: Bridgeman)*

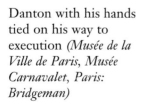

The destruction of the statue of Atheism at the Festival of the Supreme Being
(Musée de la Ville de Paris, Musée Carnavalet, Paris: Bridgeman)

French surveillance by air balloon at the battle of Fleurus *(Private Collection: Bridgeman)*

Robespierre in the
Convention, 9 Thermidor
*(Bibliothèque Nationale,
Paris)*

Robespierre lying wounded in the antechamber of the Committee of Public
Safety *(Musée de la Ville de Paris, Musée Carnavalet, Paris: Bridgeman)*

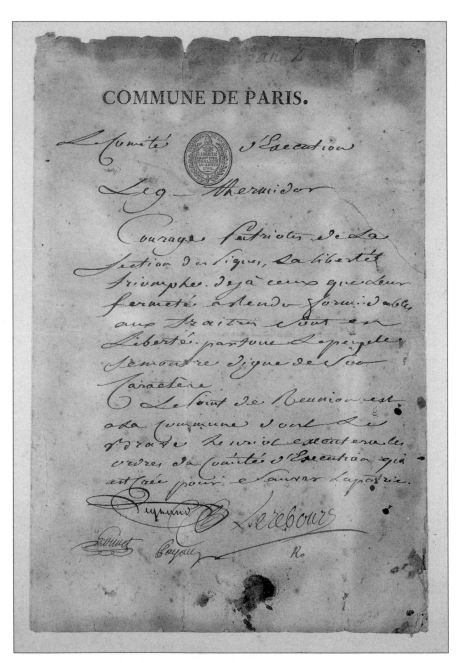

Insurrectionary summons to the Section des Piques—Robespierre's final, incomplete, signature (*Musée de la Ville de Paris, Musée Carnavalet, Paris: Bridgeman*)

In quieter times Robespierre had stalwartly defended the freedom of the press, but no longer. Now he condoned the smashing of the Girondin print shops that more violent, less articulate men than himself had already undertaken in March. At the climax of his hour-long speech he told the Jacobins that in the current crisis only the most vigorous measures could save France. If they failed, virtue would vanish from the face of the earth. It was time to see if the Jacobins truly wanted to save the human race. The club members leapt to their feet, waving hats in the air, and crying, "Yes! Yes! We want to!" Two days later, at the end of a shorter intervention, Robespierre confessed to extreme fatigue and ended with, "I have nothing more to say to you, and I have decided that, unless there is a revival of public spirit, unless the patriots make one last effort, I will wait in the seat of office to which the people have raised me for the daggers of the counterrevolution."[26]

On 11 May the sections of Paris petitioned the Convention again, still demanding the expulsion of the Girondin deputies. In reply, Isnard, a notorious hard drinker who may already have been intoxicated even though it was still early in the day, made an extremely impolitic speech:

If ever the Convention were insulted [Interruptions.]—if ever by one of those insurrections that since 10 March have been so unceasingly repeated [Violent interruptions.]—if by these incessant insurrections—any attack should be made on the national representatives, I tell you, in the name of all France [Loud negatives.]—I tell you, I repeat, in the name of all France, that Paris would be annihilated [General tumult.]—the traveller will seek along the shores of the Seine whether Paris had ever existed.[27]

The last person to utter a threat of this kind against Paris had been the Duke of Brunswick in his ill-judged manifesto of July 1792. Then the Jacobins had laughed. This time they knew at once that their lives were in danger; they had staked everything on Paris and entered a pact with the violence of its people. The suggestion that the city might be obliterated reinforced the call to arms Robespierre had recently uttered before collapsing, exhausted, into his chair. The insurrection that Isnard had condemned in advance occurred on 31 May. A great crowd of Parisian petitioners arrived at the Convention, which had recently moved from the Manège to a new chamber in the revamped Tuileries palace. The crowd entered the chamber and took possession of the deputies' seats. The Girondins protested and tried to end the session by leaving it. They returned when they saw their attempt had failed. Robespierre stepped up to the tribune and supported the petitioner's demands. "Conclude then," shouted one of the Girondins impatiently. "Yes, I shall conclude, and do so against you," he replied bitterly:

> Against you who, after the revolution of 10 August wanted to bring to the scaffold those who had accomplished it, against you who have never ceased to provoke the destruction of Paris, against you who wanted to save the tyrant, against you who conspired with Dumouriez, against you who have rabidly pursued the same patriots whose heads Dumouriez demanded [the Jacobins], against you whose criminal vengeance has provoked the same cries of indignation that you want to proscribe in those who are your victims. Ah yes! My conclusion is the decree of accusation against all the accomplices of Dumouriez and all those whom the petitioners have designated.[28]

His vehemence was vigorously applauded. But once again it had shattered him: "I am no longer capable of prescribing to the people the means of its salvation. It is a task beyond any single man's powers—certainly beyond mine, exhausted as I am by four years of revolution, and by the heart-rending spectacle of the triumph of tyranny, and of all that is most vile and corrupt."[29] There followed two further days of insurrection, during which Robespierre probably collapsed in bed while Marat, despite his debilitating skin disease, climbed the tower of the Hôtel de Ville and rang the tocsin with his own hand. On 2 June the Girondin leaders who had not already fled were provisionally arrested. François Hanriot, a former customs clerk promoted to commander of the National Guard, played a crucial part in these events. He ordered grapeshot-firing cannons, placed around the Convention, thus forcing the intimidated deputies to give in to the demands of the capital and expel the Girondins.

Mme Roland's husband was one of the Girondins who was able to flee in time, but she herself did not intend to. In the early evening she went to the Tuileries and was surprised to find that all the deputies had already gone home:

> Imagine this! A day of insurrection, when the sound of the tocsin had scarcely ceased to rend the air, when two hours previously 40,000 armed men had surrounded the Convention and petitioners were threatening members at the bar of the house. Why was the Convention not in permanent session? Had it then been entirely subjugated and agreed to do all that it was told? Was the revolutionary power now so mighty that the Convention dare not oppose it? "Citizens," I said to a bunch of sans-culottes standing around a cannon, "did everything pass off well?" "Marvellous well," they replied.[30]

Later that night she was arrested and imprisoned in the abbey of Saint-Germain-des-Prés—the scene of the first of the September Massacres, she grimly noted as she passed through the door.

IN THE MIDST of this intractable factional strife between the Jacobins and Girondins, the Convention tried to agree on France's new republican constitution. The Constitutional Committee that had been set up after the fall of the monarchy included the abbé Sieyès, still hoping to realize his elaborate theory of representative republican government, Condorcet, who had called openly for a republic in 1791, long before Robespierre dared to, and others who were loosely associated with the Girondins. On 15 April the Convention declared discussion of the constitution open and thereafter dedicated three days a week to it until it was completed. Robespierre at once intervened, insisting, against those who wanted to get on with designing the government straightaway, that the constitution must begin with a new declaration of rights, which improved on both the American example and the flawed declaration of 1789. Abstract principles were his favorite subject and as usual he spoke at length, only breaking off to remark irritably, "It is impossible for me to speak in the middle of these interruptions and sarcastic remarks!"[31] A few days later, when the discussion of specific rights began, he had this to say on the freedom of the press:

> Revolutions are made to establish the rights of man. Therefore, in the interests of these rights, it is necessary to take all measures required for the success of such revolutions. . . . The revolutionary interest might require the repression of a conspiracy founded on the liberty of the press. . . . I declare that laws expressly made for the Revolution are necessary, even if they are contrary to the freedom of the press.[32]

Thus the very same rights sought and promised by the Revolution could also be suspended, if necessary, in the Revolution's cause. Rather than hypocrisy, these views signaled a new and dangerous political pragmatism on Robespierre's part.

When discussion turned to the right to property—which had been enshrined in the declaration of 1789 alongside life and liberty—Robespierre revealed the depth of his commitment to the poor. He was not a communist before his time. He did not oppose the very existence of private property, and he deliberately distanced himself from any suggestion that the Roman *loi agraire* might be revived in revolutionary France whereby the means of subsistence would be placed in the hands of the people. "Don't worry, I don't want to touch your treasures, however impure their source," he sneeringly reassured the rich.[33] He thought making poverty honorable more important (and more practicable) than proscribing wealth. He did nevertheless go on to propose some very definite restrictions on the right to property: "The right to property is limited, like all others, by the obligation to respect the rights of others." Most significantly he called for progressive taxation, a policy that followed directly from Marat's exhortation: "Let us tax the rich to subsidize the poor." It was for this that he was eviscerated in the hostile press. "Robespierre consecrated the principle of progressive taxation, an absurd tax, destructive of equality, a tax ruinous to industry that would impede the sale of national property [confiscated from the church and émigrés]," complained the Girondin *Patriote français*, still in circulation despite recent curbs on the freedom of the press and violence directed at the

Girondin print shops.[34] While the Girondins envisaged a modern republic secured on free-market economics, Robespierre urged redistributive measures that would make a difference to the lives of the poor. After four years of revolutionary upheaval in a country that always had difficulty feeding itself, at a time when many in Paris and throughout the provinces were rioting for food, Robespierre's policy had more appeal. As he put it:

> The first social law is therefore that which guarantees the means of existence to all the members of society; all other [laws] are subordinate to this one; property is only instituted or guaranteed to affirm it. . . . It is not true that property can ever be held in opposition to man's subsistence.[35]

In other words, if the people were starving they had a right to eat, regardless of who owned the food.

Because the strife between the Jacobins and Girondins had entered so deeply into the Convention's constitutional debates—delaying and distorting them—when the Jacobins finally triumphed at the beginning of June they appointed a new committee, including Robespierre's close friends Saint-Just and Couthon, to redraft the republican constitution. This time the Convention set aside every afternoon to discuss it. France had been without a constitution for almost a year: people were becoming impatient with the protracted process of creating one. Wasting no time, the Jacobins had a draft on 10 June. "The constitution of 1793, like the world itself, was created in six days," scoffed the historian Jules Michelet.[36] It established universal male suffrage (which had seemed merely an eccentric political pipe dream when Robespierre demanded it three years earlier). The reworked Declaration of Rights made exciting new promises: welfare assistance for citizens in need and state education for all. (Robespierre had advocated both measures.) Although the new draft did not limit the right to property, Robespierre professed to be delighted: "All Europe will be constrained to admire this fine monument of human reason and of the sovereignty of a great people."[37] Europe was not currently disposed to admire France. Yet it was true that this was the most democratic constitution the modern world had seen. It was duly ratified by referendum in primary assemblies throughout the country—1,801,918 votes in favor and only 11,610 against.[38] The majority was overwhelming, but in this time of civil war the electoral turnout was low: only about a quarter of those qualified to vote cared to do so. Meanwhile, the so-called federalist revolt against the direction the Revolution had taken in Paris spread south from the town of Caen in Calvados to Bordeaux, Bourges, Lyon, Toulouse, Nîmes, Marseille, and Toulon. By mid-June, sixty of France's eighty-three departments were in open rebellion against Paris. No sooner did the new constitution come into existence than it had to be suspended. There were people in the capital who wanted—and needed—it out of the way. Saint-Just explained to the Convention:

> Your Committee of Public Safety has weighed the causes of our public misfortunes, and found them in the weakness with which your decrees are executed, in the wastefulness of the administration, in the lack of consistent policy, and in the party passions that compete for influence over the government. It has therefore resolved to explain the state of affairs to you, and to submit the measures it thinks best fitted to establish the Revolution, to confound federalism, to support and to secure abundance for the people, to strengthen the armies and to cleanse the State of the conspiracies that are the plague of its life.[39]

The Convention, in agreement with the Committee of Public Safety, or perhaps cowed by it, agreed to the continuation of provisional revolutionary government until peace was achieved at home and abroad. The Revolution was embattled and it needed a war government—strong, directive, and fearsome. Robespierre, along with Saint-Just, Danton, and Marat, had long believed that terror was the only instrument capable of saving the Revolution. None of the Jacobin leaders had pretended otherwise since the fall of the monarchy. If the Girondins had triumphed in their place, they would have needed the same weapon to restore order. "This Committee [of Public Safety] is precisely what we want," Danton had said back in April, "a hand to grasp the weapon of the Revolutionary Tribunal."[40] Three months later, after the arrest of the Girondins and the suspension of the new constitution, the path to exercising terror lay clear, demanding, and austere before the exhausted Jacobins.

* * *

THE REVOLUTION WAS an extraordinary palimpsest. With each passing year its significant dates were overwritten by still more remarkable words and events. On the eve of the fourth anniversary of the Bastille's fall, when celebrations were set to be more muted than in previous years—given the wars and the food shortages—an unknown woman of twenty-five came from Caen to Paris and inscribed her own indelible mark. Caen had become the center of Girondin resistance in the provinces. Some Girondin leaders like Pétion and Louvet, who had risen like a specter to accuse Robespierre in the Convention, had escaped arrest in the capital and reunited in Caen, from where they published a Girondin newspaper in direct defiance of the Committee of Public Safety. It was a call to rebellion that vilified the Jacobins, again singling out Marat as the most odious and culpable of them all. Charlotte Corday read this paper in her hometown and undertook a mission all her own. She traveled to Paris by coach, bought a long knife in the Palais-Royal, and called on Marat that evening in the rue des Cordeliers. He was almost always at home. He left this record of his daily regime:

> I only give two hours out of the twenty-four to sleep, and one to meals, dressing and household affairs. Besides the hours that I consecrate to my duties as a deputy of the people, I always devote six to listening to the complaints of a crowd of unfortunate and oppressed people who regard me as their defender, to forwarding their claims by means of petitions or memoranda, to reading and answering a multitude of letters, to supervising the printing of an important work that I have in the press, to making notes on all the interesting events of the Revolution, and putting my observations on paper, to receiving denunciations, and checking their veracity, and lastly to editing my paper. This is how I spend my day. I don't think I can be accused of laziness. I haven't taken a quarter of an hour's recreation for more than three years.[41]

No wonder he was ill, seeking a measure of relief from his skin disease in a medicinal bath, when Charlotte Corday came to the door. He was writing in the bath; his days were so crammed, he had to. She gave him the names of the Girondins at Caen. He thanked her and noted them down. He was making the list when she plunged the knife straight into his heart. It was not so hard to kill him, small, frail, sick, naked, defenseless figure that he was.

Robespierre, characteristically, was jealous. For months he had spoken of plots against his own life, and volunteered flamboyantly for martyrdom, while taking care to keep close to his bodyguards.[42] Now that Marat was dead he hastened to remind his colleagues at the Jacobin Club that "daggers are also marked for me."[43] He disapproved of all the interest in Marat—his poverty, his paper, his revolutionary contribution—that sprang up in the wake of his murder: "Eh! Of what importance to the republic are the financial affairs of one of its founders?"[44] Similarly, he was against honoring Marat's remains by interring them in the Pantheon. "Is it next to Mirabeau that he will be placed? [Next to] that man who merits his reputation for profound villainy? Are these the honors solicited for the Friend of the People?"[45] "Yes," interrupted a Jacobin named Bentabole, "and he shall have them despite those who are jealous of him!" Ignoring the insult, Robespierre continued: this was not the time to be distracted by funeral ceremonies—there was a war going on—Marat's honors should wait until it had been won. What should not wait was vengeance. Marat's assassin must be guillotined, along with all the other perpetrators of tyranny, all the infidel representatives of the people (the Girondins) who encouraged revolt and intended to kill the true patriots one by one. The blood of these monsters must be taken to avenge their victims, whose blood had been shed for liberty. But it was too soon to distract the Jacobins from memories of Marat. Alive, he had been a maverick in their camp, more often than not a serious embarrassment. Dead he became a hero. The next evening they voted to create a subcommittee of men of letters dedicated to keeping his spirit alive. Robespierre, meanwhile, limited himself to suggesting the Jacobin Club acquire Marat's printing presses for its own purposes.[46]

Marat's funeral became a public festival, in spite of Robespierre's advice. On the day itself he was still feeling sour and so contrived to deliver an oration in Marat's honor that pointedly avoided even mentioning his name. The artist David orchestrated the proceedings, decreeing that "Marat's burial place will have the simplicity that befits an incorruptible republican dying in honorable poverty. It was from underground that he identified the people's enemies and friends: let him rest underground in death."[47] He was interred in the garden of the Cordeliers Club. Young girls in white dresses and boys carrying branches of cypress surrounded his bier, followed by members of the Convention, the clubs, and the general public. Representatives of each of the forty-eight Paris sections filed past his grave and spoke movingly of him. His heart was suspended in an urn from the ceiling of the Cordeliers' meeting chamber—a secular relic in that requisitioned convent. In 1794, after Robespierre's own death, Marat finally made it to the Pantheon. His remains were carried in as Mirabeau's were removed, so the revolutionary and the royalist never had to lie side by side as Robespierre feared.

Why was Robespierre so sour? Did he really begrudge the murdered Marat a day of pomp and ceremony? It is only fair to point out that Robespierre felt the same way when Mirabeau died, uneasy at the distraction from the business of Revolution that a large public funeral occasioned. Back in 1791 he had been quick to remind the Jacobins that the focus of their preoccupations must remain the public interest—a grand abstraction from which personal feelings of bereavement or regard for specific individuals, whoever they were, must not detract. In 1793, too, Robespierre wanted to get on with saving the Revolution. Marat's death, now that it had occurred, might be turned to advantage in the fight against the Girondins, the rebellious departments, and the counterrevolution. He may not have cared much one way or the other for Marat as a person, but he knew a political opportunity when he saw one. It is even possible that the oration in which he failed to mention the dead man's name was itself intended to educate by example: beside the abstract principles of the Revolution mere individuals—their names, stories, and careers—no longer mattered. This reserve in Robespierre was not new. He had long prided himself, and others had never ceased to congratulate him, on being able to set the public good over his own private advantage. Like Marat, he worked incredibly hard. He attended the Convention by day and the Jacobins by night; he, too, wrote speeches, letters, and a weekly journal. There was precious little time for a private life, even if he had valued or wanted one. Nothing could come between Robespierre and the Revolution—if it had, the history of each would have been entirely different.

CHARLOTTE CORDAY WAS guillotined four days after her crime, with a beatific smile on her face. The executioner held her severed head up to the crowd and, in a fit of pro-Marat enthusiasm, slapped her cheek. Allegedly, she blushed—both her slapped and unslapped cheeks reddened—and those who were watching gasped in amazement.[48] Physiologists several years later were inspired by this story to speculate on whether human sensation ends instantly at decapitation or not. But at the time, political interests eclipsed scientific ones. From the execution of Charlotte Corday the Girondins acquired a secular saint of their own—the Jacobins had Marat, but they had a pure and beautiful young woman whose modesty did not desert her even in death. The fight between the two factions entered its final throes. It had long been a mortal combat. Now it was simply a question of how much more damage would be done to the Revolution—how much more bloodshed there would be in the provinces and at the frontier— before it was over. To try to assess the state of affairs, the Convention sent various deputies out on mission to the detachments of the army deployed on home soil. After the levy of three hundred thousand in February, the official number of men in arms had risen to 645,000, but by the summer of 1793 this was still not enough. The Convention decreed an unprecedented program of national mobilization: the *levée en masse*.[49] In August Lazare Carnot, a member of the Committee of Public Safety with special responsibility for the army, decreed that "the republic is a great city in a state of siege: France must become one vast camp and Paris its arsenal." He set out the war effort in graphic terms:

> Every Frenchman is commandeered for the needs of the armies. Young men will go to the front, married men will forge arms and carry food, women will make tents and clothing and work in hospitals, children will turn old linen into bandages, old men will be car-

ried into the squares to rouse the courage of the combatants and to teach hatred of kings and republican unity.[50]

Robespierre himself could not be parted from Paris, but his brother, Augustin, left for the south, heading for Nice via Lyon and Marseille, to report on the extent of the support for the Girondins, who were now calling openly for a federalist revolt against the capital.

When Charlotte Robespierre heard that Augustin was about to leave as a "representative on mission" together with Jean François Ricord (deputy to the Convention from Var), who was taking his wife, she demanded to be included in the party. Charlotte got her way and the four set off accompanied by only two soldiers.[51] Lyon was in revolt, but when their coach pulled up outside the town hall, things seemed calm enough. The two women waited outside while Augustin and Ricord went in. A crowd began gathering around the stationary coach and the women were drawn into conversation. "We know that the Parisians say we are counterrevolutionaries," someone said, "but they are mistaken—look at our cockades."[52] Charlotte expressed suspicions, as her elder brother would have done; after all, counterrevolutionaries, indeed the king himself, had worn the tricolor cockade back in 1789. As the women's exchange with the tense and increasingly angry crowd deteriorated, the two men were involved in a fierce altercation with municipal officers inside the town hall. It was apparent that sympathy with the Girondins was running very high in Lyon. Returning to the coach, Augustin and Ricord decided it was not safe to spend the night and they must press on to Nice. Since it was likely news of their mission had gone before them—Charlotte's conversation with the crowd was, in hindsight, very unwise—they did not dare take the main road but went cross-country via the small town of Manosque.

When they reached the bank of the river Durance, the soldiers who had gone ahead to check if it was safe to cross came rushing back warning that there were armed men from Marseille with cannons on the other side. There was no choice but to turn back to Manosque. Here, trying to be helpful, the mayor offered the party an escort of fifty local National Guardsmen. Uncertain of the sympathies of these local men, Augustin and Ricord politely refused. During their flight to Varennes, the royal family had encountered the same problem: it was always difficult to know how battalions of National Guardsmen would act since they were just ordinary citizens in arms, not professional soldiers. So the party set off again for Nice unaccompanied. En route they received a message from the well-disposed mayor that the Marseille insurgents were in pursuit. At this, they abandoned the coach and fled on horseback into the mountains bordering the Department of Vaucluse. Twelve local patriots went with them as guides—they had no choice but to trust them—and they journeyed all night through the difficult passes. By the following evening they had reached the old fortified village of Sault. Here they encountered a young doctor who had been elected to the new convention in exile that the Girondin leader Guadet was planning to convene as soon as possible at Bourges.

This doctor took Augustin and Ricord to the local Jacobin Club, where they were enthusiastically received. Considerably cheered, the party then decided to return to Manosque, this time with a band of twenty or so patriots. Their two guards went ahead to prepare their arrival. To frighten the people who had been so unwelcoming before, the guards spread the rumor that the two deputies, one of them the brother of the famous Robespierre, were about to arrive with an army of six thousand. The town of Manosque would be razed to the ground and its inhabitants slaughtered in punishment for their treatment of the national representatives. Wisely, the party moved on again before the emptiness of the rumor could become apparent. Half an hour later the men from Marseille arrived, searched everywhere for the Parisians, then fell upon their abandoned coach, dragging it off to their hometown in triumph. Augustin and Ricord demanded the return of the coach and it was sent back, vandalized. Finally they got to Nice. Here, Charlotte recalled, "public spirit was no better."[53] But the presence of a detachment of professional soldiers from the French army, as opposed to unreliable battalions of local National Guardsmen, meant that the party was at least safe from counterrevolutionary attacks. Indeed, under the protection of the army's General Dumerbion, they even felt safe enough to attend the theater. The third time they went they were pelted with rotten apples. Sympathy for the Revolution was dying in the provinces. Back in Paris, Robespierre himself described the situation in apocalyptic terms:

From the north to the Midi, from sunset to dawn, the land is strewn with corpses and the blood of patriots drenches the whole of France; the Midi revolts and joins our enemies in the north to forge chains for us; Marseille, hitherto the rampart of liberty, is today its tomb. The same fate awaits us if we do not display energy and if Paris does not rise as one to crush the hydras that are whistling in our ears.[54]

THE MEMBERS OF the Committee of Public Safety were reelected by the Convention every month, and Danton was voted off on 10 July. One of the reasons was his optimism in the face of the federalist revolt. Rejecting Robespierre's apocalyptic vision, refusing to condone Jacobin threats of violent repression in Bordeaux and elsewhere, he acted as though effort and compromise might be enough to reunite the country. Danton, for all his ferocity in the streets, understood compromise. In June he had married the young woman his first wife had picked out for him and their two small children before she died. Noting this remarriage, only four months after the extraordinary scene in the graveyard over Gabrielle's coffin, his critics conjectured that Danton was still unbalanced, distracted from public affairs, swept up in the solace of a new sexual liaison, no longer really in control of what he—still less the Revolution—was doing. Unlike Robespierre, Danton valued his private life. In a conversation between the two men during which Robespierre was speaking, as he did so often, about the importance of virtue and its role in revolutionary politics, Danton quipped, "Virtue is what I do every night in bed with my wife."[55] Robespierre, not amused, jotted this down in his notebook for future reference. Perhaps Danton did not mean it as a joke. In the circumstances in which he found himself, in the context of the life he had led since 1789—all that bloodshed, all those shattered dreams, the revolutionary fight still so far from won—sex, love, intimacy may indeed have seemed to him the best there is for human beings to hope for. Robespierre emphatically did not share that view. He may not have been as interested in sex as Danton was—he almost certainly had less experience of it, but his vision of the good life clashed drastically with Danton's despite the fact that the two men had been such close revolutionary allies. When they were together in opposition to the old regime, the king, the Feuillants, the Girondins, their differences did not matter so much. Once the Jacobins came to power and had to decide what to do with it, they became enormously significant.

ON 27 JULY, Robespierre was at last elected to the Committee of Public Safety. Now, though he had more power than ever before, he was one of twelve trying to rule France. When Danton had established the committee earlier that year, it had only nine members. Its personnel had changed over the intervening months, and three extra places had been added around the oval table at which it met in the Tuileries. There were four more changes of personnel soon after Robespierre joined, but then no more additions until after he fell.[56] Some of his fellow members were close friends: Saint-Just, Couthon (who had to be carried into meetings up what was once known as the queen's staircase), Jacques Billaud-Varenne, and Jean Marie Collot d'Herbois. The others were Barère, the honey-tongued lawyer, Carnot, Marie Jean Hérault de Séchelles, Lindet, Jean Bon Saint-André, and two unrelated men both with the surname Prieur. "Stranger set of cloud-compellers the earth never saw," Thomas Carlyle remarked of the twelve.[57] In addition to internal clashes of vision and temperament, the committee as a whole was thoroughly embattled: its power and legitimacy were disputed abroad and in the provinces. In Paris there were also clashes with the Commune, with some of the city's forty-eight sections, with the clubs, the factions, and the streets.

Robespierre began assiduously attending the committee's meetings, which were usually held in the evening, in a green-papered room inside the former palace. Elsewhere in the building the intimidated Convention still went through the motions of assembling during the day, even though the republican constitution it had been called to design was indefinitely suspended, filed away on a dusty shelf awaiting happier times. As the first anniversary of the monarchy's end approached, hope, power, and fear were focused on the nocturnal debates behind closed doors. Paris celebrated the 10 August anniversary by smashing the royal tombs at Saint-Denis. The already meager food rations for the surviving royal prisoners in the Tower were reduced further, and Marie Antoinette was transferred to the Conciergerie, pending trial. Danton's policy of conciliation in the provinces was replaced by one of repression—Lyon, where Robespierre's siblings had recently been made so unwelcome, was under siege a week after he joined the Committee of Public Safety. On the eve of his ascension to power, he had drafted a personal revolutionary catechism. It provides a window into his mind at this frenzied time:

What is our aim?
    It is the use of the constitution for the benefit of the people.

Who is likely to oppose us?
    The rich and the corrupt.

What methods will they employ?
    Slander and hypocrisy.

What factors will encourage the use of such means?
    The ignorance of the sans-culottes.

The people must therefore be instructed.

What are the obstacles to their enlightenment?
    The paid journalists who mislead the people every day by shameless distortions.

What conclusion follows?
    That we ought to proscribe these writers as the most dangerous enemies of the country and to circulate an abundance of good literature.

The people—what other obstacle is there to their instruction?
    Their destitution.

When then will the people be educated?

When they have enough bread to eat, when the rich and the government stop bribing treacherous pens and tongues to deceive them and instead identify their own interests with those of the people.

When will this be?

Never.

What other obstacles are there to the achievement of freedom?

The war at home and abroad.

By what means can the foreign war be ended?

By placing republican generals at the head of our armies and by punishing those who have betrayed us.

How can we end the civil war?

By punishing traitors and conspirators, especially those deputies and administrators who are to blame; by sending patriot troops under patriot leaders to cut down the aristocrats of Lyon, Marseille, Toulon, the Vendée, the Jura, and all other districts where the banner of royalism and rebellion has been raised; and by making a terrible example of all the criminals who have outraged liberty and spilled the blood of patriots.[58]

In Lyon and elsewhere there were plenty of terrible examples: horrific mass executions by grapeshot fired from cannons and group drownings in the Vendée—crimes against humanity that the revolutionaries would today be called to answer for under the European human rights legislation they themselves pioneered. Robespierre had argued consistently since 1789 that in a time of revolution the end justifies the means, and even his advocates have to acknowledge that he did not flinch from the bloodiest implications of his position. In 1792 the Commune of Paris had attempted to encourage France's second-largest city to imitate the Parisian September Massacres. A friend of

Robespierre's named Joseph Chalier had been sent to Lyon as an emissary. Well received at the municipal level, Chalier met with resistance from the department and the National Guard. He asked for reinforcement from Paris and corresponded regularly with another close friend of Robespierre's, Léopold Renaudin. When the counterrevolution finally triumphed in Lyon in May 1793, the members of Chalier's circle were shattered to learn that he had been executed. Afterward, Robespierre led the Committee of Public Safety's policy of repression against the rebellious city. The siege of Lyon lasted until 6 October, and in its wake the Committee decreed mass executions and the destruction of all buildings, except the houses of the poor. "Lyon is no more," said Robespierre. His friend and colleague Collot d'Herbois admired his turn of phrase.[59] Even so, Robespierre's stance on Lyon was not the most extreme. When Couthon and Collot d'Herbois tried to convince him that there were sixty thousand individuals in Lyon who would never make good patriots unless they were forcibly resettled elsewhere in France and that even then "the generations born of them would never be entirely pure," Robespierre resisted. He continued to insist that ordinary people—including the poor of Lyon—were intrinsically good. But to those deemed counterrevolutionary, he showed no mercy.

THE HARVEST OF 1793 was good—it had been a very hot summer—but many of the water mills remained dry and by autumn the flour was still not ready to send to the bakers. Since June prices had risen dramatically. In Paris food was scarce, soap had tripled in price, and even Robespierre had difficulty obtaining the silk stockings he always wore (he never abandoned his knee breeches for the humbler costume of the sans-culottes). At the end of July, the Convention fixed the price of bread and other basic necessities and imposed the death penalty on anyone convicted of hoarding. To some extent, the Convention's measures were intended to address the demands of the new best-selling newspaper, Jacques René Hébert's foul-mouthed *Père Duchesne*, which had taken over as the voice of the Parisian poor from *L'ami du peuple* after Marat's murder. Hébert was a leading figure in the Commune, the Jacobin Club, and the Cordelier Club. Robespierre already had reservations about him and was certainly not in favor of radical social leveling of the kind proposed by the *enragés*, who had been calling for price controls since the beginning of the year.

On 2 September, the first anniversary of the horrific prison massacres, news reached Paris that counterrevolutionary rebels had surrendered the great naval base at Toulon to the British. The enemy had penetrated France. Hungry, angry Parisians, impatient with the food lines that had become their way of life, panicked. The *enragés* took to the streets and another insurrection was under way. The city was completely out of control for several days. On 4 September Hébert and his allies in the Commune turned popular demands for better wages and more bread into a general strike and marched on the Convention the following day. The Jacobins were persuaded to join in, though Robespierre was reluctant. He knew that—as the current president of the Convention—he was going to have to placate the angry crowd when it burst into the debating chamber.

On 5 September, confronted once again by the mob, the Convention declared terror "the order of the day." Even though Danton had been voted off the Committee of Public Safety, he was still powerful in the Convention. Here he faced down the *enragés* and carried a controversial decree to limit the city's forty-eight sections to just two meetings per week. This ended their daily sessions (or so-called permanence) and curbed what, since 1789, had been prominent sites for popular protest. Danton also called for a "Revolutionary Army," the ordinary people in arms to act not against food hoarders (as the *enragés* wanted) but against the foreign enemy. On the spot, the Convention allocated a hundred million livres (which it did not have) to provide a musket for every man in France. In this atmosphere of patriotic unity, the main instrument for enforcing the Terror on the home front was fortified: the Revolutionary Tribunal was expanded and divided into four concurrent chambers, so that it could more rapidly process a greater number of cases. Henceforth all judges and jurors were to be appointed either by the Committee of Public Safety or the larger Committee of General Security. Finally, on 17 September, the Convention passed the terrifying Law of Suspects: anyone could now be arrested and punished with death who "either by their conduct, their contacts, their words, or their writings, showed themselves to be supporters of tyranny or of federalism or to be enemies of liberty."[60] Under the Law of Suspects everyone—not just foreigners, as had previously been the case—was obliged to carry a certificate of *civisme*, which was both an identity card and a stamp of civic virtue in one. Anyone without one of these cards could be arrested, and many thousands were.

After the declaration on 5 September, the Terror remained France's official regime for nine months. During this time approximately sixteen thousand people were formally condemned to death, most of them in the provinces, and many more unofficial victims died in custody or were lynched without trial.[61] Nearly two thousand were executed in Lyon after the city fell to the revolutionaries. Over three and a half thousand were guillotined when the revolt in the Vendée was finally suppressed, after terrible loss of life on the battlefield and the murder of an estimated ten thousand rebels and civilians in retreat. The policy of repression worked. As autumn turned to winter, the republic's armies were once again succeeding abroad and the federalist revolt unleashed by the fall of the Girondin faction was effectively over. In December Augustin Robespierre, still with the army in the south, sent news that the strategic port at Toulon had been recaptured at last. He was proud to tell his brother that he had gone into action with the troops and distinguished himself as a fighter.

BETWEEN OCTOBER AND the end of 1793, 177 people were guillotined in Paris after appearing before the Revolutionary Tribunal, now under the strict control of the Committee of Public Safety and the Committee of General Security. The trial of Marie Antoinette came early in the Terror. When the members of the royal family were first imprisoned in the Tower, Paris's Insurrectionary Commune took responsibility for guarding them. It was the Commune that sent Robespierre to check that all was quiet there while the September Massacres were taking place. During the summer of 1793, the Committee of Public Safety intervened. Louis XVI's son—Louis Capet, as the republic knew him—eight years old and ill, was separated from his mother, aunt, and sister on 9 July by the committee's decree. Marie Antoinette resisted bodily, clinging to her child and the bedpost until someone threatened to call the guard and she understood it was hopeless. Summoning all her remaining strength, she said, "My child, we are about to part. Bear in mind all I have said to you of your duties. . . . Never forget God who thus tries you nor your mother who loves you. Be good, patient, and kind and your father will look down from heaven and bless you."[62] Her son was dragged from the room, one of his manhandlers declaring, "Don't be uneasy—the nation, always great and generous, will take care of his education," before the door slammed shut.[63] In the garden where the prisoners were allowed to take exercise a new fence was erected to prevent Louis Capet from seeing his family. Marie Antoinette found a chink in it and surreptitiously glimpsed her son again three weeks after their separation. He was dressed as a miniature sans-culotte, with the red cap of liberty on his head, and accompanied by a rough, abrasive tutor, a man named Anthony Simon, who was Marat's next-door neighbor.[64] The murder of his friend and patron on 13 July, just days after he took on the role of tutor, did nothing to improve Simon's treatment of his charge. Marie Antoinette was horrified. On 2 August she was taken to the Conciergerie in anticipation of her appearance before the Revolutionary Tribunal. That same day the Commune sent her son a toy guillotine.

The queen's trial began on 14 October and lasted two days. During it, Hébert tried to prove that she had sexually abused her son. "Nature refuses to answer such a charge," Marie Antoinette retorted, "but I appeal against it to the heart of every mother who hears me."[65] Robespierre was highly irritated. "That fool Hébert will make her an object of pity!" he complained.[66] The prisoner did not want pity. She said, "I was a queen and you dethroned me. I was a wife, and you murdered my husband. I was a mother, and you have torn my children from me. I have nothing left but my blood—make haste to take it." She was guillotined before noon on 16 October. Robespierre seems to have taken little interest in this gesture of bloody vengeance. When Louis XVI went past his door on the way to execution, Robespierre turned his back in awed silence. When Marie Antoinette went past, not in a closed carriage like her husband with a priest and prayer book but in an open tumbril exposed to the braying crowd, he scarcely noticed. His mind was already on the trial of the Girondin leaders, much more politically significant for him and the Revolution than the death of one distraught, grief-stricken woman who had lost everything except her Roman Catholic faith.

The trial of the Girondins opened on 24 October, eight days after the queen's execution. Robespierre had already succeeded in opposing a vote in the Convention by *appel nominal*, which would have resembled the protracted vote over the king's fate, with all the deputies individually stepping up to the tribune to deliver an opinion and verdict, some of them simply pronouncing the word *death*, others speaking interminably long into the night for exile, imprisonment, or acquittal. Even so, he did not have complete control of the Revolutionary Tribunal, which hesitated to condemn twenty-one Girondins brought before it, among them Brissot, so long the focus of Robespierre's hatred. "I never liked Brissot as a politician," one contemporary remembered, "no one was ever more intoxicated by passion: but that does not prevent me from doing justice to his virtues, to his private character, to his disinterestedness, to his social qualities as a husband, a father and a friend, and as the intrepid advocate of the wretched Negroes."[67] Why did Robespierre hate him so much? Both were idealists—supporters of the people and the oppressed everywhere. But they had disagreed bitterly over whether France should go to war in 1792, disagreed again over the fate of the king, and disagreed with yet more vehemence about whether the new republic should have a federal structure to counter the disproportionate influence of Paris. Unlike the Incorruptible, Brissot had political skeletons in his closet. He had had shadowy dealings with the police under the old regime, had traveled to Britain and the United States, had involved himself in schemes to resolve the debts that brought France to the precipice of revolution. Robespierre had tried to have Brissot arrested in the course of the September Massacres, so he might be disposed of without due process. The plan failed. Just over a year later, Robespierre was more desperate than ever to ensure the death of his long-standing enemy. Brissot would have felt the same if their situations had been reversed.

Brissot had been one of those fortunate enough to escape arrest on

2 June; Pétion was another. Brissot headed first for nearby Chartres, where he had grown up in his father's inn. Then with a loyal friend, a false passport, minimal luggage, and a brace of pistols, he traveled south through Nevers, then on to Moulins, where he was caught and taken back to the capital. He was imprisoned in the abbey of Saint-Germain-des-Près like Mme Roland, to whom he had once written movingly of his romantic responses to books during childhood. Reading *Anson's Voyage Round the World*, for example, he had seen himself "constructing log-huts in the happy isles of Juan Fernandez and Tinian."[68] He had always been a dreamer. From prison he wrote long letters to the Convention, comparing himself to Cicero, asking to be heard, for a chance to explain himself. It was no use. Brissot and twenty other Girondins were moved to the Conciergerie to await trial before the Revolutionary Tribunal. Those who still eluded arrest were declared outlaws and hunted down. Pétion's body was found in a field, half eaten by wolves. To complete matters, Robespierre arranged to have the house of his former friend demolished.

The trial did not go well from Robespierre's point of view. He had been reluctant to let it go ahead, probably because he knew there was still a great deal of public support for the Girondins, who were eloquent and sounded convincingly patriotic. After five days, during which the possibility of acquittal—politically disastrous for the Jacobins—gathered strength, steps were taken to ensure conviction. In the Convention a Jacobin named Osselin proposed a decree to end the trial. Robespierre stepped up to the tribune and said the proposal was too vague. In its place, he offered another to "reconcile the interests of the accused men with the safety of the country":

> I propose the decree that after three days' hearing the president of the tribunal shall ask the jury whether they have enough evidence to satisfy their conscience; if they say no, the trial is to proceed until they are in a position to reach a verdict.[69]

But if they said yes, it was all over. Trial by conscience was something Robespierre had suggested before: it meant the jury's decisions could be intuitive rather than reasonable and the accused could be convicted not only for their actions but also for their dispositions and attitudes. In that frightening room above the Conciergerie dungeons, where there was one chair for the ringleader and benches behind for those destined to share his or her fate, what was on trial was a frame of mind. Individuals were beside the point; what mattered was the triumph of the revolutionary mentality over anything that might oppose, challenge, or detract from it. "Whoever trembles is guilty," Robespierre said darkly.

Guilty was the verdict on the twenty-one Girondins. When it was pronounced, one witness heard Camille Desmoulins exclaim in shock, "My God! My God! It is I who kills them."[70] He was referring to the part his newspaper had played in turning public opinion in Paris against the Girondins; Camille was sorry now, but it was too late. Another eyewitness recalled that Brissot "had scarcely heard the fatal word *death* when his arms fell to his side and his head dropped suddenly upon his breast." He wrote to his wife, "Good-bye, my darling; dry your tears; mine are wetting the paper as I write. We shall be parted, but not eternally." Like Robespierre he still believed in an afterlife. Like Robespierre, too, he had lived for ideas— progress, human rights, grand abstractions that seemed almost within reach in the middle of the Revolution. On their way to execution the Girondins sang the "Marseillaise." They sang it over the body of one of their party, Valazé, who had snuck a knife into the courtroom and stabbed himself as soon as he heard the verdict. There was talk of decapitating his corpse, but in the end it was only dragged along in the tumbril to the foot of the guillotine where the lives of the others ended. One contemporary remarked, "In the Girondins Robespierre only killed a party; in Brissot he guillotined an idea."[71] The idea in question might have been a federal French republic, on the American model that had so impressed Brissot during his transatlantic travels before 1789, or a new and original model of republican government that differed in crucial respects from Robespierre's. It is true that Robespierre thoroughly disapproved of some of Brissot's ideas, even while sharing others. But it is also indisputable that when Brissot died, Robespierre was at last rid of a thoroughly despised personal enemy. In this instance, guillotining the man meant as much to him as guillotining the ideas that menaced a republic "one and indivisible." Mme Roland followed her Girondin friends to the guillotine in early November. Gesturing toward the statue of liberty that had recently been erected on the plinth of the demolished statue of Louis XIV in the renamed place de la Révolution, she said, "Liberty, what crimes are committed in your name!"[72] Her husband was in hiding in the countryside. When he heard of her death he walked straight out of the house and committed suicide in a ditch.

ON 24 OCTOBER, the same day the trial of the Girondins began, the Convention heard the ex-actor and dramatist Philippe Fabre d'Églantine read his report on the new calendar it had requested for the new France: "We could not go on reckoning the years during which we were oppressed by kings as part of our lifetime. Every page of the old [Gregorian] calendar was soiled by the prejudices and false-hoods of the throne and the church."[73] There is evidence that Robespierre opposed this confusing and anti-Christian innovation, since he wrote in his private notebook, "indefinite adjournment of the decree on the calendar," but he did not get his way.[74] Fabre was the spokesman for the special commission that the Convention had set up to design the new calendar. He remembered seeing during his childhood what Robespierre certainly saw year in, year out in Arras: the priests going out into the fields in May to bless the growing crops. For the benefit of his audience, he put incriminating words into their mouths: "It is we, the priests, who have made this countryside green again; we who wa-ter these fields with so fair a hope. . . . Believe in us, respect us, obey us, and make us rich: otherwise hail and thunder, which are at our command, will punish you for your lack of faith, docility, and obedi-ence."[75] Now the people had arisen, the priests had fallen, and it was time for a revolutionary calendar. The new calendar was backdated to 22 September 1792, so that the day after the monarchy had been for-mally abolished became the first day of the Year I of the republic, a foundational event to rival the birth of Christ. In the new calendar, France now found herself already well into Year II of liberty:

Month of vintage	(Vendémiaire)	30 days beginning	22 September 1792
Month of mist	(Brumaire)	"	22 October
Month of frost	(Frimaire)	"	21 November
Month of snow	(Nivôse)	"	21 December
Month of rain	(Pluviôse)	"	20 January 1793
Month of wind	(Ventôse)	"	19 February
Month of seeds	(Germinal)	"	21 March
Month of flowers	(Floréal)	"	20 April
Month of meadows	(Prairial)	"	20 May
Month of harvest	(Messidor)	"	19 June
Month of heat	(Thermidor)	"	19 July
Month of fruit	(Fructidor)	"	18 August

When Robespierre was a schoolboy he used to undress in the evenings to a reading about the life of the saint whose feast fell on the following day. Now Fabre explained that not only the months were to be renamed: the days of the new ten-day week (three to a month) would be named after the objects and animals associated with agricultural laborers. Every tenth day would be a day of rest bearing the name of an implement that would be useful to laborers returning to work in the morning: plough day, roller day, spade day, sickle day, water-pot day, and so on. Other days were to be named after animals, vegetables, flowers, and other natural phenomena, and the five extra days (six in a leap year) left over from standardizing the number of days in a month were to be special *Sansculottides*, or without-breeches days, in honor of the nickname given to the workingmen of Paris without whom the Revolution would have ended long ago.

While Fabre was deploying his poetic gifts in designing the new calendar, Robespierre was contemplating the wider problem of education. Back in July, soon after the enactment—and suspension—of the new republican constitution, he had presented a bill on education to the Convention in which the formation of children's moral character was given as much attention as the instruction of their minds. It proposed centralized compulsory state education of all girls aged five to eleven and all boys aged five to twelve. Free secondary education would be offered for older children who wanted it. The cost was to be met through progressive taxation. The bill was heavily criticized for being too interventionist and expensive. Robespierre remained determined:

> For a long time we have been waiting for this: the opportunity to help a large and integral sector of society. The revolutions of the last three years have done everything for the other classes of citizens yet almost nothing for the most needy, for the proletarian citizens whose sole property is their labor. . . . If you adopt the children of citizens without property, indigence will no longer exist for them. Adopt their children and you help them in the most precious part of their being. Those young trees will be transplanted into the national nursery, where the same soil will nurture them and a vigorous culture fashion them; pressed one against another, vivified by the rays of a benign star, they will grow, develop, flourish together under the regard and gentle influence of the fatherland.[76]

Robespierre's ideas on education were far in advance of his time and reflected both his sense of the difference education had made to his own life and his commitment to raising the standard of living for the poorest sector of society. But the Convention, unwilling to infringe parental opportunities to exploit child labor or to incur the cost of the nationwide program of education he outlined, approved only a modified system of primary education. Undeterred, Robespierre continued to develop his theories of moral development and the strategic role it might play in regenerating the republic. In this he was helped and inspired by his friend Saint-Just, who was beginning to argue that the Revolution must reach far beyond politics, into the heart of civil society, and make war on all forms of moral perversity.[77]

ROBESPIERRE HAD MADE an implicit pact with street violence in order to destroy his Girondin enemies in the Convention. It had been the mob's breaking into the Convention and surrounding it in June that had forced the expulsion of the Girondin deputies. But now that they were gone he needed to restrain the violence that had helped him to power—he needed, in short, to govern. The Convention had begun the process of reasserting control over Paris on 5 September when, at

Danton's suggestion, it limited the number of section meetings to two per week. However, it had given in to the demands for price regulation of basic commodities, which culminated in the General Maximum Law on 29 September. In a rare gesture of self-indulgence, Robespierre added his own items to the list of essential comestibles: coffee and sugar. Conceding that they were artificial, as opposed to natural, needs—human beings can survive well enough without them—he argued that these two products of colonialism were nevertheless addictive and the people would be deprived without them. Fabre d'Églantine backed him up, pointing out that sugar also had medicinal uses, and in the end Robespierre got his personal necessities onto the general list of price controls. His silk stockings were more of a problem. Robespierre's friend Claude Gravier, a distiller whom he had promoted to the jury of the Revolutionary Tribunal, received a letter around this time from the postmaster general of Lyon, explaining that he was having great difficulty procuring hosiery for the Incorruptible and was sending some ham and sausage instead.[78]

Once again the Jacobin Club was torn apart by factional strife. Danton was still a member, but increasingly critical of the regime of terror. He had lost control of the Cordelier Club, distanced himself from extreme sans-culottes, and openly opposed the *enragés* and followers of Hébert, whose newspaper was still voicing violent popular demands. At the end of September Danton took his children and new wife to his country house in Arcis-sur-Aube, seemingly retiring from politics. Hébert, meanwhile, was prominent in the Commune, supported by the Cordelier Club, and still attending Jacobin meetings. Robespierre was caught up in the strife between Jacobin followers of Danton and Jacobin followers of Hébert. He struggled to keep the club together, but his own attendance declined, perhaps because of ill health or because of his all-consuming responsibilities on the Committee of Public Safety. When he did speak at the Jacobins, he addressed the subject of atheism, insisting that it was one of the most fearsome hidden enemies menacing the Revolution.

Robespierre had long opposed atheism and anticlericalism. On the day that the National Assembly moved from Versailles to Paris in 1789, he had noticed with interest, and perhaps optimism, tricolor cockades on the cassocks of clergymen lining the route. Later, back in

Arras on holiday in 1791, he was dismayed to realize that every parish priest was a potential agent of the counterrevolution. When a large number of recalcitrant priests were murdered during the September Massacres of 1792, he showed no regret. But a year later he had had enough: "Whoever tries to stop the saying of Mass is a worse fanatic than the priest who says it," he told the surprised Jacobins on 21 November (1 Frimaire). Robespierre thought atheism in a public man or legislator nothing short of insanity. He quoted Voltaire: "If God did not exist, it would be necessary to invent him":

> It will be said, perhaps, that I am a narrow-minded man, a prejudiced person, a fanatic. As I have already said, I do not speak as a private individual, or as a systematic philosopher, but as a representative of the people. Atheism is aristocratic. The conception of a great Being who watches over oppressed innocence, and punishes successful crime, is democratic through and through. . . . I have been a poor sort of Catholic ever since my College days; but I have never cooled in my friendship for, or failed in my championship of, my fellow men. Indeed, I have only grown more wedded to the moral and political ideas that I have expressed. . . . The French people pins its faith, not on its priests, nor on any superstition, or any ceremony, but on worship as such—that is to say, upon the conception of an incomprehensible power, which is at once a source of confidence to the virtuous and of terror to the criminal.[79]

Robespierre reminded the Jacobins that he had raised his voice against atheism once before at their tribune. "There is nothing superstitious in using the name of the Deity. I believe myself in those eternal principles on which human weakness reposes, before it starts on the path of virtue," he had said in spring 1792.[80] He regretted nothing. Now he returned to the topic from a position of much greater power.

Robespierre's outburst was precipitated by the proselytizing atheism of Hébert's faction, especially that of the procurator of the Paris Commune, Pierre Gaspard Chaumette. A few weeks earlier, the archbishop of Paris, an old man named Jean-Baptiste-Joseph Gobel, had been persuaded to proceed to the Convention with an entourage of prorevolutionary clergymen and renounce his belief in God at the bar.

To loud applause, he laid his staff and episcopal ring before the Convention and declared that he recognized no form of national worship except that of liberty and equality. Soon afterward Chaumette obtained a decree that closed all the churches of Paris and placed priests under even stricter surveillance. These measures were widely imitated throughout France. Meanwhile, Hébert set about organizing a new kind of devotional ceremony. He was close to a printer named Antoine François Momoro, whose wife agreed to dress up provocatively as the Goddess of Reason. On 20 Brumaire (10 November), seated high on the altar of what had once been the Cathedral of Notre-Dame but was now the Temple of Reason, she received her worshipers with an intimate kiss. When he heard, Robespierre was disgusted. He considered the recent vogue for flamboyant de-Christianization offensive and was convinced it would both exacerbate the civil war and alienate neutral foreign powers. Astutely, he pointed out that atheism must not become a religion in itself and argued passionately for liberty of worship. He agreed that it was important to keep priests under surveillance and to appropriate church wealth for the nation, but he wanted anti-Christian violence stigmatized, not encouraged by tasteless atheistic ceremonies. "Five years of Revolution directed against the priests have left them powerless," he assured the Jacobins.[81] The real danger was no longer religious fanaticism but political intrigue. The Girondin faction had been destroyed, but another had already replaced it. Robespierre turned on Hébert and his friends to unmask them: "They want our jobs. . . . Fine, let them have them," he declared for rhetorical effect. Cries of "No! No! Stay where you are!" echoed around him as he proceeded to question their dedication. "I should like to see them," he said, pointing at Hébert and his supporters, "day and night probing the wounds of the state, studying the needs of the people, and devoting their whole life to the national welfare." Claiming rationality for his own side, he continued. "It is not merely patriotism, or enthusiasm, or an ingrained love of freedom that sustains our efforts; it is reason, which will make the republic immortal; where reason reigns, the people are sovereign; and such an empire is indestructible."[82]

One of the problems, one of the sources of Robespierre's tremendous irritation with Hébert, was that he was planning to design some novel religious ceremonies for the new republic. Hébert had stolen his thunder with a louche and ridiculous spectacle. Robespierre himself was hoping to achieve more pious and constructive effects through the worship of the Supreme Being, a vague but benign otherworldly presence that would raise the level of human conduct and moral aspiration, not lower it to the level of an orgy. In his private life, Robespierre could certainly be priggish. But his views on religion are not an example of priggishness. He thought Hébert's approach irresponsible because it squandered a valuable opportunity to institute a new system of theistic morality that would benefit the poor. Atheism, he argued, is the preserve of an elite. "When the conception of God comes to be attacked, the attack will not proceed from the popular instinct, but from the rich and the privileged," he warned.[83]

1 Frimaire (21 November), the day that Robespierre lectured the Jacobins on God, was also the day that Danton returned to Paris. No one knows exactly why: perhaps after five years at the center of the Revolution he simply could not stay away, or maybe friends in Paris persuaded him to return. As soon as he entered the Jacobin Club, Hébert tried to have him expelled. When the Girondins had tried to do the same to Robespierre in 1792, Danton had leapt to his defense. Now Robespierre returned the favor. He did so in measured terms, so it was possible to hear notes of criticism within the overarching message of support. He made a point of mentioning that Danton had misjudged the treacherous General Dumouriez (so, at the time, had Robespierre himself, but this he omitted to note). Danton had also been less than enthusiastic in pursuing Brissot and the other Girondins, his friend reminded the Jacobins, but he was definitely not a traitor. Without this carefully modulated defense, Danton might have been excluded from the Jacobins. Instead, when Robespierre concluded his speech the president of the club embraced Danton and welcomed him back amid loud applause. After this slightly stilted scene of reconciliation, Danton, Robespierre, and their old friend Camille Desmoulins joined forces against Hébert's faction, which now dominated both the Commune and the Cordeliers Club. The Girondins had not been dead two months, but the Jacobins had already found a new enemy to fight. This time they were fighting against, not with, the Commune and the mob. Marat's heart was swinging in its

urn above the hall of the Cordeliers; it is difficult to guess which side he would have been on had he lived to see the Cordeliers turn on Danton.

On 14 Frimaire (4 December) the Convention passed a law designed to further strengthen and centralize the revolutionary government.[84] The new law made the Convention "the sole center of the impulse of government," and it brought public power throughout the country—departments, districts, and local communes at the lowest level—under the direct control of the Committee of Public Safety. Locally elected administrators now became "national agents" and the militant surveillance committees that had sprung up nationwide to defend republican principles and enforce the Law of Suspects found themselves integrated into a newly hierarchical system of authority. The "representatives on mission" were systematically recalled and replaced with administrators rigorously vetted by the government. From this point no one, anywhere, was allowed to raise a private army, impose taxation, or deviate from national policy—the days when "representatives on mission" could act unchecked in the provinces were over. Meanwhile, popular assemblies in Paris's forty-eight sections were suddenly answerable to the Convention over and above the municipal Commune. In effect, the Law of 14 Frimaire was an iron-fisted clampdown on all activism that was not directly sanctioned by the Committee of Public Safety.

Despite the draconian Law of 14 Frimaire, Camille Desmoulins set off on a new course of activism. He started a newspaper called *Le vieux Cordelier* (*The Old Cordelier*) in memory of the Cordelier Club as it had been before Hébert and his ultrarevolutionists took it over. The paper was dedicated to both Robespierre and Danton, "two friends of the editor," and Robespierre read the proofs of the first issue, which appeared on 15 Frimaire (5 December). The paper was a call for clemency. Under the Law of Suspects, the prisons of Paris were crammed full of ordinary men and women. It was time, Camille declared in his paper, to open the prisons. Recent news from the front line was good, the republic had repelled its foreign enemies, the Terror had served its purpose—let it end. The call for clemency got a rapturous response. The crowd grabbed copies of *Le vieux Cordelier* as they came off the press. Camille, who had roused his audience in the

Palais-Royal gardens and defined for them the meaning of the revolutionary cockade in 1789, was working his magic again, this time to end the violence he once incited so passionately. He had never been a cautious person. Feeling himself protected by both Robespierre and Danton (the latter strongly supported the move toward clemency) and emboldened by the public's enthusiastic response to his paper, Camille went further: in issue 3 he dared to call the Revolutionary Tribunal into question and to hope complete liberty of the press might soon be restored. This time Robespierre had not seen the proofs. Issue 4, fifteen days—one and a half revolutionary weeks—later, was a direct appeal to him:

> O my dear Robespierre! It is you whom I address here. . . . O, my old school friend, whose eloquent discourses posterity will read! Remind yourself of the lessons of history and philosophy: love is stronger, more lasting than fear; admiration and religion are born of generosity; acts of clemency are the ladder of pride by which members of the Committee of Public Safety can elevate themselves to the sky (the Roman Tertullian tells us this); they will never reach it through paths of blood.[85]

Not content with asking Robespierre to redirect the policy of the Committee of Public Safety—a dangerous and perhaps impossible undertaking—Camille went on to suggest that his friend had already publicly indicated willingness to do so. It would be wrong of him, Camille recklessly implied, to renege on such good intentions.

It is true that on 30 Frimaire (20 December) Robespierre had raised the possibility of forming a committee of justice to examine some of the more contentious arrests under the Law of Suspects. Camille seized on this and called for something more dramatic: a committee of clemency. Let the prisons open and the Terror resolve itself in love and reconciliation. He knew he would be accused of being reactionary (or excessively moderate), so he evoked Marat, arguing unconvincingly that, at this point in the Revolution, his own extreme clemency was the equivalent of Marat's extreme violence.[86] Robespierre had already warned him obliquely to stop being "so versatile." Robespierre's friend the printer Léopold Nicolas had warned him, too:

"Camille, you seem very close to the guillotine."[87] But Camille quipped back, "Nicolas, you seem very close to a fortune. It is only a year since you dined on baked apples, but here you are printer to the state." He was a man of great boyish charm—seemingly still at school, wisecracking in the playground and showing off his knowledge of classical literature. His wife, Lucile, adored him. "Let him save the country in his own way," she said, covering the mouth of a friend who was counseling caution.[88]

In the Jacobin Club on 18 Nivôse (7 January), Robespierre finally lost his temper with Camille. The Jacobins, as expected, were critical of Camille's moderation—it had nothing at all in common with Marat's revolutionary extremism so far as they could see. Cheekily, Camille offered to burn issue 3 of *Le vieux Cordelier* as long as his forthcoming issue 5 was read. Robespierre apologized for him, telling the club to think of him as an unthinking child who had fallen into bad company: "There is no need to expel Camille. We will burn his pamphlet."[89] Camille, so fond of, and so good at, repartee, could not resist. "Burning is no answer," he retorted. This, famously, was Rousseau's response when the Parlement of Paris burned his novel *Emile*. Camille knew exactly what Rousseau and his works meant to Robespierre. He had quoted Rousseau against his friend once before, when they had a public tiff in 1791. It was infinitely more dangerous to do so again now. Any trace of amusement left the Incorruptible's lips; any glimmer of indulgence in his weak green eyes disappeared instantly. He might not have been Camille's equal at repartee, but he was much better at anger:

> What! You still try to justify your aristocratic works! Understand this, Camille, that were you not Camille there would be no indulgence for you. Your intentions are bad. Your citation: Burning is no answer! Is it applicable here?[90]

Even Camille could see he had gone too far. He started to panic. Falling back on their long-standing connection, he said to Robespierre: "You criticize me here, but was I not in your home? Did I not give you my proofs to read and solicit your help and advice in the name of friendship?"[91] His response could only make things worse by putting Robespierre on the defensive in front of the Jacobins. "You did not show me all your proofs; I saw only the first two. Not wishing to be involved in a quarrel of any kind, I preferred not to read the rest. If I had read them, I would have been accused of dictating them." Danton intervened to try to limit the damage. He urged Camille to accept Robespierre's chastisement as well meant. Danton may or may not have believed in Robespierre's good intentions, but he wanted to end the damaging standoff. It was obvious that Robespierre genuinely cared for Camille; it was equally obvious that the Incorruptible might well pride himself on sacrificing a personal friend to the Revolution. Until now, Robespierre had only sacrificed his enemies. Perhaps Danton had some inkling that this was about to change.

The following evening Fabre d'Églantine was at the club when the discussion of Camille's *Vieux Cordelier* resumed. Despite the success of his revolutionary calendar, Fabre was feeling very nervous because his involvement in a financial scandal concerning the colonial East India Company had recently become public. As Desmoulins again came under attack, Fabre got up to leave. Robespierre noticed and turned on him as well:

> As for this fellow, who never appears without a lorgnette in his hand and is so clever at expounding theatrical plots, let him explain himself here, and we will see how he comes out of it.[92]

That lorgnette really irritated Robespierre. Fabre had an ostentatious habit of sitting in the Jacobins or the Convention and surveying the proceedings as though he were at the theater. Perhaps he just wanted to remind everyone that he had once been an actor denied civil status under the old regime. Robespierre—egocentrically—had another explanation. He suspected that Fabre was parodying his own habit of fixing the audience through eyeglasses that he moved up and down on his forehead while speaking at the tribune. If this was what Fabre was doing, he must have been as foolish as he was foppish, since the time when it was safe to poke fun at Robespierre had long since past. Stopped in his tracks skulking out of the club, Fabre heard cries of

"Guillotine him!" and fled as the Jacobins voted to strike his name from their register.

On 23 Nivôse (12 January) the Committee of Public Safety ordered Fabre's arrest on charges of corruption and forgery in connection with the East India Company. The original French East India Company (Compagnie des Indes) went bankrupt in 1769 under the old regime. But it was relaunched under royal patronage in 1785 and enjoyed a lucrative trade monopoly. Early in the Revolution this monopoly was canceled in the name of liberty, but the company continued to thrive regardless. It even managed to evade the Legislative Assembly's attempt to impose stringent taxation on transferable stock after the fall of the monarchy in 1792. In fact, the Girondin ministers had connived in this evasion, believing as they did that prosperous foreign trade was essential to the modern republic they envisaged for France. With the proscription of the Girondin deputies in June 1793, however, the company had lost its protection, and the Convention charged it with profiteering, sealed its warehouses, and forced it into liquidation. Fabre was vocal in the debates and suggested that the company's attempts to evade taxation had been inspired by foreign enemies, Prime Minister Pitt in particular. Meanwhile a group of speculators bought up falling shares in the company, anticipating that certain interested members of the Convention would force through a decree that would cause the share price to rise before the company finally went into liquidation. Fabre managed to get himself tangled up in this scam. And through Fabre, Danton was possibly implicated.

Fabre was thrown out of the Jacobins on 19 Nivôse (8 January), and two days later Camille was struck off too. Robespierre, having initially convinced his fellow Jacobins to opt for censure, now supported Camille's expulsion:

> You can see in Camille's writings revolutionary principles side by side with the maxims of a thoroughly pernicious reaction (or moderation). In one passage he raises the courage of patriots, in another he feeds the hopes of aristocrats. . . . He is a fantastic mixture of truth and falsehood, of statesmanship and absurdity, of sensible ideas and selfish

chimerical designs. In my view, Camille and Hébert are equally wrong. . . . I assure all faithful members of the Mountain that victory lies within our grasp. There are only a few serpents left for us to crush. [Applause and cries of "We will crush them."] Let us not trouble about this or that individual, but only about the country.[93]

There is no reason to think Robespierre spoke in bad faith. He thought the Terror was still needed to control the threat of counterrevolution. Against the violence of Hébert and the Commune, Camille and Danton had launched a cry for clemency. Robespierre thought treading the middle ground between these two extremes more prudent. He was irritable, tired, and unwell—Camille and Fabre (for different reasons) had annoyed him—but he was capable of setting personal feelings aside to concentrate on what he believed best for the Revolution. "Let us not trouble about this or that individual, but only about the country" is a formula as admirable as it is chilling. Robespierre had no intention of defending Camille simply because he was an old school friend, which does not mean he felt easy at the looming sacrifice of his former friends. Soon after the public quarrel with Camille, he collapsed, was ill intermittently for the rest of the month, and then between 22 Pluviôse (10 February) and 22 Ventôse (12 March) scarcely left the Duplay household. In this state of nervous strain he called Saint-Just back to Paris to help him. Saint-Just had gone on mission to the army, but Robespierre's need took precedence.

SAINT-JUST, WHO LOVED the countryside, much preferred being sent out on mission to being cooped up in Paris pacing the short distance back and forth between the Jacobin Club and the Convention. In 1794 in the month of Nivôse (January), he went to the army of the Rhine, accompanied by his friend and fellow Jacobin Philippe Lebas, who had just married Elisabeth Duplay. This small traveling party, like the one that had accompanied Augustin Robespierre earlier in the year, managed to combine business and pleasure. Saint-Just was a charming companion, reading aloud passages from Molière and Rabelais, singing Italian arias to pass the time, and fastidiously tending to the needs of his friend's new wife when she was coach sick. Arriving in

Strasbourg, he set about punishing counterrevolutionary conspirators and taxing the rich to relieve the sufferings of the poor. The soldiers did not like him; they found him too severe, unwilling as he was to recognize any form of punishment short of death. Saint-Just's second mission took him to Lille and its environs. Here he was even more severe, initiating draconian measures against all former nobles still living in the area. He was still away on 17 Pluviôse (5 February) when Robespierre, shortly before collapsing completely, delivered to the Convention one of the most important speeches of his life, *"Rapport sur les principes de morale politique qui doivent guider la Convention nationale dans l'administration intérieure de la République"* (*A Report on the Principles of Political Morality That Should Guide the Convention in the Interior Administration of the Republic*).

In this speech Robespierre developed the personal revolutionary creed that he had privately professed on the eve of his election to the Committee of Public Safety. He asked, "What is our aim?" And answered: "The peaceful enjoyment of liberty and equality and the reign of that eternal justice whose laws are engraved, not in marble or stone but in the hearts of every man—of the slave who forgets them and the tyrant who denies their truth." Then he went further, outlining the kind of morality that would obtain in his ideal republic:

> In our country, we want to substitute morality for egoism, honesty for love of honor, principles for conventions, duties for decorum, the empire of reason for the tyranny of fashion, the fear of vice for the dread of unimportance. We want to substitute pride for insolence, magnanimity for vanity, the love of glory for the love of gold. We want to replace good company with good character, intrigue with merit, wit with genius, brilliance with truth, dull debauchery with the charm of happiness. For the pettiness of the so-called great we would substitute the full stature of humanity; in place of an easygoing, frivolous and discontented people, we would create one that is happy, powerful, and stouthearted and replace the vices and follies of the monarchy with the virtues and astounding achievements of the republic.[94]

There it was, Robespierre's vision of France, a prim society of patriotic, uncorrupted, dedicated equals. In his republic there would be only innocent pleasures, no frivolous distractions, no debauchery. No one would value money above honor, and honor itself would be defined as personal integrity, just as Rousseau said it should be long before 1789. The problem was that even after five tense and traumatic revolutionary years, Robespierre's dream was still a very long way off. For this reason, he explained, the Terror must continue:

> If the basis of popular government in peacetime is virtue, its basis in a time of revolution is both virtue and terror—virtue, without which terror is disastrous, and terror, without which virtue has no power. . . . Terror is merely justice, prompt, severe, and inflexible. It is therefore an emanation of virtue and results from the application of democracy to the most pressing needs of the country.[95]

In the hands of despots, Robespierre argued, terror was a weapon of oppression. But terror wielded by virtue was the refuge of the poor. Back in 1792 he had advised the Jacobins not to sponsor the development of a new kind of musket that could fire twenty rounds a minute: what might happen if aristocrats got hold of it and turned it on the people? Now he made the opposite case, arguing that the weapons of tyranny must be appropriated by the people and used in their name. Specifically, the people, so long oppressed, must seize the weapon of terror and turn it against the republic's external and internal enemies. Robespierre had always been preoccupied with internal enemies. Since the Revolution began, however, they had multiplied dramatically; disguised and insinuating, they were not always easy to recognize, but Robespierre had been quick to spot the most prominent: General Lafayette, Mirabeau, Brissot, General Dumouriez. Now he identified the two opposing factions—Hébert's proponents of extreme violence and Danton and Camille's advocates of extreme indulgence—as the new internal enemies of the French people. Demanding a vote of confidence in the Convention for the Committee of Public Safety, doing its best to save the Revolution, he issued a double warning to its critics, both those who thought the committee too harsh and those who thought it not nearly harsh enough.

Robespierre's speech was interrupted throughout by loud applause. Afterward it was printed and widely distributed by the Convention and the Jacobins. Three days later he retired from public view. A rumor went around that he had been poisoned. When he reappeared in March (Ventôse) he said: "Would to God that my physical strength were the equal of my moral fortitude! I might then, this very day, confound the traitors and call down national vengeance on every guilty head."[96] If his illness was genuine, if the Revolution had strained him to the breaking point, his instinct was still to turn his suffering to political advantage. He was frailer than many of the other revolutionaries—a much less powerful speaker than Danton, slower than Camille Desmoulins, more circuitous than Saint-Just—but none of them had sharper political instincts. While Robespierre was ill, or possibly pretending to be ill, Saint-Just rushed back to Paris. He reiterated the message of his friend's widely praised speech, but, unlike the Incorruptible, he was alarmingly succinct:

> The republic is built on the ruins of everything anti-republican. There are three sins against the republic: one is to be sorry for State prisoners; another is to be opposed to the rule of virtue; and the third is to be opposed to the Terror.[97]

By these criteria, the friends of Hébert and the friends of Danton were all republican sinners. As usual Saint-Just thought there was only one appropriate punishment: death.

Robespierre had asked for a vote of confidence in the Committee of Public Safety to pursue the new enemies on his list. But the committee's members were far from agreed on how to save the Revolution. Collot d'Herbois, for example, thought Paris could be placated by an alliance between the Jacobins and Cordeliers (now led by Hébert), if the Jacobins could be persuaded to abandon Robespierre's censorious attitude toward extreme violence at this point. Collot was even taking up the cause of the disgraced terrorist and former representative on mission Jean Baptiste Carrier. Carrier had been in charge of the repression in Lyon and Nantes. Among other atrocities, he had instituted a new version of republican marriage, which involved tying a naked man and woman together and drowning them. When he heard of this, Robespierre, appalled, insisted on recalling Carrier to the capital.

On 14 Ventôse (4 March) Carrier proposed, and Hébert seconded, a motion at the Cordeliers Club to declare a state of insurrection. The motion was carried and the club hung black crepe over its copy of the Declaration of Rights. Plans were afoot to surround the Convention and demand the expulsion of Robespierre and his allies, a repetition of the insurrection that brought down the Girondins on 2 June 1793. But Hébert's insurrection never materialized: only two of the city's forty-eight sections were prepared to rise. Nor did the Commune rise. There are many possible explanations. Hébert was not Danton—it is not a simple task to rouse and direct a violent crowd, even in a time of revolution. Danton had a special gift for it, something to do with his astoundingly deep, strong voice and the breadth of his physical frame. Moreover, many of the poor in Paris thought Robespierre and his allies could and would help them, which diminished the appeal of Hébert's promises to intervene even more radically in the economy. Others were too jaded after five tumultuous years to take to the streets again. And some were too frightened of falling foul of the police in these brutal times—the centralizing Law of 14 Frimaire had done its work, and there were considerably more obstacles to insurrection now than there had been earlier in the Revolution.

Robespierre returned to work on 22 Ventôse (12 March), along with Couthon, who had also been ill. The next day the Jacobins gave them a rapturous welcome. Seizing the moment, Robespierre immediately denounced Hébert and his faction, who were arrested later that evening on the general charge of conspiracy. Twenty of them were tried before the Revolutionary Tribunal seven days later and, by application of the three-day rule, which Hébert himself had supported when it was introduced to secure the conviction of the Girondins, all but one were found guilty and sent to the guillotine. In the short interval between the arrest and trial of the Hébertistes, a delegation arrived at the bar of the Convention, including someone who sang a song of congratulation to the deputies and their Committee of Public Safety. Danton objected—he proposed that no one should be allowed to sing songs in the Convention, that such behavior was disrespectful and inappropriate. No one knew it at the time, but this uncharacteristically prim intervention was destined to be Danton's last. There were already some signals suggesting that, after the Hébertistes, his own faction might be next to fall. But Danton still believed that the committee and tribunal he had brought into being—not to mention the Convention, which owed its existence to his part in the fall of the monarchy—would never dare strike at him.

WHATEVER HIS PRECISE role in bringing about the downfall of the Hébertistes—his illness and absence from public life make it impossible to tell precisely—Robespierre benefited enormously from their demise. Besides the Cordelier Club, the War Ministry was the main source of Hébert's support, and it had distributed his *Père Duchesne* to the troops, greatly boosting the newspaper's circulation and influence. Carnot, Robespierre's colleague on the Committee of Public Safety, had for months been working to erode the power of the War Ministry, but soon after the executions of the Hébertistes, all six of the ministries inherited from the failed constitutional monarchy were radically restructured, purged, and downgraded to commissions. On 12 Germinal (1 April) the Convention, following the committee's recommendation, agreed to the formation of twelve new executive commissions, which Robespierre succeeded in staffing with personnel loyal to him. There were only two exceptions: the army movement commission and the finance commission. The rest were effectively under Robespierre's control. Once again, he displayed his sharp political instincts, expanding his sphere of control through patronage. In this respect, he far surpassed his colleagues on the Committee of Public Safety. Where they tended to operate as isolated individuals, carving up the committee's great power among themselves, specializing, and working alone, Robespierre—perhaps by instinct, perhaps as a result of his experience in the Jacobin Club—relied on a loyal entourage. To an outsider, it looked like a faction. To him, it was simply a network of like-minded people he could trust.

Another consequence of the downfall of the Hébertistes concerned the Commune. Hébert had been powerful within it and after his execution his superior, the atheist Chaumette, who had closed the Parisian churches, was arrested. At this point, Robespierre moved to remodel the Commune, specifically by doing away with the municipal elections through which its delegates were chosen by the Paris sections. In the autumn of 1792, after the collapse of the constitutional monarchy, Robespierre had exerted a powerful influence in the Commune and, despite its recent domination by the Hébertistes, he still had friends there. Some were representatives from his own Paris Section des Piques, and one was a former priest, Jacques-Claude Bernard, whom the Commune had deputed to escort the king to the guillotine; others included a clock maker, a bookseller, and a manufacturer of colored prints. Chaumette was replaced with a very close associate of Robespierre's, Claude Payan, originally an artillery officer from Valence, who set about developing Robespierrist support inside the Commune. Payan and his brother had come to Robespierre's attention during the federalist revolt when they played a prominent role in rallying the Jacobins of the Midi in support of the Convention and the Committee of Public Safety. Payan, like Saint-Just, was almost ten years younger than Robespierre. An ardent believer in the power of propaganda, he began a paper, the *Antifédéraliste*, which became the Committee of Public Safety's official publication. An ardent moralist as well, he hoped Robespierre would "centralize public opinion and make it uniform."[98]

There were also changes to the National Guard that indirectly benefited Robespierre after the fall of the Hébertistes. The sans-culottes' Revolutionary Army (one of the instruments of the Terror which Danton had first suggested in April 1793) was disbanded on 7 Germinal (27 March) following the execution of its commander in chief as an Hébertist. Its all-important artillery units, however, were kept intact and added to those already under the control of François Hanriot, head of the National Guard and Robespierre's close friend. Hanriot had previously displayed his loyalty to the Jacobin faction in the Convention when he used his troops to surround the Tuileries and arrest the Girondin deputies. Now, with the artillery units under his command, Hanriot had even more power at his disposal; he effectively controlled the armed forces of Paris.

ON THE EVENING of 2 Germinal (22 March), Robespierre retraced his steps to the Marais Quarter, where he had lived his first two years in Paris. He went to a dinner at which Danton was also a guest. Robespierre seemed silent and agitated. Bold as ever, Danton asked him directly why there were still so many victims of the Terror: "Royalists and conspirators I can understand, but what about those who are innocent?" "And who says anyone innocent has perished?" Robespierre retorted coldly.[99] Danton asked if they could put aside their private differences and think instead of the future of France. He should have known that the Incorruptible already thought of nothing else. If the reports of what passed between them are accurate, Danton tried to talk candidly to Robespierre, tried, as he often did in both his personal and his political life, to compromise. But Robespierre never favored compromise. His principles were paramount; everything, even his conscience, had to be tailored to fit them. To him, the idea that he and Danton were similar kinds of men who might mutually agree to set their differences aside was anathema. "At this moment, I am you," Robespierre had written when Danton's wife died. A little over a year later, there was no trace of identification left. "I suppose that a man of your moral principles would not think that anyone deserved punishment," he said sarcastically to Danton. "And I suppose that you would be annoyed if none did," came the cutting reply. Robespierre got up and left. Danton's eyes filled with tears.[100]

Later that evening Robespierre allowed the committee to add Danton's name to the list of the proscribed. Before he had violently opposed that action; now he agreed. His signature on the warrant for the arrest of Danton and his followers is the smallest: eleven tiny tight letters and half a neat line underlining them—emphatic or perhaps just resigned. Robespierre could lose his temper. He had lost it with Camille and now he had lost it with Danton. But he was not the kind to send people to the guillotine just because he was angry. He had reached the firm conclusion that his vision of the republic and the conditions for its survival had parted company with Danton's. Soon afterward, Camille went around to the Duplay household but soon came back to the flat he and Lucile still lived in, upstairs from Danton. "I am done for," he said. "I have been to call on Robespierre, and he has refused to see me."[101] There were still people loyal to Danton in the Convention and throughout the city. One of them came to tell him the warrant had been signed and he must flee to avoid arrest. Allegedly, he refused, saying, "One does not take one's country with one on the soles of one's boots," a poignant remark from someone who had his own understanding of patriotism.[102] Danton's patriotism was every bit as passionate as Robespierre's—but fatally different in other respects. He kept repeating over and over, "They will not touch me."[103]

Danton was wrong. He was arrested in the middle of the night after a joint meeting of the Committee of Public Safety and the larger but less powerful Committee of General Security. Camille Desmoulins, Fabre, and other close associates of Danton's were also arrested. They were placed in solitary confinement in the Luxembourg jail, very close to the Cordeliers Club and the building in which Danton and Camille had lived since 1789. As Danton arrived, another inmate, Thomas Paine, famous author of *The Rights of Man*, came up to greet him. Paine had made a distinguished contribution to both British politics and the American Revolution. He had come to Paris hoping for similar success, but after befriending the Girondins he had landed in prison. Danton's English was better than Paine's French. He said, "Mr. Paine, you have had the happiness of pleading in your country a cause which I shall no longer plead in mine."[104]

In the Convention the next morning, Saint-Just read out a report against the Dantonists. He stood stiffly at the tribune, his text held motionless in one untrembling hand, while he used the other to emphasize main points with a cutting gesture that reminded his audience of the guillotine:

> If you save Danton you save a personality, someone you have known and admired; you pay respect to individual talent, but you ruin the attempt in which you have so nearly succeeded. For the sake of a man you will sacrifice all the new liberty that you are giving to the whole world.[105]

He ended devastatingly with: "The words we have spoken will never be forgotten on earth." The Convention sat in stunned silence. Saint-Just's speech drew on a series of hurried notes that Robespierre had jotted down for him, notes that still survive and that show beyond a shadow of doubt the depth of the Incorruptible's complicity in the attack on his former friends.[106] In the wake of recent financial scandals, the evidence against Fabre was so strong that it hardly needed special corroboration. Nevertheless, Robespierre blamed Fabre for inspiring Camille Desmoulins to publish *Le vieux Cordelier*, implicitly repudiated his own involvement with the paper, and suggested it had been part of a counterrevolutionary plot approved by Danton. Moving on to Camille, Robespierre noted his vanity and vibrant imagination, which equipped him well for being Fabre's and Danton's henchman. He hesitated to add more—and this in itself suggests that Robespierre's notes were sincere, however distorted and fantastical; he believed what he was writing.

On Danton, he wrote much more. Danton had once been close to General Lafayette and to Mirabeau; he had associated with Barnave and the Lameth brothers (who sided with the Feuillant reactionaries when the Jacobins split after the king's flight to Varennes); he had tried to save Brissot and the other Girondins; he had been friends with the treacherous General Dumouriez. All these liaisons looked much more suspicious in retrospect than they had at the time. But this was not the kind of distinction Robespierre's fevered mind now made. The notes continued: Danton had set himself to imitate Fabre's theatrical mannerisms and had made himself ridiculous by crying at the tribune and privately in Robespierre's presence. It is true that at the end of their last meeting, Danton's eyes filled with tears—how haunted by those tears Robespierre must have been to explain them away in such an extraordinary manner. Moreover, Robespierre went on, Danton's reputation for patriotism was unwarranted. He had played no part in the rising that ended the monarchy on 10 August 1792, having left Paris for Arcis before it, and on the night itself he had to be dragged from his bed to attend the meeting of his section. In fact, Danton had been in the street that night and had sanctioned murder on the steps of the Hôtel de Ville; afterward he had been to the front line and seen blood flowing. Now Robespierre, who had never personally participated in revolutionary violence, reproached him with physical cowardice. He also accused him of being fat, lecherous, and indolent. There was bile and a touch of madness in this document—even Saint-Just could see that only bits of it could be incorporated into the official report.

After Saint-Just's speech, one of the deputies broke the silence in the Convention by proposing that Danton should be heard at the bar.

Robespierre moved at once to prevent this, arguing that it would be tantamount to granting Danton a privilege because of who he was. The Revolution, Robespierre insisted, was not about men, it was about principles. Danton must be tried by the Revolutionary Tribunal as an ordinary prisoner and not given a special opportunity to defend himself before the Convention: "No! We want no privileges! No! We want no idols!"

> I must add here that a particular duty is imposed on me to defend the purity of principles against the designs of intrigue. For they have tried to frighten me as well: they wanted me to think that if Danton were in danger, the menace would reach me, too. They represented him to me as a man to whom I ought to adhere—as a shield that could defend me, a rampart without which I would be exposed to the darts of my enemies. I have been written to—Danton's friends have sent me letters, they have persecuted me with their speeches. They thought the memory of an old friendship, former faith in feigned virtues, would induce me to slacken my zeal and my passion for liberty. Well, I declare that not one of these motives has made an impression on me. I declare that, were it true that Danton's dangers were to become my own, that if they were to cause the aristocracy to take another step toward seizing me, I would not look upon that circumstance as a public calamity. What are dangers to me? My life belongs to my country, my heart is free of fear, and if I died it would be without reproach and ignominy.[107]

Long and rapturous applause followed Robespierre's intervention. His speech was masterful, preaching the rigid application of impersonal principles, but in the distinctively self-referential rhetorical style that he had refined to perfection over the last five years. No one else spoke so insistently, so predictably, or so protractedly about himself in the Revolution. Yet no one else could have been relied upon to put his personal feelings aside with Robespierre's relentless commitment to what he believed was the common good. No friendship, no bribe, no pleasure, no pain could deflect him from pursuing what he saw as the people's cause. It is true that Danton's friends had written to him. Lucile Desmoulins's mother had even asked him to remember the joy he had felt holding his godson Horace on his knee.[108] Surely Robespierre would intervene to save Danton and Camille so they could return to their families? But it was on his ability to scrupulously set aside such feelings that the Incorruptible prided himself. He could speak about himself so often because he identified so completely with the Revolution—the two were not separate in his mind. Even more peculiarly, he was surrounded by others who also believed in this coincidence of Robespierre and the Revolution. It helped that his incorruptibility was genuine, not a fraudulent facade. Had he been implicated in a financial scandal (like Danton or Fabre), taken a bribe, indulged a streak of personal perversity (as Carrier had in Nantes), or even just been spotted, like Mirabeau, with a couple of prostitutes in the Palais-Royal gardens, Robespierre's career would have disintegrated. The strange combination of his self-centered rhetoric, clean living, clear principles, and passionate political commitment made him seem like the Revolution incarnate.

THE MORNING OF 13 Germinal (2 April) was warm for the time of year, so all the windows were open as the Revolutionary Tribunal assembled at ten to hear the Dantonists accused. They were charged with conspiring to overthrow the government (the Committee of Public Safety and Committee of General Security, both still nominally responsible to the Convention). But these charges were farfetched and conflated with accusations of corruption arising from the East India Company scandal. The public crowded into the vast room, its beautiful gilt ceiling and marble floor resonant of the old regime. Soon there was no more space, but still the people came, lining the grand staircase, pressing up around the walls of the Palais de Justice on its small island at the heart of Paris. The crowd filled the streets and quays outside and stretched back across the span of the Pont Neuf to the left and right banks of the Seine. When he spoke, Danton's deep, booming voice rang out through the open windows like the tocsin. It is said the crowd could hear him clearly across the river. He was asked for his name and address: "My abode will soon be nothingness. As for my name, you will find it in the pantheon of history."[109] When

Camille was asked his age, he replied, "Thirty-three, same age as that sans-culotte Jesus Christ."[110] It was obvious that the Dantonists were going to be defiant to the end. To mitigate their effect on the jury, judges, and crowd, Danton and his five associates (including Camille and Fabre) were put on trial with a selection of ten other prisoners allegedly implicated in the East India Company scam. During the trial a couple more prisoners were added to further confuse matters. Everyone remembered that the Revolutionary Tribunal had acquitted Marat—the outcome here was not a foregone conclusion—and this may have been one of the reasons Robespierre was initially reluctant to agree to Danton's arrest when it was first proposed in the Committee of Public Safety. On the second day the first witness, a man named Pierre Joseph Cambon, was called. Danton looked him in the eye and said, "Cambon, do you really believe we are conspirators?" Cambon could not suppress a smile. "Look, he's laughing! Write down that he laughed!" shouted Danton, laughing himself.[111] Then he began the defense that reverberated louder than the president's bell:

> You say that I have been paid, but I tell you, a man like me cannot be bought. Against your accusation—for which you cannot provide proof, not even the hint of a proof or the shadow of a witness—I pitch my entire revolutionary career. It was I who in the Jacobins kept Mirabeau from leaving Paris. I have served long enough, and my life is a burden to me, but I will defend myself by telling you what I have done. It was I who made the pikes rise suddenly on 20 June and prevented the king's journey to Saint-Cloud. The day after the massacre of the Champ de Mars a warrant was out for my arrest. Men were sent to kill me at Arcis, but my people came and defended me. I had to flee to London, but I came back. . . . At the Jacobins, I demanded the republic. It was I who knew that the court was eager for war. It was I who denounced the policy of the war.[112]

Here he was interrupted by a question: "But what did you do against Brissot and his associates?" For it was well known that whereas Robespierre had hated Brissot ever since they disagreed over the war and had fought him to the guillotine, Danton had been less active in the fall of Brissot and his Girondin friends. "I told them that they were going to the scaffold," Danton retorted. "When I was a minister [of justice] I said it to Brissot in front of the whole cabinet." He resumed:

> It was I who prepared 10 August. You say I went to Arcis. I admit it, and I am proud of it. I went there to pass three days, to say good-bye to my mother and to arrange my affairs because I was shortly to be in danger. I hardly slept that night. It was I who had Mandat killed [on the steps of the Hôtel de Ville] because he had given the order to fire on the people. . . . You reproach me for being friends with Fabre d'Églantine. He is still my friend, I still think he is a good citizen as he sits here with me. . . . With regard to those who were once my friends, I will tell you this: Marat had a volcanic character, Robespierre I have known as tenacious and firm, but I—I have served in my own way. . . . I would embrace my worst enemy for the sake of the country, and I will give her my body if she needs the sacrifice.[113]

Danton was turning the tide of the crowd—its currents responded to the pull of his powerful voice. It was exhausting work and he had to pause briefly to rest. But when he did so, the president of the tribunal, a friend of Robespierre's named Martial Joseph Armand Herman, immediately called him to order and warned him to defend himself with proof, not rhetoric. More quietly, Danton replied:

> That a man should be violent is wrong, I know, unless it is for the public good, and such violence has often been mine. . . . If I have been excessive here, it is because I have found myself accused with such intolerable injustice. [Raises his voice again.] As for you, Saint-Just, you will have to answer to posterity.[114]

Saint-Just was out of earshot. He was in the Convention preparing a motion even more stringent than the three-day rule that ended the trial of the Girondins. He proposed that "any prisoner who resists or insults national justice shall at once be debarred from pleading his case."[115] The intimidated deputies gave their consent. In addition to all their other anxieties they were frightened by a rumored revolt in the Luxembourg jail, where the Dantonists had been held after their arrest. Robespierre suggested that Saint-Just's report, and the new decree, should be taken to the tribunal and read aloud to the audience there. On the last morning of the trial this was duly done, and the prisoners were prevented from finishing their defense. The trial was summarily closed. Danton roared, "We are going to be judged without being heard."[116] Camille tore to pieces the text of the speech he had intended to make, and to avoid further trouble the prisoners were hustled out of the court before they could hear the sentence—which was death.

Danton spent most of the last twenty-four hours of his life trying to calm Camille, who was crying like a distraught child and asking distractedly, "Will they kill my wife too?" She was only twenty-three. He wrote her a long final letter that ended:

> Despite my torment, I believe that there is a God. My blood will efface my sins, my human weaknesses, and God will reward what is good in me—my virtues and my love of liberty. I will see you again one day, O Lucile! . . . Adieu, Lucile, my life, my soul, my divinity on this earth. . . . I feel the shore of life retreating before me. I still see, Lucile. I see you. My crossed arms grip you. My bound hands embrace you. My severed head rests upon you. I am going to die.[117]

Lucile never received the letter. She had already been arrested and accused of trying to incite the rumored revolt in the Luxembourg jail. A week later she did indeed follow her husband to the guillotine, as he had feared.

By the time the carts and an armed guard came for the Dantonists, late on the afternoon of 16 Germinal (5 April), Camille was more composed. The condemned saw the beauty of Paris for the last time: the soft golden light reflected from the tall windows of the houses on the right bank of the Seine, the lilac and cherry blossoms in the Tuileries gardens, the Café de l'Ecole, where Danton sat before the Revolution wooing his first wife and dreaming of life as a lawyer. Then they turned into the rue Saint-Honoré and there in the street was an artist, daring to draw the violence that was still in Danton's face. Danton lost control of himself, ranting and raving violently, only when they came to No. 366, the Duplay household, shuttered tight against the crowd as it had been on the day Louis

XVI went past on his way to execution. Somewhere inside—silent, alone—was Robespierre.

One eyewitness saw the prisoners passing along the rue Saint-Honoré and ran back afterward through the Tuileries gardens, to stand at the railings from where it was possible to get a good view over the place de la Révolution. There stood the guillotine, waiting for the prisoners beside the statue of liberty. By now it was nearly 6:00 p.m. and the sunset had turned the plaster statue red. Danton was the last to die. His shadow was immense. He told the executioner to be sure to show his head to the crowd, and he muttered, "I shall never see her again . . . no weakness."[118] He might have meant his new wife or some other woman who, for whatever reason, meant the world to him. More likely, he meant France, the country he loved passionately and had long been prepared to die for. He had already begged pardon of man and God for his part in establishing the Revolutionary Tribunal that sent him to his death. In the last few moments, another eyewitness, closer to the scene, saw him scan the crowd before lying down beneath the guillotine. She saw someone in that crowd catch his gaze, then a hand raised quickly in the priestly gesture of sacramental absolution.

10

ROBESPIERRE'S RED SUMMER

Robespierre now found himself deeply preoccupied with punishment.[1] Within hours of Danton's death he was back at the Jacobins, insisting they speak of nothing else that evening except conspiracy. "Let us now frighten aristocrats in such a way that they not only are afraid to attack us but do not even dare to try and deceive us," he suggested to the applauding audience.[2] He may have been instrumental in the immediate promotion of his friend Martial Herman from president of the Revolutionary Tribunal to the Commission for Civil Administration and Police. Like Saint-Just, Claude Payan at the Commune, and Robespierre himself, Herman was a stringent moralist.[3] The son of the registrar of the old Estates of Artois and a fellow lawyer, he had almost certainly known Robespierre in Arras long before the Revolution. Herman was at the top of Robespierre's list of patriots, "an enlightened and honest man capable of the highest employment," the perfect person to put in charge of a commission that, among other far-reaching powers, oversaw the operation of the Revolutionary Tribunal.

Ten days (one revolutionary week) after Danton's death, Robespierre supported Saint-Just's recommendations to the Convention to revise and tighten police laws. Foreigners and ex-nobles were to be expelled from Paris and from all strategic towns on the republic's borders. All political trials would henceforth be held in Paris, so the punishment of counterrevolutionary suspects could be standardized. This centralization may have been an attempt to halt the atrocities of the Terror in the provinces, but it had severe implications for the capital. There were already nearly seven thousand people crammed into the prisons of Paris, and the new laws would greatly aggravate the crisis. Nonetheless, Robespierre was determined to implement the measures and spread the news of the changes. "The more rigorous the law, the greater the need for it to be known by all citizens."[4] And so, Augustin set off again to the army (this time taking along a mistress instead of the uncongenial Charlotte). His letters to his brother were full of disturbing news from the provinces: food shortages, hunger, corruption, soldiers wracked by venereal disease, anticlerical vandalism, counterrevolutionary plots. Meanwhile in the Vendée, the civil war still festered, with burning, pillage, massacre—scenes of apocalyptic horror that Robespierre himself never saw but had no difficulty at all imagining late at night in the rue Saint-Honoré.

After supporting the fierce new police laws, Robespierre was absent from the Jacobins and the Convention between 30 Germinal (19 April) and 18 Floréal (7 May). As always, it is possible he collapsed, the strain of condemning Danton taking its toll on his overworked mind and body. Yet rumor has it that he spent the day before his reappearance, his thirty-sixth birthday, celebrating out in the countryside with the Duplays and his dog, Brount, perhaps even visiting one of Rousseau's renowned retreats at Montmorency. Robespierre, by this point, looked much older than his years. The contemporary pictures of him all show sunken, heavily lined cheeks around a grimly set mouth; his eyes were more variable—sometimes simply intense, at other times terrifyingly severe. According to another rumor, on his return to the Convention he stood at the tribune with a newfound calm and control; for the first time, there was none of the convulsive twitching, or the neurotic fiddling with his glasses, or the other agitated mannerisms of someone who, despite everything, still found it a challenge to raise his voice in public.

Robespierre's speech on 18 Floréal addressed the relationship between republican principles, religion, and morality, consolidating the public professions of personal faith he had made in the past. There was, he had no doubt, a God and an afterlife for human souls. More than this, he attempted to show how the religion of patriotism that had been implicit in the Revolution ever since the great Festival of Federation on the first anniversary of the fall of the Bastille might now be developed, institutionalized, and used to secure the social foundations of the still very precarious Republic. Here it was, at last, Robespierre's presentation of his most profound personal beliefs, his ardent faith in a public religion that he thought could save the Revolution, and the close—to some minds suspiciously close—connection between the two. Officially, he was representing the views of the Committee of Public Safety, but as so often, his approach was blazingly personal. He began with appropriate grandeur: "The world has changed. It must change again."[5] He listed evidence of man's progress and mastery of the physical world: the development of languages, the advances of agriculture, the discovery of electricity (he had not forgotten his triumph in the lightning conductor case back in Arras), the construction of terrestial and celestial maps (he had not forgotten the Coronelli globes in the library at Louis-le-Grand either), the discoveries of Newton, the artistic achievements of his friend the revolutionary artist David. Everything had changed in the physical order, and now everything must change in the moral and political order, too. He compared man's reason to the globe half in light and half in darkness; so far only the arts and sciences had been touched by enlightenment, but Robespierre wanted to venture further into the shadowy realms of morality. This was by no means an eccentric desire. The abbé Sieyès (temporarily retired from politics), the Marquis de Condorcet (dead in prison), and a fair number of the other revolutionaries Robespierre had met or known shared it, too. What made his vision distinctive was the peculiar coincidence of three major obsessions: his interest in moral development, his belief in God, and his passionate commitment to democracy. Addressing the Convention, especially those deputies inclined toward atheism, he demanded to know:

Who commissioned you to announce to the people that God does not exist? O you who are so passionate about this arid doctrine yet have no passion for your country! How does it help a man if you persuade him that blind force presides over his destiny and strikes at random, now at the virtuous, now at the criminal? Does it help him to believe that his soul is nothing but a thin vapor that is dissipated at the mouth of the tomb? Will the idea of annihilation inspire him with purer and higher sentiments than that of immortality? Will it give him more respect for himself and his fellow men, more devotion to his country, a braver face against tyranny, or a deeper disdain either for pleasure or for death? No ... the dying breath of those poor people who die beneath the blows of an assassin is an appeal to eternal justice! The innocent on the scaffold make tyrants pale in their triumphal chariots: would they have such ascendancy if the tomb made the oppressor and the oppressed equals? ... If the existence of God and the immortality of the soul were nothing but dreams, they would still be the most beautiful conceptions of the human spirit.[6]

No one could call Danton innocent—though he was not guilty of the crimes for which he was executed. No one knows if his last breath was an appeal to eternal justice—though this was certainly part of his rant outside Robespierre's door on the way to the guillotine. How, in all seriousness, could Robespierre square his passionate belief in God and eternal justice with his part in a regime of terror that was claiming more and more lives by the day? He did it by convincing himself that not a single innocent person had been condemned. "And who says anyone innocent has perished?" he had asked Danton coldly at their last meeting. But it was increasingly difficult to maintain this contorted position. The strain became obvious when, in the middle of his speech proposing public worship of the Supreme Being, Robespierre suddenly lashed out at Danton's ghost:

Danton, the most dangerous of all the enemies of the country if he had not been the most cowardly—Danton, temporizing with every crime, connected to every plot, promising criminals his protection and patriots his loyalty, artful in giving his treasons the pretext of public good, in justifying his vices by his pretended faults. He contrived through his friends to have the conspirators, who were on the point of bringing about the ruin of the republic, accused in an insignificant or favorable manner, so that he might have an opportunity

of defending them . . . and be the better able to rally all the enemies
of liberty against the republican government.[7]

This defamation of a former friend, in the midst of a speech on patriotism
and religion, may simply reflect Robespierre's habitual impulse to suborn
anything and everything fresh in the public's mind to his current political
purpose. Or perhaps it was a more personal exorcism of his confused regret at Danton's death. Either way, it was a clear warning that the new progressive and democratic religion he envisaged was perfectly compatible
with the continuation—perhaps even the intensification—of the Terror.

At the same sitting the Convention approved the decree establishing worship of the Supreme Being. Article 7 outlined the festivals to
be celebrated by the republic on successive *décadis*, or Sabbaths, occur-
ring once every ten days:

> The Supreme Being and Nature; the human race; the French people;
> the benefactors of mankind; the martyrs of freedom; liberty and
> equality; the republic; the liberty of the world; patriotism; hatred of
> tyrants and traitors; truth; justice; modesty; glory and immortality;
> friendship; temperance; courage; good faith; heroism; impartiality;
> Stoicism; love; conjugal fidelity; fatherly affection; mother love; filial
> piety; childhood; youth; manhood; old age; misfortune; agriculture;
> industry; our ancestors; posterity; happiness.

These festival plans were a straight projection of Robespierre's own
sober system of values. He saw the long-suffering ordinary people of
France as modest, stoical, and oppressed by misfortune. For them, he
wanted to inaugurate a democratic regime in which poverty would be
honorable, not shameful, and glory more meaningful than sensual
gratification. Ultimately, his model of family life was traditional: con-
jugal fidelity, fatherly affection, mother love, and filial piety—all the
things that were missing from his own disrupted childhood. The secure foundation for his values was, as it had always been, belief in
God. Earlier that year, he had been horrified to hear that the gates of
cemeteries in Lyon and Nevers were being inscribed with the atheistic
motto "Death is an eternal sleep." Now, with deep gratification, he
saw, as he walked through Paris, men on ladders painting in gold let-

ters over the doors of abandoned Christian churches, article 1 of the new religion:

> The French people recognize the existence of the Supreme Being and the immortality of the soul.

Three days after delivering his momentous speech, Robespierre and Barère, his colleague on the Committee of Public Safety, were browsing in a bookshop near the Palais-Royal. The talk that day was of Louis XVI's sister, Mme Élisabeth, who was on her way to the guillotine after nearly two years' imprisonment in the Tower. Out in the street people were blaming Robespierre for her death, although he, in fact, had argued against it on the committee. Bitter or just despondent, he turned to his colleague and said, "You see, it is always me."[8] He had done more than anyone to identify himself wholly with the Revolution, and now that the Revolution had become the Terror, he found himself identified with that, too. The next day, 22 Floréal (11 May), he decided to make an impromptu visit to the Tower. No one knows why he went. When they heard about it, his enemies spread the rumor that he was contemplating marriage to the deceased king's daughter, Mme Royale, and scheming to secure his tyranny over France by mixing his blood with that of the Capet dynasty. The princess left her own report of the incident, which mentions no such ludicrous designs:

> One day there came a man who I believe was Robespierre. The officers showed him great respect. His visit was a secret even to the people in the Tower, who did not know who he was; or, at least, would not tell me: he stared insolently at me, cast his eyes on my books, and, after joining the municipal officers in a search, retired.[9]

Whatever he was doing, or looking for, it was typical of Robespierre to be momentarily distracted by the spines of some books. Another source claims that the princess managed to pass her distinguished visitor a note:

> My brother is ill. I have written to the Convention for permission to go take care of him. The Convention has not answered me. I repeat my request.[10]

There is no record of Robespierre's having visited the young heir to the abolished throne, Louis Capet, as he was now known. The nine-year-old boy, living in squalid solitary confinement, severely beaten for saying his prayers at night, degraded, and sick, might have touched the Incorruptible's heart. What would Robespierre have said if he had known that Capet had been allowed to raise three canaries in his dank and lonely prison cell? If he had heard that those tamed and treasured birds were suddenly taken away because the pastime that had brightened his own childhood was considered too aristocratic for poor Capet? But no one bothered Robespierre with such details or dared ask him what was on his mind when he walked away from that terrible place, its child prisoners and abusive guards.

THE FIRST FESTIVAL of the Supreme Being was scheduled for 20 Prairial (8 June). Amid the frenzy of preparation—revolutionary stage sets by David and music by Gossec, as usual—there were two attempts to assassinate Robespierre. Neither was very determined. In the first, on 3 Prairial (22 May), a man named Admiral hung about in the street all day, hoping to fire at Robespierre, but ended up aiming at another member of the Committee of Public Safety, Collot d'Herbois. The gun misfired and the only person injured was a locksmith who ran to help Collot. The second attempt occurred the following evening. At about nine, a sixteen-year-old girl named Cécile Renault knocked on the Duplays' door and asked to see Robespierre. She acted very suspicious, babbled something about the old regime, and was soon arrested and found to be in possession of a knife (a fruit knife, not the kind of blade that had killed Marat). When questioned she said she had only "wanted to see what a tyrant looked like," rather as Danton had once skipped school at the time of Louis XVI's coronation "to see how they made a king." Renault's testimony was as confused and confusing as Damiens's had been after his attempt to assassinate Louis XV back in 1757. It was not even clear that she planned on murdering Robespierre, still less what her motives for doing so might have been. A rumor went around that he had staged the whole affair to boost his popularity with the people, who loved a near martyr almost as much as they loved a real one.

Whatever the real story was, Robespierre, who had been speaking regularly for the last four years of his imminent assassination, reacted with all the panic of someone who had narrowly escaped death. When the public prosecutor, Fouquier-Tinville, called on Robespierre at the Duplays' later in the evening, he found him offensively dictatorial. Robespierre persuaded the Committee of Public Safety that the situation warranted recalling Saint-Just to Paris from his latest mission with the army. Such was Robespierre's agitation that he managed to sign the document recalling his best friend twice. He also vetoed any special honors for the locksmith wounded trying to help Collot d'Herbois and made a speech in the Convention that was almost incoherent with paranoia:

> Slander, arson, poison, atheism, corruption, starvation, and murder—they [the enemies of France] have been prodigal in every sort of crime: but there still remains assassination, assassination, and again assassination.[11]

Even so, he could not disguise his pleasure at being (at last) "judged worthy of the tyrant's dagger." Let no one say city life was less dangerous than the battlefield, "we have nothing to envy our brave brothers in arms," he reassured himself and the other deputies, who had kept a safe distance from the front line. Later that evening the Jacobins were rapturous in their relief that Robespierre had survived. He rose to the occasion, announcing:

> I feel myself more independent than ever of the wickedness of man. The crimes of tyrants and the weapons of their assassins have rendered me freer and more formidable to the enemies of the people, my spirit is more disposed than ever to unmasking traitors and tearing off the masks with which they still dare to cover themselves. . . . We swear by the daggers already reddened with the blood of the Revolution's martyrs, and recently sharpened for us, too, to exterminate every single one of the criminals who want to rob us of happiness and liberty.[12]

Letters of congratulation flooded into the rue Saint-Honoré and Robespierre kept at least some of them. "Everlasting thanks to the Supreme Being, who has watched over your life!" wrote one admirer from Vesoul.[13] Whether or not Robespierre staged the first or second attempt on his life (or both), no one can doubt that he turned them instantly to political advantage. Yet this does not mean that his fear was faked. "We shall never get out of our present state. I am worried to death. I am losing my mind," he muttered in unguarded moments to his tobacconist, a pretty shopkeeper in the rue Saint-Honoré who did not matter, one way or the other, politically.

THE MORNING OF 20 Prairial (8 June), Whitsunday in the old Christian calendar,[14] was bathed in brilliant summer sunshine, and the rest of the day was destined to be the happiest of Robespierre's life. The citizens of Paris had decorated their houses with wreaths of oak, laurel, fresh flowers, tricolor ribbons, and flags.[15] Joachim Vilate, a friend of Robespierre's and a juror on the Revolutionary Tribunal who had been given lodgings in the part of the Tuileries palace known as the Pavilion de Flore, encountered him pacing around the premises at an early hour, far too nervous to have breakfast, because the day of the first Festival of the Supreme Being had arrived. Vilate persuaded Robespierre to accompany him upstairs to try to eat something. Robespierre's nerves stemmed from his election four days previously as president of the Convention, which meant he would officiate as a kind of high priest at the inaugural ceremony of the new religion that meant so much to him. From Vilate's rooms there was a wonderful view of the Tuileries gardens. Robespierre, standing at the window, was awed by the crowd beginning to assemble below. He could see women with garlands of fresh-blown roses in their hair and branches of palm or laurel in their hands, men with oak leaves in their hats, and children strewing the ground with violets and myrtle. Intoxicated with joy, he said to Vilate:

> Behold the most interesting part of humanity! Here is the universe assembled before us! Nature, how sublime, how delightful thy power! How the tyrants must turn pale at the thought of this festival![16]

That same morning, the guillotine, which had been in alarmingly frequent use within earshot of the Tuileries palace (over the previous seven days alone it had executed 119 people), was tactfully moved to the site of the demolished Bastille. Afterward it was moved even farther out of the city center because the blood pooling beneath it was beginning to pollute the city's water supply.[17]

At midday, Robespierre, dressed in a sky blue coat with an immense tricolor sash, went back down into the garden, where he joined the other deputies to the Convention, similarly attired, wearing swords and plumed hats and bearing posies made of flowers and sheaves of corn. Robespierre's posy was slightly larger than everyone else's—it had been lovingly constructed in the Duplay household. According to Vilate, Robespierre absentmindedly left it behind on an armchair on his way down to the festival and had to go back to get it. The immense crowd listened to him give a rather vague theistic speech, beginning: "The day forever fortunate has arrived that the French people have consecrated to the Supreme Being."[18] They watched him set fire to a cardboard statue of Atheism—a hideous misshapen figure with cumbersome drapery and ass's ears that the crowd had been puzzling over earlier in the day. From the flames another cardboard statue emerged—a representation of Wisdom—fair, majestic, and only slightly singed. After one more speech underscoring the meaning of this ceremony, they all sang a song to the Supreme Being and processed to the Champ de Mars (recently renamed the Champ de la Réunion).

Throughout the ceremony, Robespierre could hear behind him the sarcastic and derisive comments of fellow Convention deputies who dared to snicker at the rituals in which he had invested so much thought and hope. There was nothing he could do, short of turning around and interrupting the proceedings, but afterward he complained about it bitterly. Almost the whole population of Paris, about half a million people, had turned out for the occasion. On the old Champ de Mars—where there had already been four celebrations of the fall of the Bastille, with a fifth now imminent—the assembled congregation sang patriotic songs as the deputies filed up a papier-mâché mound (symbolic of the Jacobin Mountain) and took their seats beneath a tree of liberty at the summit. Cries of "Vive la République!" echoed all around, and the day ended with athletics, inspired by the festivals of ancient Greece. It must have seemed to

Robespierre that the optimism of the early Revolution had been revived—a new religion, a new beginning: his tremendous personal and political struggle had not been in vain.

The next day he drew up laws to further fortify the Revolutionary Tribunal and invented a new official category of criminals: enemies of the people, "those who, in any manner and no matter with what mask they have concealed themselves, have sought to thwart the progress of the Revolution and prevent the strengthening of the Republic."[19] Through his friend Couthon, who presented the proposals in the Convention, Robespierre recommended that the tribunal should now accept "moral proofs" against accused persons, who were no longer to be allowed advocates. Power to send people before the tribunal was to be extended (from the Committee of Public Safety and the larger Committee of General Security) to the Convention, to individual representatives on mission in the provinces, and to the public prosecutor, Fouquier-Tinville. Enemies of the people included anyone seeking to reestablish the monarchy, discredit the Convention, betray the republic, communicate with foreign enemies, interfere with food provision, shelter conspirators, speak ill of patriotism, suborn officials, mislead the people, spread false news, insult morality, deprave the public conscience, steal public property, abuse public office, or plot against the liberty, unity, and security of the state. The punishment for all these crimes was death. The proposals were passed by the Convention without the usual prior discussion in the Committee of Public Safety and became known as the Law of 22 Prairial, the climax of the Terror. The passing of this law made it possible to execute someone for declaring, "A fig for the nation," for producing sour wine, for hoarding, for writing to or attempting to communicate with the English. From 22 Prairial (10 June) until the arrest of Robespierre on 9 Thermidor (27 July), 1,376 people were guillotined in Paris. In those forty-seven days, the Revolutionary Tribunal condemned more people to death than it had done in all the months since Danton established it in March 1793. Was the bloodletting Robespierre's fault?

He bears direct responsibility for the Law of 22 Prairial, which was designed to both speed up and expand the Revolutionary Tribunal's work. In this simple, technical, legal sense, his hands are covered in blood. It does not matter which, or how many, individuals he intervened personally to save at the eleventh hour. He initiated the law that menaced absolutely everyone, on the most spurious grounds and without offering recourse to any form of defense. He also played a prominent part in extending the Revolution's agenda to include the moral regeneration of the people, and he was prepared to resort to the most drastic measures to achieve this. It was not enough to encourage patriotism—antipatriotic sentiment had to be exterminated. It was not enough to nurture moral rectitude—depravity had to be stamped out. In this way, the joyous Festival of the Supreme Being and the dreadful Law of 22 Prairial were all too compatible. Together they aimed at realizing the republic of virtue that Robespierre dreamed of. He may not have thought it likely to come about in his lifetime—he was ill, desperately anxious, anticipating assassination, in despair over the corruption silting up around him—but for him none of these were reasons to stop trying. And so he went on, not as a man like Macbeth, so steeped in a river of blood that "returning were as tedious as go o'er." Robespierre was no cynic. He was, as Danton told the Revolutionary Tribunal, "above all, a tenacious man," and what he held on to most tightly of all was his dream of virtue. He went on with the Terror, kept moving through that gory river, because he believed it necessary for saving the Revolution. He can be accused of insanity and inhumanity but certainly not of insincerity.

Following the Law of 22 Prairial, there was a savage quarrel in the Committee of Public Safety; they had to shut the windows to avoid a public scandal.[20] This was hardly the first big fight to erupt around the oval table in the green room. What exactly was said is unrecorded, but if Robespierre and Couthon were criticized for the manner in which they had pushed through the Law of 22 Prairial, their colleagues cannot seriously have criticized the content, which reflected common policy. The Committee of Public Safety was still an emergency wartime government; once the Terror ended and the constitution of 1793 came into effect, the committee would be annulled. All agreed that if this happened before sufficient measures had been taken to safeguard the republic from its internal and external enemies, all would be lost and the Revolution would have been in vain. Robespierre had taken the Terror to an extreme, but he had not departed from the basic principles from which the Committee of Public Safety drew its power. Serious clashes of personality and policy, however, fractured its unity of purpose. In particular, Robespierre clashed with Lazare Carnot, the army officer and stern patriot who was responsible for the conduct of the war. After the recapture of Toulon the main focus of the foreign war was once again the frontier with the Austrian Netherlands. Carnot's program of mass mobilization, combined with military reforms to integrate new recruits into a coherent fighting force, were beginning to show profit. Back in Paris, however, the war was causing political conflict. In April, Carnot had called Robespierre and Saint-Just absurd dictators. He had quarreled bitterly with Saint-Just over military issues. More recently, he had dispatched artillery units loyal to Robespierre to the front line. Robespierre suspected this action was a deliberate ploy to get those who would defend him, should the need arise, out of Paris. Since there were 700,000 armed men at the front and a constant need for reinforcements, his suspicions may have been unfounded. There was no doubt, though, that Carnot was hostile to him.

Robespierre had enemies outside the Committee of Public Safety, too. The Committee of General Security, angry at not having been consulted over the Law of 22 Prairial, began scheming to expose the Incorruptible as a dictator. Many deputies in the Convention were now frightened of being sent before the Revolutionary Tribunal—especially those who had been called back in disgrace from their provincial missions, among them Joseph Fouché and Jean Lambert Tallien, both notorious for their cruelty. Sensing so much ill feeling, Robespierre increasingly withdrew from the Convention and from meetings of the Committee of Public Safety. Instead he turned his attention to running the committee's new Police Bureau, which he had taken over on 14 Floréal (3 May) when Saint-Just left Paris again to supervise the army in the north. Saint-Just had set up the Police Bureau one revolutionary week earlier, on 4 Floréal (23 April), an act that caused immediate friction with the Convention's other executive committee, the Committee of General Security, which had had responsibility for policing ever since it was established in September 1792. That committee had not been pleased when the Committee of Public

Safety acquired the right to issue arrest warrants back in July 1793, but it was yet more threatened by the new Police Bureau. Internal security—eradicating the insidious threat of the enemy within—had been a concern of Robespierre's from the outset of the Revolution. Now in charge of the Police Bureau, he spent hour after hour assessing the reports of informers, sifting through the denunciations of unpatriotic enemies of the people pouring in from all over France. His small staff summarized each case for him, leaving a space in the margin for his decision. This work must have played on his worst nightmares. It forced him to confront on a daily basis the questions he found most tormenting: How could true and false patriots be distinguished? Who was more likely to look at a tree of liberty with indifference—the hypocrite or the real patriot? In some cases he dutifully asked for more information before making a decision; in others he simply authorized an arrest. For example, when the mayor of Mont-Rouge was accused of *incivisme*, or lack of public spirit, during the local Festival of the Supreme Being and, more specifically, of saying as he watched the celebrations, "This rabble doesn't wear undergarments. See how they dance," Robespierre directed: "Arrest the mayor of Mont-Rouge and have Herman interrogate him." However, when the popular society of Valence denounced the quartermaster of the Armée des Alpes as immoral, Robespierre questioned the esprit of the society and asked for more information from his friend Payan.[21]

Increasingly, Robespierre fell back on networks of patronage—friends and friends of the friends whom he already knew (or thought he knew) as pure of heart, "au courant" with his ideas, and "one of us."[22] His landlord, Maurice Duplay, for example, was appointed to the Revolutionary Tribunal. It is said that once, when Duplay returned home, Robespierre asked him what he had been doing on the tribunal that day. "I have never tried to find out, Maximilien, what you do on the Committee of Public Safety," replied the carpenter correctly.[23] Robespierre, in acknowledgment of Duplay's irreproachability, silently shook his hand. But virtue like this was rare. Robespierre was now in a position to appoint a considerable number of public officials to administrative jobs, but he knew comparatively few people and was soon running out of candidates. Some he summoned from Arras; his prerevolutionary acquaintance Herman recommended to Robespierre another member of the Arras criminal tribunal: "I propose one Carron for your consideration. . . . He is a good sans-culotte republican whom I consider to be one of us [*que je crois propre à être avec nous*].[24] Robespierre's printer, Léopold Nicolas, the Duplays' doctor, Souberbielle, and even their grocer also found themselves appointed to the Revolutionary Tribunal. The Duplays' next-door neighbors at 365 rue Saint-Honoré proved another source of loyal personnel. Here lodged a hat merchant, Louis Emery, and a manufacturer, Didier Fillion, who were closely linked to a faction of Lyonnais Jacobins, the Friends of Chalier, with whom Robespierre had been connected since his friend Joseph Chalier was executed during the revolt in Lyon in 1793. Robespierre ended up appointing some members of this group to administrative jobs in Paris. The fact that a provincial faction gained such influence with him highlights the essentially domestic nature of his patronage networks. Politically, he relied on those he thought he could judge instinctively, and unsurprisingly they turned out to be his friends, his neighbors, the friends of his neighbors, and so on. At the end of one of Robespierre's lists of potential candidates for appointment or promotion there is Saint-Just's brother-in-law, described as "energetic, patriotic, pure, enlightened."[25] These were the personal attributes the Incorruptible most admired. To hostile eyes, his appointments look nepotistic, his values empty excuses for promoting friends and acquaintances to positions of power. To him, this seemed the only way of finding upright, trustworthy patriots for all the urgent jobs that needed doing. He wanted to surround himself with people who believed as he did that "duty comes first when it comes to serving the republic."[26] But his labors in the Police Bureau were a daily reminder that such people were very few and far between.

By now there were unmistakable signs that Robespierre would soon turn on the deputies in the Convention whom he considered corrupt. Two in particular stood out: Tallien and Fouché. Both had been recalled from their missions to quell the counterrevolution after perpetrating infamous atrocities, Tallien in the Vendée and Bordeaux, Fouché in Nevers and Lyon. After the successful repression of Lyon, authorized by the Committee of Public Safety, Fouché remained behind in the city. His attempts to continue and even extend the repression with new excesses of brutality had led to conflict between him and the Friends of Chalier, who thought it was time for local Lyonnais patriots to resume control. Tallien, for his part, had felt personally menaced even before the Law of 22 Prairial was passed. His mistress, Thérésa Cabarrus, a twenty-one-year-old Spanish woman who had been married to a French nobleman at the age of fifteen, had been arrested earlier in the month. Tallien had met her when he was organizing the Terror in Bordeaux, spared her life, fallen in love with her, and brought her back to Paris. In his small, fastidious handwriting, Robespierre himself had written out the warrant for Therezia's arrest. Considering that France was at war with Spain and the revolutionaries regarded ex-nobles as intrinsically suspicious, the arrest of Tallien's mistress may not have reflected personal animosity on Robespierre's part. But Tallien was convinced it did. Similarly, Fouché, a militant atheist, knew he was loathed by the Incorruptible. While on mission, he had vigorously overseen the ransacking of the churches in Nivre and delighted in having the motto that Robespierre so hated, "Death is an eternal sleep," inscribed on the cemetery gates. More recently he had dared to jeer openly at the Festival of the Supreme Being. In addition to these personal reasons for hostility toward Fouché, Robespierre was encouraged to move against him by the Friends of Chalier, who, now that Fouché had been recalled to Paris, openly hoped he might be sent before the Revolutionary Tribunal and guillotined.[27]

In her memoirs, Charlotte Robespierre claims that she was present during the bitter conversation between Robespierre and Fouché that took place when Fouché returned from Lyon.[28] She says her brother severely reproached Fouché for all the bloodshed he had caused in the republic's second city. Fouché trembled, went pale, and babbled excuses for his cruelty. Robespierre told him there were no excuses for the crimes he was guilty of. True, Lyon had rebelled against the National Convention, but that did not justify killing crowds of unarmed civilians with grapeshot. According to Charlotte, Robespierre and Fouché were enemies from this day. Earlier in the Revolution, Robespierre had thought Fouché a sincere patriot and stalwart democrat and had even encouraged him to court Charlotte. Too beady-eyed to be swept up in a fanciful romance, Charlotte had understood immediately that Fouché was simply hoping to further his career by aspiring to become Robespierre's brother-in-law. So she told him coldly that the idea of marrying him was not "repugnant" to her and that she would, of course, be guided by her brother. Fouché withdrew his interest, and later Charlotte felt she and Maximilien had been equally duped by this "hypocritical, treacherous man without convictions, without morality, capable of doing anything to satisfy his wild ambition." Her account is biased as so often, but the souring of relations between Robespierre and Fouché that she describes certainly occurred. Robespierre may have thought Fouché had gone too far in Lyon, but he himself was not innocent of the bloody repression—indeed, through his connections with the Friends of Chalier, he was seriously implicated in the city's politics, much more so than Charlotte knew or understood.

At the Jacobins on 23 Prairial (11 June), when the infamous law was just one day old, Robespierre indignantly denounced Fouché for preaching atheism. The next day in the Convention he warned of a new faction trying to infiltrate the Mountain. "A member of the Mountain is a pure, reasonable, sublime patriot," he said, insisting that nothing could be worse for the country or the people than a plot to corrupt his own supporters. One deputy, Léonard Bourdon, a fervent supporter of de-Christianization, sensing that, along with Tallien, Fouché, and several others, he was being threatened without being named, interrupted to ask outright if Robespierre was calling him a scoundrel. "I demand, in the name of the country, not to be interrupted. I have not named Bourdon; shame on him who names himself." Then Robespierre continued with words to the effect of "if the cap fits wear it," whereupon another voice cried, "Name them!" "I will name them when it is necessary," he replied, meaning if and when he could be sure of arresting and guillotining them. He continued speaking in vague, abstract terms about the false patriots conspiring night and day to destroy the Mountain. He appealed to the Convention for unity and called on it to support the Committee of Public Safety:

> Give us your help; do not permit anyone to come between you and us, since we are a part of you and nothing without you. Give us the

strength to carry the immense burden, almost beyond human effort, that you have imposed on us.[29]

Tallien interrupted to say he and another deputy had been mocked in the street: the people no longer thought of them as their representatives. Robespierre turned on him—that was not true, he retorted—but what was true was that Tallien himself was seeking to degrade and menace the Convention by endlessly threatening its members with the guillotine. According to Robespierre, he had recently said: "They want to guillotine us, but first we are going to guillotine them."[30] By this point, what members of the general public thought of the Convention was entirely beside the point. Robespierre and Tallien were really arguing about the fact that under the Law of 22 Prairial the Convention's three hundred or so deputies were no longer immune from arrest and execution. Robespierre had just made it clear to anyone still in doubt that Tallien's name was on his latest list of proscriptions.

SOME OF THE atheists and supporters of de-Christianization whom Robespierre so hated decided to try to strike him before he struck them. It was obvious that a scandal would destroy his career, established as it was on personal purity. But there were no scandals where the Incorruptible was concerned. A scandal would have to be fabricated. There was an old woman in Paris who had been arrested many times under the old regime, and even interrogated in the Bastille at one point, for describing the extraordinary visions she had. Catherine Théot had grown up a serving girl in a convent. Convinced that she was destined to be the second virginal mother of God, she prophesized the final coming of the Messiah and was still expecting to give birth to him well into her eighties. Alternatively, she predicted his sudden appearance near the Pantheon amid flashes of lightning. She was almost certainly insane, but since the Revolution her sect of devoted followers had grown—these were, after all, times of tremendous turmoil and insecurity. One of her followers was an ex-monk, Dom Gerle, who had lodged with the Duplays before Robespierre did, been a member of the National Assembly, and more recently tried to involve himself in planning the worship of the Supreme Being. Thus Dom Gerle had close links to Robespierre's most intimate circle, and recently the Incorruptible had been instrumental in obtaining him a certificate of *civisme*.

These were the raw materials from which the Incorruptible's enemies in the Convention's Committee of General Security tried to concoct an embarrassing scandal. That they were driven to such desperate measures is testimony to the aptness of Robespierre's nickname. Théot was arrested on 23 Floréal (12 May), just five days after Robespierre asked the Convention, "Who commissioned you to announce to the people that God does not exist?" Then on 27 Prairial (June 15), Marc Guillaume Albert Vadier, an atheist deputy, read a report on the Théot sect (renaming it the Theos sect by a clever slip of the pen) in the Committee of General Security. Later he planned to back up the report with the news that under Théot's mattress the police had found a letter dictated but not written by the illiterate and partially paralyzed old woman, congratulating Robespierre on all he had done—by restoring belief in God—to prepare the way for her forthcoming son, the Messiah. The timing of this report was no accident: it was three days after Robespierre had publicly menaced Tallien and Fouché. According to one account, Vadier went to the green room in the old Tuileries palace the evening before he delivered his report and announced what he intended to do the next day in the Committee of General Security. Robespierre was mortified. Unsurprisingly, a quarrel ensued, Vadier called Robespierre a tyrant, and Robespierre, with tears of anger in his eyes, said, "I'm a tyrant, am I! Well, I shall release you from my tyranny and come here no more."[31] And that was the last time he attended the Committee of Public Safety. This story is exaggerated. Robespierre remained president of the Convention until 1 Messidor (19 June) and in the following week he signed a great many documents in the Committee of Public Safety. After this he does seem to have withdrawn.[32] But it is certainly true that within just a few weeks of appealing to the Convention to unite behind the committee in its awesome task of saving the republic, he effectively distanced himself from both bodies and fell back on the older sources of his political support: his friends in the Paris Commune and, of course, the Jacobins.

Whether or not he absented himself from committee meetings,

Robespierre was still a highly influential member of the government, and as such he succeeded in preventing the trial of the Théot sect. Fouquier-Tinville was sent for in the middle of the night and told by Robespierre himself that the trial was not to go ahead. The public prosecutor informed Vadier and the other conspirators that: "He, he is against it," which can hardly have come as a surprise to them.[33] What was surprising, indeed frightening, was that one man had this power to impose his will on the Convention and its Committee of General Security, even when he was personally embattled in the smaller Committee of Public Safety. Robespierre's formidable power derived from both formal and informal sources: his reputation for patriotism, his patronage networks, revolutionary experience, official responsibilities, control of the Police Bureau, popularity at the Jacobins, and support in the Commune. But taken together these do not add up to the powers of a dictator. Nevertheless, this was how his enemies perceived him. And when he quashed the trial of the Théot sect, he did indeed appear dictatorial. Soon afterward, Robespierre's supporter in the Commune Claude Payan wrote urging him to secure his victory over the conspirators with a denunciation of fanaticism. Payan, like Saint-Just and Robespierre, was interested in the possibility of centralizing moral as well as physical government. But these were long-term objectives. Much more pressing was the need to eliminate the faction in the Convention that had dared to strike at Robespierre.

Two days after the atheists failed to embroil the Incorruptible in their fabricated scandal, there was a terrible scene at the guillotine, even by the standards to which Paris had become accustomed (not for nothing had the royalist abbé Maury, back in 1791, warned against depraving the people by inuring them to the sight of blood). It was now two and a half revolutionary weeks since Cécile Renault's confused attempt to assassinate Robespierre, and the days were getting warmer with the approach of midsummer. The inhabitants of the rue Saint-Honoré must have been relieved that the guillotine was still positioned outside the city center, so they no longer had to contend with the noise and stench of the crowd accompanying the tumbrils past their doorsteps every day. As a result, Robespierre probably did not see his would-be assassin on her way to execution on 29 Prairial (17 June). She was accompanied by her father, brother, and aunt, along with a random assortment of other prisoners, all clothed in the red shirts of parricides. Before the Revolution, Robespierre had written his first essay for the Academy of Arras against the tradition of bad blood. Under the old regime, the concept of guilt by association, used to implicate a criminal's entire family in his or her shame, had been repugnant to him. How had it lost its horror for him under the republic? No wonder people began to suspect him of wanting to become king when they saw Cécile Renault and her family go by, costumed for their execution.

Also among the prisoners that day were three members of the outstandingly good-looking Sainte-Amaranthe family—a mother and her two children, aged nineteen and seventeen. It was unclear what their crime was. A story went around that Robespierre had been to dinner at their house, got uncharacteristically tipsy, spoken somewhat indiscreetly about his political intentions, and so had the whole family condemned to death to keep them quiet. But there is another story to set against this. Allegedly, on the night that Vadier went to the Committee of Public Safety to announce his forthcoming report on the Théot sect, he also threatened to propose the indictment of the Sainte-Amaranthe family. "You will do no such thing," said Robespierre imperiously. "I will," retorted Vadier. "I have plenty of evidence." "Evidence or not, if you do so I shall attack you," came the Incorruptible's reply. If the first story suggests he was a ruthless tyrant, the second suggests this was exactly how his enemies wanted to make him appear. Another prisoner among the sixty-one executed in that appalling throng was the underage servant girl of someone who had once been mistress to an Hébertist. When her small body went under the guillotine there were cries of "No children!" from the crowd, whose depravity, despite everything, still knew some bounds. We will never know for sure if the 29 Prairial executions were the revenge Robespierre demanded for a supposed attempt on his life or if those actively plotting his downfall staged them against his will. His friends and his enemies can choose the version they prefer.

Two days after the executions, Robespierre ceased to be president of the Convention and turned his attention to reorganizing the Police

Bureau. The Committee of Public Safety agreed to increase the number of staff members under him, ordering them to work every day from eight-thirty to three-thirty and, if necessary, in the evenings, too. Despite the additional help the paperwork remained chaotic and Robespierre testily complained on 5 Messidor (23 June):

> The absence of dossiers that are mentioned but often found to have gone astray perhaps stems from the poor organization of the bureau, which means that the dossiers are not put back where they should have been.[34]

He had always been fastidious. He lost his temper when he could not put his hand on the file he needed. It was a great relief when Saint-Just came back from the army in the north and took over the bureau again at the end of June. Then Robespierre could stay all day in his orderly room at the Duplays' and Saint-Just could run around the corner and straight up the outside staircase to ask his advice if he needed it. During this period, the number of people guillotined grew steadily. The sixty-one who died on 29 Prairial set a gruesome new record. It was soon surpassed on 19 Messidor (7 July) when sixty-seven were executed and almost equaled on 21 Messidor (9 July) when a further sixty went under the guillotine. Fouquier-Tinville, the public prosecutor, was often summoned in the night to receive his orders for the next day. He said that ghosts trailed him on those dark walks, hideous ghosts appearing in defiance of the argument against clemency that Barère presented to the Convention: "It is only the dead who never come back."[35] In the month that followed, there were only four days on which fewer than twenty-eight people were executed: one of these was a *décadi*, a revolutionary day of rest, and another was the fifth anniversary of the fall of the Bastille. The Police Bureau shared joint responsibility for this bloodshed with the Committee of Public Safety and the Committee of General Security. It is impossible to know exactly how the responsibility was divided but implausible that none of it was Robespierre's. Yet when he fell from power, those who pushed him gave not his extremism but his moderation as their reason. The atheist Vadier, for example, accused him "of having endeavored to save from the scaffold the enemies of the people and of having officiously interfered with Fouquier-Tinville to suspend the execution of conspirators."[36] Vadier may have meant the Sainte-Amaranthe family, over whom he and Robespierre allegedly quarreled, but there were perhaps others the Incorruptible also wanted to save.

WHEN SAINT-JUST ARRIVED back in Paris and burst through the doors of the Committee of Public Safety on the night of 10 Messidor (28 June), Robespierre was immensely relieved for both personal and political reasons. Saint-Just brought exciting news. The Revolutionary Army had just won a decisive victory against the Austrian army at Fleurus in Belgium. In doing so, it had secured the road to Paris against the foreign enemy. The battle of Fleurus was the first in history to be won by the use of air surveillance: from a manned air balloon tethered to the ground by two long cables the French had been able to observe the enemy's tactics from on high. The Committee of Public Safety received Saint-Just's news nervously. Recently it had had to move to a new room on the top floor of the Tuileries palace, so that its violent disputes could not be overheard if the windows were opened because of the stifling summer heat.[37] It was a war government. Once the war was won, there were sure to be calls for a return to constitutional government. Back in 1791, an air balloon trailing tricolor ribbons above Paris had announced the inauguration of the ill-fated constitutional monarchy. Many in the Convention now thought the air balloon floating over the battle of Fleurus should herald the institution of the long-postponed republican constitution of 1793. Robespierre, for all his differences with his colleagues on the Committee of Public Safety, did not want to see the war government disbanded until all the internal, as well as the external, enemies of the Revolution had been dealt with. In this he was supported by his friends in the Commune and Jacobin Club and by Saint-Just and Couthon on the Committee of Public Safety.

It was at the Jacobins that Robespierre had always been surest of himself. There on 21 Messidor (9 July) he tried to define patriotism— the heart of virtue and the cornerstone of the dream republic he was still fighting for. His fatigue and disillusionment showed in his speech. "There are few generous men who love virtue for itself and ardently desire the happiness of the people," he admitted with resignation, obviously numbering himself among the few.[38] Reaching imaginatively back to the beginning of the Revolution, he recalled that Necker, Louis XVI's chief minister, with whom he had once been invited to dine at Versailles, was a tyrant in his own home. Nothing astonishing there—a man who lacks public virtue cannot have private virtue either, remarked the Incorruptible. Similarly the Girondin minister Roland, married to that pretty woman so much younger than himself, displayed the kind of false virtue that Robespierre considered "diametrically opposed to heroism and humanity."[39] Then there was Hébert secretly trying to destroy the liberty of France, and the moderate Dantonists endangering the safety of the Revolution. Now there was a new plot against the revolutionary government and tribunal, which the Jacobins must alert the Convention to.

Robespierre was terribly tired. He urged the Jacobins to be suspicious, to hold fast to their principles, to fight on against the Revolution's internal enemies, so pernicious and yet so hard to identify. "It is necessary always to return to these principles: public virtue and supreme justice are the two sovereign laws under which all those charged with the interests of the country must bow."[40] His words and themes were what they had always been, but much of the vigor was gone. Did any of the Jacobins still bother about Necker or Roland? Why did Robespierre think their names might stir his audience when so many terrible things had happened since the fall of the monarchy? Everyone knew he had more immediate enemies now, and the time was fast approaching when he must move against them or die at their hands. "I will name them when I must," he had told the Convention weeks before. The confrontation was long overdue, and still he continued with swirling abstractions, first principles, the public expression of his own private conscience, his pride, and his purity.

The twenty-sixth of Messidor (14 July) marked the fifth anniversary of the Bastille's fall. How would Paris—traumatized, frightened, disillusioned—celebrate? Some of the city's sections organised fraternal banquets (*repas fraternels*), simple communal meals—"a bit of cold beef, a plate of haricots verts, and a salad"—consumed in the street on the warm, bright summer evening.[41] A number of Robespierre's closest associates saw no harm in these alfresco meals: François Hanriot, his friend in charge of the National Guard, Martial Joseph Armand Herman, his friend on the Revolutionary Tribunal, and Claude Payan, his friend in the city's Commune, all took part in them. Robespierre did not. He celebrated the anniversary of the Bastille's fall by attending the Jacobins, as usual, and trying for the second time to denounce Fouché. Here he was as sure as ever of acting impartially for the public good: "I begin with the declaration that the individual Fouché interests me not at all." What, he asked, was Fouché afraid of? "Is it perhaps the eyes and ears of the people? Is it perhaps that his wretched face proves him too clearly the author of a crime?"[42] What crime did Robespierre mean? He specified it only in vague terms at the very end of his speech: "These men have used the Terror to force patriots to keep silent; they have put patriots in prison because they dared break their silence. This is the crime of which I accuse Fouché."[43] This was enough for the Jacobins, and they immediately expelled the ferocious promoter of de-Christianization whom Robespierre so hated.

Two days later he criticized the fraternal banquets, reminding the Jacobins that the time for fraternity had not arrived when so many internal enemies still remained. Those who called for an end to revolutionary government in the wake of the battle of Fleurus were false patriots, since Robespierre was convinced the banquets and conspiracies were closely linked. Together beneath the clear blue sky at the Festival of the Supreme Being, the people had been united, grand, sublime. But divided into little groups, seated around trestle tables, they were vulnerable to the schemes of intriguers: "How indeed could one mistrust a man with whom one has drunk from the same cup, on whose lips one has encountered the language of patriotism?"[44] Even at this point in the Revolution, the shattered symbolism of the Catholic Mass retained enough power to make it worth fighting over. Robespierre asked the Jacobins to consider whether those who drank from one cup at the fraternal banquets were sincere in expressing unity with the people. "Share my fear," he had urged the Jacobins in the past. Now he tried asking them again. His associates who had misread the signs and participated in the banquets wrote groveling letters excusing themselves: "Judge, judge what I must suffer at the thought of having involuntarily contributed to placing those instruments of mischief in the hands of our enemies," wrote one abject member of the Revolutionary Tribunal.[45]

Soon after, another member of the Revolutionary Tribunal, Joachim Vilate, who had given Robespierre breakfast on the morning of the Festival of the Supreme Being, allegedly made a list of those whom the Incorruptible planned to proscribe. It had supposedly been dictated by Bertrand Barère, Robespierre's colleague on the Committee of Public Safety—why is a mystery. Even more of a mystery is why Vilate left the list lying on a desk in his charming apartment in the Pavilion de Flore, overlooking the Tuileries gardens, where the trees that shed their leaves early in the year the monarchy fell now sweltered in the heat. The list was still there a few days later on 3 Thermidor (21 July) when the Committee of General Security arrested Vilate. The list is lost, but the names of Fouché, Tallien, Vadier, and other members of the Convention probably figured on it. By now there were no walls thick enough, no rooms sufficiently high or soundproof, to conceal the personal and political differences tearing the Convention and its two committees apart. Saint-Just and Barère tried to act as peacemakers. Twice they convened joint meetings of the Committee of Public Safety and the Committee of General Security. Robespierre, now practically a recluse, except when at the Jacobins, went to the second of these meetings, on 5 Thermidor (23 July). He was cold and reserved—nothing new—but left his friends and enemies alike with the impression that he was prepared to compromise, that some headway had been made toward uniting the two committees. But he never did compromise. In his thirty-six years there are no examples, except, just possibly, when he agreed to the death of Danton. Compromise, to Robespierre, was corruption—the betrayal of his absolute principles, the stars by which he had steered his extraordinary political career.

After the meeting, he went off on his own. Secluded in his room above the carpentry yard, he wrote for three days and nights preparing the text of a new speech. He consulted no one, not even Saint-Just. Perhaps he was offended by the younger man's opening to compromise inside the Committee of Public Safety, or perhaps, however close they seemed to outsiders, Robespierre had kept something back from even this, the most significant of his personal and political alliances.

On the morning of 8 Thermidor (26 July) he got dressed carefully, as he always did, drank coffee, and went out for the first time in days. It was a very short distance to the Convention. There he spoke for two hours—sincerely, passionately, truthfully—explaining what he had done in the Revolution and why. Who knows if before he opened his mouth the unwelcome thought crossed his mind that it was precisely this privilege—this opportunity to defend himself before the Convention—that he and Saint-Just had denied Danton. "I am going to unveil the abuse that is bringing about the ruin of the country, the abuse that your probity alone can repress."[46] This was his familiar vocabulary. His audience had heard him say such things before. This time was going to be different:

> The French Revolution is the first to have been founded on the theory of the rights of humanity and the principles of justice. Other revolutions required nothing but ambition; ours imposes virtue. Ignorance and power absorbed the others in a new despotism; ours, emanating from justice, stands alone. The republic, led insensibly by the force of circumstance and by the struggle of the friends of liberty against continually reborn conspiracies, has slid, so to speak, through all the factions. . . . It has been persecuted constantly since its birth, as have the men of good faith who have fought for it. And so, to preserve the advantage of their position, the heads of the factions and their agents have been obliged to hide themselves behind the edifice of the republic. . . . All the deceivers have adopted, each more convincingly than the last, all the formulas and all the rallying words of patriotism.[47]

Here was the problem that had driven Robespierre mad: How can you tell a sincere man in politics? When the language of those who work for the public good is so easily adopted by those who work only for themselves, who can tell a true from a false patriot? And how? Robespierre, absolutely sincerely, did not see himself as the leader of just another faction. He saw himself as one of the persecuted, someone who had fought for the republic against "tyrants, men of blood, oppressors of patriotism."[48] After his death his enemies turned the very same words against him—he became the tyrant, the man of blood, responsible for the worst excesses, if not the entire system, of the Terror.

He would not have been surprised. The slipperiness of language, that great gulf between what is said and what is true, was precisely what he complained of in this last of his astonishing speeches.

He went on to defend the actions of both the executive committees. Each had only *charged* people—it was the Revolutionary Tribunal, in the name of the Convention, that had actually *condemned* them. Quite why Robespierre thought there was a valid distinction to be made between charging and condemning people under the Law of 22 Prairial, is a difficult question to answer. He was personally implicated in passing the infamous law that transformed the Revolutionary Tribunal's work into something still more brutally perfunctory. Was his statement pure hypocrisy? Complete self-delusion? Or did he, insanely, believe that a true patriot would have been acquitted by the Revolutionary Tribunal despite everything? By now he certainly knew that innocent people had died. The best he could come up with was to say: It was not my fault, not even the fault of the Committee I sat on, it was the fault of the Convention to which I now appeal. His strategy was not admirable, but he did think his claim was true. Moreover, he believed there was a case for continuing with the Terror: "The guilty complain of our rigor—the country, more justly, complains of our weakness."[49]

Robespierre's was a characteristically personal speech. He spoke of the ridiculous calumnies against him: who could believe that he wanted the Convention "to cut its own throat with its own hands" and so open the bloody path to his dictatorship? "The monsters who charge me with such insanity are the real cutthroats who meditate the sacrifice of all the friends of their country." It hurt him deeply "to become an object of terror" to the people he loved and revered:

> They [the real conspirators] call me a tyrant. If I were one, they would grovel at my feet. I would shower them with gold and they would be grateful. When the victims of their perfidy complain, they excuse themselves by saying, "Robespierre will have it so." To the nobles they say, "He alone persecutes you." To the patriots they say, "Robespierre protects the nobles." To the clergy they say, "He's the one persecuting you." To the fanatics they say, "He's the one who destroyed religion." All the grievances that I have tried in vain to redress are still imputed to me: "He did all of it," "He won't prevent it," "Your fate is in his

hands alone." Spies are hired and stationed in our public places to propagate these calumnies. You see them at the sittings of the Revolutionary Tribunal. You find them around the scaffold when the enemies of the people expiate their crimes—you hear them saying, "These are the unhappy victims of Robespierre." Above all, they strive to prove that the Revolutionary Tribunal is a tribunal of blood, created and guided by me alone. . . . When a deputy on mission to a department is recalled, they tell him it is I who recalls him. Obliging persons have been found to attribute to me more good than I have done in order to impute to me mischief in which I had no hand. They kindly repeat to my colleagues everything that I happened to say, and, above all, everything that I did not say. If any measure of the government was likely to displease anyone, it was I who did all, exacted all, commanded all! It was never to be forgotten that I was the dictator.[50]

"You see, it is always me," Robespierre had complained to his colleague Bertrand Barère in a bookshop earlier that year—always him whom people blamed. Why was he surprised? He identified himself with the Revolution. He had insisted over and over again, in the Estates General, the National Assembly, the Jacobins, the Commune, the Convention, and the Committee of Public Safety, that there simply was no distinction: he was the living embodiment of the eternal principles upon which the Revolution was founded. Of course people blamed him for its excesses and failures. In his own mind, Robespierre had slid (as he put it) with the Revolution past all the factions that had tried to possess it for their own corrupt purposes. He and the Revolution had remained pure, and together they had eluded all those grasping hands that sought to sully his beautiful dream of a just and virtuous democracy. Now, inevitably, he thought the time had almost come to move against the latest set of conspirators:

You will ask who are the authors of this system of calumny [against himself]. I answer, in the first place, the Duke of York, Mr. Pitt [the British prime minister], and all the tyrants who are in arms against us. But who next? [Long, dramatic pause.] Ah! I dare not name them at this moment and in this place—I cannot bring myself to a resolution to tear away altogether the veil that covers this profound mystery of iniquity.[51]

Everyone in the room had a good idea whom he meant: Fouché, Tallien, Vadier, and perhaps even Barère, among others. Not naming, but only alluding to them at this point in his speech was extremely imprudent, leaving the whole Convention to tremble with fear. Whatever did he hope to achieve by it? In his isolation, perhaps he had failed to recognize that the time for insinuation at the Convention was long since past, since none of the deputies felt safe from the tribunal. Terrified and divided, they spent their days whispering the names of the soon-to-be-proscribed along the benches. Many had stopped sleeping at home, scared of a knock on the door in the middle of the night and an arresting hand on their shoulder. Now Robespierre, last seen in the Convention on 24 Prairial, two days after the infamous law was passed, had reappeared, speaking with devastating passion, but stopping short of actually naming names. Saint-Just, hearing only at the last minute what Robespierre intended to do, probably rushed to the Convention to watch his friend bare his soul and expose both their lives. Sitting there listening, Saint-Just would have felt like putting his head in his hands in a gesture of black despair. Camille Desmoulins had once jeered at him for carrying his beautiful head about like a sacred host, but those days, too, were gone.

Robespierre even hinted that the list on Vilate's desk was part of the plot against him: "Inoffensive, ordinary people are tormented and patriots are every day cast into dungeons. Have not even members of the Convention been designated as victims on secret and odious lists of proscription? Has not this imposture been propagated with such combined artifice and audacity that a great number of deputies have not ventured to sleep in their own residences?"[52] Next he discussed the plot to make him look ridiculous by association with Catherine Théot. Then he gave heartfelt thanks to the Convention for supporting his new religion of the Supreme Being:

> Immortal thanks to the Convention for that decree, which is in itself a revolution and has saved the country. You have struck with the same blow atheism and priestly despotism! . . . You have won over to the Revolution every pure and generous heart! . . . O day forever fortunate! When the French people rose altogether to offer to the Author

of Nature the only homage worthy of him, what a touching assemblage was there of all the objects that can fascinate the eyes or attract the hearts of men! O honored old age! O generous and ardent youth! O pure and playful joy of childhood! O delicious tears of maternal fondness! O divine influences of innocence and beauty! O the majesty of a great people, happy in the contemplation and enjoyment of its own strength and glory and virtue![53]

If anyone had been in any doubt that the Festival of the Supreme Being was the happiest day of Robespierre's life, they were no longer. Remembering it, he was moved to pray aloud in the Convention: "Being of beings, was the day on which the universe came forth from your creative and almighty hands brighter or more acceptable to your eyes than that recent day when the first People of the world, bursting the bonds of crime and error, appeared before you worthy of your favor and of its own destiny?" The best of his friends must have wondered what on earth he thought he was doing. What had "delicious tears of maternal fondness" got to do with the desperate crisis he found himself in? French mothers had wept ever since the Revolution began. Marie Antoinette had appealed to them when the Revolutionary Tribunal accused her of child abuse; the mothers of those lynched in the street, the mothers of those killed in battle, the mothers of those massacred in prison, the mothers of those sent to the guillotine—who could find their tears delectable? For the last time, Robespierre publicly described his vision of the republic as he thought it should be. The reality—as he was the first to admit—was far removed. Finally he turned on his enemies:

No, Chaumette! No, Fouché! Death is not an eternal sleep. The French people will not submit to a desperate and desolating doctrine that covers nature itself with a funeral shroud, that deprives virtue of hope, and misfortune of consolation, and insults even death itself. No, we will efface from our tombs your sacrilegious epitaph and replace it with the consolatory truth DEATH IS THE BEGINNING OF IMMORTALITY.[54]

Interestingly, and in the face of plentiful hints to the contrary, Robespierre did not feel himself close to death at this point. As usual, he announced that he was more than willing to sacrifice his life for the

Revolution. And, as Danton had done when close to the end, he claimed life had become a burden: "Why should I regret escaping from the eternal torture of seeing this horrible succession of traitors, who, concealing the turpitude of their souls under the veil of virtue, and even of friendship, will leave posterity in doubt which was the greater, their cowardice or their crimes?"[55] His conclusion was a self-referential remark of superb insight: "I was made to oppose crime, not to control it." He knew and understood himself as no biographer ever could. However, when the Convention discussed its response to his two-hour address, Robespierre was genuinely shocked that it turned against him. Instead of immediately lauding, printing, and circulating his speech, the Convention referred it to the Committees of Public Safety and General Security. He had serious enemies on both. He tried to protest: "What! My speech is to be sent to be examined by the very deputies I accuse!" And so, in one spontaneous sentence, he suddenly revealed what he had tried to bury so carefully in the text of his long, bizarre oration. He had returned to the Convention to swing it against its own committees. There was no further need for him to name the conspirators—their identities were clear to everyone listening. Pierre Joseph Cambon, head of the finance commission and one of the few "monsters" who were eventually mentioned by name in Robespierre's speech, was the first to denounce him. He began by defending himself and other members of the finance commission against Robespierre's implicit charges of corruption and conspiracy, but then he went a step further and announced: "It is time to tell the whole truth: one man is paralyzing the National Convention; that man is the one who has just made a speech; it is Robespierre." Soon afterward Barère intervened to distract everyone with a buoyant speech about recent military victories and the republic's bright future. Barère's purposes were unclear—and his feelings about Robespierre at best ambivalent—but he succeeded in deflecting the immediate crisis, and there was no call for Robespierre's arrest.[56]

If Robespierre decided not to consult Saint-Just before he made his speech because he thought his friend might try to talk him out of it, he was right. Saint-Just thought the way forward was to work with, not against, the committees, which, after all, still formed the locus of revolutionary government. Robespierre's flamboyant, unilateral, and unmistakably personal intervention had seriously damaged any chance of compromise. That evening, Robespierre, accompanied by Couthon, went off to the Jacobins to make sure the club rallied behind him. But Saint-Just went alone to the Tuileries palace and sat in the meeting room of the Committee of Public Safety. Perhaps he had not yet decided what to do. Because he had played such an important role on mission to the army and been present for the decisive battle of Fleurus, Saint-Just's revolutionary identity was not simply conflated with Robespierre's. They had been, and still were, personally and ideologically close. They meant the same thing by the reign of virtue and were passionately committed to realizing it in France. But if Robespierre was going to fall, there was a good chance that Saint-Just might save himself. Wondering what was going on around the corner at the Jacobins on that warm summer evening, wondering if compromise might still, even now, reunite the two committees, Saint-Just must have turned over in his mind the possibility of betraying the Incorruptible.

Meanwhile at the Jacobins things were, as usual, going in Robespierre's favor. Despite some initial opposition, he succeeded in rereading his speech to the club. At the end he said it was his last will and testament and, identifying now with Socrates, declared: "If you forsake me see how calmly I shall drink the hemlock."[57] At this the artist David, emotional as always, shouted: "I will drink it with you." (David, who had been close to the Incorruptible for a long time and deeply involved in designing the Festival of the Supreme Being, survived his fall and lived to be Napoleon's painter too.) Most of the other Jacobins also backed Robespierre. They turned on Collot d'Herbois and Billaud-Varenne, two of his hostile colleagues on the Committee of Public Safety, and drove them from the club. The pair, furious and humiliated, stormed off to the Tuileries palace, where they found Saint-Just sitting at the committee's table, bent over the text of his speech for the following day. Carnot, Barère, and some of the other members of the committee were there, too. There was another loud quarrel—they had become a habit. Finally, Saint-Just, "cold as marble," agreed to submit the draft of his speech to the committee before reading it to the Convention the next morning. Having secured this promise, Collot d'Herbois and Billaud-Varenne set off to reassure Fouché, Tallien, and the other deputies who were afraid of being proscribed by Robespierre. Saint-Just sat on in the committee room until 5:00 a.m.—he felt the insults of his colleagues branding his soul. When he left at last, he went to find Robespierre.

Maybe Robespierre persuaded him. Maybe Saint-Just had already decided. But whatever he was thinking as he ascended—perhaps with a heavier tread than had been his wont—the outside staircase that led directly to the Incorruptible's room, he no longer believed in compromise with the committees when he came back out. On that beautiful summer morning he did not submit to the Committee of Public Safety, as he had promised to do, the draft of the speech he intended to deliver to the Convention. Instead he sent his colleagues a dramatic note: "You have seared my heart. I intend to open it to the Convention."[58] Saint-Just, who had wavered, had thrown in his lot with Robespierre and that morning would see a fight to the death. Leaving the Duplay household for what everyone knew might be the last time, Robespierre turned to his host and said, "Don't be alarmed. The majority of the Convention is pure; I have nothing to fear."[59] Saint-Just, pasty from his sleepless night, went out with him, carrying the amended speech. Together they entered the Convention, where Couthon and Robespierre's brother were waiting for them. Fouché, Tallien, Bourdon, and others determined to bring down Robespierre were there too, rallying moderate or undecided deputies to their cause. Unfortunately for Robespierre and his supporters, Collot d'Herbois happened to be the current president of the Convention. He was going to help Tallien and the others stop Saint-Just and Robespierre from speaking.

Saint-Just began. He had scarcely finished his first sentence when Tallien interrupted, complaining that, like Robespierre the day before, the speaker had isolated himself from the committees and spoke only for himself. Saint-Just's speech had not been sanctioned by the Committee of Public Safety, still less the Committee of General Security. Before Saint-Just could resume, Billaud-Varenne described how he and Collot d'Herbois had been expelled from the Jacobins the evening before. He accused Robespierre directly of plotting against the Convention. At the tribune, Saint-Just froze. He had stood there before and never trembled when he delivered those razor-sharp interventions on the fate of Louis XVI and afterward Danton. "The words we have spoken will never be forgotten on earth," he had announced so proudly.[60] Now, suddenly, he could find no more words. Robespierre saw and ran forward to interrupt Billaud-Varenne. But his enemies were prepared, and by prearrangement shouts of "Down with the tyrant!" rang out around the hall. No one could hear Robespierre in the tumult. From the chair, Collot d'Herbois ignored his requests to speak and instead allowed Tallien to do so again. Every time Robespierre tried to interrupt, cries of "Down with the tyrant!" deafened him. After Tallien, who proposed arresting Hanriot (Robespierre's friend at the Commune), among others, it was Vadier's turn. Vadier chose this moment to reveal that a letter implicating Robespierre in the Catherine Théot sect had been found under the old woman's mattress at the time of her arrest. He developed this ridiculous line of attack until Tallien stopped him irritably: "I demand the floor to bring the discussion back to the real point." "I could bring it back," yelled Robespierre with all his might, making his voice heard at last in the fight. But they would not let him. "It is the blood of Danton that chokes you!" someone shouted, remembering that Robespierre, in his time, had prevented others from speaking. "Danton! Is it, then, Danton you regret? Cowards! Why did you not defend him?" he yelled as the din broke over his voice again and silenced it.[61]

They voted for Robespierre's arrest. Augustin at once asked to be arrested with his brother and no one objected. Next the deputies attacked the crippled Couthon, "thirsty for blood" and hoping "to make of our corpses so many steps to mount the throne." "Oh yes! I wanted to get a throne," said Couthon, gesturing at his wheelchair with bleak irony.[62] Finally Saint-Just and Robespierre's friend Lebas were arrested, too. The five were assembled before the bar and had to listen to a moralizing speech from Collot d'Herbois, the Convention's far-from-neutral president. They were probably still in shock, knowing full well what failure meant in a time of revolution. Robespierre and Saint-Just had theorized, justified, and legalized the draconian punishment of death for anyone and everyone who failed the Revolution. Both had said they did not value life in and of itself: "I despise the dust that forms me and speaks to you," said Saint-Just before his eloquence deserted him.[63] Now they really were very close to death. Despite everything, it came as a surprise.

*   *   *

WHEN NEWS OF the events in the Convention reached the Commune, it rose in support of Robespierre. The city gates were closed and the tocsin rang out from the Hôtel de Ville as it had before the fall of the monarchy and later the Girondins. Armed men began assembling and dragging out any cannons that had not yet been sent from Paris to the front line. Robespierre's friend Hanriot, who had also been threatened with arrest, ordered the city prisons to refuse admittance to prisoners sent by the Convention. Meanwhile the Jacobins went into permanent session, periodically sending messages of support to the Commune throughout the night. The problem was that the Commune did not have complete control over the city's forty-eight sections, many of which disregarded the orders they received. Some sections went further and came out in support of the Convention. By ten that evening only thirteen of the forty-eight had sent armed men to the Hôtel de Ville to fight for Robespierre. Where was he? Hanriot had set off to find out and discovered the five arrested deputies in the rooms of the Committee of General Security, where they had been given dinner. When he arrived, Hanriot was arrested, too, so that made six. For some reason, Lebas was allowed to go home, watch the police seal his papers, and say good-bye properly to his wife, Elizabeth, and their tiny son. Afterward he was taken to the prison of La Force, where he joined Augustin, whom the prison of Saint-Lazare, following orders, had refused to admit. Robespierre was taken to the Luxembourg, close to the apartments where Danton and his wife and Camille and Lucile Desmoulins had lived. Couthon was wheeled to the Bourbe, and Saint-Just escorted to the Ecossais. Hanriot was still at the Tuileries palace when an armed deputation from the Commune arrived to liberate him. Unexpectedly, this proved quite easy.

The Convention had just begun its evening session when news arrived that the men it had arrested earlier in the day were at large again: none of the prisons had wanted to detain them in defiance of orders from the Commune. Indeed, Robespierre had been spotted getting out of a cab with a white handkerchief over his mouth (perhaps he had been sick on the journey) and walking into the town hall, where he fell into the arms of the mayor's staff. They reassured him that he was still among friends. Augustin had given a speech at the Commune. And by 1:00 a.m. all five, together with Hanriot, were at the Hôtel de Ville waiting for the insurrection to begin. Robespierre had hoped to avoid a resort to violence, would have preferred a proper opportunity to win the Convention around, but eventually was persuaded that, in the circumstances, there was no alternative. The Convention's committees responded by declaring the prisoners outlaws, to be taken dead or alive and executed without trial. And so, Robespierre and his friends became hunted men, just like the Girondins had been a year before. But unlike the Girondins, who had fled Paris and scattered throughout France, Robespierre and his accomplices remained in a single room in the Hôtel de Ville. From here they sent out rousing proclamations to the Paris sections and arrest warrants for their enemies in the Convention. Robespierre's own section was to receive the following:

> Courage, patriots of the Pikes Section! Liberty is winning the day! Those men whose constancy made them feared by the traitors have already been released. Everywhere the people are showing themselves worthy of their reputation. The rallying point is the Commune, where the brave Hanriot will carry out the orders of the Executive Committee [Robespierre and friends] that has been set up to save the country.
>
> Signed: Lerebours, Legrand, Louvet, Payan, Ro . . .

Robespierre's signature is incomplete and the document is blood-splattered. There is dispute about whose blood made the stains. Some historians think it is Robespierre's own. According to one version, he was carefully adding his signature when the door flew open and soldiers sent by the Convention fired at him, shattering his jaw and knocking him forward bleeding onto the document. The soldiers had got past the Commune guards by guessing their not very difficult password: "Vive Robespierre!" Other, more skeptical historians think the blood could be anyone's, may not even have got onto the paper during the early hours of 10 Thermidor (28 July), and there will never be a proper explanation for Robespierre's broken signature. He was, after all, in something of a catatonic state even before half his jaw was shot off—perhaps he broke off his signature simply to be sick again and, since there was so much going on, never got back to complete it.

What is certain is that soldiers from the Convention did burst into the room and, one way or another, Robespierre suffered a bullet wound that shattered his jaw. The most likely explanation for this outcome is a bungled suicide attempt. When the soldiers came in Augustin escaped through a window, edged his way along a ledge overlooking the square below, holding his shoes in one hand, holding on with the other, but slipped suddenly and smashed onto the steps outside the Hôtel de Ville, to the horrified amazement of the people assembled there for the insurrection. An eyewitness observed that "the body had fallen on a sabre and a bayonet, and knocked down the two citizens who carried them."[64] Augustin was picked up later half dead. Hanriot jumped, or was pushed, through another window on the third story of the building, which overlooked an inner court. He landed in an open sewer and was found there several hours later, covered in excrement, in horrendous pain, and begging to be finished off. Couthon, who could not walk, pulled himself out of his wheelchair, only to fall down a staircase and cut his head open. Lebas, the only one who had been home since the defeat in the Convention, had two pocket pistols on him. He handed one to Robespierre and blew his own brains out with the other. Robespierre, who had probably never fired a gun in his life, may have tried to do the same but pulled the trigger too soon with a very shaky hand. Saint-Just, cold as marble, sat there like a statue, waiting.

Lying on a plank, Robespierre was carried back to the Committee of Public Safety between one and two in the morning. He was bleeding profusely from the wound to his left lower jaw. He tried to stop the blood flow by pressing with a white leather pistol bag. Later someone noted the words inscribed on it: "Lecourt, gun maker to the king and to the army, rue Saint-Honoré, near the rue des Poulies, Paris."[65] Probably it was the bag for the pistol that Lebas gave Robespierre to shoot himself with—it might still have been in his left hand after he pulled the trigger with his right. He was only semiconscious by the time his rough stretcher was carried up the stairs of the Tuileries and put down on a table in the antechamber to the committee's meeting room. Someone placed a small box, containing samples of bread intended for the army in the north, under his head as a pillow. He was unconscious for an hour or so and seemed unlikely to last the night. But around three or four in the morning he opened his eyes again and tried to remove some of the blood from his mouth with the pistol bag. At one point someone handed him some sheets of paper for this purpose. The leather bag must have been too soiled to be of further use. At about six a surgeon was called in to dress the wound. Two or three teeth were extracted and the shattered jaw bandaged tightly. Sometimes Robespierre looked steadily at the people around him, but mainly he looked up at the ceiling. He made very little noise even though he must have been in terrible pain. Suddenly he sat bolt upright on the table. He pulled up his stockings, which were hanging down around his ankles, stood up, crossed the room, and seated himself in a vacant armchair. He was wearing the same sky blue coat that he had worn for the Festival of the Supreme Being. Fastidious to the end, he asked for some clean linen.

At 9:00 a.m. Couthon was brought to the Tuileries, also on a makeshift stretcher—or, possibly, in a wheelbarrow. Before he was carried up the grand staircase, Collot d'Herbois, Billaud-Varennes, and Barère, who were all inside the committee room, decided to send the prisoners to the Conciergerie. By this time, Saint-Just, in much better physical shape than his friends, had joined them. He stood motionless before the framed copy of the Declaration of Rights that hung in the antechamber to the Committee of Public Safety. Finally he raised his arm, pointed, and said composedly, "And yet it was I who did that."[66] It was true. He had helped draft the democratic constitution of 1793 that never came into effect. Robespierre was carried down the stairs in the armchair he was sitting in. Legend has it he struck at the men carrying him, but it seems very unlikely he had the strength left.[67] Later that morning, the five deputies who had stood before the bar of the Convention the previous day, been arrested, escaped, and been hunted through the night were at last assembled before the Revolutionary Tribunal. Augustin may have been dead already, Lebas certainly was, and Couthon and Robespierre were both physically mangled. Only Saint-Just remained on his feet. The five were joined by seventeen other prisoners considered loyal to the Incorruptible, including Hanriot. Outside, the carts were already waiting for them, and the guillotine had been brought back into the city center and reassembled in the place de la Révolution especially for the occasion. By early evening, enormous crowds filled the streets and the banks of the Seine. Everyone wanted to see Robespierre go past.

There was not much to see. The bandage covered most of his face. He showed no emotion and closed his eyes. Perhaps he opened them again when he felt the cart jolt to a halt suddenly. They had stopped outside the Duplay house on the road that led to the guillotine. The windows were all closed, as they had been on the days that Louis XVI and later Danton passed that way. Amid all the terrible jeering and bitter rejoicing, someone threw a bucket of animal blood against the bolted outer door. Madame Duplay was not behind it; she was in prison, where she later killed herself. Eléonore Duplay might have been at home—afterward they called her the Widow Robespierre.[68] One witness saw a woman in the crowd pull herself up on the railing of the cart to curse the Incorruptible face to face: "Monster spewed up from hell. The thought of your punishment intoxicates me with joy." He looked at her sadly as she added, "Go now, evil one, go down into your grave loaded with the curses of the wives and mothers of France."[69] The carts at last moved on. The first contained the Robespierre brothers and Hanriot; Saint-Just was in the second, and Couthon behind in the third. Some of the condemned had to be carried up the scaffold, but not Robespierre. He went last but one, ascending the steps on his own, a frail figure in sky blue. If he looked around when he got to the top, he would have seen the Tuileries again, from which, only six weeks before, he had emerged so proudly as the high priest of a new religion. His coat came off. Just before they strapped Robespierre to the plank, the executioner decided to rip off the bandage that was holding his face together. Perhaps the executioner—so experienced by now—thought the bandage was thick enough to get in the way of the descending blade; perhaps he wanted to be cruel. Robespierre let out a scream. It was the deep, sharp cry of a man in excruciating pain that you hear sometimes in hospitals—the violent protest of a wounded human animal that, however brave or bent on self-control, cannot stop the voice of torment.

The scream was the last act of the man who had tried as no one else did to embody the Revolution. It was the point of severance, when Robespierre's precious vision of a democratic republic, pure and founded on virtue, must have finally left him. A "tenacious" man, Danton had called him. And indeed he carried his vision right to the end, only surrendering it in those last few seconds before he was guillotined. Perhaps it went out into the world on the back of that scream. It is certainly true that friends and later followers of Robespierre in France, and elsewhere, tried to keep fighting for it, as he would have done. And some of them are still trying, for all the damage inflicted on left-wing political dreams by the collapse of communism across Europe and beyond. But the vision itself has never been clearly understood: a democracy for the people, who are intrinsically good and pure of heart; a democracy in which poverty is honorable, power innocuous, and the vulnerable safe from oppression; a democracy that worships nature—not nature as it really is, cruel and disgusting, but nature sanitized, majestic, and, above all, good. "The end of the Revolution is the triumph of innocence," Robespierre believed.[70] Many of those claiming to be inspired by his vision have shared it only in part. The most honest always admit that there is something peculiar and elusive about it. If the vision was entirely clear to him—as he sat alone in his room at the Duplays', as he walked out in the countryside with his dog, or as he lay there on the table in the Tuileries staring up at the ceiling through the long last night of his life—he never succeeded in making it so to others. One historian describes that scream as "the end of the bright hope for a democratic Republic."[71] Others hear it as a rallying cry to continue the fight. As a biographer, I hear it as the agonized separation of Robespierre and the Revolution: the man and what he lived for. When it finally came to it, what was pushed under the guillotine on 10 Thermidor (28 July) was as limp, frail, and meaningless as a puppeteer's marionette. The real severance had already happened—it happened when he screamed and the picture in his mind went blank.

CODA

A few days later, in England, the poet William Wordsworth was crossing Morecambe Bay after visiting the grave of his former school-teacher. Like his compatriot the agronomist Arthur Young, Wordsworth had traveled in France on the eve of the Revolution, and he, too, had been to Arras in 1789:

> I paced, a dear companion at my side,
> The town of Arras, whence with promise high
> Issued, on delegation to sustain
> Humanity and right, "that" Robespierre,
> He who thereafter, and in how short a time!
> Wielded the sceptre of the Atheist crew.

Wordsworth resented that memory of joy and hope in the streets of Arras. It seemed to mock him in the wake of all the horror and bloodshed that the Revolution brought with it. Wordsworth had seen some of it for himself. He was there at the Convention watching in 1792 when Louvet rose before the tribune and said, "Yes, Robespierre, it is I who accuse you!" He wrote about it afterward, and about the storming of the Tuileries palace, the royal prisoners in the Tower, the September Massacres, the war, and the Revolutionary Tribunal. It is all in Book 10 of *The Prelude*. It was in Morecambe Bay that he heard the news of Robespierre's death:

> As I advanced, all that I saw or felt
> Was gentleness and peace. Upon a small
> And rocky island near, a fragment stood
> (Itself like a sea rock) the low remains
> (With shells encrusted, dark with briny weeds)
> Of a dilapidated structure, once
> A Romish chapel, where the vested priest
> Said matins at the hour that suited those
> Who crossed the sands with ebb of morning tide.
> Not far from that still ruin in the plain
> Lay spotted with a variegated crowd
> Of vehicles and travellers, horse and foot,
> Wading beneath the conduct of their guide
> In loose procession through the shallow stream
> Of inland waters; the great sea meanwhile
> Heaved at a safe distance, far retired. I paused,
> Longing for skill to paint a scene so bright
> And cheerful, but the foremost of the band
> As he approached, no salutation given
> In the familiar language of the day,
> Cried, "Robespierre is dead!"

Wordsworth uttered a hymn to everlasting justice on those open sands. He was among the first to get Robespierre completely wrong. How could he call him, of all things, the leader of "the Atheist crew"? How could he not know that the small, ruined, shell-encrusted chapel would have moved the Incorruptible? Robespierre, too, would have liked the procession of simple working or traveling people, their horses, and their motley vehicles. He, like Wordsworth, might have longed to sketch the scene. For he, too, loved nature in all its majesty—even though, so far as we know, he never once saw the splendor of the sea.

Notes

Preface

1. Croker (1967), p. 277.
2. Croker (1835), pp. 565–66.
3. Croker (1857), p. 384.
4. Ibid., p. 299.

Introduction

1. Forsyth (1989), p. 133; Rœderer (1853–59), vol. 3, pp. 270–71. Rœderer's depiction of Robespierre was based on personal acquaintance and first published, under the name Merlin de Thionville, in 1794.
2. Pierre Choudieu quoted in Thompson (1989), pp. 243–44.
3. O'Brien (1837?), pp. 6–7.
4. Robespierre (1828), vol. 2, p. 14.
5. Furet (1978), p. 64.
6. M. Bloch quoted in Haydon and Doyle (1999), p. 212.
7. When the Maison Robespierre was purchased by the city of Arras in 1990, the town council decided to entrust its refurbishment to the Compagnons de France, who would receive in payment for their work the right to use part or all of the house. Les Amis de Robespierre pour le Bicentenaire de la Révolution (ARBR), a society established in Arras to ensure that Robespierre's

contribution to the Revolution is not overlooked, campaigned hard to retain space for a small museum devoted to him. The ARBR continues working today to raise Robespierre's profile in Arras and beyond. See http://www.amis-robespierre.org/.

8. Forsyth (1989), p. 128; Rœderer (1853–59), vol. 3, p. 267.

9. Dumont (1832), p. 250.

10. There is dispute over whether Robespierre's famous sky-blue coat was different from the blue coats worn by the other deputies to the National Convention as their official dress. Vilate (1825), p. 197, suggests that it was not.

11. Thompson (1989), p. 223.

12. Ibid., p. 224.

13. For a summary of the dispute about the decor of Robespierre's room at the Duplays, see M. Cumming in Haydon and Doyle (1999), pp. 180–81. Also Jordan (1985), p. 58.

1: *Child of Arras*

1. On Arras, see Bougard (1988) and Héricourt and Godin (1856).

2. On Robespierre's ancestry, see Robespierre (1910–67), vol. 1, pp. 197–203, and Thompson (1939), pp. 1–4.

3. Paris (1870), p. 17.

4. Palmer (1975), p. 43.

5. Proyart (1803), p. 220.

6. Rousseau (1993), p. xxi.

7. Ibid., p. 1.

8. Ibid., p. 12.

9. Robespierre (1910–67), vol. 1, pp. 211–12.

10. Palmer (1975), pp. 70–71.

11. Quoted in Horne (2003), p. 170.

12. Palmer (1975), p. 84.

13. Proyart (1803), pp. 217–20.

14. Desmoulins (1980), vol. 1, p. 521.

15. Little is known of the childhood acquaintance of Robespierre and Desmoulins. One source says they were neither rivals nor close friends because their age difference meant they were not in the same class; see *Le vieux Cordelier*, p. 3.

16. Robespierre (1828), vol. 1, pp. 154–55.

2: *The Lawyer-Poet Back Home*

1. Paris (1870), p. 18. This institution was founded by Marianne and Joseph Manarre in 1674. It admitted deserving girls between the ages of nine and eighteen, who were taught to read, write, sew, and make lace.

2. Bougard (1988), p. 178.

3. Robespierre (1910–67), vol. 3a, p. 25.

4. Ibid., p. 26.

5. Ibid., p. 27.

6. Ibid., vol. 1, p. 241; Laponneraye (2002), p. 106. Charlotte Robespierre implies that this was a later poem, composed during the Revolution.

7. Robespierre (1910–67), vol. 3a, p. 22.

8. Laponneraye (2002), pp. 44–45.

9. Ibid., pp. 47–48.

10. Lewes (1899), p. 39.

11. See Riskin (1999); also Huet (1989).

12. Robespierre (1910–67), vol. 2, p. 357.

13. Laponneraye (2002), p. 59.

14. Robespierre (1910–67), vol. 1, p. 44.

15. *Archives parlementaires*, vol. 9, p. 393.

16. Robespierre (1910–67), vol. 1, p. 24.

17. Ibid., p. 28.

18. Ibid., p. 42.

19. Ibid., p. 31. The term *l'être suprême* was a well-established way of referring to God in Christian vocabulary since the seventeenth century. Later in the Revolution Robespierre imbued it with new meaning; see Deprun (1972).

20. Thompson (1939), pp. 22–23.

21. Rœderer (1853–59), vol. 3, p. 9.

22. Babeuf (1961), p. 7.

23. Wogue (1894), p. 267.

24. Robespierre (1910–67), vol. 1, p. 94.

25. Ibid., p. 89.

26. Ibid., p. 114.

27. Ibid., pp. 244–46; Thompson (1939), p. 32. The story of Charlotte's disapproval was told to Sainte-Beuve by an old bookseller named Isnard, who had taught at the Collège d'Arras.

28. Ibid., p. 223.

29. Ibid., p. 224.

30. Ibid., vol. 3a, pp. 30–31.

31. Thompson (1939), p. 21.

32. Robespierre (1910–67), vol. 3a, p. 24.

33. Ibid., p. 33.

34. Joseph Garat remembered that during the Revolution Robespierre kept *La nouvelle Héloïse* open on his desk as a literary and oratorical model; see Proyart (1850), p. 224.

35. Rousseau (2000), p. 418.

36. Rousseau (1987), pp. 58–59.

37. Robespierre (1910–67), vol. 3a, pp. 33–34.

38. Paris (1870), p. 187.

39. See Carr (1972), ch. 8, pp. 79–96, for an argument connecting the Rosati Society and Freemasonry in Arras.

40. Robespierre (1910–67), vol. 1, p. 194.

41. Dickens (1988), p. 11.
42. Paris (1870), p. 124.

3: *Standing for Election in Arras*

1. Doyle (1990), p. 76.
2. Palmer (1959), vol. 1, p. 454.
3. Lamoignon (1787), p. 3.
4. Robespierre (1910–67), vol. 8, p. 307.
5. Young (1929), p. 97.
6. Ibid., p. 97.
7. Ibid., p. 97.
8. Doyle (1990), p. 14.
9. Hufton (1974), p. 12.
10. Robespierre (1989), p. 5.
11. Crook (1996), p. 10.
12. The municipality of Arras traced its origins back to the eleventh century.
13. Stage 1 was elections by parish, corporation, or *quartier*, stage 2 the town assembly, stage 3 the secondary *baillage* assembly (Artois was divided into seven *baillages*), and stage 4 the principal *baillage* assembly, from which the final delegates of the third estate would be chosen.
14. The most notable was Gracchus Babeuf.
15. Hampson (1974), p.41.
16. Robespierre (1910–67), vol. 6, p. 18, gives the precise composition of this assembly.
17. Proyart (1850), pp. 42–43.
18. Ibid., p. 40.

4: *Representing the Nation at Versailles*

1. Pierre L'Enfant, who designed the 1791 street plan for Washington, D.C., had spent time in Versailles as a child.
2. Young (1929), p. 151.
3. Ibid., p. 13.
4. La Morandière [1764] quoted in Corbin (1986), p. 27.
5. See Alison Patrick's article in Blanning (1996), pp. 236–66, for a full explanation of how and why the number of deputies fluctuated. Also Tackett (1996).
6. Ferrières (1932), p. 34.
7. Ibid., p. 43.
8. Stäel (1983), p. 140.
9. Mirabeau (1790), p. 40.
10. Dumont (1832), p. 144.
11. Hampson (1974), pp. 17–18.

12. Staël (1983), pp. 313–14.

13. Jones (2002), p. 262.

14. Ibid., p. 310.

15. Doyle (1990), p. 94.

16. Rousseau (1962), vol. 1, p. 255.

17. Robespierre (1910–67), vol. 3a, p. 41.

18. Hampson (1974), p. 47.

19. Aulard (1889–97), vol. 1, pp. ii–xvii. The history of the Breton Club is difficult to reconstruct and it is not clear when exactly Robespierre joined it.

20. Schama (1989), p. 331.

21. Dumont (1832), p. 64.

22. Mirabeau (1790), vol. 1, p. 14.

23. Ibid., p. 15.

24. Dumont (1832), pp. 60–61.

25. Ibid., pp. 61–62. The deputy Reybaz, sitting next to Dumont, said this to him.

26. Doyle (1990), p. 105.

27. Dumont (1832), p. 93.

28. Robespierre (1910–67), vol. 3a, p. 42.

29. Desmoulins (1980), vol. 1, p. 77.

30. Robespierre (1910–67), vol. 3a, pp. 42–50.

31. Schama (1989), pp. 389–94.

32. Godechot (1970), pp. 219–20.

33. Robespierre (1910–67), vol. 3a, p. 44.

34. *New Annual Register*, p. 25.

35. Robespierre (1910–67), vol. 3a, pp. 44–45.

36. *New Annual Register*, p. 28.

37. Doyle (1990), p. 113.

38. Robespierre (1910–67), vol. 3a, p. 45.

39. Ibid.

40. Godechot (1970), p. 327.

41. Thompson (1989), p. 46.

42. Godechot (1970), p. 331.

43. Mirabeau (1835–36), p. 204.

44. Dumont (1832), p. 138.

45. Robespierre (1910–67), vol. 3a, p. 48.

46. Lefebvre (1973), pp. 35–56.

47. Lefebvre (2002), pp. 135–36.

48. Robespierre (1910–67), vol. 3a, pp. 46–47.

49. Dumont (1832), p. 138.

50. See K. M. Baker in Van Kley (1994), pp. 154–99.

51. *Archives parlementaires*, vol. 9, p. 236.

52. Dumont (1832), p. 140.

53. Ibid., p. 143.

54. Ibid., p. 146.

55. Ibid., p. 147.

56. Robespierre (1910–67), vol. 6, p. 58.
57. Ibid., p. 59.
58. Ibid., p. 61.
59. Robespierre (1910–67), vol. 6, p. 66.
60. Tour du Pin (1979), p. 100.
61. Robespierre, (1910–67), vol. 6, p. 107.
62. Tour du Pin (1979), p. 104.
63. Ibid., p. 103.
64. Roudinesco (1991), p. 27.
65. *L'ami du peuple*, vol. 1, p. 249.
66. *Révolutions de France et de Brabant*, vol. 5, p. 369. Desmoulins's account of Marat's involvement in the march to Versailles was retrospective and possibly exaggerated.
67. Robespierre (1910–67), vol. 6, pp. 108–9.
68. Ibid., pp. 110–15.
69. Villiers (1802), p. 5.

5: *The National Assembly in Paris*

1. The house no longer exists. In his correspondence, Robespierre gives the address as No. 30, but for a summary of the dispute about how the house was numbered and where it was in the street, see Thompson (1939), p. 65, and Michon (1924).
2. Villiers entrusted a friend with publishing his haphazard memoirs in 1802. On the dubious status of his evidence, see R. Garmy in Soboul (1967), pp. 19–33.
3. Villiers (1802), p. 1.
4. Ibid.
5. Ibid., p. 2.
6. Ibid., p. 5.
7. Ibid., p. 3.
8. Ibid., p. 2.
9. One other scrap of possible evidence turned up in 1909 in the form of a drawing of a woman by Claude Hoin, inscribed *La dévouée Hortense Delannoye, maîtresse du traître Robespierre*; see Thompson (1939), p. 66.
10. On Robespierre's relations with women, see Fleischmann (1908) and Mantel (2000).
11. Robespierre (1910–67), vol. 3a, p. 57.
12. Ibid.
13. Dumont (1832), p. 280.
14. Doyle (1990), p. 123.
15. Villiers (1802), p. 3.
16. Hufton (1974), p. 23.
17. Thompson (1939), pp. 82–83.
18. Sieyès (1989), vol. 2, sec. 13, pp. 1–2.

19. Robespierre (1910–67), vol. 6, pp. 349–50.

20. Sieyès (1989), vol. 2, sec. 11, p. 41.

21. Ibid., sec. 16, pp. 14–15.

22. Robespierre (1910–67), vol. 6, p. 319.

23. Ibid., p. 193.

24. Ibid., pp. 386–87.

25. Walter (1989), pp. 144–45.

26. Robespierre (1910–67), vol. 3a, p. 82.

27. Villiers (1802), p. 4.

28. Hampson (1974), p. 35.

29. English historians differ over whether to describe this building as a convent or monastery, but since the occupants were male, the latter seems more appropriate, even though the French word is *couvent*.

30. Initially, Robespierre resisted officially adopting the name Jacobins, because he thought it more pejoratively suggestive of factionalism than "The Society of the Friends of the Constitution"; see Robespierre (1910–67), vol. 8, pp. 206–8.

31. Ibid., vol. 3a, p. 73.

32. Ibid., pp. 73–74.

33. Ibid., p. 82.

34. Ibid., p. 68.

35. Ibid., p. 69.

36. Ibid., p. 71.

37. *Chronique de Paris*, 11 October 1790.

38. *Archives parlementaires*, vol. 15, p. 517.

39. Croker (1857), p. 107.

40. *Révolutions de France et de Brabant*, vol. 4, p. 191.

41. Ibid., pp. 192–93.

42. The identity of the priest is disputed: some say it was Denis Bérardier from Louis-le-Grand, others that it was M. de Pancemont of Saint-Sulpice. One account of the wedding claims that Camille was moved to tears by the religious ceremony and that Robespierre said nastily, "Cry then, hypocrite!" See Paris (1870), p. 26, and *Le vieux Cordelier*, pp. 4–6.

43. Robespierre (1910–67), vol. 3a, pp. 87–88.

44. Ibid., p. 83.

45. Schama (1989), p. 509.

46. McManners (1998), p. 8.

47. Thompson (1989), p. 43.

48. Ibid., p. 52.

49. *L'ami du peuple*, vol. 2, p. 1121.

50. Thompson (1989), p. 171.

51. Robespierre (1910–67), vol. 6, p. 497.

52. Ibid., p. 489.

53. Hampson (1974), p. 64.

54. The deputy was Duquesnoy.

55. Robespierre (1910–67), vol. 6, p. 490.

56. Dumont (1832), p. 283.

57. Thompson (1989), p. 219.

58. Ibid., p. 29.

59. Ibid., p. 33.

6: The Constitution

1. Dumont (1832), pp. 266–67.

2. *L'ami du peuple*, vol. 3, p. 1826.

3. Dumont (1832), pp. 22–23.

4. Cabanis (1791), p. 11.

5. Dumont (1832), p. 310.

6. Cabanis (1791), p. 60.

7. Robespierre (1910–67), vol. 7, p. 178.

8. Mirabeau (1835–36), p. 216.

9. Robespierre (1910–67), vol. 7, p. 235.

10. Ibid., vol. 3a, p. 99.

11. Dumont (1832), p. 290.

12. Jones (2002), p. 226.

13. Foucault (1979), p. 4.

14. *Archives parlementaires*, vol. 26, p. 332.

15. Croker (1857), p. 525.

16. Ibid.

17. Ibid.

18. The last execution with the Halifax gibbet was in 1648.

19. Robespierre (1910–67), vol. 7, p. 433.

20. Croker (1857), p. 318.

21. Robespierre (1910–67), vol. 7, p. 325.

22. Ibid., p. 138.

23. The advertisement appeared in *L'orateur du peuple*, vol. 6, no. 18; see Thompson (1939), p. 138. There is no record of the speech's being found.

24. Andress (2000), p. 64.

25. Ibid., p. 48.

26. Robespierre (1910–67), vol. 6, p. 611.

27. Robespierre (1910–67), vol. 3a, p. 100.

28. Ibid., vol. 6, p. 622.

29. Ibid., vol. 7, p. 266.

30. Wrigley (2002), pp. 135–86.

31. Ibid., p. 151.

32. Robespierre (1910–67), vol. 7, p. 268.

33. *L'ami du peuple*, vol. 5, pp. 2745–51.

34. Blanning (1986), pp. 69–96.

35. *Archives parlementaires*, vol. 25, p. 201.

36. Croker (1857), p. 121.

37. Robespierre (1910–67), vol. 7, p. 514.

38. Thompson (1989), p. 74.

39. Shuckburch (1989), pp. 170–71.

40. Ibid., p. 82.

41. Robespierre (1910–67), vol. 7, p. 519.

42. Croker (1857), p. 150.

43. Tackett (2003), pp. 116–18.

44. *L'ami du peuple*, vol. 3, p. 1870.

45. *Archives parlementaires*, vol. 27, pp. 602–60. Tackett (2003), p. 134.

46. By one count, seventeen petitions of this kind were drawn up between 21 June and 17 July and rejected out of hand by the assembly; see Tackett (2003), p. 113.

47. Thompson (1939), p. 162.

48. Laponneraye (2002), p. 73.

49. Robespierre still gave his address as rue Saintonge on 9 August, which suggests a brief period of transition between the two lodgings; see Thompson (1939), p. 178.

50. The fact that the assembly voted to exonerate Louis XVI after the flight to Varennes is difficult to explain, given both the fierce opposition of radical deputies like Robespierre and hostile public opinion. The final vote on this issue was not recorded. See Tackett (2003), p. 141.

51. There is dispute about the exact date of the premature welcome party; see Walter (1989), p. 204.

7: *War*

1. Robespierre had already demanded a serious discussion of the émigré problem earlier in the Revolution; see Robespierre (1910–67), vol. 7, pp. 87–88.

2. Ibid., vol. 3a, p. 127.

3. Burke (1989), p. 469.

4. Robespierre (1910–67), vol. 3a, pp. 127–28.

5. Ibid., pp. 129–30.

6. Ibid., p. 130.

7. Ibid., vol. 8, p. 26.

8. Walter (1989), p. 257. By this point, the circulation of major speeches had become customary, so the long debate provoked by Robespierre suggests the Parisian Jacobins were deeply divided over Brissot's speech.

9. Robespierre (1910–67), vol. 8, pp. 47–48.

10. Ibid., pp. 128–32.

11. Doyle (1990), p. 179.

12. Thompson (1939), p. 209; Robespierre (1910–67), vol. 8, p. 151.

13. Robespierre resigned his job as Public Prosecutor on 10 April 1792. The court to which he had been appointed only came into existence in February 1792, and he resigned before its first formal session. See Thompson (1939), p. 225.

14. Robespierre (1910–67), vol. 8, p. 248.

15. Hardman (1999), p. 43.

16. Robespierre (1910–67), vol. 8, p. 157.

17. Ibid., pp. 160–61.

18. Ibid., p. 165.

19. Ibid.

20. *Guillaume Tell*, a drama set to music by A. E. M Gréty, was performed for the first time at the Comédie italienne, Paris, on 9 April 1791. Voltaire's *Brutus*, first staged in 1730, was popular during the Revolution. M. J. Chénier's *Caius Gracchus* opened at the Théâtre de la République on 9 February 1792.

21. Robespierre (1910–67), vol. 8, pp. 179–80.

22. W. A. Miles to H. J. Pye, 1 March 1791; quoted in Thompson (1989), p. 143.

23. Belloc (1910), p. 191.

24. Robespierre (1910–67), vol. 4, p. 92.

25. Shuckburch (1989), p. 61.

26. Robespierre (1910–67), vol. 3a, p. 139.

27. Ibid., vol. 4, p. 34.

28. Ibid., vol. 8, p. 315.

29. Ibid., vol. 8, p. 90.

30. Ibid., vol. 8, pp. 59–60.

31. Ibid., p. 233.

32. Ibid., pp. 233–34.

33. Ibid., p. 241.

34. Hardman (1999), p. 34.

35. Thompson (1939), p. 184.

36. Ibid., p. 183.

37. Ibid.

38. Madame Élisabeth (1868), p. 416.

39. Robespierre (1910–67), vol. 3a, p. 147.

40. Danton (1910), pp. 28–32.

41. Robespierre (1910–67), vol. 8, p. 313.

42. Aulard (1889–97), vol. 3, p. 576.

43. Robespierre (1910–67), vol. 4, p. 2.

44. Ibid., p. 9.

45. Ibid., p. 33.

46. Danton (1910), p. 28.

47. Robespierre (1910–67), vol. 3a, p. 160.

48. Ibid., vol. 8, p. 163.

49. Ibid., vol. 4, p. 52.

50. Shuckburch (1989), p. 62.

51. Doyle (1990), p. 185.

52. Thompson (1989), p. 57.

53. Robespierre (1910–67), vol. 8, p. 383.

54. Croker (1857), p. 185.

55. *Archives parlementaires*, vol. 45, pp. 411–12.

56. Croker (1857), p. 199.

57. Madame Élisabeth (1868), pp. 416–21.

58. Thompson (1989), p. 57.

59. Robespierre (1910–67), vol. 4, p. 225.

60. Ibid., p. 232.

61. Ibid., p. 259.

62. Ibid., vol. 3a, p. 150.

63. Ibid., p. 151.

64. Aulard (1889–97), vol. 4, p. 160. Brunswick's manifesto was dated 25 July 1792, known in Paris on 28 July, and published in *Le moniteur* on 3 August.

65. Thompson (1989), p. 118.

66. Rœderer (1853–59), vol. 3, p. 221.

67. Desmoulins (1995), p. 94.

68. Rœderer (1853–59), vol. 3, p. 226.

69. Doyle (1990), p. 189.

70. Robespierre (1910–67), vol. 4, p. 352.

8: The King's Trial

1. Mathiez (1921), p. 83.

2. Thompson (1939), p. 274.

3. Croker (1857), p. 246.

4. Blanc (1847–69), vol. 7, p. 192.

5. Croker (1857), p. 535.

6. Danton (1910), p. 52.

7. Belloc (1910), p. 225.

8. Doyle (1990), p. 193.

9. Croker (1857), p. 343.

10. Robespierre (1910–67), vol. 8, pp. 460–61.

11. Robespierre (1910–67), vol. 3a, p. 152; Thompson (1939), pp. 263–64.

12. Croker (1857), p. 348.

13. Ferrières (1932), p. 43.

14. Of the 749 deputies elected to the National Convention, only 83 had sat in the National Assembly, compared with 200 who had sat in the Legislative Assembly. This time there was no self-denying ordinance precluding members of the earlier assemblies from standing for election to the National Convention. See Doyle (1990), p. 193.

15. Price (2003), pp. 315–16.

16. Robespierre (1910–67), vol. 5, p. 17.

17. Rousseau (1962), vol. 2, p. 51.

18. Robespierre (1910–67), vol. 5, p. 19.

19. Ibid., vol. 9, p. 20.

20. *Archives parlementaires*, vol. 52, p. 158.

21. Thompson (1989), p. 171.

22. *L'ami du peuple*, vol. 7, p. 3965.

23. Ibid., vol. 8, p. 4756.

24. Ibid., p. 4757.

25. Ibid., p. 4790.

26. Asprey (2000), p. 61.

27. *Archives parlementaires*, vol. 53, p. 49.

28. Ibid., p. 53.

29. Croker (1857), p. 358.

30. *Chronique de Paris*, 9 November 1792.

31. Walter (1946), p. 634.

32. Robespierre (1910–67), vol. 9, pp. 80–81.

33. Ibid., p. 93. The one innocent victim whom Robespierre alluded to was an alleged case of mistaken identity.

34. Ibid., p. 89.

35. Ibid., p. 88.

36. Thompson (1989), p. 102.

37. Laponneraye (2002), p. 75.

38. Ibid., p. 76.

39. Robespierre (1910–67), vol. 9, p. 144.

40. Thompson (1939), pp. 295–96.

41. *L'ami du peuple*, vol. 5, pp. 2649–50.

42. Walzer (1974), p. 111.

43. Robespierre (1910–67), vol. 3a, p. 87.

44. Walzer (1974), pp. 121–25.

45. Ibid., p. 131; Robespierre (1910–67), vol. 9, pp. 121–22.

46. Walzer (1974), p. 138; Robespierre (1910–67), vol. 9, p. 122.

47. Walzer (1974), p. 133; Robespierre (1910–67), vol. 9, p. 123.

48. Robespierre (1910–67), vol. 9, p. 89.

49. Ibid., p. 122.

50. Ibid., p. 130.

51. Saint-Just (1908), vol. 1, p. 2.

52. Ibid., pp. 298–99.

53. *Archives parlementaires*, vol. 55, p. 7.

54. Walzer (1974), p. 176.

55. Walzer (1974), p. 192; Robespierre (1910–67), vol. 9, p. 198.

56. Walzer (1974), p. 192; Robespierre (1910–67), vol. 9, p. 198.

57. Croker (1857), p. 360.

58. Robespierre (1910–67), vol. 9, p. 205.

59. Thompson (1939), p. 308.

60. Mercier (1800), pp. 230–31; Croker (1857), p. 361.

61. Belloc (1910), p. 243.

62. Robespierre (1910–67), vol. 9, p. 228.

63. Ibid., p. 232.

64. Croker (1857), p. 257.

65. Mme d'Angoulême quoted in Croker (1857), p. 257.

66. Jones (2002), p. 6.

67. Prudhomme quoted in Croker (1857), p. 560.

68. Croker (1857), p. 259. The April 1770 date was that of Marie Antoinette's marriage by proxy, a familiar practice where the marriage of a princess to a foreigner was concerned; see Fraser (2001), p. 40. Her wedding in France took place later, on 16 May 1770.

9: *The Pact with Violence*

1. Price (2003), p. 328.
2. 30 March 1793, William Bentley Papers, American Antiquarian Society.
3. Doyle (1990), pp. 197–200. See also Blanning (1986) and (1996).
4. Robespierre (1910–67), vol. 3a, p. 160.
5. Ibid., vol. 9, p. 315.
6. *Archives parlementaires*, vol. 59, pp. 717–18.
7. Croker (1857), p. 436. Later the Committee of General Security and the Committee of Public Safety sometimes intervened in making appointments to the tribunal.
8. Doyle (1990), p. 227. The armed bands that smashed the print shops where Girondin journals were produced were in disguise but probably organized by Jacques René Hébert, a radical journalist and editor of the increasingly popular *Père Duchesne*.
9. For important recent work on the *comités de surveillance*, see Guilhaumou and Lapied (2004).
10. The establishment of the Committee of Public Safety was preceded by a complicated sequence of short-lived committees of government. Between 4 and 25 March there was the Committee of General Defense, set up in response to the foreign and domestic crises. It was succeeded by the *Commission de salut public*, which had twenty-five members drawn from both the Mountain and Girondin factions. This was too large and disunited to function and was finally replaced by the famous Committee of Public Safety on 6 April.
11. Biard (1998), pp. 3–24.
12. Robespierre (1910–67), vol. 9, p. 320.
13. Ibid., vol. 9, p. 320.
14. Ibid., p. 346.
15. Ibid., p. 318.
16. Ibid., p. 363.
17. Ibid., p. 377.
18. Thompson (1989), p. 170.
19. Robespierre (1910–67), vol. 9, p. 420.
20. Ibid., p. 418.
21. *Archives parlementaires*, vol. 61, pp. 624–25.
22. Ibid., vol. 62, p. 34.
23. Thompson (1989), p. 181.
24. Croker (1857), p. 365.
25. Robespierre (1910–67), vol. 9, p. 490.

26. Ibid., p. 513.

27. Croker (1857), p. 366.

28. Robespierre (1910–67), vol. 9, p. 541.

29. Thompson (1939), p. 333.

30. Shuckburch (1989), pp. 34–35.

31. Robespierre (1910–67), vol. 9, p. 437.

32. Ibid., pp. 452–53.

33. Ibid., p. 459.

34. *Le patriote français*, no. 1354, p. 1.

35. Robespierre (1910–67), vol. 9, p. 112.

36. Michelet (1979), vol. 2, p. 452.

37. Robespierre (1910–67), vol. 9, p. 548.

38. Doyle (1990), p. 246.

39. Thompson (1989), p. 195.

40. *Archives parlementaires*, vol. 61, p. 279.

41. Thompson (1989), pp. 179–80.

42. There is dispute as to whether Robespierre had bodyguards. The Jacobins living in or near his street often walked home with him, but this may only have been because they were going in the same direction.

43. Robespierre (1910–67), vol. 9, p. 623.

44. Ibid.

45. Ibid., p. 624.

46. Ibid., p. 625.

47. Thompson (1989), p. 182.

48. Croker (1857), p. 561.

49. Jones (1990), p. 204.

50. Carnot's decree of August 1793, *Archives parlementaires*, vol. 73, p. 121.

51. Charlotte does not date this trip in her memoirs, but Augustin wrote to Buissart in Arras on 20 July 1793 telling him he had agreed to go on mission; see Robespierre (1910–67), vol. 3a, p. 176. It was during this trip that Augustin and Charlotte first met Napoleon Bonaparte, who later gave Charlotte a state pension of thirty-six hundred francs when he became premier consul; see Laponneraye (2000), p. 113.

52. Laponneraye (2002), pp. 87–88.

53. Ibid., p. 94.

54. Robespierre (1910–67), vol. 9, p. 539.

55. Thompson (1939), p. 446; Mathiez (1973), p. 138.

56. Lazare Carnot and Claude Prieur joined the Committee of Public Safety on 14 August, just over a fortnight after Robespierre, then Jacques Billaud-Varenne and Jean Marie Collot d'Herbois joined on 6 September; see Palmer (1965), p. 4.

57. Carlyle (1848), vol. 3, p. 277.

58. Robespierre (1828), vol. 2, pp. 13–15.

59. Hardman (1999), p. 112.

60. *Archives parlementaires*, vol. 74, pp. 303–4.

61. Doyle (1990), p. 253.

62. Croker (1857), p. 263.
63. Ibid.
64. Ibid., p. 264.
65. *Le moniteur*, vol. 18, p. 146.
66. Croker (1857), p. 357.
67. Thompson (1989), p. 89.
68. Ibid., p. 70.
69. Robespierre (1910–67), vol. 10, p. 159.
70. Claretie (1908), pp. 194–95.
71. Thompson (1989), p. 90.
72. Croker (1857), p. 564.
73. *Archives parlementaires*, vol. 77, p. 500.
74. Robespierre (1920), p. 3.
75. *Archives parlementaires*, vol. 77, pp. 500–501.
76. Robespierre (1910–67), vol. 10, pp. 32–33.
77. Saint-Just (1908), vol. 2, pp. 492–536.
78. Hardman (1999), p. 114.
79. Thompson (1939), p. 430.
80. Robespierre (1910–67), vol. 8, p. 233.
81. Ibid., vol. 10, p. 195.
82. Thompson (1939), p. 428; Robespierre (1910–67), vol. 9, p. 194.
83. Belloc (1927), p. 281.
84. Palmer (1965), p. 127.
85. *Le vieux Cordelier*, p. 73.
86. Ibid., p. 75.
87. Aulard (1889–97), vol. 5, p. 569; Belloc (1927), p. 284.
88. *Le vieux Cordelier*, p. 14.
89. Robespierre (1910–67), vol. 10, p. 309.
90. *Le vieux Cordelier*, p. 20.
91. Robespierre (1910–67), vol. 10, p. 309.
92. Aulard (1889–97), vol. 5, p. 603.
93. Ibid., pp. 601–2.
94. Robespierre (1910–67), vol. 10, p. 352.
95. Ibid., p. 357.
96. Ibid., p. 374.
97. Thompson (1989), p. 129.
98. Hardman (1999), p. 137.
99. Hamel (1987), vol. 2, p. 335.
100. Thompson (1989), p. 129. Williams (n.d.), p. 128, describes Danton's conversations with prisoners in the Conciergerie.
101. The source of this story is a friend of a friend of E. Hamel. See Thompson (1939), p. 463; Hamel (1987), vol. 2, p. 337.
102. Danton (1910), p. 247.
103. Michelet (1979), vol. 2, p. 753.
104. Belloc (1910), p. 301.
105. Saint-Just (1908), vol. 2, pp. 305–32.

106. There is evidence to suggest that Robespierre's notes were written in response to an initial draft of Saint-Just's speech, in which case the collaboration between them was even more complex. See Mathiez (1973), pp. 121–56.

107. Robespierre (1910–67), vol. 10, p. 414.

108. Desmoulins (1874), pp. 389–91.

109. Danton (1910), p. 248.

110. Michelet (1979), vol. 2, p. 745.

111. Danton (1910), p. 250.

112. Ibid., pp. 257–58.

113. Ibid., pp. 259–64.

114. Ibid., pp. 251–52.

115. *Archives Parlementaires*, vol. 88, pp. 151–52.

116. Danton (1910), p. 271.

117. *Le vieux Cordelier*, p. 170.

118. Belloc (1910), p. 336, claims a Mme Gély was the source of this story. See also Claretie (1908), pp. 285–86 (who assumes Danton was thinking of his wife when he muttered "I shall never see her again"), and Michelet (1979), vol. 2, p. 758.

10: Robespierre's Red Summer

1. The title "Robespierre's Red Summer" is borrowed from Richard Cobb. See also Hardman (1999), p. 125.

2. Robespierre (1910–67), vol. 10, p. 426.

3. Hardman (1999), p. 162; Robespierre (1828), vol. 2, p. 7.

4. Robespierre, (1910–67), vol. 10, p. 437.

5. Ibid., p. 444.

6. Ibid., p. 452.

7. Ibid., p. 448.

8. Thompson (1939), p. 530.

9. Croker (1857), p. 279.

10. Ibid., p. 279.

11. Ibid., p. 500.

12. Robespierre (1910–67), vol. 10, p. 471.

13. Ibid., vol. 3b, pp. 127–28.

14. Belloc (1927), p. 310.

15. Williams (n.d.), p. 142.

16. Favone (1937), pp. 49–50. On the extent of popular support for Robespierre's new religion, see Vovelle (1988).

17. Croker (1857), p. 447.

18. Robespierre (1910–67), vol. 10, p. 481.

19. Hardman (1999), p. 143.

20. Thompson (1939), p. 548.

21. Hardman (1999), pp. 154–56.

22. Ibid., p. 109.
23. Stéfan-Pol (1900), p. 75.
24. Hardman (1999), p. 109.
25. Ibid., p. 131.
26. Ibid., p. 132.
27. Ibid., p. 182.
28. Laponneraye (2002), pp. 106–9.
29. Robespierre (1910–67), vol. 10, p. 496.
30. Ibid., p. 497.
31. Croker (1857), p. 401. The original source is A. Lamartine, whose accuracy Croker doubts.
32. Relying on the Committee of Public Safety's register, Belloc (1927), p. 315, claims Robespierre was only absent six times during the period between 22 Prairial and 9 Thermidor, but Thompson (1939), p. 540, doubts the accuracy of the register and notes that Robespierre's signature appears only three times on the committee's documents during this period.
33. Croker (1857), pp. 400–401.
34. Hardman (1999), p. 150.
35. *Archives Parlementaires*, vol. 87, p. 100.
36. Ibid., vol. 93, p. 553.
37. Thompson (1939), p. 550.
38. Robespierre (1910–67), vol. 10, p. 519.
39. Ibid., p. 520.
40. Ibid., p. 522.
41. Hardman (1999), p. 139.
42. Robespierre (1910–67), vol. 10, p. 528.
43. Ibid., p. 529.
44. Ibid., p. 534.
45. Croker (1857), p. 397; Hardman (1999), pp. 138–39.
46. Robespierre (1910–67), vol. 10, p. 543.
47. Ibid., pp. 544–45.
48. Ibid., p. 546.
49. Ibid., p. 547.
50. Ibid., pp. 554–55; Croker (1857), pp. 406–7.
51. Ibid., p. 560.
52. Ibid., p. 559.
53. Ibid., p. 561.
54. Ibid., p. 575.
55. Ibid., p. 576.
56. Croker (1857), p. 413.
57. Robespierre (1910–67), vol. 10, p. 587.
58. Saint-Just (1908), vol. 2, p. 477.
59. Thompson (1939), p. 567.
60. Saint-Just (1908), vol. 2, p. 332.
61. Croker (1857), p. 421; *Archives parlementaires*, vol. 93, pp. 553–54.

62. *Archives parlementaires*, vol. 93, p. 555.

63. Palmer (1965), p. 380.

64. Croker (1857), p. 423.

65. Robespierre (1828), vol. 2, p. 72.

66. Ibid., p. 74.

67. Ibid.

68. It was rumored that Robespierre had secretly married Eléanore Duplay with Saint-Just as a witness; see Proyart (1850), pp. 208–9.

69. Proyart (1850), p. 210; Pernoud and Flaissier (1960), p. 336.

70. Aulard (1889–97), vol. 5, p. 594.

71. Palmer (1965), p. 381.

Bibliography

Robespierre's Writings

With few exceptions (the holograph speech of 8 Thermidor in his own writing, for example), what is known of Robespierre's political speeches is known through newspaper reports that are subject to slight variations. These have been collated in the *Œuvres complètes*. On the day of Robespierre's arrest, his close friend Eléanore Duplay hid what she could of his papers. Another member of the Duplay family, still fearing recrimination in 1815, burnt them. The rest of his papers were seized, and E. B. Courtois was commissioned to present an official report on them to the Convention. In doing so, Courtois suppressed a quantity of evidence that was later published.

(1910–67) *Œuvres complètes*, ed. E. Hamel, 10 vols., Société des études Robespierristes, Paris: Ernest Leroux.

(1920?) *A Facsimile and Transcript of the Manuscript Notes Found in Robespierre's Possession at His Arrest*, Paris: [s.n.].

(1906) *De Robespierre à Fouché. Notes de Police. Documents inédits*, preface J. Claretie, Paris: Ernest Flammarion.

(1795) *Rapport fait au nom de la commission chargée de l'examen des papiers trouvés chez Robespierre et ses complices . . . dans la séance du 16 nivôse, an IIIe de la république française, etc.*, by E. B. Courtois, Paris: Imprimerie Nationale des Lois.

(1828) *Papiers inédits trouvés chez Robespierre, Saint-Just, Payan, etc. supprimés ou omis par Courtois; précédés du rapport de ce député à la Convention nationale*, 3 vols., Paris: Baudouin Frères.

(1989) *A la nation artésienne, sur la nécessité de reformer les Etats d'Artois, nouvelle edition, considérablement augmentée de nouveaux faits, recueillis depuis la première*, French Revolution Research Collection, Oxford: Pergamon Press.

Revolutionary Journals and Newspapers

L'ami du peuple, reprinted in Marat, J.P. (1989) *Œuvres politiques, 1789–1793*, ed. J. Cock and C. Goëtz, 10 vols., Brussels: Pole Nord.

Archives parlementaires de 1787 à 1860, débats législatifs et politiques des chambres françaises, sous la direction de M. J. Mavidal et de M. E. Laurent, première série, 1787–99, 82 vols., Paris: Libraire Administrative de Paul Dupont, 1885.

Courier français (1789–), Paris: Imprimerie de Gueffier.

Chronique de Paris (24 August 1789–25 August 1793), Paris: Imprimerie de Fiévée de la Chronique.

Le moniteur, réimpression de l'ancien Moniteur: Depuis la réunion des États-généraux jusqu'au Consulat (mai 1789–novembre 1799) avec des notes explicatives, 30 vols., Paris: Au Bureau Central, 1840–45.

The New Annual Register, or General Repository of History, Politics, and Literature, for the Year 1791, London: G. G. J. and J. Robinson, Pater-noster-row, 1791.

Le Patriote français, Paris: [s.n.], 1793.

Le républicain, ou le défenseur du gouvernement représentatif par une société de républicains, 10 July 1791–23 July 1791, Paris: [s.n.], 1791. Only four issues of this journal appeared, the first two published together on 10 July, the third on 16 July, and the fourth on 23 July.

Révolutions de France et de Brabant, reprinted in C. Desmoulins, *Œuvres de Camille Desmoulins*, 10 vols., Munich: Kraus Reprint, 1980.

Révolutions de Paris … publiées par L. Prudhomme, Paris: Imprimerie de Prudhomme, 1789–93.

Le vieux Cordelier, reprinted in *Collection des mémoires relatifs à la Révolution française, avec des notices sur leurs auteurs*, Paris: Baudouin Frères, 1825.

Books and Articles

Acton, J. E. E. D. (1910) *Lectures on the French Revolution*, ed. J. N. Figgis and R. V. Laurence, London: Macmillan.

Alméras, H. d' (1905) *Les dévotes de Robespierre: Catherine Théot et les mystères de Dieu*, Paris: Société français d'imprimerie et de libraire.

Andress, D. (2000) *Massacre at the Champ de Mars: Popular Dissent and Political Culture in the French Revolution*, Woodbridge: Boydell Press.

———. (2005) *The Terror: Civil War in the French Revolution*, London: Little, Brown.

Artarit, J. (2003) *Maximilien Robespierre ou l'impossible filiation*, Paris: La Table Ronde.

Asprey, R. (2000) *The Rise and Fall of Napoleon Bonaparte*, vol. 1, London: Abacus.

Aulard, F. A. (1889–97) *La Société des Jacobins*, 6 vols., Paris: Librairie Jouaust.

———. (1889–1951) *Recueil des actes du comité de salut public avec la correspondance officielle des représentants en mission et le registre du conseil exécutif provisoire*, 12 vols., Paris: Imprimerie Nationale.

———. (1901) *Histoire politique de la Révolution française: Origines et développement de la démocratie et de la République (1789–1804)*, Paris: Librairie A. Colin.

Babeuf, G. (1961) *Correspondance de Babeuf avec l'Académie d'Arras (1785–1788)*, ed. M. Reinhard, Paris: Presses Universitaires de France.

Baczko, B. (1989) *Comment sortir de la Terreur: Thermidor et la Révolution*, Paris: Gallimard.

Badinter, E. and Badinter, R. (1988) *Condorcet, 1743–1794 : Un intellectuel en politique*, Paris: Fayard.

Baker, K. M. (1975) *Condorcet: From Natural Philosophy to Social Mathematics*, Chicago: University of Chicago Press.

———. (1994) "The Idea of a Declaration of Rights," in D. Van Kley (ed.), *The French Idea of Freedom: The Old Regime and the Declaration of Rights of 1789*, Palo Alto: Stanford University Press, pp. 154–99.

Barnave, A. (1960) *Introduction à la Révolution française*, text established and presented by F. Rude, Paris: Armand Colin.

Belloc, H. (1910) *Danton: A Study*, London: Thomas Nelson and Sons.

———. (1927) *Robespierre: A Study*, London: Nisbet and Co.

Ben-Israel, H. (1968) *English Historians on the French Revolution*, Cambridge: Cambridge University Press.

Bentley, W. (1905–14) *The Diary of William Bentley, Pastor of the East Church*, Salem, Mass.: Essex Institute.

Berthe, L.-N. (1969) *Dubois de Fosseux, secrétaire de l'Académie d'Arras, 1785–1792 et son bureau de correspondence*, Arras: L'auteur, 103, rue d'Amiens.

Biard, M. (1998) "Les pouvoirs des représentants en mission sous la Convention," *Annales historiques de la Révolution française*, no. 311, pp. 3–24.

Blagdon, F. W. (1803) *Paris as It Was and as It Is, or A Sketch of the French Capital, Illustrative of the Effects of the Revolution, with Respect to Sciences, Literature, Art, Religion, Education, Manners, and Amusements*, 2 vols., London: C. and R. Baldwin.

Blanc, L. (1847–69) *Histoire de la Révolution française*, 12 vols., Paris: Langlois et Leelereq.

Blanc, O. (1984) *La dernière lettre: Prisons et condamnés de la Révolution, 1793–1794*, preface M. Vovelle, Paris: R. Laffont.

Blanning, T. C. W. (1986) *The Origins of the French Revolutionary Wars*, London: Longman.

————. (1996) *The French Revolutionary Wars, 1787–1802*, London: Arnold.

————. (1996) (ed.) *The Rise and Fall of the French Revolution*, Chicago: Chicago University Press.

Bougard, P. (1988) (ed. with Y. M. Hilaire and A. Nolibos), *Histoire d'Arras*, France: Editions de Beffrois.

Bouloiseau, M. (1956) *Robespierre*, Paris: Presses Universitaires de France.

Brightfield, M. F. (1940) *John Wilson Croker*, London: George Allen and Unwin.

Brissot, J.-P. (1911) *Correspondance et papiers*, ed. C. Perroud, Paris: Picard et Fils.

Brodhurst, A. C. (1979) (revised) "French Revolution Collections in the British Library: List of the Contents of the Three Special Collections of Pamphlets, Journals, and Other Works in the British Library, Relating Chiefly to the French Revolution," compil. G. K. Fortescue, London: British Library.

Brunel, F. (1989) *Thermidor: La chute de Robespierre, 1794*, Brussels: Editions Complexe.

Büchner, G. (1971) *Danton's Death* [1835], trans. V. Price, Oxford: Oxford University Press.

Buffenoir, H. (1910) *Les portraits de Robespierre*, Paris: Ernest Leroux.

Burke, E. (1989) *The French Revolution 1790–1794: The Writings and Speeches of Edmund Burke*, ed. L. G. Mitchell, vol. 8, Oxford: Oxford University Press.

Cabanis, P. J. G. (1791) *Journal de la maladie et de la mort d'Honoré-Gabriel-Victor Riquetti Mirabeau par P. J. G. Cabanis docteur en medicine, et de la Société philosophique de Philadelphie*, Paris: Chez Grabit.

Campan, J. L. H. (1823) *Mémoires sur la vie privée de Marie-Antoinette, reine de France et de Navarre: Suivis de souvenirs et anecdotes historiques sur les règnes de Louis XIV, de Louis XV et de Louis XVI*, Paris: Baudouin Frères.

Carlyle, T. (1848) *The French Revolution*, 3 vols., London: Levey, Robson and Franklyn.

Carr, J. L. (1972) *Robespierre: The Force of Circumstance*, London: History Book Club.

Claretie, J. (1908) *Camille Desmoulins*, Paris: Librairie Hachette.

Cobb, R. (1955) *Les armées révolutionnaires des départements du Midi (automne et hiver de 1793, printemps de 1794)*, Toulouse: Soubiron.

————. (1961–63) *Les armées révolutionnaires: Instrument de la Terreur dans les départements, avril 1793–floréal an II*, Paris: Mouton.

Cobban, A. (1971) *Aspects of the French Revolution*, London: Paladin.

Cochin, A. (1920–35) *Les actes du gouvernement révolutionnaire (23 août 1793–27 juillet 1794), recueil de documents publiés pour la Société d'histoire contemporaine par A. Cochin et C. Charpentier*, Paris: A. Picard et Fils.

————. (1936) *Précis des principales opérations du gouvernement révolutionnaire; publié pour la Société de l'histoire de France (série postérieure à 1789), préparé par A. Cochin et mis au point par M. de Boüard*, Paris: Honoré Champion.

————. (1921) *Les sociétés de pensée et de la démocratie: Etudes d'histoire révolutionnaire*, Paris: Plon.

Corbin, A. (1986) *The Foul and the Fragrant: Odor and the French Social Imagination*, Cambridge: Harvard University Press.

Croker, J.W. (1835) "Robespierre," *Quarterly Review* (September), pp. 517–80.

———. (1857) *Essays on the Early Period of the French Revolution*, London: John Murray. Reprinted from the *Quarterly Review* with additions and corrections.

———. (1967) *The Croker Papers: 1808–1857*, London: Batsford.

Crook, M. (1996) *Elections in the French Revolution: An Apprenticeship in Democracy, 1789–1799*, Cambridge: Cambridge University Press.

Crouzet, F. (1989) *Historians and the French Revolution: The Case of Maximilien Robespierre*, Swansea: University College of Swansea.

Danton, G.J. (1910) *Discours de Danton*, ed. A. Fribourg, Paris: Edouard Cornely.

Darnton, R. (2003) *George Washington's False Teeth: An Unconventional Guide to the Eighteenth Century*, New York: Norton.

Darnton, R. and Roch, D. (1989) (eds.) *Revolution in Print: The Press in France, 1775–1800*, Berkeley: University of California Press.

Dauban, C.A. (1867) *La démagogie en 1793 à Paris (ou histoire, jour par jour, de l'année 1793, accompagnée de documents contemporains rares ou inédits)*, Paris: Henri Plon.

Deprun, J. (1972) "A la fête suprême: Les 'noms divins' dans deux discours de Robespierre," *Annales historiques de la Révolution française*, no. 44, pp. 161–80.

Desmoulins, C. (1874) *Œuvres de Camille Desmoulins*, 2 vols., ed. J. Claretie, Paris: Charpentier.

Desmoulins, C. (1980) *Œuvres de Camille Desmoulins*, 10 vols., Munich: Kraus Reprint.

Desmoulins, L. (1995), *Journal 1788–1793*, introd. P. Lejeune, Paris: Editions des Cendres.

Dickens, C. (1988) *A Tale of Two Cities* [1859], ed. A. Sanders, Oxford: Oxford University Press.

Dinaux, A. (1850) "La société des Rosati à Arras," in *Archives Historiques et litteraires du Nord de la France et du Midi de la Belgique*, 3rd series, vol. 1, Valenciennes: A. Prignet, pp. 63–99.

Dingli, L. (2004) *Robespierre*, Paris: Flammarion.

Domecq, J.P. (1989) "Robespierre and the Être-Suprême Celebration—Political Neutrality between Revolution and Christianity," *Esprit*, vol. 9, pp. 91–125.

Doyle, W. (1990) *The Oxford History of the French Revolution*, Oxford: Oxford University Press.

Dumont, E. (1832) *Souvenirs sur Mirabeau et sur les deux premières assemblées législatives* [posthumous, published by M.J.L. Duval], Paris: C. Gosselin, et Chez H. Bossange.

Duplay, M. (1929) *Robespierre, amant de la patrie*, Paris: Albin Michel.

Edmonds, E.W. (1988) *Jacobinism and the Revolt of Lyon, 1789–1793*, Oxford: Oxford University Press.

Egret, J. (1975) *Necker, ministre de Louis XVI*, Paris: H. Champion.

Ehrard, J. (1996) (ed.) *Images de Robespierre, Actes du colloque international de Naples, 27–29 septembre 1993*, Naples: Vivarium.

Eude, M. (1937) *Etudes sur la Commune Robespierriste*, Paris: Mellottée.

Fauré, C. (1999) *Des manuscrits de Sieyès, 1773–1799, sous la direction de Christine Fauré, avec la collaboration de Jacques Guilhaumou et Jacques Valier*, Paris: Honoré Champion.

Favone, M. (1937) *Dans le sillage de Maximilien Robespierre: Joachim Vilate*, Paris: Librairie des Sciences Politiques et Sociales.

Ferrières, C. E. Marquis de (1932), *Correspondance inédite* [1789, 1790, 1791], ed. H. Carré, Paris: Armand Colin.

Fleischmann, H. (1908) *Robespierre et les femmes*, Paris: Albin Michel.

———. (1910) *Les coulisses du Tribunal révolutionnaire : Fouquier-Tinville intime, avec des lettres inédites de Fouquier-Tinville, de sa veuve, de ses enfants, et de nombreux documents nouveaux tirés des cartons du Tribunal révolutionnaire aux Archives nationales*, Paris: Société d'Éditions et de Publications Parisiennes.

———. (1911) *Le masque mortuaire de Robespierre*, Paris: Ernest Leroux.

Forsyth, M. (1987) *Reason and Revolution: The Political Thought of the Abbé Sieyès*, New York: Leicester University Press, Holmes and Meier.

———. (1989) *Pierre-Louis Rœderer: The Spirit of the Revolution of 1789 and Other Writings of the Revolutionary Epoch*, Aldershot: Scholar Press.

Foucault, M. (1979) *Discipline and Punish*, trans. A. Sheridan, Middlesex: Penguin.

Fraser, A. (2001) *Marie Antoinette: The Journey*, London: Weidenfeld and Nicolson.

Furet, F. (1978) *Penser la Révolution française*, Paris: Gallimard.

———. (1987) "La monarchie et le règlement électoral de 1789," in K. M. Baker (ed.), *The Political Culture of the Old Regime*, Oxford: Pergamon Press, pp. 375–387.

Furet, F. and Halévi, R. (1989) (eds.) *Les Constituents*, vol. 1 of *Orateurs de la Révolution française*, Paris: Gallimard.

———. (1996) (eds.) *La monarchie républicaine: La constitution de 1791*, Paris: Fayard.

Furet, F. and Ozouf, M. (1989) (eds.) *Dictionnaire critique de la Révolution française*, trans. A. Goldhammer, Cambridge: Belknap Press of Harvard University Press.

———. (1991) (eds.), *La Gironde et les Girondins*, Paris: Payot.

Gallo, M. (1984) *L'homme Robespierre: Histoire d'une solitude*, Paris: Librairie Académique Perrin.

Garmy, R. (1967) "Aux origines de la légende antirobespierriste: Pierre Villiers et Robespierre," *Actes du colloque Robespierre, XIIe Congrès international des sciences historiques*, introd. A. Soboul, Paris: Société des Etudes Robespierristes, pp. 19–35.

Garrioch, D. (2002) *The Making of Revolutionary Paris*, Berkeley: University of California Press.

Gauchet, M. (1989) *La révolution des droits de l'homme*, Paris: Gallimard.

———. (1995) *La révolution des pouvoirs: La souveraineté, le peuple et la représentation 1789–1799*, Paris: Gallimard.

Gauthier, F. (1992) "The French Revolution and the Colonial Problem, Slavery, and Constitutional Laws: The Case of Robespierre," *Annales historiques de la Révolution française*, no. 288, pp. 169–92.

Gillion, A. (1989) "Robespierre Remembered in Arras, 1794–1939," *Revue du Nord*, vol. 71, pp. 1037–50.

Godechot, J. (1967) "L'historiographie française de Robespierre," *Actes du colloque Robespierre, XIIe Congrès international des sciences historiques*, Paris: Société des Etudes Robespierristes, pp. 167–89.

———. (1970) *The Taking of the Bastille*, trans. J. Stewart, London: Faber and Faber.

———. (1983) "Laponneraye, Historian of Robespierre," *Annales historiques de la Révolution française*, no. 251, pp. 154–56.

Godineau, D. (1998) *The Women of Paris and Their French Revolution*, trans. K. Streip, Berkeley: University of California Press.

Goethe, J. W. von (1849) *Campaign in France in the Year 1792*, London: Chapman and Hall.

Goulet, J. (1983) "Robespierre, the Death Penalty, and the Terror," *Annales historiques de la Révolution française*, no. 251, pp. 38–64.

Grimsley, R. (1961) *Jean-Jacques Rousseau: A Study in Self-Awareness*, Cardiff: University of Wales Press.

Gueniffey, P. (1991) "Brissot," in F. Furet and M. Ozouf (eds.), *La Gironde et les Girondins*, Paris: Payot, pp. 437–64.

———. (1993) *Le nombre et la raison: La Révolution française et les élections*, Paris: Editions de l'Ecole des Hautes Etudes en Sciences Sociales.

———. (1994) "Cordeliers and Girondins: The Prehistory of the Republic?" in B. Fontana (ed.), *The Invention of the Modern Republic*, Cambridge: Cambridge University Press, pp. 86–106.

———. (2000) *La politique de la Terreur: Essai sur la violence révolutionnaire*, Paris: Fayard.

Guilhaumou, J. and Lapied, M. (2004) "Comités de surveillance et pouvoir révolutionnaire," *Rives*, no. 18 (*Comités de surveillance et Révolution française*), http://rives.revues.org/document122.html.

Hamel, E. (1865–67) *Histoire de Robespierre d'après des papiers de famille: Les sources originales et des documents entièrement inédits*, Paris: A. Lacroix, Verboeckhoven and Co.

———. (1987) *Histoire de Robespierre et du coup d'état du 9 Thermidor*, 2 vols. [1865–67], Paris: Ledrappier.

Hampson, N. (1974) *The Life and Opinions of Maximilien Robespierre*, London: Duckworth.

———. (1988) "La patrie," in *The Political Culture of the French Revolution*, vol. 2 of *The French Revolution and the Creation of Modern Political Culture*, ed. C. Lucas, Oxford: Pergamon Press, pp. 125–39.

———. (1991) *Saint-Just*, Oxford: Basil Blackwell.

Harcourt, F. (1979) *Escape from the Terror: The Journal of Madame de la Tour du Pin*, London: Folio Society.

Hardman, J. (1993) *Louis XVI*, New Haven: Yale University Press.

———. (1999) *Robespierre*, Profiles in Power Series, Harlow: Pearson Education/Longman.

Harris, R. D. (1986) *Necker and the Revolution of 1789*, Lanham: University Press of America.

Haydon, C. and Doyle, W. (1999) (eds.), *Robespierre*, Cambridge: Cambridge University Press.

Héricault, C. d' (1878) *La révolution de thermidor, Robespierre et le Comité de salut public*, Paris: Didier.

Héricourt, A. d' and Godin, A. (1856) *Les rues d'Arras: Dictionnaire historique*, Arras: Editions Cultures et Civilisation.

Higonnet, P. (1985) "The Social and Cultural Antecedents of Revolutionary Discontinuity: Montagnards and Girondins," *English Historical Review*, vol. 100, pp. 513–44.

———. (1998) *Goodness beyond Virtue: Jacobins during the French Revolution*, Cambridge: Harvard University Press.

Hont, I. (2005) *Jealousy of Trade: International Competition and the Nation-State in Historical Perspective*, Cambridge: Harvard University Press.

Horne, A. (2003) *Seven Ages of Paris*, London: Pan.

Huet, M. H. (1989) "Thunder and Revolution—Franklin, Robespierre, Sade," *Eighteenth-Century Theory and Interpretation*, vol. 30, pp. 13–32.

Hufton, O. H. (1974) *The Poor of Eighteenth-Century France, 1750–1789*, Oxford: Oxford University Press.

Ireland, B. (2005) *The Fall of Toulon: The Last Opportunity to Defeat the French Revolution*, London: Orion.

Jacob, L. (1938) *Robespierre vu par ses contemporains*, Paris: A. Colin.

Jaume, L. (1989) *Le discours jacobin et la démocratie*, Paris: Fayard.

Jaurès, J. (1968) *Histoire socialiste de la Révolution française*, Paris: Editions Sociales.

Jessenne, J.-P. et al. (1994) (eds.), *Robespierre: De la nation artésienne à la République et aux nations: Actes du colloque, Arras, 1-2-3 avril 1993*, Villeneuve d'Asq : Centre d'Histoire de la Région du Nord et de l'Europe du Nord-Ouest, Université Charles de Gaulle–Lille III.

Jones, C. (2002) *The Great Nation: France from Louis XV to Napoleon*, London: Penguin.

———. (2005) "Michel Vovelle and the French Revolution," *French History*, vol. 19, pp. 168–76.

Jordan, D. P. (1985) *The Revolutionary Career of Maximilien Robespierre*, New York: Free Press; London: Macmillan.

Kates, G. (1985) *The Cercle Social, the Girondins, and the French Revolution*, Princeton: Princeton University Press.

Kennedy, M. (1982) *The Jacobin Clubs in the French Revolution: The First Years*, Princeton: Princeton University Press.

———. (1988) *The Jacobin Clubs in the French Revolution: The Middle Years*, Princeton: Princeton University Press.

Kerr, W. B. (1927) *The Reign of Terror, 1793–4: The Experiment of the Democratic Republic and the Rise of the Bourgeoisie*, Toronto: University of Toronto Press.

Kuscinski, A. (1973) *Dictionnaire des conventionnels*, Breuil-en-Vexin: Vexin Français.

Lamartine, A. (1848) *Histoire des Girondins*, 3 vols., trans. H. T. Ryde, London: Henry G. Bohn.

Lamoignon, C.-F. de (1787) *Discours de M. de Lamoignon, garde des sceaux de France, à la séance du roi au parlement, le 19 novembre 1787*, Paris: Imprimerie de Philippe-Denys Pierres.

Laponneraye, A. (2002) *Mémoires de Charlotte Robespierre sur ses deux frères* [1835], Paris: Phénix Editions.

Le Blond de Neuvéglise (1795) *La vie et les crimes de Robespierre, surnommé le Tyran, depuis sa naissance jusqu'à sa mort*, Augsbourg: [s.n.].

Lefebvre, G. (1973) *The Great Fear of 1789*, trans. J. White, London: NLB.

——. (2002) *The French Revolution*, trans. E. M. Evanson, London and New York: Routledge.

Lenôtre, G. [pseud. L. L. T. Gosselin] (1926) *Robespierre et la "Mère de Dieu,"* Paris: Librairie Académique Perrin.

Lewes, G. H. (1899) *The Life of Maximilian Robespierre (with Extracts from His Unpublished Correspondence)*, London: Chapman and Hall.

Lewis, G. (1972) *Life in Revolutionary France*, London: Batsford.

Lucas, C. (1991) (ed.) *Rewriting the French Revolution*, Oxford: Clarendon Press.

Madame Élisabeth (1863) *Correspondance de Madame Élisabeth de France: sœur de Louis XVI*, Paris: Henri Plon.

Mantel, H. (1992) *A Place of Greater Safety*, London: Viking.

——. (2000) "What a Man This Is, with His Crowd of Women around Him!" *London Review of Books*, vol. 22, pp. 3–8.

Marat, J. P. (1877) *Placards de Marat, l'ami du people*, ed. F. Chevremont, Paris: Chez l'Auteur.

——. (1908) *La correspondance de Marat*, annotated C. Vellay, Paris: Librairie Charpentier et Fasquelle.

——. (1989) *Œuvres politiques, 1789–1793*, ed. J. Cock and C. Goëtz, 10 vols., Brussels: Pole Nord.

Margerison, K. (1983) "P. L. Rœderer: Political Thought and Practice during the French Revolution," *Transactions of the American Philosophical Society*, vol. 73, pp. 1–161.

Mathiez, A. (1904) *Les origines des cultes révolutionnaires 1789–1792*, Paris: Bellais.

——. (1910) (ed.) *Le club des Cordeliers pendant la crise de Varennes et le massacre du Champ de Mars; documents en grande partie inédits publiés avec des éclaircissements, des notes et une planche*, Paris: H. Champion.

——. (1921) *Robespierre terroriste*, Paris: La Renaissance du Livre.

——. (1922) *La Révolution française*, Paris: Librairie Armand Colin.

——. (1926a) *Autour de Robespierre*, Paris: Payot.

————. (1926b) *Autour de Danton*, Paris, Payot.

————. (1927) *La vie chère et le mouvement social sous la Terreur*, Paris: Payot.

————. (1930) *Girondins et Montagnards*, Paris: Firmin-Didot.

————. (1973). *Études sur Robespierre, 1758–94*, Paris: Éditions sociales.

Maury, l'Abbé (1789) *Opinion de M. l'abbé Maury, député de Picardie, sur la propriété des biens ecclésiastiques, prononcée dans l'Assemblée nationale le mardi 13 octobre 1789*, Paris: Chez Baudouin.

McManners, J. (1998) *Church and Society in Eighteenth-Century France*, 2 vols., Oxford: Oxford University Press.

Méda, C. A. (1825) *Précis historique des événements qui se sont passés dans le soirée du 9 thermidor*, reprinted in *Collection des mémoires relatifs à la Révolution française, avec des notices sur leurs auteurs*, Paris: Baudouin Frères.

Mercier, L. S. (1800), *New Picture of Paris*, 2 vols., London: C. Whittingham, for H. D. Symonds.

Michelet, J. (1979) *Histoire de la Révolution française*, 2 vols., Paris: Robert Laffont.

Michon, G. (1924) "La maison de Robespierre rue de Saintonge, à Paris," *Annales historiques de la Révolution française*, vol. 1, pp. 64–66.

Mirabeau, G.-H. de R. Comte de (1790) (attrib.), *Gallery of Portraits of the National Assembly, Supposed to Be Written by Count de Mirabeau*, 2 vols., Dublin: H. Chamberlaine and Rice.

————. (1835–36) *Mémoires de Mirabeau, biographiques, littéraires et politiques, écrits par lui-même, par son père, son oncle, et son fils adoptif*, 8 vols., Paris: A. Auffray.

Montesquieu, C. L. S. Baron de (1950–61) *De l'ésprit des loix* [1748], critical ed. by J. Brethe de la Gressaye, Paris: Société Les Belles Lettres.

Nicolet, C. (1982) *L'idée républicaine en France (1789–1924): Essai d'histoire critique*, Paris: Gallimard.

O'Brien, B. (1837?) *The Life and Character of Maximilian Robespierre*, London: J. Watson.

————. (1857) *An Elegy on the Death of Robespierre*, London: G. J. Holyouke & Co.

O'Brien, C. C. (1985) "Virtue and Terror," *New York Review of Books*, vol. 32, pp. 28–31.

Ording, A. (1930) *Le bureau de police du Comité de salut public: Etude sur la Terreur*, Oslo: J. Dybwad.

Ozouf, M. (1989) *La fête révolutionnaire (1789–1799)*, Paris: Gallimard.

Palmer, R. R. (1939) *Catholics and Unbelievers in Eighteenth-Century France*, Princeton: Princeton University Press.

————. (1959) *The Age of the Democratic Revolution*, vol. 1, Princeton: Princeton University Press.

————. (1965) *Twelve Who Ruled: The Year of the Terror in the French Revolution*, New York: Atheneum.

————. (1975) (ed.), *The School of the French Revolution: A Documentary History of the College of Louis-le-Grand and Its Director, Jean-François Champagne, 1762–1814*, Princeton: Princeton University Press.

————. (1985) *The Improvement of Humanity: Education and the French Revolution*, Princeton: Princeton University Press.

Paris, J. A. (1870) *La jeunesse de Robespierre et la convocation des Etats généraux en Artois* [based on articles in *Mémoires de l'Académie d'Arras*], Arras: Rousseau-Leroy.

Pasquino, P. (1998) *Sieyès et l'invention de la constitution en France*, Paris: Odile Jacob.

Pernoud, G. and Flaissier, S. (1960) *The French Revolution*, trans. R. Graves, London: Secker and Warburg.

Price, M. (2003) *The Fall of the French Monarchy, Louis XVI, Marie Antoinette, and the Baron de Breteuil*, London: Pan Macmillan.

Proyart, Abbé (1803) *Louis XVI détrôné avant d'être roi: Ou, tableau des causes de la Révolution française, et de l'ébranlement de tous les trônes*, Paris: Chez l'Auteur.

Proyart, J. M. (1850) *La vie de Maximilien Robespierre*, Arras: Chez Théry Libraire.

Prudhomme, L. M. (1789) *Résumé général, ou extrait des cahiers de pouvoirs, instructions demandes & doléances, remis par les divers bailliages, sénéchaussées & pays d'états du royaume, à leurs députés à l'Assemblée des etats généraux, ouverts à Versailles le 4 mai 1789 avec une table raisonnée des matiéres/par une société de gens de lettres*, Paris: [s.n.].

————. (1797) *Histoire générale et impartiale des erreurs, des fautes et des crimes commis pendant la Révolution française, à dater du 24 août 1787, contenant le nombre des individus qui ont péri par la Révolution, de ceux qui ont émigré, et les intrigues des factions qui pendant ce temps ont désolé la France. Ornée de gravures et de tableaux*, 6 vols., Paris: [s.n.].

Ratineau, F. (1992) "The Books of Robespierre on 9 thermidor," *Annales historiques de la Révolution française*, vol. 287, pp. 131–35.

Rigney, A. (1990) *The Rhetoric of Historical Representation: Three Narrative Histories of the French Revolution*, Cambridge: Cambridge University Press.

Riley, P. (2001) (ed.) *The Cambridge Companion to Rousseau*, Cambridge: Cambridge University Press.

Riouffe, H. (1795) *Mémoires d'un détenu, pour servir à l'histoire de la tyrannie de Robespierre*, Paris: Chez de Boffe.

Riskin, J. (1999) "The Lawyer and the Lightning Rod," *Science in Context*, vol. 12, pp. 61–99.

Robespierre, A. B. J. (1891) *Lettres inédites de Augustin Robespierre à Antoine Buissart*, ed. V. Barbier, Arras: Rohard-Courtin.

Rœderer, P.-L. (1853–59) *Œuvres du comte P. L. Rœderer*, 8 vols., Paris: Firmin-Didot Frères.

Roudinesco, E. (1991) *Madness and Revolution: The Lives and Legends of Théroigne de Méricourt*, trans. M. Thom, New York: Verso.

Rousseau, J.-J. (1962) *The Political Writings*, ed. C. E. Vaughan, 2 vols., Oxford: Basil Blackwell.

————. (1987) *La nouvelle Héloïse*, trans. J. H. McDowell, University Park: Penn State University Press.

————. (1993) *Emile*, trans. B. Foxley, London: Everyman.

————. (2000) *Confessions*, trans. A. Scholar, Oxford: Oxford University Press.

Roux, L. F. (1794) *Liste de proscription des patriots*, Paris: Lejebure.

Roux, P. de (1986) (ed.) *Mémoires de Madame Roland*, Paris: Mercure de France.

Sanson, C. H. (1911) *Mémoires de Sanson, exécuteur des jugements criminaels*, Paris: A. Michel.

Sardou, V. (1895) *La maison de Robespierre (réponse à E. Hamel)*, Paris: Paul Ollendorf.

Saint-Just, A. L. L. (1908) *Œuvres complètes*, 2 vols., ed. C. Vellay, Paris: Charpentier et Fasquelle.

Schama, S. (1989) *Citizens: A Chronicle of the French Revolution*, London: Penguin.

Shapiro, B. M. (1993) *Revolutionary Justice in Paris, 1789–1790*, Cambridge: Cambridge University Press.

Shuckburch, E. (1989) *The Memoirs of Madame Roland*, London: Barrie and Jenkins.

Sieburg, F. (1937) *Robespierre*, trans. J. Dilke, London: Geoffrey Bles.

Sieyès, E.-J. (1989) *Œuvres de Sieyès*, 3 vols., Paris: Edhis.

Soboul, A. (1958) *Les sans-culottes parisiens en l'an II: Mouvement populaire et gouvernement révolutionnaire, 2 juin 1793–9 thermidor an II*, Paris: Clavreuil.

————. (1967) (ed.) *Actes du colloque Robespierre, XIIe Congrès international des sciences historiques*, Paris: Société des Etudes Robespierristes.

————. (1973) *1789, l'an un de la liberté: Etude historique, textes originaux*, Paris: Editions Sociales.

————. (1981) *Comprendre la Révolution: Problèmes politiques de la Révolution française (1789–1797)*, Paris: F. Maspero.

————. (1980) (ed.) *Girondins et Montagnards: Actes du colloque, Sorbonne, 14 décembre 1975*, Paris: Société des Etudes Robespierristes.

Sonenscher, M. (1997) "The Nation's Debt and the Birth of the Modern Republic: The French Fiscal Deficit and the Politics of the Revolution of 1789," *History of Political Thought*, vol. 18, pp. 65–103, 267–325.

————. (2003) (ed.) *Emmanuel Joseph Sieyès, Political Writings, including the Debate between Sieyès and Tom Paine in 1791*, Cambridge: Hackett.

Springer, C. (1981) "Far From the Madding Crowd: Wordsworth and the News of Robespierre's Death," *Wordsworth Circle*, vol. 12, pp. 243–45.

Stäel, A. L. G. de (1983) *Considérations sur la Révolution française*, Paris: Tallandier.

Stéfan-Pol [pseud.] (1900) *Autour de Robespierre: Le conventionnel Le Bas d'après des documents inédits et les mémoires de sa veuve*, pref. V. Sardou, Paris: Ernest Flammarion.

Tackett, T. (1996) *Becoming a Revolutionary: The Deputies of the French National Assembly and the Emergence of a Revolutionary Culture (1789–1790)*, Princeton: Princeton University Press.

————. (2003) *When the King Took Flight*, Cambridge: Harvard University Press.

Thomas, W. (2000) *The Quarrel of Macaulay and Croker: Politics and History in the Age of Reform*, Oxford: Oxford University Press.

Thompson, J.M. (1939) *Robespierre*, Oxford: Basil Blackwell. First published, in two volumes, in 1935.

———. (1970) *Robespierre and the French Revolution*, London: English Universities Press Ltd.

———. (1989) *Leaders of the French Revolution*, Oxford: Basil Blackwell.

Tour du Pin, H.L. Marquise de la (1979) *Escape from the Terror: The Journal of Madame de la Tour du Pin*, ed. and trans. F. Harcourt, London: Folio Society.

Van Kley, D. (1994) (ed.) *The French Idea of Freedom: The Old Regime and the Declaration of Rights of 1789*, Palo Alto: Stanford University Press.

———. (1996) *The Religious Origins of the French Revolution: From Calvin to the Civil Constitution, 1560–1791*, New Haven: Yale University Press.

Vermorel, A. (n.d.) *Œuvres de Vergniaud, Gaudet, Gensonné*, Paris: Libraire Editeur.

Vilate, J. (1825) *Causes secrètes du 9 thermidor*, reprinted in *Collection des mémoires relatifs à la Révolution française, avec des notices sur leurs auteurs*, Paris: Baudouin Frères.

Villiers, P. (1802) *Souvenirs d'un déporté, pour server aux histoirens, aux romanciers, aux compilateurs d'ana*, Paris: Chez l'Auteur.

Vovelle, M. (1972) *La chute de la monarchie, 1787–1792*, Paris: Editions du Seuil.

———. (1988) *La révolution contre l'eglise: De la raison à l'Être Supreme*, Brussels: Editions Complexe.

———. (1993) *Combats pour la Révolution française*, Paris: Société des Etudes Robespierristes.

Walter, G. (1946) *Maximilien de Robespierre* (with appendix "Robespierre devant les hommes") Paris: Gallimard.

Walter, G. (1989) *Maximilien de Robespierre*, Paris: Gallimard.

Walzer, M. (1974) (ed.) *Regicide and Revolution: Speeches at the Trial of Louis XVI*, Cambridge: Cambridge University Press.

Whatmore, R. (2000) *Republicanism and the French Revolution: An Intellectual History of Jean-Baptiste Say's Political Economy*, Oxford: Oxford University Press.

Williams, H.M. (n.d.) *Memoirs of the Reign of Robespierre* [1795, 1796], ed. F. Funck-Brentano, London: John Hamilton.

Wogue, J. (1894) *J.-B.-L. Gresset: Sa vie, ses œuvres*, Paris: Lecène, Oudin et Cie.

Wordsworth, W. (1995), *The Prelude: The Four Texts (1798, 1799, 1805, 1850)*, ed. J. Wordsworth, London: Penguin.

Wrigley, R. (2002) *The Politics of Appearances: Representations of Dress in Revolutionary France*, Oxford: Berg.

Young, A. (1929) *Travels in France during the Years 1787, 1788, 1789*, ed. C. Maxwell, Cambridge: Cambridge University Press.

Acknowledgments

Parts of *Fatal Purity* were researched and written alongside my work as a British Academy Postdoctoral Fellow in the Politics Department of Cambridge University. I acknowledge the valuable support of the academy, my colleagues, and my students.

An earlier version was generously read and improved by two eminent historians of the French Revolution: Professor Norman Hampson (whose own book on Robespierre is a lasting bequest to scholarship in the field), and Dr. Michael Sonenscher (teacher, colleague, and friend of a decade in King's College, Cambridge). I am beholden to both. All remaining inaccuracies and infelicities are certainly my own.

I am extremely grateful to Sara Bershtel at Metropolitan Books for her highly intelligent and tirelessly generous editorial work, as well as to Riva Hocherman for her valuable suggestions, Roslyn Schloss for her excellent copyediting, and Kate Levin for her organizational acumen. At Chatto and Windus, my thanks to Jenny Uglow, with whom it is a privilege to work, and to Alison Samuel and Poppy Hampson. I'm grateful also to Lindsay Duguid, Nick Laird, and Erica Wagner, who all took the time to read and comment at length.

My agent, Peter Straus, has helped in countless ways, and I am grateful also to Rowan Routh at Rogers, Coleridge and White and to Melanie Jackson in the United States.

I have always been courteously assisted by staff at the Cambridge University Library, the British Library, the London Library, the Archives nationales, and the Bibliothèque nationale de France.

For professional advice of different kinds, thank you: Alex Butterworth, Rebecca Carter, Heather Glen, Istvan Hont, Sunil Khilnani, Robert MacFarlane, Brian McDonnell, Angus McKinnon, Andrew Wilson, Bee Wilson (who first encouraged me to begin this book), and Brian Young.

I apologize to Charles, Polly, and Rosalind Dunn for encroachments on their weekends and childhood holidays.

And I thank, above all, John Dunn, for our fierce conversations and everything else he has given me.

Index

MR = Maximilien Robespierre

Academy of Amiens, 49–51
Academy of Arras, 45–49, 52, 56, 76, 178
Academy of Metz, 45, 47–48
Achilles, 39
A la nation artésienne, sur la nécessité de réformer les États d'Artois (pamphlet), 69–71
Alexander the Great, 39
Altar of the Fatherland, 133–34, 167–70, 212
American Revolution, 63, 84, 97, 135, 151, 159, 192
    bills of rights and, 101–2
Ami des noirs (abolitionist society), 162
Ami du peuple, L' (newspaper), 106, 136–37, 234, 241, 284
Anson's Voyage Round the World (Walter), 288
Antifédéraliste (newspaper), 308
Arles, archbishop of, 219
Arras
    elections and taxation and, 118
    Estates General and, 10, 80–81, 84, 86
    on eve of Revolution, 68–69
    history and economy of, 17–19
    Jacobin Club in, 126–27, 228
    judicial system in, 40–41

MR elected to Estates General for, 67–77
MR practices law in, 36–37
MR visits, 172–74, 177–80, 203–4
shame surrounding MR in, 10–11
Arras, bishop of, 123
Arras Commune, 228
Artois, Count of (brother Louis XVI), 95, 100
Artois province, 17, 41, 43, 74–75, 114, 118–19
    counterrevolution in, 126–27
atheism and de-Christianization, 293–96, 320–21, 327, 334–37, 342
Audrein, Yves-Marie, 29, 30
Austria, 136, 137, 158, 165
    war with, 192, 197–98, 261, 340
Austrian Netherlands, 185, 257, 258, 330

Bacon, Francis, 47
bad blood, 45–48, 147–48, 338
Bailly, Jean Sylvain, 87, 91, 96–97, 100, 121, 162, 169
Barère, Bertrand, 239, 247, 250, 261, 280, 323, 339, 343, 346, 347, 349, 350, 356
Barnave, Antoine, 95, 166, 167, 181, 311
Bastille, 56, 93, 108, 243

Bastille, fall and demolition of, 92–95,
98–99, 107, 120, 216–17. *See also*
Festival of Federation
first anniversary of, 133–36
second anniversary of, 167–68
fifth anniversary of, 339, 341–42
Bastille of Artois, 71
Beaumarchais, Pierre-Augustin Caron de,
73
Beauvais, bishop of, 219
Beccaria, Cesare, 44
Becket, Saint Thomas, 38
Belgium, 258, 260, 340
Bentabole, Pierre-Louis, 274
Bentley, William, 257
Bergasse, Nicolas, 86
Bernard, Jacques-Claude, 308
Bertrand, Francis, 2
Bicêtre reformatory massacre, 220
Billaud-Varenne, Jacques, 280, 350,
351–52, 356
Bonnet rouge, 156–57, 163
Bouillé, Marquis de, 156, 159–61, 168, 186
Bourbon alliance, 128–29
Bourbon dynasty, 252
Bourdon, Léonard, 334
Boyer-Fonfrède, Jean-Baptiste, 266
bread prices, 32, 283
bread riots of 1789, 76, 98, 103–6
Bréard, Jean, 261
Breton Club, 86–87, 125
Brissot, Jacques ("Phédor"), 172, 258, 304,
311, 314–15
advocates republic, 168, 189, 199–205
background of, 162–64
Danton and, 296
expelled from Jacobins, 235
fall of monarchy and, 207, 218
influence of, with Louis XVI, 188–91,
205–7
leads Girondins, 227, 230, 232–33, 236,
248–49
leads pro-war party, 182–84
MR attacks, 199–201, 221, 226, 263,
264, 287–90
trial and execution of, 261, 287–90
British constitutional model, 114
Brunswick, Duke of, 213, 219–20, 223–24,
267
Brutus, 33
Brutus (play), 187
Buissart, Antoine "Barometer," 41, 42,
45–46, 48–50, 73, 84, 85–86, 91–96,
113–14, 127–28, 181

Buissart, Mme, 41, 173
Buonarotti, Philippe, 194
Burke, Edmond, 179–80

Cabanis, Pierre Jean George, 139, 142, 143
Cabarrus, Thérésa, 333
Caen Girondins, 273–74
Caesar, 39, 243
Cambon, Pierre Joseph, 261, 314, 349
Capet, Hugh, 252
Carlyle, Thomas, 280
Carmelites, convent of, 219
Carnot, Lazare, 276, 280, 307, 330, 350
Carraut, Jacqueline Marguerite (mother),
19, 22
Carraut, (maternal grandparents), 20–22,
36–37
Carrier, Jean Baptist, 305–6, 313
Catherine de Médicis, 129
Catherine the Great, Czarina of Russia,
257
Catholic Church, 26–27
confession debate, 181–82
counterrevolution and, 178–79
National Assembly debates future and
wealth of, 121–25
tithes stopped, 102, 103, 122, 124
Catiline, 33
censorship, 136–37, 151–52
Cercle Social, 153
certificate of *civisme*, 285, 336
Chalier, Joseph, 283, 332
Champ de Mars massacre, 169–70, 177,
184, 187, 200–201, 205, 212, 243
Charles I, king of England, 200
Châteauvieux rebellion (Nancy mutiny),
156–57, 159, 186, 195, 243
celebration of freed soldiers, 195–97,
207
Châtelet massacre, 219
Chaumette, Pierre Gaspard, 294, 295,
307–8, 348
Cherubini, Luigi, 154
Chronique de Paris, 128, 153, 237
Cicero, 288
Cietty, Pierre, 194
citizens, active vs. passive, 117–18, 155–56,
224
Civil Constitution of the Clergy, 123–24,
126, 143, 154, 165, 179, 203
signed by Louis XVI, 158
civil war. *See* federalist revolt
threat of, in 1790, 139
Clavière, Etienne, 188, 218

clergy, 32, 62, 69, 103
  Estates General and, 66, 75, 79, 80,
    88–90
  MR defends, 293–95
  National Assembly and, 121–25
  resistance by, 126–27, 154, 178–80,
    203–6, 219–20
  Revolution and, 96
Collège d'Arras, 22, 24, 72
Collège Louis-le-Grand (Paris), 22–24,
  26–35, 49
Collot d'Herbois, Jean Marie, 280, 283,
  305, 324, 350–52, 356
comités de surveillance, 260
Commission for Civil Administration and
  Police, 318
Committee of General Security, 261, 284,
  285, 310, 330–31, 336–37, 339,
  343–44, 349–53
Committee of Public Safety, 273, 276–77,
  279–81, 283, 297, 301, 304–8, 325,
  329–31, 334–37, 339, 340, 343–44
  created, 261–62
  Dantonists trial and, 309–17
  MR trial and, 349–53, 355–56
  suspends constitution, 272
  Terror initiated by, 284–85, 293
Condé, Prince de, 38, 137, 161, 178
Condorcet, Marquis de, 42, 236–37, 251,
  269, 320
Confessions (Rousseau), 53
Conseil d'Artois (Council of Artois), 40,
  42, 48, 61
Constitutional Committee, 162
Cook, James, 128
Corday, Charlotte, 273–74, 276
Cordeliers Club, 120–21, 166, 198, 207,
  238, 275, 284, 307
  Danton loses control of, 293, 297
  fall of monarchy and, 168–69, 214
  led by Hébert, 305, 306
Coronelli, Vincenzo, 28
Correspondence Committee of Paris
  Jacobin Club, 184, 204
counterrevolution, 149, 152–53, 165–66,
  178–80, 198, 203–5, 234, 283
Courier français, 103
Couthon, Georges, 180, 213, 271, 280,
  306, 328, 340, 350–53, 355–57
criminal code, 62, 64, 74, 114
Crinchon river, 17
Croker, John Wilson, 1–3, 148
Cromwell, Oliver, 200, 243
Cunosse, Melanie, 2

Dalibard, Thomas-François, 42
Damiens, Robert-François, 145–47, 222,
  324
Danton, Gabrielle, 258, 279
Danton, George Jacques, 172, 183, 185,
  227, 229, 238, 261, 324, 329
  advocates deposition of king, 168–69
  "audacity" speech by, 223
  Champ de Mars massacre and, 169–70
  Cordeliers led by, 120–21
  death of wife and, 202, 258–59
  defends MR, 199, 233, 235–36, 239
  fall of, 293, 298, 300–302, 304–7
  fall of monarchy and, 213–14, 218
  Hébert opposed by, 296–98
  insurrection of 1793 and, 284
  Louis XVI and, 32–33, 158
  on MR, 358
  personality of, 198, 201–2, 279–80
  remarriage of, 279
  Revolutionary Tribunal and, 258–59
  September Massacres and, 220–21, 223
  Terror advocated by, 272
  trial and execution of, 309–17, 321–22,
    343, 349, 352
  trial of Louis XVI and, 250, 251
  voted off CPS, 280, 281
  war and, 188, 197–98, 258, 260–61
Dantonists, 341
Dauchez, Jean Baptiste, 10
David, Jacques-Louis, 90–91, 227, 229,
  265, 274–75, 320, 324, 350
death penalty, 44–45, 147–50, 222–23, 233,
  259, 338–40
  for Louis XVI, 244–45, 250–51
debtors law, 43–44
Declaration of Rights of Man and Citizen,
  8, 101–3, 118, 122, 211, 269–71, 356
Défenseur de la constitution, Le (journal),
  199–202, 210–13
Deflue, Louis, 93
Delacroix, Jean, 261
De l'esprit des lois (Montesquieu), 46–47
Delmas, Jean, 261
democracy, 47, 116–18, 232, 271–72
democratic war, 183, 223
Descartes, René, 42
Deshorties, Anais, 53, 54, 178
Desmoulins, Camille, 106, 125, 130–32,
  135–36, 150, 151, 155, 165–66, 200,
  347
  early censorship of, 136–37
  early friendship with MR, 31, 34
  execution of Girondins and, 289

Desmoulins, Camille (*cont'd*)
  fall and execution of, 296–302, 304–6,
    309–11, 313, 314, 316–17
  fall of monarchy and, 214
  National Convention and, 227, 229, 243
  Paris riots and, 92, 96
Desmoulins, Lucile Horace, 131, 214, 299,
    309, 312, 316
Dickens, Charles, 56
dioceses, number reduced by National As-
    sembly, 124
Dubois de Fosseux, 48–49, 51, 55, 73,
    75–76, 126–27
Duchesne, James, 2
Dumerbion, Pierre, 278
Dumont, Pierre Étienne Louis, 142, 143,
    145
Dumouriez, Charles, 260–61, 263, 268,
    296, 304, 311
Duplay, Eléonore, 194–95, 357
Duplay, Elisabeth, 194, 253–54, 302
Duplay, Maurice, 171–72, 177, 180,
    193–95, 199, 224, 240, 331
Duplay, Françoise-Eléonore, 171, 228–29,
    239–40, 357
Duplay family, 12, 193–95, 214, 228–29,
    309, 320, 324, 327
Dupond, M., 56–57, 107
Dutch Republic, 258, 260

East India Company, 301, 313, 314
Edgeworth de Firmont, Henry Essex,
    252–52
education issue, 70, 187, 271, 291–92
Élisabeth, Mme (sister of Louis XVI), 160,
    167, 196–97, 209, 323
Eloge de la Rose (speech), 55–56
Emery, Louis, 332
émigrés, 178, 182, 188, 192
Émile (Rousseau), 24–25, 27, 29, 30, 299
Enemies of the Fatherland Unmasked, The
    (pamphlet), 74–75, 231
"enemies of the people (or within),"
    137–38, 154, 165–66, 183, 185–87,
    191–92, 200–202, 226–27, 230–32,
    304–5, 328
enragés, 260, 264, 284, 293
equality, 102, 118, 134
Estates General
  election chaos, 75–76, 87, 119
  Louis XVI agrees to convene, 64–67,
    71–73
  meetings of, 84–90
  MR elected to, 6, 69–77

opening ceremony, 76, 79–82
  third estate declares itself National
    Assembly, 90–92
Estates of Artois, 67, 69, 71–72
executive power, 103, 150–51, 231–32
executive veto, 114–17

Fabre d'Églantine, Philippe, 290–91, 293,
    300–301, 310–11, 314, 315
Fauchet, Claude, 153
federalist revolt, 261–62, 272–85, 308
federal republic idea, 289
Ferrières, Marquis de, 80, 229
Festival of Federation, 133–36, 168, 186,
    320
Festival of the Supreme Being, 8, 324,
    326–29, 331, 333, 336, 342, 343, 348,
    350
feudalism, 18, 62, 101
Feuillants Club, 166, 170, 177–78, 181,
    225, 311
Fillion, Didier, 332
Flesselles, Jacques, 94, 97, 215
Fleurus, battle of, 340, 342, 350
Fouché, Joseph, 330, 332–34, 336, 342–43,
    347–48, 350–51
Foulon, Jospeh François, 94, 100
Fouquier-Tinville, Antoine, 259, 325, 337,
    339–40
France
  declares war on Holy Roman Emperor,
    197–98
  fall of monarchy (10 August 1792),
    210–16, 228, 280–81
  monarchy, 46–47, 56–57, 63–65
  monarchy abolished, 230
  provisional government of, 218
  Republic declared by National
    Convention, 229–30
Francis II, Holy Roman Emperor, 197
Franklin, Benjamin, 42, 43, 101, 106, 111,
    196
freedom of press, 103, 151–52, 267, 270,
    281
freedom of religion, 103
freedom of speech, 151–53
Freemasons, 55
French Academy of Sciences, 87
French army, 156–57, 185
  levee en masse and, 276–77
  new federal, 203–6, 212–13, 215
French constitution of 1791 (consitutional
    monarchy), 202–3, 210, 242
  accepted by Louis XVI, 169, 172

escape of royal family threatens, 162, 166–71
fall of, 210–16
written, 114–17, 128–30, 139, 150–51
French republican constitution of 1793, 340
suspended, 272
written and ratified, 269–72
French Revolution of 1789, 90–107
causes of, 69
complexity and vividness of, 5–9
Jacobins as guardians of, 126
Lafayette and Louis XVI and, 135
MR as embodiment of, 6, 8–9, 57
Fréron, Louis Marie Stanislaus, 34, 193
Friends of Chalier, 332–34
Furet, François, 5, 8–9

Galileo, 42
General Maximum Law (1793), 293
general strike of 1793, 284
George III, king of England, 192
Gérard, François, 194
Gerle, Dom, 335–36
Girondins, 230, 233, 235–37, 239, 242, 259–61, 311
constitution and, 270–71
Danton and, 296, 314–15
expelled from National Convention, 263–69
execution of, 287–90, 301
Lyon revolt and, 277, 278
Marat assassination and, 273–76
Paine and, 310
private property and, 263–64
trial of Louis XVI and, 247–49, 251
Gobel, Jean-Baptiste-Joseph, 294–94
Goethe, Johan Wofgang von, 223–24, 229
Gossec, François-Joseph, 144, 167, 324
Gouges, Olympe de, 237
Gouvon, Geneviève, 2
Gracchus (play), 187
Gravier, Claude, 293
Great Britain, 128–29
war with, 257–58, 284
Greece, ancient, 28
Grenoble riots, 64
Gresset, Jean Baptiste, 49–51
Guadet, Marguerite-Elie, 264, 278
Guillotin, Joseph-Ignace, 45, 82–83, 90, 147–49
guillotine, 146–48, 222–23, 327
Guyton, Louis, 261

Hanriot, François, 268, 308, 342, 352–55, 357
Hardman, John, 9
Harduin, Alexandre, 48
Harvey, William, 42
Hébert, Jacques René, 283–84, 286, 293–97, 302, 304, 306–8, 341
Helvétius, Claude-Adrien, 240
Henry, Jean Baptiste, 2
Henry II, king of France, 129
Henry IV, king of France, 252
Hérault de Séchelles, Marie Jean, 280
Hérivaux, abbé, 31, 33
Herman, Martial Joseph Armand, 315, 318–19, 331–32, 342
Historic Doubts on the Life and Reign of King Richard III (Walpole), 230
honor, 46–48

Insurrectionary Commune, 214–15, 218–21, 225–26, 228, 235–36, 238–39, 285
Invalides, storming of, 93
Isnard, Maximin, 266

Jacobin Club of Paris, 157, 284, 340
assassination attempt on MR and, 325
Billaud-Varenne and Collot d'Herbois expelled by, 350, 351
Brissot and, 163, 182–84, 201–2, 235
Brissot and Louvet expelled by, 239
Châtcauvieux soldiers and, 195
clubs in provinces affiliate with, 126
Danton and, 198, 293
Desmoulins expelled from, 299–302
elections of 1792 and, 225
expulsion policy established, 126
fall of monarchy and, 213, 216
fall of MR and, 350–51, 353
Feuillants split from, 166, 177–78
formed, 125–26
Fouché expelled by, 342
Girondins battle with, 247–49, 251, 263–69, 276
Lafayette denounces, 206
Marat assassination and, 274–76
Mirabeau and, 143, 144, 240–41
Mme Roland and, 163
mob violence and, 260
MR addresses, on arming for war and internal enemies, 184–88
MR addresses, on atheism, 294–96
MR addresses, on *citoyens passif* and National Guard, 155–56

Jacobin Club of Paris (*cont'd*)
MR addresses, on conspiracy after death of Danton, 318–19
MR addresses, on escape attempt of Louis XVI, 164–66
MR addresses, on freedom of press and speech, 151–53
MR addresses, on massacre of Champ de Mars, 169–72
MR addresses, on patriotism, 340–41
MR addresses, on religious faith, 192–93
MR becomes president of, 181–82
MR defends Danton vs. Hébert in, 296–97
MR denounces Desmoulins, Danton, and Hébert, 305
MR denounces fraternal banquets, 342–43
MR dominates, 236
MR power at height of terror and, 337
MR's rise to power and Danton, 279–80
MR vs. Louvet and, 239
new federal army and, 204–5
petition on deposition of king and, 168–69
protests of 20 June 1792 and, 207
republican constitution and, 271
separation of power ended by, 263
speeches published by, 126
Terror supported by, 272
war debated in, 182–84, 188, 197–99, 201–2, 204
Jansenists, 23
Jefferson, Thomas, 101
Jemappes, battle of, 257
Jesuits, 23, 24, 28, 30, 49, 50
Jews, 119
Journal de Louis XVI et de son peuple (newspaper), 149
Jura revolt, 282

"Korff, Baroness de," 160

Labille-Guyard, Adélaide, 145, 172
Lafayette, Marquis de, 101, 105, 135, 196, 198, 205–7, 222, 260, 304, 311
Danton vs., 120, 121
flees country, 218
flight to Varennes and, 158, 160–61, 166–67
Louis XVI and, 97, 139, 140, 169
MR vs., 135, 192, 201, 206, 210–12
National Guard and, 99–100, 104, 156
runs for mayor of Paris, 181

La Force prison massacre, 219–20
Lally-Tollendal, Triophime Gérard, Marquis de, 100
Lamballe, Princesse de, 219–20
Lameth brothers, 311
Lamoignon, Chrétien François de, 63–66, 91
Lamoignon Edicts (8 May 1788), 61, 63–65, 75, 201
Lanthenas, François-Xavier, 153
La Salpêtrière prison massacre, 220
la Tour du Pin, Henriette Lucie Dillon, Marquise de, 104
Launay, Bernard-René, 93–95, 215
Law of 14 Frimaire, 297–98, 306
Law of 22 Prairial, 8, 328–29, 333–35, 345
Law of Suspects, 284–85, 297, 298
Lebas, Elizabeth, 353, 355
Lebas, Philippe, 302, 352, 353, 356
Le Gay, M., 48, 54
Legislative Assembly, 181–83, 185–87, 203–4, 218, 224, 243, 301
Châteauvieux soldiers and, 195
fall of monarchy and, 215
20 June 1792 and, 207–9
ultimatum to Leopold II, 183, 192
legislative power, 103, 114–15, 150–51
Leopold II, Holy Roman Emperor, 136, 183, 192
Lettres à ses commettans (journal), 230–31
lettres de cachet, 56–57, 64, 93, 107
levée en masse, 276–77
Lewes, G. H., 42
libel, 151–53
Lindet, Jean, 261, 280
Loizelier, Frances, 2
Louis XIII, king of France, 252
Louis XIV, king of France (Sun King), 28, 78, 105, 252
Louis XV, king of France, 23, 108, 145–46, 242, 252, 324
Louis XVI, king of France
absolute power of monarchy and, 63
armed intervention of major powers requested by, 182
Austria threatens war, after Revolution vs., 137
bankruptcy of, 66
bodyguard of, abolished, 203–4
Bourbon threat of war vs. Britain and, 128–29
captured by women and returned to Paris, in 1789, 104–7
constitution of 1791 signed by, 172

coronation and early reign of, 30–33
dismisses Brissot ministers, 206
dismisses ministers and appoints Brissot
    circle, 188–89
Estates General convened by, 65–66,
    71–72, 79–81, 87
fall of constitutional monarchy and,
    210–16
Festival of Federation and, 133–35
Feuillants ministers appointed by, 181
flight to Varennes and, 157–70, 200
imprisoned in Temple, 221, 230
Lafayette's last audience with, 210
Lamoignon Edicts and, 62–65
lettres de cachet and, 57
life of, at Versailles, 79
list of complaints vs. National Assembly
    and constitution, 162
Mirabeau and, 138–40, 143
MR advocates deposition of, 117
MR welcome speech to, at Collège
    Louis-le-Grand, 32–33
Napoleon on fall of, 235
National Assembly debates executive
    veto by, 114–17
protests of 20 June 1792 and, 206–10
Revolution of 1789 and storming of
    Bastille and, 90–98
trial and execution of, 242–54, 257–58,
    286
in Tuileries as virtual prisoner, 129–30,
    138–39
veto threat by, on refractory priests and
    federal army, 202–6
Louis, Antoine, 148
Louis Capet (dauphin, son of Louis XVI),
    129, 130, 159, 167, 246–47, 252,
    285–86, 324
    regency threatened, 260
Louison, Antoine, 222
Louvet, Jean Baptiste, 198–99, 200,
    235–36, 239, 273, 359–60
Lyon, revolt and siege of, 277–79, 281–83,
    332–33
Lyonnais Jacobins, 332

Maillard, Stanislas, 104
Maison Robespierre, 10, 37
Malesherbes, Chrétien Guillaume de Lam-
    oignon de, 251–52
Malouet, Pierre-Victor, 85, 86, 136
Mandat, Marquis de, 215
Marat, Jean-Paul, 42, 151, 155, 158, 184,
    200, 234, 260, 270, 296, 298, 299, 315

assassination of, 273–76, 284
censorship and, 136–37
early arrest of, 106–7
Jacobins vs. Girondins and, 264–65
insurrection of Paris and, 268
Louis XVI and, 168
Mirabeau and, 141–42, 241
MR and, 236–39
National Convention and, 224, 227, 229,
    233–34, 236–38, 249
Revolutionary Tribunal and, 265–66
Terror and, 272
Marboeuf, Henrietta Frances de, 2
Marie Antoinette, queen of France, 33, 55,
    79, 80, 90, 97, 104, 130, 136, 140, 143,
    183, 223, 348
    execution of, 281, 285–87
    execution of Louis XVI and, 252–53
    fall of monarchy and, 214–16
    flight to Varennes and, 157–61, 167
"Marseillaise," 213, 289
Marseille Jacobins, 166
martial law, 169–70, 187
Maury, Jean-Sifrein, abbé, 148, 149, 337
*Mémoires authentiques de Maximilien Robes-
    pierre* (1830 forgery), 25–26
Mercure de France, 42, 137
Michelet, Jules, 105, 271
Miles, William Augustus, 188
Mirabeau, Comte de, 81, 85–86, 88, 91–92,
    98, 99, 102–3, 107, 115, 121, 124,
    128–29, 148, 180, 223, 274, 275, 304,
    311, 313
    death of, 138–45, 150, 154, 157, 159,
    166
    on MR, 217
    secret letters to Louis XVI discovered,
    240–41, 244
mob violence, 99–100, 105–6, 136, 150,
    154–55, 167, 169, 208, 215–16,
    219–22, 233–36, 238–39, 259–60,
    292–93, 296–97
Molière, 302
Momoro, Antoine, François, 295
Montesquieu, Baron de, 46–47, 67, 150,
    246
Montmorin, Comte de, 181
Moore, John, 235–236, 239
morality, 47–48, 328, 329
Morison, Charles, 242
Mort de Mirabeau, La (Pujoulx), 154
Mounier, Jean-Joseph, 86
Mountain, 230, 233, 235, 239, 242,
    248–49, 260, 266, 334

Mozart, Wolfgang Amadeus, 73
Musée Carnavalet, 76

Napoleon Bonaparte, 235, 350
Narbonne, Comte de, 181
National Assembly
  Bastille storming and, 95, 98–99
  censorship and, 136–37
  closes Versailles session and reconvenes
    in Paris, 108
  death penalty and penal code reform,
    147–50, 222
  debate in, over church and clergy,
    121–27
  debate in, over constitution, 101–3,
    107–8, 114–19, 125
  debates in, over Paris municipal govern-
    ment, 119–21
  declared by third estate, creating Revo-
    lution, 90–93
  ends feudalism and monarchy, 102–3
  Festival of Federation and, 133–35
  Jacobin Club and, 126–27
  last day of, after signing of constitution,
    172
  letters of Duke of Artois and, 100–101
  Louis XVI and, 90–92, 95–98, 138–40,
    158–59, 162, 165–70, 248
  Mirabeau and, 138–45
  mob violence and, 95
  MR proposes prohibition of deputies
    from becoming ministers of king,
    150–51
  MR's pay as deputy to, 111
  war threat and, 137–38, 186
  war threat and, and monarch's right to
    declare war, 128–31
  women's delegation to Versailles and,
    104–6
National Convention
  Committee of Public Safety created by,
    261
  constitution suspended and Terror by,
    280, 283–85, 320, 339
  Danton's arrest and execution and,
    309–12, 315
  declares war on England, Dutch Repub-
    lic, and Spain, 258
  East India Company and, 301
  education reform and, 292
  end to separation of powers and, 262–63
  establishes worship of Supreme Being,
    322–23
  formation of, 225–30

Girondins attacked and arrested,
    263–69, 288
  Girondins battle Mountain in, 232–37
  Law of 14 Frimaire and, 297
  Law of 22 Priarial and, 328, 330, 334–35
  Louis XVI tried and sentenced to death
    by, 242–52
  MR addresses, on 8 Thermidor on patri-
    otism leading to his arrest, 344–53
  MR addresses, on public morality and
    Terror, 304–5
  MR as president of, 336–38
  new executive commissions created by,
    307
  Paris insurrection and storming of Tui-
    leries and, 268
  price controls and, 292–93
  republican constitution adopted by,
    269–72
  revolutinary calendar and, 290–91
  second Revolutionary Tribunal estab-
    lished by, 259
National Guard, 104–5, 120, 133–35, 140,
    144, 154–57, 160–61, 173, 177–78,
    183, 185, 197, 207–9, 214–15, 268,
    277–78, 308
  Champ de Mars massacre and, 169–70
  formed of citizen militia, 97, 99–100
  limited to active citizens, 118, 155–57
  new federalist army to replace, 203–5
  professional army vs., 156–57
Necker, Jacques, 66, 72, 81–84, 87, 90–92,
    95, 341
Necker, Suzanne Curchod, 83–84
Neerwinden, battle of, 260
Neuvéglise, Le Blond de, 28
Newton, Isaac, 320
Nicolas, Léopold, 298–99, 332
Nîmes, archbishop of, 89, 122
nobility, 32, 88–89
  Estates General and, 66, 69, 75–76, 79,
    80, 82
  parlements and, 61–62
  privileges abolished, 102–3, 112
  taxation and, 62
Nootka Sound dispute, 128
Nouvelle Héloïse, La (Rousseau), 53–54

*Offrande a la patrie (Offering to the Father-
    land)* (Marat), 106
Orateur du peuple, L', 153
Organt (Saint-Just), 132
Osselin, Charles Nicholas, 288
Othryades, 92

Paine, Thomas, 310
Palloy, Pierre-François, 98, 221
Pantheon, 144, 145, 275
Paris, 27
 bread riots of 4 October 1789, 104–6
 daily life in, of 1791, 153–54
 Estates General and, 87–88
 48 sections, 154–55, 185, 212–13, 249,
  251, 297
 Insurrectionary Commune and, 214
 insurrection of 1793, 259–60, 267–69,
  284
 insurrection of 1794 fails to materialize,
  306
 Municipal Assembly, 162
 municipal elections abolished, 307–8
 municipal government of, 96–97,
  119–21, 158–59, 207, 214
 National Convention and, 227–28,
  233–34
 Pétion elected mayor of, 181
 punishment centralized in, 320
 Revolution of 1789 and, 90–98
Paris, University of, 23, 28–30
Paris Commune, 121, 247, 259, 266, 280,
  282–84, 286, 294, 296–97, 307–8, 337,
  340, 353–54
Parlement of Besançon, 81
Parlement of Bordeaux, 62
Parlement of Paris, 61–66
parlements, 61–65, 102
Patriote français, 162, 240–41, 270–71
patriotic cockade, 96–97, 103–4
Payan, Claude, 308, 318, 331, 337, 342
Peel, Robert, 1, 3
Pelletier, Nicholas Jacques, 222, 223
Père Duchesne (newspaper), 283–84, 307
Pétion, Jérôme, 129, 145, 156, 162, 164,
  167, 168, 170, 172, 207, 209, 212
 flees to Caen, 273, 288
 Girondins and, 230
 as mayor of Paris, 180–81, 186, 196–97,
  218
 MR opposes, 190, 197, 263–65
 National Convention and, 225–27,
  229–30
 petition for dethronement of Louis XVI
  (17 July 1791), 168–70, 200
Pitt, William, 128, 257, 258, 263, 301, 346
Plaisant, Mary Angelica, 2
Plutarch, 163
Poitou clergy, 89–90
Police Bureau, 330–31, 332, 337–39
police laws of 1794, 320

poor, 18, 32, 41, 69–70, 89, 104–5, 118,
  123, 127, 264, 271, 283–84
pope, 124, 143
Pope, Alexander, 49
Prelude, The (Wordsworth), 360
Premonstratensians of Dommartin (reli-
  gious order), 19
price controls, 283, 284, 292–93
Prise de la Bastille, La (Gossec), 167
prison massacres of 1792, 219–22
prisons, 219, 297–98
property rights, 122, 142, 263–64, 270–72
protests of 20 June 1792, 206–10
Provence, Count of (brother of Louis
  XVI), 95
Proyart, Liévin-Bonaventure, abbé, 28–30,
  33–35
Prudhon, Pierre Paul, 194
Prussia, 165, 223–24, 229
Pujoulx, Jean-Baptiste, 154
Pye, Henry James, 188

Quarterly Review, 3
*Qu'est-ce que le Tiers Etat? (What Is the
  Third Estate?)* (Sieyès), 106, 122

Rabelais, François, 302
Racine, Jean, 63
Raigecourt, Marquise de, 196, 209
Rape of the Lock, The (Pope), 49
Renaudin, Léopold, 283
Renault, Cécile, 324, 337–38
Réplublicain, Le (journal), 200
Report on the Principles of Political Morality
  (speech of 5 Feb. 1794), 303–5
republican government, theory and debate
  over, 29–31, 46, 168–69, 189,
  200–204, 246
Resolution (ship), 128
*Rêveries du Promeneur solitare, Les (Reveries
  of the Solitary Walker)* (Rousseau), 26
Revolutionary Army, 262, 340
revolutionary calendar, 290–91
Revolutionary Tribunal
 first, 222, 223, 259
 second, 3, 152, 258–59, 261, 265–66,
  272, 284–85, 287, 298, 306–7,
  312–18, 328–29, 331–32, 343, 345,
  356–57
Révolutions de France et de Brabant
  (Desmoulins newspaper), 106, 135–36,
  155
Reybaz, Etienne Salomon, 124
Ricord, Jean François, 277, 278

rights of excluded groups, 119
Rights of Man, The (Paine), 310
riots
 of 1775, 32
 of 1788, 64
Robespierre, Augustin (brother), 35, 36,
  134, 124–25, 277–78, 285, 320
 arrest and execution of, 351–56
 childhood of, 20–22
 Jacobins in Arras and, 126–27
 MR's visit to Arras and, 173
 National Convention and move to Paris,
  228–29
Robespierre, aunt and uncle, 36–37
Robespierre, Charlotte (sister), 20–22, 27,
  33–34, 36–37, 40, 41, 44–45, 53, 54,
  111, 134, 171
 Fouché and, 333–34
 mission to Lyon and, 277–78
 MR visits in 1791, 172–74
 in Paris, 228–29, 239–40
Robespierre, Henriette (sister), 20–21, 36
Robespierre, Jacqueline Marguerite Carraut (mother), 19–20, 25
Robespierre, Maximilien de (father),
  19–22, 36–37, 40
Robespierre, Maximilien de (grandfather),
  19, 20, 40, 55
Robespierre, Maximilien Marie Isidore de
  (MR)
 academic success of, 34–35
 Academy of Arras and, 45–46, 48–49
 antiwar arguments of, 7, 182–84,
  190–92
 antiwar position reversed, 210–12
 appearance of, 6, 11–12, 112
 arming people as leaders of Revolution
  advocated by, 185–87
 Arras grievance list and, 74–75
 arrest and execution of, 351–58
 Artois pamphlet of 1788 and, 70
 assassination attempts on, 324–26,
  337–38
 atheism and anticlericalism opposed by,
  293–96, 335–37
 attacks enemies after Law of 22 Prairial,
  330–31
 attitude toward in contemporary Arras,
  10
 awarded prize for essay on bad blood,
  47–48
 awarded prize on leaving Louis-le-
  Grand, 35
 baptism of, 20

Bastille storming of 14 July and, 92–95,
  98–99, 108, 341–42
battle of Valmy and, 224
biographers and interpretation of, 3,
  9–10, 28–29
birth of, 11, 17–20
Breton Club and, 86–87
Brissot and Roland denounced by, 221
Brissot vs., 182–91, 199–204, 205–6,
  232–37, 263–69, 287–90
brother Augustin and, 35, 228–29
Buissart family and, 41–42, 45–46
calls for end of separation of powers to
  save republic, 262–64
Champs de Mars massacre and,
  169–72
Châteauvieux rebels and, 156–57,
  195–97
childhood of, 20–23
chronology of, xiii–xvii
civil war in provinces and, 262–64,
  278–79
clergy and, 122–25
clothing and vanity of, 11–12, 23–24
Committee of Public Safety and,
  280–81, 343–44
constitution signed by Louis XVI and,
  172
counterrevolution feared by, 149
Danton and, 198, 202, 258, 279–80, 293,
  296–98
Danton and Desmoulins trial and execution and, 304–6, 309–19, 321–22
death of, 6
death of Mirabeau and, 143–45
death of mother and, 20–21
death of sister Henriette and, 33–34
death penalty and, 148–49
Declaration of Rights and, 103
Delaroche and, 27
Desmoulins and, 34, 130–32, 137
Desmoulins denounced by, 297–302,
  304–6
domestic life of, in Paris, 110–13, 125
Duplay family and, 12–13, 171–72,
  193–95, 228–29, 239–40
early career of, in Arras, 36–38, 40–45,
  48, 56–57
early essay on decapitation, 44–45
early essay on political honor, 46–47
early life of, 5–6
educational reform and, 291–92
education of, 22–31
elections of 1792 and, 224–26

enemies of the people and, 70–71,
191–92
enemies within and paranoia of, 137–38,
325
Estates General and, 66–67, 69–77, 80–89
executive commissions of 1794 and, 307
extraordinary courts advocated by,
100–101
fall of monarchy and, 210–17
Festival of Federation and, 133–35
Feuillants of Arras and, 177–78
finances and poverty of, 111–12
food preference of, 37
Fouché denounced by, 342
fraternal banquets criticized by, 342–43
Freemasons and, 55
friendship with Brissot, Roland, and Pétion, 162–64
Girondins opposed by, 247–49, 263–69,
287–90
health of, 112
Hébert denounced by, 306–8
Hérivaux influences, 31, 33
ideal lawgiver and, 231–32
ideal society and, 13
illnesses of, 45
illnesses of, after denouncing
Desmoulins and Danton, 302, 305
illnesses of, after self-defense in National Conventon, 239–40
instrument of Providence, 13
Insurrectionary Commune and, 218–19
Insurrection of Paris of 1793 and,
268–69, 284
integrity and conscience of, 152
Jacobins and attacks on, with outbreak
of war, 198–99
Jacobins formation and, 125–27
Jacobins of Versailles and, 161–62
Jacobins schism, and opposition to constitutional monarchy, 166–67
journal of, *Le défenseur de la constitution*,
199–202
journal of, relaunched as *Lettres à ses
commettans*, 230–32
Lafayette and, 135, 210–12
Lamoignon Edicts and, 64–65
Law of 22 Prairial and, 328–31
life of, as crescendo, 10
Louis XVI and, 31–33, 57, 162, 164–70
Louis XVI return to Paris during Revo-
lution and, 95–98
Louis XVI trial and execution and, 117,
242–54

Louvet's accusation of, 235–40
Marat and, 234, 237–38, 241
Marat assassination and, 274–76
Marie Antoinette trial and execution
and, 286–87
Mirabeau and, 91–93, 138
Mirabeau's death and, 145–47
Mirabeau's letters to Louis XVI and,
240–41
mistress of, 112–13
Mme de Staël on, 84
Mme Roland friendship cools,
189–90
mob violence used by, 221–22
Mountain and, 230
moves to Paris, with National Assembly,
108
National Assembly and, 91–93, 103,
107–8, 113–17, 122–25, 128–31,
137–38, 148–51
National Convention and, 225–30
National Guards and, 100, 155
Necker and, 83–84
new federalist army and citizen soldier,
203–5
paintings and, 28
Paris municipal elections abolished by,
307–8
Paris sixty vs. forty-eight debate and,
120–21
patriotism concept of, 84–85
patronage and, 331–32
personality of, 6–8, 27–29, 33–40,
45–46, 50, 86, 107–8, 191, 226–27
personality of, as embodiment of revolution, 8–9, 313
personality of, vs. Danton, 201–2,
279–80
Pétion and, 180–81, 190, 197, 225–27
Police Bureau and, 330–31, 338–39
political isolation of, in 1792, 190–94
political shrewdness of, 205
poor and oppressed defended by, 8
popularity of, 174
portraits of, 10–13, 91, 145, 172, 228
poverty of, 23–24, 111
power and, 26, 337
price controls and, 292–93
principles of, 45, 112
protests of 20 June 1792 and, 206–8
Proyart on, 29–30, 33
purity of, 113
reading by, as youth, 28, 29
recordkeeping of, 112

Robespierre, Maximilien Marie Isidore de (MR) (*cont'd*)
religion and, 26–27, 122–23, 178–80, 203
religion and cult of Supreme Being and, 8, 322–28
religious faith defended by, to Jacobins, 192–93
republican constitution and, 269–72
resigns office as public prosecutor, 190
revolutionary calendar and, 290–91
revolutionary catechism drafted by, 281–82
Revolutionary Tribunal reestablished, 259
romance with A. Deshorties, 53–54
romance with E. Duplay, 194–95
Rosati society and, 54–56
Rousseau influences, 25–26, 53–54, 84–85, 131, 152, 187, 190–91, 231–32, 304
Saint-Just and, 132–33, 242–46
secret list of, 343–44
September Massacres and, 220–22, 238
siege of Lyon and, 283
speaking style of, 12
speech of, 8 Thermidor leading to downfall, 344–51
speech of, comparing 1789 to 1792, 216–17
speech of, *Eloge de la Rose* to Rosati, 55–56
speech of, on flight of Louis and enemies within, 164–66
speech of, on freedom of press and libel, 151–53
speech of, on National Guard, 155–57
speech of, on National Guard and democratic war, 183
speech of, on republican principles, religion and morality, 319–22
speech of, on trial of Louis XVI, 244–45
speech of, on veto published, 116–17
speech of, opposing foreign war and decrying enemies, 182–88
speech of, *Report on Principles of Political Morality* defends Terror, 303–5
suspicions and paranoia of, 123, 127–28, 137–38
Tallien and Fouché attacked by, 332–35
Terror and, 9, 272–73, 320, 338–40
Théot sect and, 337
trial by character and, 152–53

vertu concept and, 8, 245–46, 248, 279–80, 329
vision of, 358
visits Arras in 1791, 172–74, 177–80
visits Carins and Sens in 1783, 38–40
visits daughter of king, during Terror, 323–24
voting rights and, 117–19
war with Austria and, 197–99
war worries of, and National Guard and, 178, 182–83
women and, 51–55, 104, 113, 236–37
Wordsworth on, 359–60
work habits of, 275–76
writings of, *A la nation artésienne* pamphlet, 69–71
writings of, early poetry, 39, 51, 54–55
writings of, *Les ennemis de la patrie démasqués* pamphlet, 74–76
writings of, on bad blood, honor, and monarchy, 45–48, 74
writings of, on enemy within, 230–32
writings of, on Gresset, 49–51
writings of, on visit to Carvins and Sens of 1783, 38–39
Robespierre, Robert de (15th century ancestor), 19
Robespierre, Robert de (16th century ancestor), 19
Roederer, Pierre-Louis, 47, 170, 207, 214, 215, 222
Roland, Jean Marie, 163, 171, 188, 189, 203, 205–6, 218, 221, 235, 236, 269, 341
suicide of, 290
Roland, Manon Phlipon, 162–64, 171, 189–90, 205–6, 223, 233
arrest of, 269, 288
death of, 261, 290
Rome, ancient, 28, 31, 33, 39, 243
Rosati (Arras literary society), 48, 54–56, 178
Rousseau, Jean-Jacques, 24–27, 29, 49, 50, 131, 150, 190–91, 196, 240, 299, 304, 320
affinity of MR with, 25–26
citizen militia and, 155–57
education and, 24–25, 30
innate goodness and, 152, 187
on Paris, 27
patriotism and, 84–85
romance and, 53–54
Social Contract, 106, 187, 231–32
vertu and, 246

royal council, 64
Royale, Mme (daughter of Louis XVI),
159, 167, 323–24
royalists, 86, 137–38, 145–46, 219, 225
Russia, 257

Sade, Marquis de, 22, 81, 93
Saint-André, Jean Bon, 280
Saint-Denis tombs smashed, 281
Sainte-Amaranthe family, execution of,
338, 340
Saintes, bishop of, 219
Saint-Firmin massacre, 220
Saint-Germain-des-Près, abbey of, 288
Saint-Germain-des-Près, abbey of, mas-
sacres, 219, 220, 269
Saint-Just, Louis Antoine Léon de, 271–72,
280, 292, 318, 320, 325, 330, 332, 337,
339, 343
arrest and execution of, 352–57
Dantonists and, 305–6, 310–11, 315–16
fall of MR and, 347, 349–52
friendship with MR, 132–33, 245–46
travels with army, 302–3, 340
trial of Louis XVI and, 242–47
Saint-Norbert, 19
Saint-Vaast, abbey of, 18, 22, 37, 75, 123
Salle Episcopale (Bishop's Court), of Arras,
40, 44
sans-culottes, 196, 221, 293, 308
Sanson, Charles Henri, 222
Sauvage, John, 2
September Massacres, 219–23, 225,
233–36, 238, 282–84
Servan, Joseph, 188, 204, 205, 218
Seven Years War, 62, 63
Sévigné, Marie de Rabutin Chantal,
Marquise de, 63
Sidney, Algernon, 196
Sieyès, Emmanuel-Joseph, abbé, 49, 87–88,
91, 102–3, 106, 115–16, 119, 122, 124,
170, 269, 320
Simon, Anthony, 286
Social Contract (Rousseau), 106, 187,
231–32
Society of the Friends of the Constitution
(*later* Jacobin Club), 125
Sommerville, Marie, 43–44
Souberbielle, Dr., 194–95, 332
Spain, 128–29, 257, 333
war declared on, 258
Staël-Holstien, Anne-Louise-Germaine
Necker, Baronne de, 81, 83–84
Staël-Holstein, Baron de, 84

Stuart, Charles Edward (Young Pretender),
19, 117
Swiss Guard, 80, 92, 214–16, 234–35

Tale of Two Cities, A (Dickens), 56
Talleyrand-Périgord, Charles Maurice,
135, 143
Tallien, Jean Lambert, 330, 332–36, 343,
347, 350–52
Target, Guy-Jean-Baptiste, 85–86, 90
taxation, 18, 32, 62–63, 86, 90, 102–3,
117–19, 301
progressive, 270, 292
Tennis Court Oath, 90–91, 161–62, 207–9
Terror. *See also* Committee of Public
Safety; Committee of General Security; Revolutionary Tribunals; *and specific people and laws*
begins, 284–85
Danton opposes, 293
executions and, 1–3, 285, 328
hopes embodied in, 5
Law of 22 Prairial and, 328–29
MR and, 6–9, 302, 304–5, 322
Théot, Catherine, 335–38, 347, 352
third estate, 32, 62, 63, 69
coronation of Louis XVI and, 32–33
declares National Assembly, 90–92
Estates General and, 66–67, 72–77, 80,
82–83, 85–90
as nation, 87–88, 106
Thompson, J. M., 138
Tocqueville, Alexis, 251
Toulon, 282, 284–85
Treilhad, Jean-Baptiste, 261
trial by character, 152–53
trial by conscience, 288–89
Tuileries palace, 129–30, 138–39
protests of 20 June 1792 and, 207–10
royal family wishes to leave, 157–59
storming of 10 August 1792, 214–17,
234–35, 243

Vadier, Marc Guillaume Albert, 336, 337,
338, 339–40, 343, 347, 352
Valazé, Charles Éléonor Dufriche, 289
Valmy, battle of, 223–24, 257
Varennes, flight to, 157–61, 166–67, 248,
277
Vendée, revolt in, 261–62, 282, 285, 320
Versailles, 63, 78–79
Jacobin Club of, 161–62
women's march to, 103–6
vertu (virtue), 46, 245–46, 248, 279, 329

Ver-Vert (Gresset), 49
Vieux Cordelier, Le (newspaper), 297–301,
    311
Vilate, Joachim, 326, 327, 343, 347
Villiers, Pierre, 111–13, 117, 125
Virolle, Mary Magdalen, 2
Vissery de Bois-Valé, Charles Dominique
    de, 41–43
Voltaire, 22, 49, 196, 294
voting rights, 117–19, 271

Walpole, Horace, 230
War Ministry, 307
war of defense vs. conquest, 184–88

war of liberty vs. intrigue, 210–12
war with European powers, 165, 178,
    182–89, 192, 206, 260–61, 282, 330
    conscription for, 261–62
    declared on Holy Roman Empire,
        197–98
    execution of Louis XVI and, 257–58
    threat of, 128–29, 136–37, 139, 182–83
Washington, George, 97
welfare assistance, 271
William Tell (play), 187
Wordsworth, William, 359–60

Young, Arthur, 68–69, 78–79, 359

About the Author

Born in 1971, Ruth Scurr studied at Oxford and Cambridge, where she currently teaches politics and history. A prominent literary critic, she has written for *The New York Review of Books* and *The Times Literary Supplement*. *Fatal Purity* is her first book.